# T. S. ELIOT:

*A Selected Critique*

# T. S. ELIOT:

A SELECTED CRITIQUE

EDITED BY

LEONARD UNGER

------------

NEW YORK / RUSSELL & RUSSELL

1966

# ACKNOWLEDGMENTS

All the articles in this collection have been reprinted with the permission of the following authors, agents, publishers and holders of copyright, to whom especial thanks are due:

*Conrad Aiken*, Brewster, Massachusetts, and *Brandt & Brandt*, New York, N. Y.: Pages 203–205 from SCEPTICISMS by Conrad Aiken.

*Edward Arnold & Co.*, London, and *Harcourt, Brace and Company, Inc.*, New York, N. Y.: Pages 89–96 from ABINGER HARVEST by E. M. Forster.

*C. L. Barber*, Amherst, Massachusetts, and *Louisiana State University Press*, Baton Rouge, Louisiana: "Strange Gods After T. S. Eliot's *The Family Reunion*," from *The Southern Review*, Vol. VI, No. 2.

*R. P. Blackmur*, Princeton, New Jersey: Pages 184–218 from THE DOUBLE AGENT by R. P. Blackmur.

*Jonathan Cape Limited*, London: Pages 132–149, 153–167, from THE DESTRUCTIVE ELEMENT by Stephen Spender.

*Chatto & Windus*, London: Pages 75–91, 112–132 from NEW BEARINGS IN ENGLISH POETRY by F. R. Leavis.

*The Clarendon Press*, Oxford, England: Pages xxi–xxiii from William Butler Yeats' Introduction to THE OXFORD BOOK OF MODERN VERSE.

*Malcolm Cowley*, Gaylordsville, Connecticut: Pages 123–128 from EXILE'S RETURN by Malcolm Cowley.

*The Dial Press, Inc.*, New York, N. Y.: Pages 181–191 from LITERARY STUDIES AND REVIEWS by Richard Aldington.

*E. P. Dutton & Co., Inc.*, New York, N. Y.: Pages 218–227 from OPINIONS OF OLIVER ALLSTON by Van Wyck Brooks.

*Harcourt, Brace and Company, Inc.*, New York, N. Y., and *George Routledge & Sons, Ltd.*, London: Pages 289–295 from PRINCIPLES OF LITERARY CRITICISM by I. A. Richards.

*Harper & Row*, New York, N. Y.: Pages 205–221, 246–255 from THE WIND BLEW FROM THE EAST by Ferner Nuhn.

v

*Mark Van Doren c/o Nannine Joseph, New York, N.Y.,*
Pages 212–216 from THE PRIVATE READER by Mark Van
Doren.

*Granville Hicks, Grafton, N.Y.*                    Pages 268–271 from
THE GREAT TRADITION by Granville Hicks.

*Louis L. Martz,* New Haven, Connecticut, and *The Sewanee
Review,* Sewanee, Tennessee: "The Wheel and the Point" from *The
Sewanee Review,* Winter, 1947 issue.

*New Directions,* Norfolk, Connecticut: Pages 135–138, 141–143
from POLITE ESSAYS by Ezra Pound; Sections I, II, III and VI
from THE NEW CRITICISM by John Crowe Ransom; and Pages
120–167 from THE ANATOMY OF NONSENSE by Yvor Winters.

*Oxford University Press,* New York, N. Y.: Pages 132–149 from
THE ACHIEVEMENT OF T. S. ELIOT, Revised Edition, by
F. O. Matthiessen.

*Partisan Review,* New York, N. Y.: "T. S. Eliot as the International Hero" by Delmore Schwartz, from *Partisan Review* (Spring,
1945), Vol. XII, No. 2.

*Mario Praz,* Rome, Italy, and *Louisiana State University Press,*
Baton Rouge, Louisiana: "T. S. Eliot and Dante" by Mario Praz,
from *The Southern Review,* Vol. II, No. 4.

*Random House, Inc.,*          New York, N. Y.: Lines 405–439,
610–614, 731–738, 1119–1123, 1716–1748, from ESSAY ON RIME by
Karl Shapiro.

*George Routledge & Sons Ltd.,* London: Pages 91–112 from
THE PERSONAL PRINCIPLE by D. S. Savage.

*The Saturday Review of Literature,* New York, N. Y.: Review
of T. S. Eliot's "Selected Essays" by P. E. More, from *The Saturday
Review of Literature.*

*Charles Scribner's Sons, New York, N.Y.:*   Pages 93–131 from
AXEL'S CASTLE by Edmund Wilson.

*James Johnson Sweeney,* New York, N. Y., and *Louisiana State
University Press,* Baton Rouge, Louisiana: "East Coker: A Reading" by James Johnson Sweeney, from *The Southern Review,* Vol.
VI, No. 4.

*Leonard Unger,* Minneapolis, Minnesota, and *Louisiana State
University Press,* Baton Rouge, Louisiana: "Ash Wednesday" by

Leonard Unger, from *The Southern Review*, Vol. IV, Pages 745–770, and "T. S. Eliot's Rose Garden" from *The Southern Review*, Vol. VII, Pages 567–589.

*University of North Carolina Press,* Chapel Hill, North Carolina: Pages 136–173 from MODERN POETRY AND THE TRADITION by Cleanth Brooks.

*The Viking Press, Inc.,* New York, N. Y.: Pages 96–100, 180–182 from FAITH, REASON AND CIVILIZATION by Harold J. Laski.

*Allan Swallow, Denver, Colo.: pp. 210-220 from* COLLECTED ESSAYS *by Allen Tate.*

# CONTENTS

# INTRODUCTION

FEW figures in contemporary literature have been so seriously and so extensively written about as T. S. Eliot. (How many essays on Eliot begin with a sentence to this effect!) There is scarcely an area of intellectual and literary opinion in which Eliot has not served as a subject of discussion and as a point of reference for the formulation of characteristic attitudes. In its cumulative aspect the comment on his work provides a survey of modern criticism from a perspective that is constant and specific.

In many instances the writers who have appraised Eliot are important figures by virtue of their own accomplishment, and their discussions are sometimes most significant as self-revelation. For example, the statements of William Butler Yeats and Harold J. Laski are interesting for what they reveal about the thought of these writers, as well as for what they may contribute to the evaluation of Eliot's work.

The comment is self-revealing in a still larger sense. To the extent that the voices that have spoken on Eliot are representative of the age in its literary and intellectual aspect, they show the reaction of the age to its outstanding poet and most influential critic. This is not to say that many of the questions about Eliot have been settled. Since the appearance of his first poems and essays, especially since *The Sacred Wood* (1920) and *The Waste Land* (1922), Eliot has been a favorite subject of heated and vigorous contention among the literary critics. Perhaps no name was mentioned so often, and almost always the name was a cue for the critic to take a stand. While the comment is no longer so abundant or so aroused in temper, it continues to appear—at what some might call a more normal pace.

Almost every approach to Eliot implies issues which are controversial. Some of the reasons for this become apparent when he is compared to Yeats, who emerged gradually from a literary landscape which was conventional and familiar, a landscape to which he seemed to belong, however much he came to dominate it and transform it. Eliot appeared suddenly, with his "peculiarities" fully developed and he soon proved unpredictable, a figure who, for many observers, fitted into no landscape or who did not even fit together. Despite (and in some ways because of) the fact that there is so much in Yeats's work that is bizarre, private and "invented," the consistency and continuity of the various aspects of his prose statement and poetic practice have remained relatively unquestioned. His work has been regarded as self-contained, some parts significant almost wholly by reason of illuminating other parts. In contrast, the interrelatedness of Eliot's work has not been so generally acknowledged; indeed, critics range from finding it all of a piece to finding it in several unrelated pieces. A familiar complaint was made by Paul Elmer More, who found Eliot "cleft" into the critic of formal and traditional principles with whom he sympathized, and the poet whose "obscurity of language" and "license of metrical form" he deplored, in *Ash Wednesday* as much as in *The Waste Land*. Charges like those made by Ernest Boyd—that Eliot's "aesthetic theory bears no relation whatsoever to his practice"—and by More—that Eliot "seems to be leading us in two directions at once" were disputed by Richard Aldington, F. R. Leavis, H. Ross Williamson, George Williamson, F. O. Matthiessen, and others. These critics would not allow that any division exists. They called witness to Eliot's consistency by careful and generous reference to his work. They showed how key terms from the criticism—tradition, objective correlative, auditory imagination, levels of meaning, fusion of thought and feeling, etc.—may be applied to the poetry, and how the favorite texts of the criticism—the French symbolist poets, the metaphysicals, the Elizabethan and Jacobean dramatists, Dante—are reflected by the poetry. Finally, they elaborated Eliot's own answer to the charge of division: that while one is concerned with ideals in criticism, one must confront actualities in the practice of poetry.

These arguments were not the last word. They did not convince, for example, such close critics as John Crowe Ransom and Yvor Winters of the unity of Eliot. Ransom, though sympathetic with much of Eliot, with his wide learning and his skepticism of popular modern values, still found a poetical Hyde and critical Jekyll in Eliot. His early judgment that *The Waste Land* was disordered and incomplete remained unchanged, and he could find no justification for the poetry in the "conservative" criticism, which "was heavily against the drift of the poetry." Like Paul Elmer More, neither Ransom nor Winters would admit that disorder and fragmentariness are appropriate in the organization of a poem because they are the poet's subject and milieu.

While critics like Leavis, Matthiessen and George Williamson used Eliot's criticism in support of his poetry, there were others—Louis Grudin, Wyndham Lewis, Frank Swinnerton, and, more recently, Ransom, Winters, and D. S. Savage—who would not allow that the criticism was free of contradictions and inconsistencies. A common judgment made—with varying emphasis—by such critics was that Eliot was at his best when dealing with specific subjects, but that he did not provide a general theory of aesthetics; and that when he did approach, or imply, the more inclusive generalizations he fell into contradictions.

If the debate over whether there is unity or division in Eliot remains unsettled, there is no doubt that it was worth having—and even continuing. The close examination of a writer who has had the acclaim and influence of Eliot is perhaps even more valuable than it is inevitable. One of the several benefits of such an activity is to make the individual critics more cautious and reflective and also more outspoken, and to indicate the extent to which contemporary thinkers are thinking and writing in the same language. Thus far the argument suggests that they are not quite doing so—suggests that an ideal definition of terms would reveal some differences in initial premises. A difference is in fact already apparent. Often those who will not interpret Eliot's criticism as consistent with his poetry are in emphatic disagreement with one or more points in the criticism. Such disagreement is implicit (perhaps unconscious) in More, and quite explicit in Ransom. Among those who do interpret the criticism as consistent with the poetry there is little or no questioning of the criticism. Eliot's critical terms and the preoccupations of his prose are used to interpret the poetry—and quite successfully. And that is the great contribution of the votaries of the "wholeness" of Eliot. They make the kind of selection from the prose and the poetry which illuminates both— which shows that both are the product of the same sensibility, the same mind, the same personality. Eliot is a whole Eliot by identity. They have helped us enjoy and understand Eliot by proving that there is a consistency of temperament from the prose to the poetry— by approaching Eliot on his own terms; but by making Eliot his own arbiter they have not quite refuted the charges of logical inconsistency. And while accepting Eliot's critical conclusions and principles, these critics as a rule fail to commit themselves on political, sociological and religious questions which are inseparable from Eliot's whole critical position.

F. O. Matthiessen's *The Achievement of T. S. Eliot* is probably the best single introduction to Eliot's work—for certain purposes. It provides preeminently a general understanding of the wholeness of Eliot, of the interrelationship among the several features of his prose and poetry—by taking its cues from the prose. This is apparent in its chapter titles, which are phrases quoted either directly or in effect from Eliot's criticism. Matthiessen provides much instructive information about the poems and about Eliot's critical position. In demonstrating how Eliot lives up to his own principles and in defending those principles, he returns again and again to the more important poems, but he never gives a thorough and uninterrupted analysis of any of them (until the revised edition, 1947, which has two additional chapters, one on Eliot's plays and one on *Four Quartets*). The tendency of his treatment is to provide a general orientation to all of Eliot's work, to establish a sympathy with Eliot's intentions and an appreciation of the extent to which they are achieved. This tendency is more or less common to all the defenders of Eliot's unity and makes their comment more interpretative than judicial. A later example of such treatment is found in Ronald Peacock's *The Poet and the Theatre,* where *Murder in the Cathedral* and *The Family Reunion* are assessed by Eliot's own principles.

For all its contribution, such sympathetic treatment is open to objection—objection that it is begging the question and reaffirming what Eliot has already affirmed. Objection has been made not only to the logical basis and general limitation of this kind of treatment, but to the frequent tone of pious righteousness and *me too* snobbishness with which Eliot is echoed. Matthiessen has noted this tone in one of his fellow critics: "Mr. Leavis's interpretation of Eliot . . . suffers from a certain over-intensity. He seems to be writing continually on the defensive as though he were the apostle of modern art to an unappreciative world. As a result his criticism, though eager, is somewhat wanting in balance and perspective." Similar charges might be brought against critics like Bonamy Dobrée, George Williamson, H. Ross Williamson and Matthiessen himself. An extreme example of the strained and precious deference toward Eliot practised by these critics may be found in H. Ross Williamson. The second chapter of his book on Eliot is called "The Man Behind the Poetry" and opens with a quotation of Eliot's entry in *Who's Who* (1932). "These things constitute everything about the man behind the poetry that it is necessary to know or mannerly to inquire." With this pronouncement the man behind the perfect manners completes the "necessary" one-page chapter. It is only fair to add that since *New Bearings in English Poetry* and *The Achievement of T. S. Eliot,* both Leavis and Matthiesson have discussed Eliot with greater independence of judgment but not with less respect and appreciation. We should remember, too, that the criticism which "suffers from a certain over-intensity" was written at a time when there was over-intensity on both sides and the outcome of the battle was still in doubt. Among the more sympathetic interpreters of Eliot's poetry and criticism, R. P. Blackmur is distinguished in this respect. His acceptance or rejection of any of the elements in Eliot's position has had scarcely any effect on the tone of his comment. The intensity of his appreciation is supported by the originality of his insights and definitions and his objective analysis of Eliot's insights and definitions. It is Blackmur's kind of criticism which is most likely to be persuasive where persuasion is possible.

A frequent issue in much of the controversy over Eliot has been his influence as poet and critic. Rarely, if ever, has a writer been considered with so much attention to his place in and effect on literary history while the history was still being made. It has been often noted as remarkable that Eliot became an influence so early in his career and that so meager a body of writing should have provided such a strong and widespread effect. Those who admired Eliot without reservations and defended his wholeness and self-consistency hailed his influence as entirely beneficial, while those who saw contradictions in Eliot and/or were annoyed with the tone of his most ardent votaries questioned the effects of his influence and in some cases utterly deplored it. An article by Sherry Mangan (in *Pagany,* Spring, 1930) develops a characteristic attitude which is expressed clearly enough in its title: "A Note: On the Somewhat Premature Apotheosis of Thomas Stearns Eliot." The same general attitude is reflected by G. W. Stonier's use of the term *Eliotism* in his article, "Eliot and the Plain Reader" (*Gog-Magog,* 1933). Frank Swinnerton in 1935 wondered whether Eliot's influence has not been more harmful than beneficial, and in 1943 Yvor Winters saw it as "the most dangerous and nearly the least defensible of our time." The strong feeling with which Eliot's influence was debated may be represented by quotation

from an exchange of verbal blows between I. M. Parsons and Rebecca
West in the pages of *The Spectator* in 1932:

> *I. M. Parsons:* It is not only that Mr. Eliot's prose has a quality, a
> texture, which stamps it at once as the product of an adult and
> trained sensibility: others besides he can justly lay claim to that.
> It is not even that he has been instrumental in rehabilitating the
> work of certain great writers of the past, though that alone is an
> achievement for which he deserves our gratitude, and one in
> which his powers of analysis and appreciation continually compel
> our admiration. It is that by his scholarship, his perception, and
> above all by the exact and scrupulous use of language, he has
> made it possible to discuss literature with a new precision and
> with a living vocabulary once more at one's command. It is, per-
> haps, even more than this, that alone among contemporary critics
> he has maintained a consistent standard of judgment and pre-
> served an authentic scale of values. Just how supremely important
> the latter may be, only those who are purblind to the plight of
> modern culture will fail to appreciate.
>
> *Rebecca West:* Mr. Parsons cannot think. But he is sure he can
> think because he is a follower of Mr. Eliot; and he is sure other
> people cannot think because they are not followers of Mr. Eliot.
> And he knows all the proper patter to use to impress the casual
> reader with the sense that he is on the right side—"scholarship,"
> "perception," "exact and scrupulous use of language," "adult and
> trained sensibility," and so on. "The plight of modern culture" is
> due to the prevalence of this intellectual tarantism among the
> young as much as to any one single cause.

At these extremes and along the whole scale between them, scores
of critics have evaluated Eliot's influence.

An issue closely related to the value of his influence has been
Eliot's general position—expatriate, traditionalist, aristocratic, Anglo-
Catholic. When Ransom said that Eliot's success "was a greater success
than an American could have had in America, or an Englishman in
England, it was an international success, and pleased everybody" he
must have meant, only and simply, that Eliot was very popular and
much admired in the world of letters. For certainly there were many
who were not pleased, and many who were pleased, but with marked
reservations. A characteristic complaint was that Eliot had fled from
America and the present to seek refuge in the past of Europe. In an

article called "The Harvard Exiles" (1934), Dixon Wecter placed Eliot with Henry James, Henry Adams and Santayana, men who had fled, geographically and historically, into the past. They belonged, Wecter observed with satisfied confidence, to an era that had closed. It had not closed so firmly, however, or receded so completely for some critics who shared Wecter's ojections but lacked his confidence. The argument against Henry James and Eliot was a very present issue, raised with fresh force and bitterness some years later by Van Wyck Brooks's "Oliver Allston", who found Eliot's concept of tradition artificial, negative, egotistical. Ferner Nuhn, even more recently, made the same definition of Eliot's position, but he attacked it with more subtlety and a deeper understanding of Eliot's intentions. Nuhn acknowledged the brilliance of the essays and responded to the poetry; he respected "the sensibility to the position," but he insisted that Eliot's position rests on a "failure of reconciliation and integration." Criticisms similar to those of Wecter, Brooks and Nuhn were made from a British point of view. For example, David Daiches and D. S. Savage saw something typically American, naïve and artificial in Eliot's doctrine of acquiring culture and tradition. Writers of the political left, of course, rejected rather than questioned Eliot's traditionalism, branding his work as reactionary and including him among the representatives of a decadent culture—although some of them, like Malcolm Cowley, John Strachey, Granville Hicks and Harold J. Laski, granted the astuteness and brilliance of his literary accomplishments.

A frequent criticism of Eliot, made not only by those who from a partisan viewpoint attack his traditionalism and its political implications, is that he lacks patience with the average human qualities and sympathy for what is simply human. This observation has been made in a number of ways and it has served as the basis for a number of conclusions. Francis Fergusson, discussing "T. S. Eliot and His Impersonal Theory of Art" (1927), saw Eliot as "doomed to sterility in the effort to make art out of art" because he lacked "any sympathy with non-creative types." In seeking an explanation for the difficulty of *The Waste Land* E. M. Forster suggested that Eliot has had a vision of horror and has "declined to say so plainly" because he has underestimated "the general decency of his audience." According to Stephen Spender, the effect of Eliot's poetry—in which the bank clerk, Sweeney, Mrs. Porter, the pub conversationalists "are all part of the world of *things"*—derives from the poet's blindness "to the existence of people outside himself." For all the limitations which may be ascribed to Eliot's lack of a sense of humanity, or whatever it may be called, the response to his poetry indicates a considerable human sympathy with him. If his poetry has often been read with mixed feelings, one of the feelings has been that his sensibility to the life of his time is not uncommon, but uncommonly well articulated.

Extremely opposite judgments are a characteristic of the comment that has been made on Eliot's work. An absurd example of one extreme has been provided by Bernard De Voto. Writing during the war (*The Literary Fallacy,* 1944), he waved the flag of oversimplification in an attack on Eliot's lack of faith in humanity. De Voto rescued the typist-home-at-tea-time and the young-man-carbuncular from the indignity of *The Waste Land* to proclaim glowingly their "fortitude, sacrifice, fellowship; they were willing to die as an act of faith for the preservation of hope. They were hope, the soul and body of hope. They were staunchness, resolution, dedication. In fact they were incommensurable with what Mr. Eliot's poem said they were." Also writing during the war, Delmore Schwartz took a position at the other extreme, squarely in the line of De Voto's fire—and this should and does mean, of course, that Schwartz understands Eliot's intentions. Eliot, however, becomes a strange god in Schwartz's presentation of him as an international culture hero, one of the heroic and international hallmarks being Eliot's concern with the related difficulties of making love and having religious beliefs.

It is likely that Eliot's work—the methods and principles of his criticism and the broader implications of his poetry—will continue to serve as the specific issue for controversial comment and the development of disparate attitudes. Interpretations and analyses of his poetry, however, have tended to become more specialized, more strictly in the academic vein. Argument in such writing is seldom more than the courteous expression of differences among scholars. This situation contrasts strikingly with the welter of irate and impatient differences of opinion which followed the appearance of *The Waste Land.* The first issue of *Time* (March 3, 1923) reported the rumor that *The Waste Land* was written as a hoax, and that this possibility was considered immaterial by some of its supporters, who claimed that results, and not intentions, were the concern of literature. *Ash Wednesday* was equally successful in setting up opposing camps of bewilderment:

Max Eastman called the poem an "oily puddle of emotional noises" and Conrad Aiken said that it approaches "the kind of heavenly meaninglessness which we call pure poetry." It is true, of course, that many enlightening studies were made by writers who combined scholarly analysis with the presentation of their own critical and ideological attitudes. One may notice a cooperative effort from Edmund Wilson's *Axel's Castle* (which is of abiding value), through the work of such critics as Leavis and Matthiessen, to Cleanth Brooks's extensive and detailed analysis of *The Waste Land*. While Brooks's treatment has general implications sympathetic to Eliot's position, these are always integral to his interpretation, and the occasional points of dispute raised by Brooks are all on the order of scholarly correction. Although Brooks's essay might be revised on a few points in the light of later studies, it remains the most thorough exegesis of *The Waste Land*. In recent years—the last decade, approximately— similar studies have been made of individual poems of Eliot and of specific issues relating to the poems. A few of such studies, for example, are those on *Murder in the Cathedral* by Leo Shapiro, Louis L. Martz, and Francis Fergusson; on *The Family Reunion* by Maud Bodkin and C. L. Barber; on *Four Quartets,* in whole or in part, by Helen Gardner, James Johnson Sweeney, Philip Wheelwright and Raymond Preston. The special significance of such studies is that they are not primarily critical appraisals—although critical appraisal is often implicit in the interpretations of the poetry. These studies are significant beyond their individual contributions.

It must be obvious that in this essay I have not given an exhaustive report of all questions relating to Eliot. My intention has been to indicate, after reading the critical literature, what impressed me as the most important considerations. A glance at the bibliography will make it obvious, too, that I have named here and included in the book only a few of the critics that have written on Eliot. My choice has been determined not only by the physical limitations of a book, but by the desire to achieve some economy, to present a picture that is balanced with both the intrinsically valuable and the significantly representative, even if they do not always overlap.

LEONARD UNGER

# T. S. ELIOT:

*A Selected Critique*

# CONRAD AIKEN *

M R. T. S. ELIOT, whose book "Prufrock and Other Observations" is really hardly more than a pamphlet, is also a realist, but of a different sort. Like Mr. Wilfred Wilson Gibson, Mr. Eliot is a psychologist; but his intuitions are keener; his technique subtler. For the two semi-narrative psychological portraits which form the greater and better part of his book, "The Love Song of J. Alfred Prufrock" and "The Portrait of a Lady," one can have little but praise. This is psychological realism, but in highly subjective or introspective vein; whereas Mr. Gibson, for example, gives us, in the third person, the reactions of an individual to a situation which is largely external (an accident, let us say), Mr. Eliot gives us, in the first person, the reactions of an individual to a situation for which to a large extent his own character is responsible. Such work is more purely autobiographic than the other—the field is narrowed, and the terms are idiosyncratic (sometimes almost blindly so). The dangers of such work are obvious: one must be certain that one's mental character and idiom are sufficiently close to the norm to be comprehensible or significant. In this respect, Mr. Eliot is near the border-line. His temperament is peculiar, it is sometimes, as remarked heretofore, almost bafflingly peculiar, but on the whole it is the average hyperaesthetic one with a good deal of introspective curiosity; it will puzzle many, it will delight a few. Mr. Eliot writes pungently and sharply, with an eye for unexpected and vivid details, and, particularly in the two longer poems and in "The Rhapsody of a Windy Night," he shows himself to be an exceptionally acute technician. Such free rhyme as this, with irregular line lengths, is difficult to write well, and Mr. Eliot does it well enough to make one wonder whether such a form is not what the adorers of free verse will eventually have to come to. In the rest of Mr. Eliot's volume one finds the piquant and the trivial in about equal proportions.

* *Varieties of Realism: Wilfrid Wilson Gibson, William Aspenwall Bradley, T. S. Eliot,* from SCEPTICISMS: Notes on Contemporary Poetry, pp. 203–5, Copyright, 1919, by Alfred A. Knopf, Inc.

3

# RICHARD ALDINGTON *

T O define twentieth-century literature when it is only beginning to emerge is a feat one may be excused from attempting. But one may note a certain homogeneity in the writings of M. Marcel Proust and Mr. James Joyce, of Miss Sitwell and Mr. Huxley, of Miss More and H. D., of Jean Cocteau and Paul Morand and T. S. Eliot. They are intellectually contemporaries; they are post-war; they are sufficiently unlike each other to reward curiosity and sufficiently similar to show the first outline of a period. The typical modern poet whose affinities are chiefly with the writers above mentioned, is something extremely unlike the conventional idea of a poet. Some day, when the first authoritative collection of writings by these poets is issued, the editor should put as an epigraph two quotations from "Une Saison en Enfer"—

> Quant au bonheur établi, domestique ou non . . . non, je ne peux pas.

> Je vais dévoiler tous les mystères: mystères réligieux ou naturels, mort, naissance, avenir, passé, cosmogonie, néant. Je suis maître en fantasmagories.

This (hypothetical) modern poet is not amiable or romantic or tender or tranquil; but neither is the age in which he lives. And as irreverence and indocility are qualities of this decade, so are they of this decade's poets. The platoons of poets "going through the motions" of verse in unison at the word of some invisible commander are superannuated for ever. The new poet is the "poète contumace" of Laforgue. His indocility is extreme and nearly as disturbing to the godly as his determination to accept none of the official wax effigies as realities, to take nothing seriously until it has been proved worthy of seriousness. His thought is pessimistic and disillusioned; his modes of expression sarcastic and his chief weapon an acrid wit. He is psychologically subtle and intellectually acute; his culture is extensive. He is

---

* *The Poetry of T. S. Eliot,* from LITERARY STUDIES AND REVIEWS, pp. 181–191. The Dial Press, New York, 1924.

4

not a democrat though he observes popular habits. He is a cosmopolitan, but he enjoys the flavour of nationality. He writes for an audience
equipped to understand him, and is indifferent to popular success.
His mind is exceedingly complex and moves with a rapidity incomprehensible to sluggish wits. He is perilously balanced among the
rude forces of a turbulent mechanical age; he walks the tight-rope
over an abyss and he knows it. His work has the gusto of peril.

The works of Mr. James Joyce may be taken as typical of the
best original prose of this school; the poetry of Mr. Eliot occupies a
similar position. The plan of this article forbids discussion of Mr.
Eliot's criticism, but it is essential to observe that the faculty of
analysis which makes the "Sacred Wood" so valuable is equally characteristic of "Prufrock" and "Ara vos prec." When Mr. Eliot analyses
as a critic he clarifies one's ideas, enlarges one's comprehension, purifies
one's taste. And the author of the "Sacred Wood" is of one piece with
the author of "Ara vos prec." That is a conclusion not to be dodged.
You cannot accept the "Sacred Wood" and ignore Mr. Eliot's poetry;
each is a different facet of the same talent; and that talent cannot be
disposed of by a little cheap journalism. As a character in one of Mr.
Eliot's poems says, interpreting so strangely well one's sensation of his
thoroughness and impeccable restraint, his strength of purpose—

> You are invulnerable, you have no Achilles' heel.
> You will go on, and when you have prevailed
> You can say: at this point many a one has failed.

The reader will almost certainly have noticed that when the
syllables "T. S. Eliot" are pronounced, the reply "Laforgue" is elicited
as invariably as an automatic machine produces a very small piece of
chocolate when pressed with a penny. Now it is certainly true that Mr.
Eliot's poetry has some affinity with Laforgue's poetry; but is it not a
perfect example of muddled thinking to deduce imitation from affinity
of mind, just as the same muddled thought deduces affinity of mind
from imitation? Is it not certain that such people have never worked
out even this simple distinction? And yet, with so faulty an equipment,
they will undertake to analyse a work as profound and complex as
"Ara vos prec." To say that Mr. Eliot imitates Laforgue because they
have a common faculty for unexpected juxtapositions of ideas expressed with ironic wit is as foolish as it would be to say that Mr. Eliot
imitates Ausonius because both frequently quote other poets in their

verse. Moreover, Mr. Eliot has quite as much affinity with Rimbaud and Corbière. Mr. Eliot's "Mélange adultère de tout" depends for its full effect upon the reader's comprehending the reference to Corbière's "Épave mort-né." But Mr. Eliot has completely purged out Cobière's querulous romanticism and self-pity; he is hard on himself—

> En Amérique, professeur;
> En Angleterre, journaliste;
> C'est à grands pas et en sueur
> Que vous suivrez à peine ma piste.
> En Yorkshire, conférencier;
> A Londres, un peu banquier;
> (Vous me paierez bien la tête.)
> C'est à Paris que je me coiffe
> Casque noir de jemenfoutiste.
> En Allemagne, philosophe
> Surexcité par Emporheben
> Au grand air de Bergsteigleben;
> J'erre toujours de-ci de-là
> A divers coups de tra-la-la
> De Damas jusqu'à Omaha;
> Je célébrai mon jour de fête
> Dans un oasis d'Afrique
> Vêtu d'une peau de girafe.
>
> On montrera mon cénotaphe
> Aux côtes brûlants de Mozambique.

The intention of parody, the reference to Verlaine, the compression, the tone of badinage in which the experiences of a varied life are dismissed, are characteristic of the modern poet. All Mr. Eliot's poems in French fit in perfectly with the development of the younger French poets. The tone of disillusion of "Lune de Miel" and the singular dialogue with a dirty waiter, called "Dans le Restaurant," would be highly approved by our "chers confrères." At least we may be certain that he would be greeted as a poet by the author of the following lines, whose inferiority to those of Mr. Eliot is apparent—

> Voyez le vieux Goethe; il sautille
> Comme une chèvre sur le Vésuve;
> Il porte un livre grec, un herbier,
> Un filet à papillons;
> Il casse des gros morceaux de Vésuve

Et en rempli ses poches,
Car la fin des vacances d'Eckermann
Approche . . . *etc.*

It is not a question of imitation or even of similarity of manner, but
of having reached a similar stage of intelligence.

Mr. Eliot's English poetry is often attacked as incomprehensible
and heartless; which is simply another way of saying that it is subtle
and not sentimental. His desire for perfection is misrepresented as
puritan and joyless, whereas it is plain he discriminates in order to
increase his enjoyment. But, of course, refinement will not be applauded by those who cannot perceive it, nor will intelligence be
appreciated by those who cannot understand it; literary criticism is
not the only human activity wherein ignorance is made a standard.
Mr. Eliot's poetry makes very high demands on a reader's intelligence
and knowledge. It is caviare to the general. And yet this poetry can at
once be assimilated into tradition, may be placed at once as the last
development of two currents of thought, one French and the other
English. The common perception of the affinity between "Ara vos
prec" and "Les Complaintes" may be extended to "Les Illuminations"
and "Les Amours Jaunes." And when the reader has granted that, he
has simply admitted that one side of Mr. Eliot's poetry is a development of the secular tradition of "poètes contumaces" or "poètes liber-
tins," which runs from the poets of to-day to Laforgue and Verlaine,
to Rimbaud and Corbière, to Aloysius Bertrand, to Saint-Amant, to
Théophile, back to Villon, and beyond him to a shadowy host of
mediaeval "pinces-sans-rire," "goliards" and satiric "goguenards,"
whose sharp tongues spared neither the Church nor the rich nor the
pretty ladies. That tradition of poignant, witty, derisive verse has survived many centuries and passed through many transformations; it
has been stifled underground for a generation or more, but has always
sprung up in some new form—that sharp French mind whose watch-
word is "ne pas être dupe." So that when we find in Mr. Eliot agreeable
sarcasms of this sort—

> The sable presbyters approach
> The avenue of penitence;
> The young are red and pustular,
> Clutching piaculative pence,

our mind runs at once to

Sur mol duvet assis, ung gros chanoine,

and

> Ce fanfaron de Ferradine,
> Qui pare son affreuse mine
> D'un grand et vilain chifreneau,
> Aura beau tordre ses bigottes,
> Beau renasquer à hautes nottes, *etc.*

If the reader will take the trouble to spend a few days with the poets quoted he will appreciate the point at issue. It is not required to prove that these generations of poets imitated each other, but simply that they belong to a category of the intelligence which has produced remarkable poetry and shown extraordinary persistence and vitality.

When this aspect of Mr. Eliot's poetry is explained, there remains the more serious and difficult problem of his so-called obscurity. Now the charge of "obscurity" may be just, for all verse which on analysis proves to have no intellectual or emotional content is "obscure"; obscure because it pretends to possess a meaning which it has not. But the obscurity of Mr. Eliot is as much a myth of lazy people as the obscurity of Browning. Indeed, Mr. Eliot's verse never makes the heavy demands on a reader that were made by "Sordello." But this subtlety of mind which makes necessary an effort for full comprehension is not something invented by Browning, but goes far beyond him to the so-called metaphysical poets, to Donne and Davies and Chapman. Compare the following paragraphs—

> History has many cunning passages, contrived corridors
> And issues; deceives with whispering ambitions,
> Guides us by vanities. Think now
> She gives when our attention is distracted,
> And what she gives, gives with such supple confusions
> That the giving famishes the craving. Gives too late
> What's not believed in, or if still believed
> In memory only, reconsidered passion. Gives too soon
> Into weak hands what's thought can be dispensed with
> Till the refusal propagates a fear.
>
> Oh, of what contraries consists a man!
> Of what impossible mixtures! vice and virtue,
> Corruption and eterness, at one time,
> And in one subject, let together, loose!

We have not any strength but weakens us,
No greatness but doth crush us into air.
Our knowledges do light us but to err,
Our ornaments are burthens: our delights
Are our tormentors; fiends that, raised in fears
At parting shake our roofs about our ears.

Is there so great disparity between the modern and the Elizabethan? Does not the modern poet speak with the accents of his great
predecessors, though the matter of his speech be remote from theirs?
Is it not certain that this feigned obscurity is no obscurity, but simply
density of thought?

If space and the patience of readers permitted, there would be a
great pleasure in carrying these comparisons into every aspect of Mr.
Eliot's poetry. Let us take but one more instance where the modern
poet and the poets of the seventeenth century have "unveiled death,"
have forced themselves to look unmoved on dreadful horrors—

> . . . saw the skull beneath the skin;
> And breastless creatures under-ground
> Leaned backward with a lipless grin.
> Daffodil bulbs instead of balls
> Stared from the sockets of the eyes!
> He knew that thought clings round dead limbs
> Tightening its lusts and luxuries.
>
> What that? O, fatal! he throws earth upon me!
> A dead man's skull beneath the roots of flowers!
>
> I prithee, yet remember,
> Millions are now in graves which at last day
> Like mandrakes shall rise shrieking.
>
> . . . they'll re-marry
> Ere the worm pierce your winding-sheet, ere the spider
> Make a thin curtain for your epitaphs.
>
> Or as sometimes in a beheaded man,
> Though at those two red seas which freely ran,
> One from the trunk, another from the head,
> His soul be sail'd to her eternal bed,
> His eyes will twinkle, and his tongue will roll,
> As though he beck'ned and call'd back his soul. . . .

It is a long step from the dense thought of Mr. Eliot's "Gerontion"
and the sombre horrors of his "Whispers of Immortality" to the pleasant little rhymes now current. Between these rhymes, however pretty
and melodious, and the intellectual poetry of Mr. Eliot, there is a
wide gulf. Few will contest the originality of the mind expressed in
his poetry, and yet the comparisons instituted show that Mr. Eliot's
poetry is traditional, linking up on the one hand with the ironic
French poets and, on the other, with the stately, subtle-minded
Englishmen of the Renaissance. The poetry of Mr. T. S. Eliot is a
healthy reaction against the merely pretty and agreeable, against shal-
lowness and against that affectation of simplicity which verged on
dotage. Mr. Eliot is to be honoured as a poet who has brought new
vigour to the intellectual tradition of English poetry.[1]

---

[1] Written before the publication of "Waste Land." I have been censured
by an old friend for mixing quotations from Mr. Eliot and the Elizabethans,
without indicating the authors. My object is merely to surprise the reader into
admitting how "traditional" this "revolutionary" poet is.

# E. M. FORSTER *

I T was during the war that I first came across Mr. Eliot's work. It was Egypt, no danger or discomfort; still it was the war, and while waiting for a tram in Cairo I sprained my ankle upon the asphalt pavement and was carried into the garden of a friend. Literature was available. I lay for two or three weeks among the oleanders and bananas, watched from over the wall by a friendly and rakish minaret, and reading whatever was least likely to be bracing. Huysmans's *A Rebours* is the book of that blessed period that I remember best. Oh, the relief of a world which lived for its sensations and ignored the will—the world of des Esseintes! Was it decadent? Yes, and thank God. Yes; here again was a human being who had time to feel and experiment with his feelings, to taste and smell and arrange books and fabricate flowers, and be selfish and himself. The waves of edifying bilge rolled off me, the newspapers ebbed; Professor Cramb, that profound philosopher, and Raemekers, that inspired artist, floated out into an oblivion which, thank God, has since become permanent, and something resembling reality took their place. Perhaps it was not real, but it was not helpful, and in 1917 that was enough to make me repeat after the muezzin on my minaret "Thank God." And in the hasty uncritical fashion of those days I tacked on to Huysmans some poems which had come out in a sort of paperish volume from England: *Prufrock, The Portrait of a Lady,* and a few more.

The poems were not epicurean; still they were innocent of public-spiritedness: they sang of private disgust and diffidence, and of people who seemed genuine because they were unattractive or weak. The author was irritated by tea-parties, and not afraid to say so, with the result that his occasional "might-have-beens" rang out with the precision of a gong.

> I should have been a pair of ragged claws,
> Scuttling across the floors of silent seas.

* ABINGER HARVEST, pp. 89–96, Copyright, 1936, by E. M. Forster. Harcourt, Brace & World, Inc. New York, and Edward Arnold & Co., London.

Here was a protest, and a feeble one, and the more congenial for being feeble. For what, in that world of gigantic horror, was tolerable except the slighter gestures of dissent? He who measured himself against the war, who drew himself to his full height, as it were, and said to Armadillo-Armageddon "Avaunt!" collapsed at once into a pinch of dust. But he who could turn aside to complain of ladies and drawing-rooms preserved a tiny drop of our self-respect, he carried on the human heritage. And in all the years that have followed, years in which Mr. Eliot has gone both beyond me and behind, this early fragmentary sympathy has remained, so that still when I read him it is for the witty resentment followed by the pinch of glory.

> Yet there the nightingale
> Filled all the desert with inviolable voice
> And still she cried, and still the world pursues,
> "Jug Jug" to dirty ears.

This simple reaction of mine was not unsound. But it was too facile. There was much more in his work than black followed by white. Even the early poems, when studied, revealed crossing shadows, and in time one discerned blends, or it might be confusions, of colours. Here was a poet whose gesture, whatever its ultimate intention, certainly was not a handshake, and here was a critic who held that a poet does not possess a personality, but is "only a medium, in which impressions and experiences combine in peculiar and unexpected ways." Here was a character habitually urbane, but liable to sudden spleen, which was vented on Milton or Hobbes or Mr. Bernard Shaw so as rather to take the breath away. Here, in a word, was a difficult writer. And it is my aim now to sort the difficulties presented by him into two heaps. For though I cannot solve them, into two heaps I am convinced they will go.

One heap—and it is a large one—will contain all those difficulties that are due to our own incompetence or inattention. Mr. Eliot does not write for the lazy, the stupid, or the gross. Literature is to him a serious affair, and criticism not less serious than creation, though severely to be distinguished from it. A reader who cannot rise to his level, and who opens a book as he would open a cigarette case, cannot expect to get very far. There is abundance of beauty and even of amusement awaiting us, there is all the treasure of a richly-stored and active mind, but we are expected to do our share, and if (to take a concrete test) we cannot do it over the little essay in *The Sacred Wood* entitled *Hamlet and His Problems,* it means that we are not up to his standard, and must keep to ready-made stuff. I instance the Hamlet essay because it is both sensitive and lucid (two of Mr. Eliot's great merits), because it handles with amazing skill problems both of historical criticism and of psychology, and because it never attempts to mystify. If we find difficulties here, the fault is ours.

But is the fault always ours? Are there not cases where we turn away because there was no way in? And if our check is due to the writer, why is it that, having set out to address us, he should change his intention, and mislead?

It is natural, at this point of our inquiry, to ask help of the young. For Mr. Eliot's work, particularly *The Waste Land,* has made a profound impression on them, and given them precisely the food they needed. And by "the young" I mean those men and women between the ages of eighteen and thirty whose opinions one most respects, and whose reactions one most admires. He is the most important author of their day, his influence is enormous, they are inside his idiom as the young of 1900 were inside George Meredith's, they are far better qualified than their elders to expound him, and in certain directions they do expound him. But they are averse to answering leading questions. "What is *The Waste Land* about?" provokes no enthusiastic reply. Yet it is, to my mind, a pertinent question, and to be told that the poem is simply a poem or just a work of art is unsatisfying. Who is the drowned sailor in it? What does the scrap-heap of quotations at the end signify? Is it helpful, here and elsewhere, to know where the quotations come from? or to read Miss Weston's *From Ritual to Romance,* or the other authorities recommended in the notes? No answer comes, or perhaps a sly rejoinder that questions as to Mr. Eliot's meaning are only asked by those whom they will lead deeper into confusion. It is implied that if he sees a reader floundering he might amuse himself by setting an additional trap. And I am afraid there is a little truth in this.

There is no reason why a writer should not play tricks on his audience; Samuel Butler and André Gide have done it with success. But it denotes a divided purpose, a shifting energy, and in Mr. Eliot's case pure love of fun will scarcely be the cause. His is rather the love of the cryptogrammatic. "I hope," he says, in his *Homage to John Dryden,* "that these three papers may, in spite of and partly because of their defects, preserve in cryptogram certain notions which, if expressed directly, would be destined to immediate obloquy, followed by perpetual oblivion." What is he trying to put across us here? Something which we should dislike and forget. Why, if he believes in it, can he not say it out straight and face the consequences—the very trivial consequences? And not only here, but again and again we have the sense of being outwitted, which is agreeable to the young, who always take a sell in good part, but which nevertheless needs analysing. Whose fault has it been? Into which heap is the difficulty to be thrown? The verse always sounds beautiful, but often conveys nothing. The prose always conveys something, but is often occupied in tracing the boundaries of the unsaid. The more we look into the fabrics, the more intellectual and emotional reservations do we find.

Mr. Eliot is quite frank about this. He admits to the reservations, and he offers an apology for them which we must now examine. Tradition is the keynote of it. An English writer, to be great, must create in the English tradition. He will not, of course, be imitative, and he need not be erudite, but he will acquire the sense of the past, that is to say he will feel the past of Europe present in him while he composes, and within it he will feel the past of England. Such a feeling can only be gained at a price. To acquire tradition, the writer must give up all personal idiosyncrasies, he must not indulge in private mythologies like Blake or facile reactions like Mr. Arthur Symons; even as a critic he must submit to discipline, while as a creative artist he will engage in "a continual self-sacrifice, a continual extinction of personality." And it will be readily understood that with so much in his bones he cannot speak to the reader as man to man; indeed, while he creates he has ceased to be a man in the hand-shaking sense, he has disassociated himself for the reception of something else, something timeless. Reticence, mental and emotional, is to be expected, and the reader who has likewise the sense of the past will appreciate this, while the reader who has not got it must expect to feel baffled and slighted. This argument, adumbrated in *The Sacred Wood,* has been underlined in *For Lancelot Andrewes,* where it is shown to entail classicism in literature, royalism in politics, and Anglo-Catholicism in religion—none of these three ideals being quite what, in our haste, we might suppose them to be. And the "uncommon reader" who is further interested is referred to three small volumes which Mr. Eliot has in preparation.

The argument draws no clear line between literary and social tradition, and one has a feeling at moments that the Muses are connected not so much with Apollo as with the oldest county families. One feels, moreover, that there is never all this talk about tradition until it has ceased to exist, and that Mr. Eliot, like Henry James, is romanticizing the land of his adoption. However, criticisms such as these are beside the point. They do not affect the apology, which is a serious one, and which does explain his work. The poems—so novel, startling, subtle, coarse—are not offered as the product of a private whim. They belong to the succession of Ben Jonson, Marvell, and Donne; they are a protest against the personal raptures of the Lake School. And when they are evasive and when the prose evades, it is because the writer is following an inner rule—some canon of wit, elegance, taste, or Divine Grace, the working of which is not apparent to the indisciplined reader. That is the explanation. When there are difficulties, the fault is always ours.

It is not an explanation under which I propose to sit down. Let me go straight to the heart of the matter, fling my poor little hand on the table, and say what I think *The Waste Land* is about. It is about the fertilizing waters that arrived too late. It is a poem of horror. The earth is barren, the sea salt, the fertilizing thunderstorm broke too late. And the horror is so intense that the poet has an inhibition and is unable to state it openly.

> What are the roots that clutch, what branches grow
> Out of this stony rubbish? Son of man,
> You cannot say, or guess, for you know only
> A heap of broken images.

He cannot say "Avaunt!" to the horror, or he would crumble into dust. Consequently, there are outworks and blind alleys all over the poem—obstacles which are due to the nature of the central emotion, and are not to be charged to the reader. *The Waste Land* is Mr. Eliot's greatest achievement. It intensifies the drawing-room premonitions of the earlier poems, and it is the key to what is puzzling in the prose. But, if I have its hang, it has nothing to do with the English tradition in literature, or law or order, nor, except incidentally, has the rest of his work anything to do with them either. It is just a personal comment on the universe, as individual and as isolated as Shelley's *Prometheus*.

In respect to the horror that they find in life, men can be divided

into three classes. In the first class are those who have not suffered
often or acutely; in the second, those who have escaped through horror
into a further vision; in the third, those who continue to suffer. Most
of us belong to the first class, and to the elect outside it our comments
must sound shallow; they may feel that we have no right to comment
at all. The mystics, such as Dostoevsky and Blake, belong to the
second class. Mr. Eliot, their equal in sensitiveness, distinct from them
in fate, belongs to the third. He is not a mystic. *For Lancelot Andrewes*
contains several well-turned compliments to religion and Divine
Grace, but no trace of religious emotion. Is he relegating it to another
place? No; if it exists, it cannot be relegated. He has not got it; what
he seeks is not revelation, but stability.[1] Hence his approval of institutions deeply rooted in the State, such as the Anglican Church,
hence the high premium he places upon statesmanship. "These fragments I have shored against my ruins." Hence the attempted impersonality and (if one can use the word here) the inhospitality of
his writing. Most writers sound, somewhere or other in their scale,
a note of invitation. They ask the reader in, to co-operate or to look.
Gerard Manley Hopkins is a case in point—a poet as difficult as Mr.
Eliot, and far more specialized ecclesiastically, yet however twisted
his diction and pietistic his emotion, there is always a hint to the
layman to come in if he can, and participate. Mr. Eliot does not want
us in. He feels we shall increase the barrenness. To say he is wrong
would be rash, and to pity him would be the height of impertinence,
but it does seem proper to emphasize the real as opposed to the apparent difficulty of his work. He is difficult because he has seen
something terrible, and (underestimating, I think, the general decency
of his audience) has declined to say so plainly.

I have called that terrible thing Armadillo-Armageddon, and
perhaps another personal reminiscence may conclude this very personal approach. It is of a bright August morning in 1914. I am lying
in bed. The milkman below calls as usual with the milk, and through
the clink of the handle I hear him say: "We've gone in." This, in its
small way, is the kind of experience that must have beset Mr. Eliot,
and rooted itself in the soil of his mind. Most of us forget such an experience, or do not feel it acutely. Only here and there does it expand
and contort into

---

[1] In view of Mr. Eliot's later work (not here considered) I would modify
these remarks.

The circles of the stormy moon
Slide westward toward the River Plate,
Death and the Raven drift above
And Sweeney guards the horned gate.

(1928)

# EZRA POUND *

### 1

. . . $\text{M}$R. ELIOT and I are in agreement, or 'belong to the same school of critics', in so far as we both believe that existing works form a complete order which is changed by the introduction of the 'really new' work.

His contempt for his readers has always been much greater than mine, by which I would indicate that I quite often write as if I expected my reader to use his intelligence, and count on its being fairly strong, whereas Mr. Eliot after enduring decennial fogs in Britain practically always writes as if for very feeble and brittle mentalities, from whom he can expect neither resilience nor any faculty for seeing the main import instead of the details or surfaces.

When he talks of 'commentation and elucidation' and of the 'correction of taste', I go into opposition, or rather, having been there first, I note that if I was in any sense the revolution I have been followed by the counter-revolution. Damn your taste, I would like if possible to sharpen your perceptions, after which your taste can take care of itself.

'Commentation' be damned. 'Elucidation' can stand if it means 'turn a searchlight on' something or preferably some work or author lying in shadow.

### 2

Mr. Eliot's flattering obeisance to 'exponents of criticism', wherein he says that he supposes they have not assumed that criticism is an 'autotelic activity', seems to me so much apple-sauce. In so far as the bureaucracy of letters has considered their writing as anything more than a short cut to the feeding trough or a means of puffing up their

---

* *Prefatio Aut Cimicium Tumulus,* from POLITE ESSAYS, pp. 135–138, 141–143. New Directions, Norfolk, Connecticut.

personal importances, they have done little else for the past thirty years than boost the production of writing about writing, not only as autotelic, but as something which ought to receive more attention from the reading victim than the great books themselves.

Granted that nobody ought to be such a presumptuous imbecile as to hold up the autotelic false horizon, Mr. Eliot describes a terrestrial paradise and not the de facto world, in which more immediate locus we observe a perpetual exchange of civilities between pulex, cimex, vermiformis, etc., each holding up his candle before the shrines of his similars.

A process having no conceivable final limit and illustratable by my present activity: I mean on this very page, engaging your attention while I talk about Mr. Eliot's essay about other essayists' essays. In the course of his eminently professorial volume he must have mentioned at least forty-five essayists whom to-morrow's readers will be most happy not to hear mentioned, but mention of whom must have contributed enormously to Mr. Eliot's rise to his deserved position as arbiter of British opinion.

### KRINO

'Existing monuments form an ideal order among themselves.' It would be healthier to use a zoological term rather than the word monument. It is much easier to think of the *Odyssey* or *Le Testament* or Catullus' *Epithalamium* as something living than as a series of cenotaphs. After all, Homer, Villon, Propertius, speak of the world as I know it, whereas Mr. Tennyson and Dr. Bridges did not. Even Dante and Guido with their so highly specialized culture speak of a part of life as I know it. ATHANATOS.

However, accepting for the moment Mr. Eliot's monumental or architectural simile: the KRINO, 'to pick out for oneself, choose, prefer' (page 381 my edition of Liddell and Scott) which seems to me the major job, is to determine, first, the main form and main proportions of that order of extant letters, to locate, first the greater pyramids and then, possibly, and with a decently proportioned emphasis, to consider the exact measurements of the stone-courses, layers, etc.

Dryden gives T.S.E. a good club wherewith to smack Milton. But with a modicum of familiarity or even a passing acquaintance with Dante, the club would hardly be needed. . . .

### MR. ELIOT'S GRIEF

Mr. Eliot's misfortune was to find himself surrounded by a horrible and microcephalous bureaucracy which disliked poetry, it might be too much to say 'loathed' it. But the emotion was as strong as any in the bureaucratic bosom. Bureaucracy has no loves and is composed mainly of varied minor dislikes. The members of this bureaucracy, sick with inferiority complex, had just enough wits to perceive that Eliot was their superior, but no means of detecting his limits or measuring him from the outside, and no experience that would enable them to know the poisons wherewith he had been injected. For that diagnosis perhaps only a fellow American is qualified, one having suffered an American University. The American University is or was aware of the existence of both German and English institutions, being younger and in a barbarous country, *its* inferiority complex impelled it to comparison and to a wish to equal and surpass, but gave it no immunity from the academical bacilli, inferiority complex directed against creative activity in the arts.

That there is a percentage of bunk in the *Selected Essays* Mr. Eliot will possibly be the last to deny, but that he had performed a self-analysis is still doubtful.

This kind of essay assumes the existence of a culture that no longer subsists and does nothing to prepare a better culture that must or ought to come into being. I say 'better', for the new paideuma will at least be a live paideuma not a dead one.

Such essays are prepared NOT for editors who care about a living literature or a live tradition, or who even want the best of Eliot's perception applied to an author of second or third or fourth category (per ex. Seneca), they want to maintain a system wherein it is possible to receive fifteen guineas for an article of approximately 3000–4000 words, in a series to which Mr. Eliot's sensitivity and patience will give lustre and wherein his occasional eminence will shed respectability on a great mass of inferior writing.

Their mentality is not far from that of a publisher of cheap editions who occasionally puts in a good book, so that the serious German will think that the miscellany is intellectual (*ipse dicebat*). Given the two or three real books in his series he believes the German highbrow will buy the rest thinking it the right thing to do.

# MARK VAN DOREN *

THIS is a new edition of "For Lancelot Andrewes," the volume of essays which Mr. Eliot published eight years ago with a preface announcing his position as royalist in politics, classicist in literature, and Anglo-Catholic in religion. He omits the preface now because it has "more than served its turn" and because it has misled too many readers into supposing that in his mind "all these three are inextricable and *of equal importance*." The italics are Mr. Eliot's, and refer to an ascending importance which time has established among the famous three. Nothing is said any more, indeed, about royalism at all. And classicism informs but a single discourse. The emphasis is all upon religion; by which Mr. Eliot means the Christian religion and more particularly Anglo-Catholicism; and in the high light of which he examines the contemporary world. Two of the essays which he has struck out of the present edition, those on Middleton and Crashaw, were perhaps too merely literary to please him. The essay on Machiavelli would have continued to serve his purpose had he kept it here where it so brilliantly belongs. For some reason he has not kept it; but for certain very plain reasons he has added three un-collected pieces on the eternal aspects of literature, politics, and edu-cation, and he has been content to represent himself as a critic of writing with two further pieces of Pascal and Tennyson.

The position he maintains here—maintaining it with that unique talent of his for being at the same time delicately ironic and fanatically firm—was anticipated in the essay on Irving Babbitt's humanism which he has held over from the earlier book. Mr. Eliot's objection to Mr. Babbitt's morals was that they were after all personal to Mr. Babbitt; lacking the religious reference as they did, they were simply one more attempt by modern man to save himself. Mr. Eliot has grown more and more sure during these eight years that man cannot save himself, and his review of the current chaos is a series of nods

* From *A Review of Essays Ancient and Modern* from THE PRIVATE READER, pp. 212–216, Copyright, 1942, by Mark Van Doren.

in the direction of schemes which will not work because their authors have taken the short view and ignored "the primacy of the supernatural over the natural life." Contemporary literature is by and large "degrading" because it knows no other life than this one; contemporary affairs are mismanaged because we have lost respect for that "otherworldly wisdom" without which worldly wisdom can never be complete; and contemporary education is meaningless because most teachers have forgotten that their problem is at bottom religious. The universal sin is secularism, under whose blind guidance we follow low ideals to the inevitable moment of disillusion—it is only the Catholic, with his absolute ideals and his moderate expectations, who cannot be disillusioned—and then stumble off, still hopeful, in another wild direction. Fascism and socialism, not to speak of the elective system in education, are heresies because their glance is ahead, not up; and because they subscribe to the tragic faith that man is sufficient unto himself. Confidence in the League of Nations is for Mr. Eliot an illustration of "that exaggerated faith in human reason to which people of undisciplined emotions are prone"; and the notion of letting students educate themselves is a sign of our having forgotten that "no one can become really educated without having pursued some study in which he took no interest—for it is a part of education to *learn to interest ourselves* in subjects for which we have no aptitude."

All of this is interesting, and it would be folly in the present state of affairs to assume without question that it is untrue. There is more truth in Mr. Eliot than there is in many a contemporary prophet to whom he will sound archaic and fantastic. The strange thing is that he speaks in the end with so little force and gives so little assurance that it is the world which he desires to save. The suspicion that it is himself—that he is only one step beyond Mr. Babbitt in the personal race for cover from the hailstones of our unbalmy time—arises if nowhere else from the circumstances that his essay on Pascal's "Pensées" is so much the most powerful essay here; and from the intimation of an affinity which he has felt for one who possessed in such high degree "the sensibility to feel the disorder, the futility, the meaninglessness, the mystery of life and suffering," as well as the need to "find peace through a satisfaction of the whole being." But the suspicion may be entertained by any serious reader on any page of this after all too tentative book. Mr. Eliot has suggested rather than substantiated a human world order, and his humility in doing so is perhaps more exquisite than it should be. What are we to make, considering the sternness with which he has announced the necessity of our learning to interest ourselves in subjects for which we have no aptitude, of his protestations again and again that he knows almost nothing about politics, economics, and science? How then are we to know which "ways of reorganizing the mechanisms of this world" are good in the degree to which such things in his opinion can be good? For he cannot tell us. He can merely reiterate, sometimes with an inflection like that of any curate, his faith in the enduring primacy of God's kingdom. And nothing that he says puts down the suspicion that he is as innocent of theology as he is of economics. If this is so, then he cannot be serious. He remains a literary critic of great charm and acumen; one furthermore who is skillful in the art of announcing distinctions—between mediation and compromise, say, or between unity and uniformity—which there never is time to exhaust; but one who, straying into immense subjects with only his "sensibility" to guide him, may add at best a few grace notes to the already roaring confusion.

# PAUL ELMER MORE *

WHEN T. S. Eliot came from London to Harvard as Professor
of Poetry for the year on the Charles Eliot Norton Foundation, the selection was generally applauded, though a few may have
asked cynically what Mr. Norton himself, with his kinship to the
old preaching Eliots of Massachusetts and his uncompromising notions of art, would have thought of such an appointment. The
significant fact is that the present scion of the family is perhaps the
most distinguished man of letters today in the British-speaking world,
and that his home-coming was the occasion of much comment, favorable and unfavorable, and of much searching of our critical principles. For myself I have this personal interest, that his grandfather,
a cousin, I believe, of the former President of Harvard, was Chancellor
of the little university (at that time little) in St. Louis to which I owe
my academic allegiance, and that I had the privilege of teaching one of
the grandsons in a school conducted under the charter of the University, though that office has not been extended in any form to my
pupil's brother.

As for the distinguished position of Mr. Eliot, no one is likely to
dispute the fact who is familiar with the English press and knows
with what frequency and respect his name occurs. More significant
even is his following among the younger thinking men of England,
especially in the universities. Nor is this following confined to his
adopted country. I can well remember the furor of enthusiasm aroused
among the youthful intelligentsia of Princeton a few years ago when
I proposed that he should be invited to lecture here. Whatever the
more sober part of the world may think of him, his name acts, or certainly has acted, like a spell upon the forward pushing minds of two
countries.

The fact of Mr. Eliot's reputation is indisputable. But if one asks
the reason for it, the answer is not so quickly at hand. As a critic he
stands high. For myself I have been going through the volume of his

---

* Review of SELECTED ESSAYS by T. S. Eliot, from *The Saturday Review of
Literature,* Copyright, 1932, by Saturday Review Associates, Inc.

"Selected Essays" (it is so comprehensive as almost to justify the title "collected"). Undoubtedly the author comes well through this ordeal of continuous reading. There is capable scholarship in these essays, particularly in those that deal with the Elizabethan and Jacobean dramatists; there is a play of alert and penetrating thought, and above all a certain unassumed gravity of judgment, a certain note of authority, not readily defined but instinctively felt. The "metaphysical" poets, from whom Mr. Eliot rightly draws his spiritual lineage, will have a new value for anyone who has read his analysis of their method. Yet there are sides to his critical work which are not so easily reconciled with his reputation. His apparent blindness to the real greatness of Milton may be explained by the fact that Milton stands at the head of the line of development which to Mr. Eliot's disciples, if not to Mr. Eliot himself, has acted like a damper upon English poetry until the advent of the modern "metaphysicals"; but that cavalier judgment will not please many whose taste was formed in an older school, nor those younger advocates of a return to Milton of whom Professor Elliott, of Amherst, is a leader. And, on the other hand, the critic's pages are sprinkled with pungent sayings that must shock and sting the complacent enthusiasts of modernism. Who then are the authenticators of this critical renown, the conservatives or the modernists?

But Mr. Eliot is a poet as well as a critic, or, more precisely, a poet primarily; and it might be presumed that the source of his great reputation could be found in his verse rather than in his prose. And this in a sense is true. Yet here too difficulties arise, which perhaps may be best exhibited by relating a bit of personal experience. I am myself a staunch admirer of his "Ash Wednesday," though the poem has been pretty harshly judged by certain narrow champions of his earlier style. Well, I have read the poem aloud five or six times to variously composed groups of listeners (and reading aloud is about the final test of a poet), with invariably the same result. Without exception, whether their taste was of the older or the newer model, the auditors have been deeply impressed. For one thing they have felt the sonority of the lines and have been stirred by the cadences of a music which is extremely rare in our free verse. And this is not the melody of merely prettily selected and adroitly adjoined words, independent of their sense, but suggests the profounder harmony—if one could only find it—of an organically constructive genius behind the superficial disarray of the phrases. Yet without exception also the poem—and generally it was read aloud two or three times consecutively to the same group—failed to convey any clear meaning. Regularly the comment was the same: This is beautiful, this holds our attention; but we have the vaguest notion, if any notion, of what it is all about. Ordinarily the complaint was made by way of disparagement, whether of the poet's intelligence or the hearer's capacity. But not always. On one occasion the poem selected for reading was "The Hippopotamus," which ends, as will be remembéred, with this rather startling comparison:

> He shall be washed as white as snow,
> By all the martyr'd virgins kist,
> While the True Church remains below
> Wrapt in the old miasmal mist.

At the conclusion of the reading I turned to one of the most attentive auditors, an enthusiast to whom Mr. Eliot is the sublimest poet since Milton (the concession to Milton being, I suspect, of the lips only), with the query: Now this has the ring of poetry; but what in the name of sense *is* the hippopotamus? "Does it make any difference?" cried he, almost jumping out of his chair at the indignity of such a question. And his answer, if it did not elucidate Mr. Eliot, explained several things to me in the taste of the younger generation. (I may add that on a later occasion the poet himself, with his sly ironic smile, put me off by intimating that possibly the writer could not—he meant would not—expound my riddle.)

Now all this points to a curious discrepancy in Mr. Eliot's position. I find a good many poetry lovers of the older tradition simply neglecting him as unintelligible and unimportant; and this indifference I can understand, though I do not share it. A few also of the ultra modern type repudiate him with equal finality, but with an added note of supercilious contempt which is rather characteristic of the fully emancipated mind. Miss Rebecca West, for instance, ridicules his "flustered search for coherence," and a preposterous contributor to the Boston *Transcript* ends a long diatribe with the complaint: "He still is lost in his Waste Land and, whether with malice or not, is still pointing out false roads to the oasis to those travelers who seek from him the way"—rather than from Mr. Calverton. Other radicals distinguish for their own satisfaction between the poet of the past and the critic of the present. I once asked a young student of very advanced ideas about art and life how he, as an admirer of Mr. Eliot, reconciled the "Waste Land" with the program of classicism and royalism (i.e., the divine right of kings) and Anglo-Catholicism announced in a recent preface. His reply was quick and decisive: "I don't reconcile them; I take the one and leave the other." And to this rebuke I had nothing to say, since it pointed to a cleft in Mr. Eliot's career to which I am myself sensitive, though my young friend's order of values is the reverse of my own.

There it is, the dilemma that confronts those who recognize Mr. Eliot's great powers; somehow they must reconcile for themselves what appears to be an inconsequence between the older poet and the newer critic, or must adjust their admiration to what cannot be reconciled. It is not that we have to do with an author who is strong in one phase of his work and weak in another, but that this power is so differently directed here and there. The writer of the "Waste Land" and the other poems of that period appeals to us as one struck to the heart by the confusion and purposelessness and wastefulness of the world about him, and as dismayed by the impoverishment of our human emotions and imagination in a life so divested of meaning and so dull of conscience. And to that world his verse will be held up as a ruthlessly faithful mirror. The confusion of life will be reflected in the disorganized flux of images; its lack of clear meaning in the obscurity of language; its defiance of authoritative creeds in a license of metrical form; its dislocated connection with the past in the floating debris of allusion; while its flattened emotions will be reproduced realistically, without comment. If there be any salvation from such a whirligig of chance and time it is only into the peace of utter escape—"*Shantih, shantih!*"

And now against this lyric prophet of chaos must be set the critic who will judge the world from the creed of the classicist, the royalist, and the Anglo-Catholic, who will see behind the clouds of illusion the steady decrees of a divine purpose, and who has gone so far at least in that program as to compose a long pamphlet (included in the "Selected Essays") of "Thoughts after Lambeth." And what has the young rebel who rejoices in the disillusion of the "Waste Land" to do with the Bishops of the Church assembled in solemn conclave to unravel the purposes of Deity? In one sense it would be easy to

reconcile such a *volte face* by saying simply that the author has under-
gone a deep conversion; and that explanation is in a way true. But
the embarrassing fact remains that somehow the poet contrives to carry
on the old shop into the new market. I think, for instance, that a sensitive mind cannot read "Ash Wednesday" without an uneasy perception of something fundamentally amiss in employing for an
experience born of Anglo-Catholic faith a metrical form and a freak-
ishness of punctuation suitable for the presentation of life regarded as
without form and void. Such a discord manifestly was felt by those
to whom I have read the poem, though one and all they responded
to the mere magic of the language in itself. And I am sure it is this
same disharmony between subject and mode of expression that drives
a friendly critic like Mr. McGreevy to complain of being fairly dis-
concerted by "the distinct falling off in vigor and vividness, in pregnancy, suggestiveness of words, in technical adequacy to the subject,
not only from the quality of the 'Waste Land' but from that of the
much earlier 'Prufrock.' " I am sure it is not inadequate technique
that disconcerts Mr. McGreevy, for there is no falling off in adequacy,
but wrong technique, which is quite another thing.

No, it is not the revolution in Mr. Eliot's views of life, his conversion if you prefer the word, that troubles his true admirers, but the
fact that his change on one side is complicated and disrupted by lack
of change on the other side. And here I would like to recall a bit of
conversation with him, trusting that I may do so without any breach
of confidence or betrayal of the intimacies of friendship (if Mr. Eliot
will allow me the honor of calling myself a friend). It was in his London home; I was lauding the audacity of the critical conversion announced in the preface to his "Lancelot Andrewes," then recently
published, and I concluded with the query: "And now, when you
have completed this heroic program and have returned, as your intention is, to verse, will you cling to the old impossible (so I expressed
it) manner of the 'Waste Land'?" "No," he exclaimed, losing for a
moment his armor of placid irony, and shaking a defiant fist in the
air,—"No; in that I am absolutely unconverted!"

I am not at all confident that I have interpreted Mr. Eliot correctly, or that, in particular, I have grasped his state of mind when he
composed the earlier poems; his is an elusive, though an unmistakable,
genius. But my perplexity over some unreconciled paradox, at once
provocative and baffling, in his attitude towards life and letters has

been confirmed by too many witnesses to leave me in doubt of its justification. Mr. Eliot, I am sure, would disavow any ambition to pose as a leader of men; but he is a leader, and a very influential leader. Our difficulty is that he seems to be leading us in two directions at once.

# MALCOLM COWLEY *

TO American writers of my own age, or at any rate to those who went abroad in 1921, the author who seemed nearest to themselves was T. S. Eliot. Essentially the picture he presented was that of the local-boy-makes-good. He was born in St. Louis; he was graduated from Harvard, where he took courses that any of us might have taken and managed to belong to three or four undistinguished clubs; he continued his studies at a French provincial university and got a job in London—now, ten years after leaving Cambridge, he was winding himself in a slow cocoon of glory. But his glory, his making good, was not in the vulgar sense of making money, making a popular reputation: in 1921 the newspapers had never heard of this clerk in Barclay's Bank. His achievement was the writing of perfect poems, poems in which we could not find a line that betrayed immaturity, awkwardness, provincialism or platitude. Might a Middle Western boy become a flawless poet?—this was a question with which we could not fail to be preoccupied.

But it was not the only question that Eliot answered, nor the only door by which he entered our secret minds. His early critical writings were concerned in large part with the dispute between form and matter, and he aligned himself with what we had learned to call our side of it. He effectively defended the intellect as against the emotions, and the conscious mind as against the libido, the dark Freudian wish. His poems, from the first, were admirably constructed. He seemed to regard them moreover, as intellectual problems—having solved one problem, he devoted himself to another. From his early sketches in free verse, he moved on to *Portrait of a Lady* and *Prufrock;* thence he moved on to his Sweeney poems, thence to *Gerontion;* and it was certain that his new ambitious work soon to be published in the *Dial* would mark another departure. For he never repeated himself and never, in those days, persisted in any attitude or technique; once having suggested its possibilities, he moved on.

---

* *Readings from the Lives of the Saints* from EXILE'S RETURN, pp. 123–128, Copyright, 1934, by Malcolm Cowley.

Eliot, of course, did not originate the idea of "moving on." It was part of the general literary atmosphere, part of a long tradition—for example, it closely resembled the "theory of convolutions" that developed among my high school friends. But Eliot's influence had the effect of making the idea vastly popular among young writers. They began to picture the ideal poet as an explorer, a buffalo hunter pressing westward toward new frontiers—from the Shenandoah he marches into unknown Tennessee, thence into the Blue Grass, thence into Missouri, always leaving the land untilled behind him, but who cares?—there will be disciples to follow the plow. No other American poet had so many disciples as Eliot, in so many stages of his career. Until 1925, his influence seemed omnipresent, and it continued to be important in the years that followed. But in 1922, at the moment when he was least known to the general public and most fervently worshiped by young poets, there had been a sudden crisis. More than half of his disciples began slowly to drop away.

When *The Waste Land* first appeared, we were confronted with a dilemma. Here was a poem that agreed with all our recipes and prescriptions of what a great modern poem should be. Its form was not only perfect but was far richer musically and architecturally than that of Eliot's earlier verse. Its diction was superb. It employed in a magisterial fashion the technical discoveries made by the French writers who followed Baudelaire. Strangeness, abstractness, simplifications, respect for literature as an art with traditions—it had all the qualities demanded in our slogans. We were prepared fervently to defend it against the attacks of the people who didn't understand what Eliot was trying to do—but we made private reservations. The poem had forced us into a false position, had brought our consciously adopted principles into conflict with our instincts. At heart—not intellectually, but in a purely emotional fashion—we didn't like it. We didn't agree with the idea that the poem set forth.

Yet the idea is simple. Beneath the rich symbolism of *The Waste Land,* the wide learning expressed in seven languages, the actions conducted on three planes, the musical episodes, the geometrical structure—beneath and by means of all this, the poet is saying that the present is inferior to the past. The past was dignified; the present is barren of emotion. The past was a landscape nourished by living fountains; now the fountains of spiritual grace are dry. . . . Often in his earlier poems Eliot had suggested this idea; he had used such symbols of dead glory as the Roman eagles and trumpets or the Lion of St. Mark's to emphasize the vulgarities of the present. In those poems, however, the present was his real subject. Even though he seemed to abhor it, even though he thought "of all the hands that are raising dingy shades in a thousand furnished rooms" and was continually "aware of the damp souls of housemaids sprouting despondently at area gates," still he was writing about the life that all of us knew—no, more than that, he was endowing our life with distinction by means of those same distinguished metaphors in which he decried and bewailed it. *The Waste Land* marked a real change. This time, he not only expressed the idea with all his mature resources, but carried it to a new extreme. He not only abused the present, but robbed it of vitality. It was as if he were saying, this time, that our age cannot even find words of its own in which to lament its barrenness; that it is forever condemned to borrow and patch together the songs of dead poets.

The seven-page appendix to *The Waste Land,* in which Eliot paraded his scholarship and explained the Elizabethan or Italian sources of what had seemed to be his most personal phrases, was a painful dose for us to swallow. But the truth was that the poet had not changed so much as we ourselves had changed. We were becoming less preoccupied with technique. In the midst of poems admirable in structure, we were groping for those that portrayed our own picture of the world. As for the problem presented by Eliot, whether the values of past ages were superior or inferior to present values, it was a question on which we could bring no objective evidence to bear. Values are created by living men. If they believe—if their manner of life induces them to believe—that greatness died with Virgil, Dante, or Napoleon, who can change their opinion or teach them new values? It happened that we were excited by the adventure of living in the present. The famous "post-war mood of aristocratic disillusionment" was something that affected us not in the least. It happened that Mr. Eliot's subjective truth was not our own.

I say "it happened" although, as a matter of fact, our beliefs were inevitable. I say "we" although I can refer only to a majority, perhaps two-thirds, of those already influenced by T. S. Eliot. When *The Waste Land* first appeared, it made visible a social division among writers that was not a division between capitalist and proletarian. The literary profession included not many who, in the strict sense, were members of either great social order. There were, it is true, some writers of my age whose parents were factory workers or tenant farmers, but these few, having received the education of the middle class, had for the most part adopted its standards. The middle class was beginning to dominate the world of letters; the dominant educational background was that of the public high school and the big Middle Western university. And the writers of this class—roughly corresponding to Marx's petty bourgeoisie—were those who began to ask where Eliot was leading and to travel in other directions.

But there were also many young writers who had been graduated from good preparatory schools, usually Episcopalian, before attending Yale, Harvard, or Princeton, Williams or Amherst. Whether rich or poor, they had received the training and acquired the standards of that small American owning and ruling class, the bourgeoisie proper. These, in general, were the "young poets old before their time" who not only admired *The Waste Land* but insisted on dwelling there; who, as Edmund Wilson says, "took to inhabiting exclusively barren beaches, cactus-grown deserts and dusty attics overrun with rats"— their special education, their social environment and also, I think, their class feeling of mingled power and insecurity had prepared them to follow T. S. Eliot in his desert wanderings toward a goal that must have been visible to others before he saw it himself.

There were many exceptions in both groups. Eliot continued to be fervently admired behind the dingy shades of a thousand furnished rooms; he continued to be violently attacked by many writers of the class to which he would shortly proclaim his allegiance. But slowly it became evident that writers and their theories were moving toward two extremes (though few would reach either one or the other). The first extreme was that of authority and divinely inspired tradition as represented by the Catholic Church; the second was Communism. In Paris, in the year 1922, we were forced by Eliot to make a preliminary choice. Though we did not see our own path, we instinctively rejected his. In the future we should continue to honor Eliot's poems, and the integrity, the clearness of his prose, but the Eliot picture had ceased to be our guide.

# GRANVILLE HICKS *

WHEN Eliot began writing the enthusiasms of the renaissance were reverberating about him, but the esthetes who followed him at Harvard quickly recognized that he was closer to them than were the poets of the middle generation, and both his mood and his method won him admirers. The method borrowed something from the imagists, but it relied largely on the device, practiced by Ezra Pound among others, of using quotation and allusion to suggest the contrast between the grandeur of the past and the meanness of the present. No one expressed better than Eliot the beliefs and attitudes of the esthetes: the mixture of rebellion and condescension in their relations with their contemporaries, their self-conscious modernity and their wistful admiration for the poets of bygone days, their strange self-contempt and their boundless egotism.

But Eliot was so bitterly aware of the emptiness of modern life, the sterility of its negations and the futility of its hopes, that he desperately sought for some abiding place of faith and peace. At first he found a kind of refuge in his art, even though that art celebrated uncertainty and unrest, but in time that refuge proved inadequate. Not long after he had feebly announced his prostrate helplessness in "The Hollow Men," he defined his general point of view as "classicist in literature, royalist in politics, and Anglo-Catholic in religion." He had turned for support to what were, for him, the only institutions that offered strength and permanence, the British Church and State. We need not ask how so melodramatic a skeptic can accept the dogmas of Anglicanism, or what so intelligent an observer can expect from the King of England, or why so resolute an experimenter should affirm his allegiance to the laws of ancient art. The need for security was too strong to pay any attention to common sense or logic.

But the poetry Eliot has written since his conversion suggests that he has gained little—and may have lost much. In his critical pronouncements he can dogmatically affirm his new faith, but the poems

---

* From THE GREAT TRADITION, pp. 268–271, Copyright, 1933, 1935, by The Granville Hicks

34

in *Ash Wednesday* are as weak and elegiac as any he wrote in his unregenerate state. In fact Mr. Eliot's principles seem to be strangling his poetic gifts: he can now speak neither as poet of faith nor as poet of doubt. The unity of tone that once made his poems memorable has disappeared, and nothing of comparable value has taken its place. "A Song for Simeon" and "The Journey of the Magi," for example, are full of the old despair, and yet, merely as statements of that despair, they are less moving than "The Waste Land" or "J. Alfred Prufrock."

Mr. Eliot continues, however, to have his following. Allen Tate, John Crowe Ransom, and John Brooks Wheelwright are among the defenders of the faith, and the interest in religion has spread, influencing many men who have not joined the Church. Catholicism, whether Roman or Anglican, provides the writer with a body of ideas that have the dignity of age and, for that reason, the appearance of stability. It offers him, moreover, the support of a thoroughly dignified tradition. Poets do not join the Baptist Church or the Methodist. The evangelical Protestant churches are strongholds of the lower middle class, against whose standards the poets are in rebellion. It is to Anglicanism that the writer usually turns, grateful for its traditional association with aristocracy, its historic friendliness to the arts, and its complacent assertion of a realm of values outside the comprehension of the average American business man.

# HAROLD J. LASKI *

THE tragedy of the intellectuals of our time has been their relative indifference to one of the supreme battles in the history of
civilization, or, alternatively, that, like Sorel and Kipling, like Barrès
and Maurras, and, if in a lesser degree, even Charles Péguy, they had
enlisted in the army of reaction. It is worth noting that there is hardly
an evil against which Dickens and Charles Reade, Ruskin and Matthew Arnold and William Morris warned the Victorians which has
not, as it has been neglected, poisoned our social organization. The
crime of the intellectuals was not, as Benda thought, that some of
them went into the battle. The crime was the very different one that
most of them did not know that a battle was being waged, and that,
of those who did, a majority was willing to fight on the wrong side.
It was not merely that, as in the war of 1914, the men of letters and
the artists were willing, with rare exceptions, to glorify the conflict
and even take pride in the effectiveness with which they served a
social order the decadence of which was proved by the fact of war.
What was even worse was the fact that, when the peace came in
1919, they entered the waste land instead of embarking upon the task
of reconstruction. Occasionally, we listened to the voice of a poet
who, like W. H. Davies, had the great gift of natural song. Occasionally, also, some angry sonnet of Mr. Siegfried Sassoon would show
that the poet's divine power of passionate anger could still express
itself. But that Mr. T. S. Eliot should have been the outstanding influence in Anglo-American poetry between the two wars is not less
significant than Professor Lynd's report of a Christianity which, as
in Middletown, has come to terms with the money-changers in return for the right to retain a small room in the temple.

It was not that Mr. Eliot had not great gifts, learning, the power
of superb phrase, a mastery of the ironic epithet unsurpassed in our
time. But the most important thing in Mr. Eliot was his horror of
the common man, his shrinking from any contact with the masses,

* From FAITH, REASON AND CIVILIZATION, pp. 96–100, 180–182, Copyright,
1944, by The Viking Press, Inc., New York.

the fastidious sensitiveness which seemed to regard whatever is democratic as in its nature vulgar and ugly and barbarous. Mr. Eliot
showed, as no other poet of his time, that we were reaching the end
of a culture as surely as in the days when Claudian celebrated in his
epic the last great triumph of Roman poetry. For he neither sought
nor desired to make his music heard by ordinary people. He spoke
to an *élite* the real pride of which lay in its deliberate cultivation of
remoteness from ordinary people. There was no spontaneity of feeling in what he wrote, but rather a mannered disdain for a world
in which the overwhelming majority would have no more chance of
understanding his poems than they would of following a paper by
Einstein or some development by Littlewood of the mathematical
theory of inequalities. If it be said that it is not the business of an
eminent poet to write so that the half-literate masses may follow his
thought, it is surely a sufficient answer that the cultivation of a conscious aloofness from the world is at least as artificial a procedure as
a refusal to write down to the level of the masses. When the poet
ceases to be Shelley's "unacknowledged legislator of the world," it is
because he has ceased to find meaning in the world; he has so divorced thought from action that he has hardly wanted even an audience to address. The poet who thus cuts himself off from his fellows
is cutting himself off from life. And that is, as hardly anything else
can be, a denial that life has meaning. For the poet to whom his art
denies the necessity of the fullest communication that is open to him
is in truth denying that he has anything it is essential to say. His art
becomes a form of narcissism in which he whispers to himself, afraid,
above all, lest he be overheard; and even when, as with Mr. Eliot, he
writes with brilliance for a special band of acolytes, it is rather the
echo of his own voice than the message he has to proclaim that is of
importance to him. At that point, surely, what has withered in him is
humanism, and he has exchanged the full range of imaginative insight for a mysticism which blacks out the living world. I cannot
think that it is the function of poetry thus to deny the validity of life.
But the poet who performs this function is as profoundly guilty as
any of those whom M. Benda impeaches of the treason of which he
accuses them. Like the Desert Fathers, he has gone into self-chosen
exile because he fears the battle which is waging. That is an abandonment of the positive life which it is difficult to distinguish from betrayal of it.

I am not arguing that one ought to criticize Mr. Eliot because the view he recommends to us has become, in fact, a tradition based on values which repose on both sanctions and on hopes which are largely irrelevant not only to our problems but, also, to the dearly purchased achievements of modern historical scholarship. Every society in crisis produces small groups of thinkers who seek to provide, as Mr. Eliot has sought, an alternative outlook to the predominant habits of thought in and through which he finds release from the misery these cause him. No one can read Mr. Eliot's writings without the admiring conviction that he loathes with all his heart the degradation it imposes by the standards to which it is committed. No one, either, can doubt his deep anxiety to find a way out of that degradation.

My criticism is the different one, first, that he accepts as inevitable that degradation for all but a small band of precious souls, and, second, that this leads him to address these only in what is almost wilfully a special language in the obscurities of which he quite obviously has a peculiar pleasure; he thus deliberately turns his back upon the supreme issue of whether it is in our power to elevate the standards of value and taste throughout our society; one is always reminded, in reading Mr. Eliot, of the great Hebrew scholar, Dr. Schechter's remark, of Oxford—"they mistake fastidiousness for holiness." I accept the fact not only that he has given profound satisfaction to his disciples, even that he has expressed the disillusion of this generation more vividly than any other contemporary figure. But I suspect that the satisfaction he has given them derives less from the inherent beauty of what he has written than from the fact that, as they apprehend the meaning of his exotic remoteness, they are made to feel that they, too, by that power to apprehend, are set apart, with their master, from the multitude.

So that the real effect of Mr. Eliot's work is to abandon the great mass of men and women to those who impose upon our civilization the very standards he is denouncing. He has, so to say, found his way out of the waste land through a door he leaves half-hidden still, even while he proclaims that no one can find the clue to salvation unless he passes through that door. So that those who through poverty, or the ills, physical and social and cultural, which accompany it, not merely receive no call to seek for the vision he himself has seen; Mr. Eliot seems to have a sense almost of delight in insisting that a glimpse of the vision is beyond their powers. The character our society gives to men leads him to an almost Platonic disdain of ordinary persons, and the inference that they are unfit to join the pilgrimage on which he has set out; and, alongside that inference, he turns round to denounce them fiercely for their refusal to see the beauty and the truth of the vision he is painting. He leaves them to struggle in a corruption they did not cause, and blames them contemptuously for not perceiving the depth of their corruption. The note of disdain and contempt for the masses is omnipresent; and I call this a betrayal of culture, a form of intellectual treason, because it leaves those prisoners of the dark forces in society to whom it might have sought to communicate their way to emancipation. It is important, moreover, to add with emphasis that, in terms of the Christian tradition to which Mr. Eliot seeks a return, the contrast between the massive simplicity of its founders, with their deliberate appeal to the poor and the humble and the despised, and the complex aloofness of its restatement, is significant indeed. It is the measure in which the democratic ideal is assumed to be an aristocracy which stands apart and remote from the daily struggle.

I agree at once that it is not the task of imaginative literature to be didactic; still more, that the inculcation of any specific creed is not a duty to which any of the arts is called. I agree that the artist must report what he sees, and that, if he dons the uniform of a Church or a party, there is danger that his vision will be dimmed. But great literature cannot be either a means of escape merely from the tragic burden of life, nor can it seek to provide the artist with no more than a means of self-realization without regard to the price society pays for that fulfilment. For the logic of that view becomes, in the end, the claim that the rest of mankind must be content to be no more than instruments who make possible the artist's godlike satisfaction. Great art, in all its media, is surely the communication of an intense emotion which, at its deepest level, gives new insight to all who hear its call. It seeks to be an understanding shared, not a secret withheld. Whether it is Homer singing his epic into the memory of all Greek history, or Paul of Tarsus journeying in endless anxiety to communicate his good tidings, the function it performs is a spiritual elevation which reaches the higher the more supreme its quality. In the degree that it withdraws its secret, and leaves the masses in the waste land, it leaves them, also, to become the victims of men like Hitler and Mussolini, or mean cults and ugly illusions, of the crude habits which mistake power and pomp for truth and beauty. And, in the end, the artist shares the fate of the masses he thus abandons; for when they have lost their power to differentiate between good and evil, between great art and poor art, they enter a prison whose jailer demands from the artist himself that he announce no message which might make his captives seek to break their prison bars. Great artists can only be free when they call the world to freedom. . . .

"When morals cease to be a matter of tradition and orthodoxy," Mr. T. S. Eliot has written,[1] "that is, of the habits of the community, formulated, corrected and elevated by the continuous thought and direction of the Church—and when each man is to elaborate his own, then personality becomes a thing of alarming importance." It would be difficult to find a sentence which reveals more fully than this the final bankruptcy of our social order. For while it perceives that the moral quality of a system must be, as it were, a function of the community as natural to it as the phenomena of life and death, and while, too, it recognizes that the moral quality must change and grow, it assumes that its fate is to be entrusted to a Church and that the alternative is an individualism which rapidly assumes the character of a *Fuhrer-prinzip*. Like his predecessor in fastidiousness, Henry James, he is appalled at the breakdown in values; but while James's judgment is a verdict upon that rich *bourgeoisie* whose devotion to property is their outstanding characteristic, the one in terms of which all the social relations of his novels are constructed, Mr. Eliot's judgment is a verdict upon the common people whose vulgarity so appals him that he is led by his distaste for them into hostility, as a critic, to poets like Milton who had played, even if only for a time, a progressive role in their age. Mr. Eliot does not ask himself what it is, alike in the ethical and intellectual record of the Church, that has made it incapable of retaining the guardianship of morals in our civilization. He does not examine its relation to the evolution of a tradition which has made personality "alarming in its importance." He merely looks backwards for the revival of a leadership which had risen and established its orthodoxy under circum-

---

[1] Cf. "Tradition and the Individual Talent" in T. S. Eliot, *Selected Essays* (1941), with *The Idea of a Christian Society* (1940).

stances completely different from those Mr. Eliot should himself
have been observing. Henry James may not have understood that
the morals of a society in which a small class of wealthy people are
parasitic upon the labour of the masses are predestined to corruption;
but, at least, he recognized the corruption when he encountered it.
Mr. Eliot saw that same corruption; yet it did not occur to him that
it could extend, as it had in fact for nearly two thousand years extended, to the very Church which he proposed to make the safeguard
against its invasion of society. He did not understand that a Church
which does not insist upon the inclusion of the masses within the
culture of a civilization is bound to fail, in the long run, to perform
that task of moral elevation he has assigned to it.

The truth is, of course, that the small, wealthy class had made
the morals of our civilization no more than an argument for the
defence of its own claims. As soon as the case against those claims
was stated, with a force which, since the Industrial Revolution, has
never ceased to gather momentum, it became increasingly obvious
that they were ethically inadequate to the issues they sought to meet.
They failed altogether to recognize the driving forces of the society
in which they sought acceptance. It was really no use to ask that
men should recognize how wretched they were, deformed by original sin, yet capable, as Mr. Eliot himself has said, of "apprehending
perfection," if the working of the social and economic system in fact
confines that apprehension—the idea of a Christian society—to a
chosen few the very condition of whose existence as an *élite* is the
inevitable exclusion of the overwhelming majority of men and women
from the prospect even of being aware that such apprehension is possible. I think Mr. Eliot is wholly right in his view that the outcome
of the moral decay he has seen so clearly and depicted with such
incisive force is the glorification of power; and I think it is right to
emphasize that when power, as such, has once been glorified, the
emergence of the type like Hitler is only a matter of time and the
occasion. But Hitler is, after all, no more than the final term in a
series in which the feudal lord, the nobleman of the Renaissance, the
aloof Whig aristocrat of Eighteenth-century England, the Prussian
general who built his conduct on the model of Frederick the Great,
the ruthless millionaire of that America which had not yet finished
the exploitation of the frontier, were also terms; and there was none
of them with whom the Church, to which Mr. Eliot looks for libera-

tion, was not willing eagerly to make its peace. If there is to be the chance of liberation, it is in other directions we must search.

For, at bottom, the Christian society of which Mr. Eliot writes so eloquently is not a means of liberating the masses, but a technique of escape for a few chosen souls who cannot bear the general spectacle of civilization in decay. It is a monastery, a retreat in the wilderness, which enables its inhabitants to turn their back upon the universe. That they are to do so in humble recognition of their miserable natures, I do not for one moment doubt Mr. Eliot believes; but I suggest that, beneath the announcement of humility, there is, as in Pascal, by whom it is evident that Mr. Eliot has been profoundly influenced, a limitless pride which recognizes with gratitude that the new Desert Fathers are not as other men are. And the plea, in any case, breaks down, partly because there is, in fact, no Church genuinely prepared to break with the world and thus surrender its hope of ultimately controlling the world, and, in part for the vital reason that, in the conditions of our time, that glorification of power which can result in the emergence of a Hitler means, inescapably, a totalitarian society in which the men who rule dare not allow the separate spiritual *élite* which Mr. Eliot recommends to us, since its very existence is an explicit criticism of their right to power. We are driven back, in short, not to the need to recover a tradition which our circumstances render an anachronism, but to the discovery of the principles which make a democratic society no longer a formality of use when rhetoric is in order, but a living reality which captures the heart and mind of the common man.

# DELMORE SCHWARTZ *

A CULTURE hero is one who brings new arts and skills to mankind. Prometheus was a culture hero and the inventors of the radio may also be said to be culture heroes, although this is hardly to be confounded with the culture made available by the radio.

The inventors of the radio made possible a new range of experience. This is true of certain authors; for example, it is true of Wordsworth in regard to nature, and Proust in regard to time. It is not true of Shakespeare, but by contrast it is true of Surrey and the early Elizabethan playwrights who invented blank verse. Thus the most important authors are not always culture heroes, and thus no rank, stature, or scope is of necessity implicit in speaking of the author as a culture hero.

When we speak of nature and of a new range of experience, we may think of a mountain range: some may make the vehicles by means of which a mountain is climbed, some may climb the mountain, and some may apprehend the new view of the surrounding countryside which becomes possible from the heights of the mountain. T. S. Eliot is a culture hero in each of these three ways. This becomes clear when we study the relationship of his work to the possible experiences of modern life. The term, possible, should be kept in mind, for many human beings obviously disregard and turn their backs upon much of modern life, although modern life does not in the least cease to circumscribe and penetrate their existence.

The reader of T. S. Eliot by turning the dials of his radio can hear the capitals of the world, London, Vienna, Athens, Alexandria, Jerusalem. What he hears will be news of the agony of war. Both the agony and the width of this experience are vivid examples of how the poetry of T. S. Eliot has a direct relationship to modern life. The width and the height and the depth of modern life are exhibited in his poetry; the agony and the horror of modern life are represented as inevitable to any human being who does not wish to deceive him-

* T. S. Eliot as the International Hero, from Partisan Review, Vol. XII, No. 2 (Spring, 1945), pp. 199–206, Copyright, 1945, by Partisan Review.

self with systematic lies. Thus it is truly significant that E. M. Forster, in writing of Eliot, should recall August 1914 and the beginning of the First World War; it is just as significant that he should speak of first reading Eliot's poems in Alexandria, Egypt, during that war, and that he should conclude by saying that Eliot was one who had looked into the abyss and refused henceforward to deny or forget the fact.

We are given an early view of the international hero in the quasi-autobiographical poem which Eliot entitles: "Mélange Adultère De Tout." The title, borrowed from a poem by Corbière, is ironic, but the adulterous mixture of practically everything, every time and every place, is not ironic in the least: a teacher in America, the poem goes, a journalist in England, a lecturer in Yorkshire, a literary nihilist in Paris, overexcited by philosophy in Germany, a wanderer from Omaha to Damascus, he has celebrated, he says, his birthday at an African oasis, dressed in a giraffe's skin. Let us place next to this array another list of names and events as heterogeneous as a circus or America itself: St. Louis, New England, Boston, Harvard, England, Paris, the First World War, Oxford, London, the Russian Revolution, the Church of England, the post-war period, the world crisis and depression, the Munich Pact, and the Second World War. If this list seems far-fetched or forced, if it seems that such a list might be made for any author, the answer is that these names and events are *presences* in Eliot's work in a way which is not true of many authors, good and bad, who have lived through the same years.

Philip Rahv has shown how the heroine of Henry James is best understood as the heiress of all the ages. So, in a further sense, the true protagonist of Eliot's poems is the heir of all the ages. He is the descendant of the essential characters of James in that he is the American who visits Europe with a Baedeker in his hand, just like Isabel Archer. But the further sense in which he is the heir of all the ages is illustrated when Eliot describes the seduction of a typist in a London flat from the point of view of Tiresias, a character in a play by Sophocles. To suppose that this is the mere exhibition of learning or reading is a banal misunderstanding. The important point is that the presence of Tiresias illuminates the seduction of the typist just as much as a description of her room. Hence Eliot writes in his notes to *The Waste Land* that "what Tiresias *sees* is the substance of the poem." The illumination of the ages is available at any moment, and when the typist's indifference and boredom in the act of love must be represented, it is possible for Eliot to invoke and paraphrase a lyric from a play by Oliver Goldsmith. Literary allusion has become not merely a Miltonic reference to Greek gods and Old Testament geography, not merely the citation of parallels, but a powerful and inevitable habit of mind, a habit which issues in judgment and the representation of different levels of experience, past and present.

James supposed that his theme was the international theme: would it not be more precise to speak of it as the transatlantic theme? This effort at a greater exactness defines what is involved in Eliot's work. Henry James was concerned with the American in Europe. Eliot cannot help but be concerned with the whole world and all history. Tiresias sees the nature of love in all times and all places and when Sweeney outwits a scheming whore, the fate of Agamemnon becomes relevant. So too, in the same way exactly, Eliot must recognize and use a correspondence between St. Augustine and Buddha in speaking of sensuality. And thus, as he writes again in his notes to *The Waste Land,* "The collocation of these two representatives of eastern and western asceticism as the culmination of this part of the poem is not an accident." And it is not an accident that the international hero should have come from St. Louis, Missouri, or at any rate from America. Only an American with a mind and sensibility which is cosmopolitan and expatriated could have seen Europe as it is seen in *The Waste Land.*

A literary work may be important in many ways, but surely one of the ways in which it is important is in its relationship to some important human interest or need, or in its relationship to some new aspect of human existence. Eliot's work is important in relationship to the fact that experience has become international. We have become an international people, and hence an international hero is possible. Just as the war is international, so the true causes of many of the things in our lives are world-wide, and we are able to understand the character of our lives only when we are aware of all history, of the philosophy of history, of primitive peoples and the Russian Revolution, of ancient Egypt and the unconscious mind. Thus again it is no accident that in *The Waste Land* use is made of *The Golden Bough,* and a book on the quest of the Grail; and the way in which images and associations appear in the poem illustrates a new view of consciousness, the depths of consciousness and the unconscious mind.

The protagonist of *The Waste Land* stands on the banks of the Thames and quotes the Upanishads, and this very quotation, the command to "give, sympathize, and control," makes possible a comprehensive insight into the difficulty of his life in the present. But this emphasis upon one poem of Eliot's may be misleading. What is true of much of his poetry is also true of his criticism. When the critic writes of tradition and the individual talent, when he declares the necessity for the author of a consciousness of the past as far back as Homer, when he brings the reader back to Dante, the Elizabethans and Andrew Marvell, he is also speaking as the heir of all the ages.

The emphasis on a consciousness of literature may also be misleading, for nowhere better than in Eliot can we see the difference between being merely literary and making the knowledge of literature an element in vision, that is to say, an essential part of the process of seeing anything and everything. Thus, to cite the advent of Tiresias again, the literary character of his appearance is matched by the unliterary actuality by means of which he refers to himself as being "like a taxi throbbing waiting." In one way, the subject of *The Waste Land* is the sensibility of the protagonist, a sensibility which is literary, philosophical, cosmopolitan and expatriated. But this sensibility is concerned not with itself as such, but with the common things of modern life, with two such important aspects of existence as religious belief and making love. To summon to mind such profound witnesses as Freud and D. H. Lawrence is to remember how often, in modern life, love has been the worst sickness of human beings.

The extent to which Eliot's poetry is directly concerned with love is matched only by the extent to which it is concerned with religious belief and the crisis of moral values. J. Alfred Prufrock is unable to make love to women of his own class and kind because of shyness, self-consciousness, and fear of rejection. The protagonists of other poems in Eliot's first book are men or women laughed at or rejected in love, and a girl deserted by her lover seems like a body deserted by the soul.

In Eliot's second volume of poems, an old man's despair issues in part from his inability to make love, while Sweeney, an antithetical character, is able to make love, but is unable to satisfy the woman with whom he copulates. In *The Waste Land,* the theme of love as a failure is again uppermost. Two lovers return from a garden after a moment of love, and the woman is overcome by despair or pathological despondency. A lady, perhaps the same woman who has returned from the garden in despair, becomes hysterical in her boudoir because her lover or her husband has nothing to say to her and cannot give her life any meaning or interest: "What shall I do now?" she says, "what shall I ever do?" The neurasthenic lady is succeeded in the poem by cockney women who gossip about another cockney woman who has been made ill by contraceptive pills taken to avoid the consequences of love; which is to say that the sickness of love has struck down every class in society: "What you get married for, if you don't want children?" And then we witness the seduction of the typist; and then other aspects of the sickness of love appear when, on the Thames bank, three girls ruined by love rehearse the sins of the young men with whom they have been having affairs. In the last part of the poem, the impossibility of love, the gulf between one human being and another, is the answer to the command to give, that is to say, to give oneself or surrender oneself to another human being in the act of making love.

Elsewhere love either results in impotence, or it is merely copulation. In "The Hollow Men," the hollow men are incapable of making love because there is a shadow which falls between the desire and the spasm. The kinship of love and belief is affirmed when the difficulty of love and of religious belief are expressed in the same way and as parallels, by means of a paraphrase and parody of the Lord's Prayer. In "Sweeney Agonistes," Sweeney returns to say that there is nothing in love but copulation, which, like birth and death, is boring. Sweeney's boredom should be placed in contrast with the experience of Burbank, who encountered the Princess Volupine in Venice, and found himself impotent with her. A comparison ought also to be made between Sweeney and the protagonist of one of Eliot's poems in French who harks back to a childhood experience of love: "I tickled her to make her laugh. I experienced a moment of power and delirium." Eliot's characters when they make love either suffer from what the psychoanalysts term "psychic impotence," or they make love so inadequately that the lady is left either hysterical or indifferent when the episode is over. The characters who are potent and insensitive are placed in contrast with the characters who are impotent and sensitive. Grishkin has a bust which promises pneumatic bliss, while Burbank's kind, the kind of a man who goes to Europe with a Baedeker, has to crawl between the dry ribs of metaphysics because no contact possible to flesh is satisfactory. The potent and the insensitive, such as Sweeney, are not taken in by the ladies, the nightingales and the whores; but Burbank, like Agamemnon, is betrayed and undone.

This synoptic recitation might be increased by many more examples. Its essence is expressed perfectly in "Little Gidding": "Love is the unfamiliar name." But we ought to remember that the difficulty of making love, that is to say, of entering into the most intimate of relationships, is not the beginning but the consequence of the whole character of modern life. That is why the apparatus of reference which the poet brings to bear upon failure in love involves all history ("And I Tiresias have foresuffered all") and is international. So too the old man who is the protagonist of "Gerontion" must refer to human beings of many nationalities, to Mr. Silvero at Limoges, Hakagawa, Madame de Tornquist, Fräulein von Kulp and Christ [the tiger] and he finds it necessary to speak of all history as well as his failure in love. History is made to illuminate love and love is made to illuminate history. In modern life, human beings are whirled beyond the circuit of the constellations: their intimate plight is seen in connection or relation with the anguish of the Apostles after Calvary, the murder of Agamemnon, the insanity of Ophelia and children who chant that London bridge is falling down. In the same way, the plight of Prufrock is illuminated by means of a rich, passing reference to Michelangelo, the sculptor of the strong and heroic man. Only when the poet is the heir of all the ages can he make significant use of so many different and distant kinds of experience. But conversely, only when experience becomes international, only when many different and distant kinds of experience are encountered by the poet, does he find it necessary to become the heir of all the ages.

Difficulty in love is inseparable from the deracination and the alienation from which the international man suffers. When the traditional beliefs, sanctions and bonds of the community and of the family decay or disappear in the distance like a receding harbor, then love ceases to be an act which is in relation to the life of the community, and in immediate relation to the family and other human beings. Love becomes purely personal. It is isolated from the past and the future, and since it is isolated from all other relationships, since it is no longer celebrated, evaluated and given a status by the community, love does become merely copulation. The protagonist of "Gerontion" uses one of the most significant phrases in Eliot's work when he speaks of himself as living in a *rented* house; which is to say, not in the house where his forbears lived. He lives in a rented house, he is unable to make love, and he knows that history has many cunning, deceptive, and empty corridors. The nature of the house, of love and of history are interdependent aspects of modern life.

When we compare Eliot's poetry to the poetry of Valèry, Yeats and Rilke, Eliot's direct and comprehensive concern with the essential nature of modern life gains an external definition. Yeats writes of Leda and he writes of the nature of history; Valèry writes of Narcissus and the serpent in the Garden of Eden; Rilke is inspired by great works of art, by Christ's mother and by Orpheus. Yet in each of these authors the subject is transformed into a timeless essence. The heritage of Western culture is available to these authors and they use it many beautiful ways; but the fate of Western culture and the historical sense as such does not become an important part of their poetry. And then if we compare Eliot with Auden and with Pound, a further definition becomes clear. In his early work, Auden is inspired by an international crisis in a social and political sense; in his new work, he writes as a teacher and preacher and secular theologian. In neither period is all history and all culture a necessary part of the subject or the sensibility which is dealing with the subject. With Pound, we come closer to Eliot and the closeness sharpens the difference. Pound is an American in Europe too, and Pound, not Eliot, was the first to grasp the historical and international dimension of experience, as we can see in an early effort of his to explain the method of the *Cantos* and the internal structure of each *Canto:* "All times are contemporaneous," he wrote, and in the *Cantos,* he attempts to deal with all history as if it were part of the present. But he fails; he remains for the most part an American in Europe, and the *Cantos* are never more than a book of souvenirs of a tour of the world and a tour of culture.

To be international is to be a citizen of the world and thus a citizen of no particular city. The world as such is not a community and it has no constitution or government: it is the turning world in which the human being, surrounded by the consequences of all times and all places, must live his life as a human being and not as the citizen of any nation. Hence, to be the heir of all the ages is to inherit nothing but a consciousness of how all heirlooms are rooted in the past. Dominated by the historical consciousness, the international hero finds that all beliefs affect the holding of any belief (he cannot think of Christianity without remembering Adonis); he finds that many languages affect each use of speech (*The Waste Land* concludes with a passage in four languages).

When nationalism attempts to renew itself, it can do so only through the throes of war. And when nationalism in America attempts to become articulate, when a poet like Carl Sandburg writes that "The past is a bucket of ashes," or when Henry Ford makes the purely American remark that "History is the bunk," we have only to remember such a pilgrimage as that of Ford in the Peace Ship in which he attempted to bring the First World War to an end in order to see that anyone can say whatever he likes: no matter what anyone says, existence has become international for everyone.

Eliot's political and religious affirmations are at another extreme, and they do not resemble Ford's quixotic pilgrimage except as illustrating the starting-point of the modern American, and his inevitable journey to Europe. What should be made explicit here is that only one who has known fully the deracination and alienation inherent in modern life can be moved to make so extreme an effort at returning to the traditional community as Eliot makes in attaching himself to Anglo-Catholicism and Royalism. Coming back may well be the same thing as going away; or at any rate, the effort to return home may exhibit the same predicament and the same topography as the fact of departure. Only by going to Europe, by crossing the Atlantic and living thousands of miles from home, does the international hero conceive of the complex nature of going home.

Modern life may be compared to a foreign country in which a foreign language is spoken. Eliot is the international hero because he has made the journey to the foreign country and described the nature of the new life in the foreign country. Since the future is bound to be international, if it is anything at all, we are all the bankrupt heirs of the ages, and the moments of the crisis expressed in Eliot's work are a prophecy of the crises of our own future in regard to love, religious belief, good and evil, the good life and the nature of the just society. *The Waste Land* will soon be as good as new.

# JOHN CROWE RANSOM *

E LIOT'S criticism antedates that of Richards a little. But the two
critics are not exactly in competition; they have impressed
rather different sets of readers for rather different reasons. The accuracy of Eliot's scholarship, and its always pointed application to the
niceties of criticism, and even the distinction of his prose style, did
not necessarily excite some young writers who were looking for
something in the way of large and bold ideas; to these Richards was
coming with radical critical theories which they would be able to regard as a triumph in revolutionary thinking; Empson was coming
with unquestionable literary discoveries.

But when Eliot, after Harvard, left America to have a literary
career in England, he resembled those young men in Grimm or in
Andersen who go far out into the world "to seek their fortunes." The
success that came to him presently was a spectacular success and
carried twice as far. It was a greater success than an American could
have had in America, or an Englishman in England; it was an international success, and pleased everybody.

Exciting to the literary public also was the early sense of a complex personality behind the criticism. There were other Eliots besides
the critic. Specifically, there were three Eliots, and the other two were
the poet and the religionist. The first book of criticism was published in 1921, but the first volume of poetry had appeared a year
before. The poems were very brilliant, in structure and tone they
were rather revolutionary; the criticism though it was original was
conservative. But in 1922 appeared "The Waste Land," the most
famous poem of our age. Here were the largeness and the boldness
for the young men. And the poet clashed with the critic. The critical
Eliot was Jekyll, the poetical Eliot was Hyde; and it was wonderful
to imagine that somewhere in Jekyll's pervasive wisdom was the
word which justified the Hyde; both the Jekyll and the Hyde were
studied the harder in the effort to harmonize them. I think it can-

* T. S. Eliot: The Historical Critic, from THE NEW CRITICISM, pp. 135–158,
192–208, Copyright, 1941, by New Directions, Norfolk, Connecticut.

not be done, and the word was not there. The drift of the criticism was heavily against the drift of the poetry. Lesser works both of verse and criticism appeared intermittently, and still nothing to resolve the division in the personality. In no formal sense did the poetry become more traditionary. But I confess that I generalize rather simply about the poetry.

In 1928 the third aspect of Eliot's personality [1] appeared startlingly in the book, *For Launcelot Andrewes.* The essays composing it discuss religious prose literature, devotional literature. The title essay begins:

> The Right Reverend Father in God, Launcelot Bishop of Winchester, died on September 25, 1626.

The introduction declares the famous series of alignments: classicist in literature; royalist in politics; and Anglo-Catholic in religion. A public man could hardly have written a more conservative ticket. It makes the literary and religious affirmations; but it does not support the author's poetry; it does not bear very directly on the great body of his criticism. Eliot now had his triple personality, and each part was reinforced in interest equally by the relatedness and the unrelatedness of the others. We may say roundly that his has been the most interesting literary personality we have had in these times.

I generalize a little further. Eliot's critical taste was fastidious—in his own word it was "classicist"—and its studies and interests were apparently for poems quite different from his own. The significance of this is that his own creative mode was not allowed to usurp his critical judgment. (And *vice versa* too, but that is not here our concern.) But now I wish to say also that his religious convictions never dictated his critical obligation to poetry. One of the best things in his influence has been his habit of considering aesthetic effect as independent of religious effect, or moral, or political and social; as an end that is beyond and is not coordinate with these. He talked about poetry as *autotelic,* and was equally ready to give patient appreciation to the perfectly secular poet, to even the irreligious poet, and to the religious one; for instance, he wrote much oftener, and even more sympathetically, about the godless Elizabethans than about the religious poets of the 17th Century. I believe his critical attitude is

---

[1] I am disregarding the fact that since 1922 Eliot was editing the *Criterion,* in which his religious interests sufficiently appeared.

still unchanged. But the religionist in Eliot has gained on the critic as he has gained on the poet: in the distribution of energies. The poems have become more religious. The religious writings have almost displaced the critical essays. Eliot's prose work now is religious, political, and philosophical; it rarely consists in strict literary criticism, like the early work.

## 2.

I call Eliot a historical critic, and with about such propriety, I think, as there would be for our way of referring to certain academic literary scholars as having the historical scholarship. These scholars know the threads of factual and intellectual history which connect some English poet with the incidents of his own life, with the "thought" and "interests" of his age, and with contemporary and earlier poets in the same "school" or "tradition." It will probably occur to us that they seem ordinarily to stop with knowing these connections; they do not use their historical learning for the literary understanding of the poet, and so the rather disparaging tone in which they are often referred to as simply "historical scholars." A scholar may know a great many facts and still stay within a curiously limited area of intelligence.

It is Eliot who uses his historical studies for the sake of literary understanding, and therefore might be called a historical critic. If the title conferred upon him seems quaint, I mean the formality to stand for the fact that he is learned in the precise learning of the scholars, a Pharisee of the Pharisees. I have not heard of any serious impeachment of his learning coming out of the universities. If the academic scholars do not recognize him as one of themselves, it is because he turns his scholarship to pointed critical uses, whatever they may do with theirs. Perhaps it is also because he writes prose of great suppleness and charm, for his criticism of literature has some of the value of literature.

It must look strange, except that we are far too used to the dullness of the official custodians of literature, that a critical achievement like Eliot's should be a phenomenon so rare, and seem so fabulous when it comes. The learning behind it is perfectly regular, and based generally on the academic sources of learning. The universities should have produced scores of Eliots, so far as his kind of intelligence is concerned, though one might wish to make reservations about its quickness, or its depth, which would probably be superior in any age. Eliot is a critical scholar on the order of Dryden, or Doctor Johnson; but that is a kind of scholar which our wonderfully organized Departments of Literature, offering advantages far greater than those earlier scholars ever possessed, have simply not turned out, nor dreamed of turning out. We should in the future expect better of them, I imagine, assuming that Eliot with his unvaryingly correct learning has won their respect. As for the comparative intelligence of Eliot beside Dryden or Johnson, or other famous critics in our language, I think surely he does not yield to any of them; he is "closer" and more patient than the two mentioned. It is likely that we have had no better critic than Eliot. And if Eliot is one of the most important sources of a new criticism, it is because here the new criticism is in part the recovery of old criticism.

But presently the absolute aesthetician, the philosophical critic, offers what sounds like a serious objection to a historical critic if he sets up as one of the legitimate varieties of critic. What is a historical critic exactly? And how does historical learning offer any basis for criticism? Eliot professes commonly to be in search of the poetic practice which is standard in the sense that it is furnished by the main stream or "tradition" of English poetry—unless it is the still bigger and more authoritative stream of European poetry. But the judgment that a poetic practice is in accord with it, or not in accord with it, remains a historical judgment; it is not a critical judgment. The critical judgment would want to determine whether a poetic practice was a good practice, and that might conceivably be settled without any reference to history or tradition. Though a critic must feel reassured if he can know that a good practice is a traditional practice, it need not be, and he cannot always know it. Comparing a practice with tradition, a critic tests its traditionalism, or its orthodoxy; he does not test its aesthetic value.

I do not mean to say that it does not occur to Eliot to discuss poetic effects in critical terms which will not be historical or comparative terms. It does occur to him, and prompts critical judgments. But what occurs to him most characteristically, and most makes him the powerful critic he is, is that it can never cease to be instructive to see a poem in the light of other comparable poems; and perhaps that a critic's fertility derives from his power and patience to observe the limits within which the like poems differentiate themselves and branch off from each other. Eliot has nothing like a formula ready in advance; he looks at the poem against its nearest background to see what sort of criticism it needs; he comes up presently with a set of judgments which are comparative in the first instance, but critical in the end. I open his book of selected essays at random, and the second thing I hit on, if not the first, is the essay on Swinburne, and Eliot remarking on people's habit of saying: "The beauty of Swinburne's verse is the sound; he had little visual imagination." And how is such a thing to be determined, how is either part of this judgment to be safely determined, except on comparative grounds? Eliot fingers his texts, so to speak, and goes to work:

> What we get in Swinburne is an expression by sound, which could not possibly associate itself with music. For what he gives is not images and ideas and music, it is one thing with a curious mixture of suggestions of all three.
>
> > Shall I come, if I swim? wide are the waves, you see;
> > Shall I come, if I fly, my dear Love, to thee?
>
> This is Campion, and an example of the kind of music that is not to be found in Swinburne. It is an arrangement and choice of words which has a sound-value and at the same time a coherent comprehensible meaning, and the two things—the musical value and meaning—are two things, not one. But in Swinburne there is no *pure* beauty—no pure beauty of sound, or of image, or of idea.
>
> > Music, when soft voices die,
> > Vibrates in the memory;
> > Odours, when sweet violets sicken,
> > Live within the sense they quicken.
> >
> > Rose leaves, when the rose is dead,
> > Are heaped for the beloved's bed;
> > And so thy thoughts, when thou art gone,
> > Love itself shall slumber on.
>
> I quote from Shelley, because Shelley is supposed to be the master of Swinburne; and because his song, like that of Campion, has what Swinburne has not—a beauty of music and a beauty of content; and because it is clearly and simply expressed, with only two adjectives. Now, in Swinburne the meaning and the sound are

one thing. He is concerned with the meanings of the word in a
peculiar way: he employs, or rather "works," the word's meaning. And this is connected with an interesting fact about his
vocabulary: he uses the most general word, because his emotion
is never particular, never in direct line of vision, never focused;
it is emotion reinforced, not by intensification, but by expansion.

> There lived a singer in France of old
>   By the tideless dolorous midland sea.
> In a land of sand and ruin and gold
>   There shone one woman, and none but she.

You see that Provence is the merest point of diffusion here.
Swinburne defines the place by the most general word, which has
for him its own value. "Gold," "ruin," "dolorous": it is not
merely the sound that he wants, but the vague associations of
idea that the words give him. He has not his eye on a particular
place, as:

> Li ruscelletti che dei verdi colli
> Del Casentin discendon giuso in Arno. . . .

It is, in fact, the word that gives him the thrill, not the object.
When you take to pieces any verse of Swinburne, you find always
that the object was not there—only the word. Compare

> Snowdrops that plead for pardon
> And pine for fright

with the daffodils that come before the swallow dares. The snow-
drop of Swinburne disappears, the daffodil of Shakespeare remains. The swallow of Shakespeare remains in the verse of
*Macbeth;* the bird of Wordsworth

> Breaking the silence of the seas

remains; the swallow of "Itylus" disappears. Compare, again, a
chorus of *Atalanta* with a chorus from Athenian tragedy. The
chorus of Swinburne is almost a parody of the Athenian: it is
sententious, but it has not even the significance of commonplace.

This is Eliot's sort of criticism. Little is "formulated" in this
essay in the technical terms of some critical theory, even of some
theory of his own. The idea is to set some Swinburne lines close by the
lines of some of his peers, and see what happens. Something happens.
Something always happens under Eliot's acute observation. Here per-

haps it is this: "It is the word that gives him the thrill, not the object." It seems very important, if we are technically curious; and very tantalizing, mentioned and dropped like that. We perhaps pick it up and study it. Could there be a critical principle here, on this order: that there is a poetry which stops with words instead of going through words to their objective referents; a verbal poetry? The proof that the poet stops on the words, not uses the words to go beyond them, is said to be that neither a music nor a meaning is completely realized, only a half-music and a half-meaning, put together and enjoyed together, inseparably. But such a statement of principle, looked at abstractedly, taken ever so carefully from the tissue of Eliot's prose, looks like an overstatement, looks like a falsification of Eliot. Eliot does not encourage us to find sweeping critical principles in his work. He declines to be responsible for them as principles: they are remarks. In this case I should not care to answer for the fate of the remark if stiff critical theorists should pounce upon it, remove it, put it technically, and evaluate it. I do not know what would survive but I should be apprehensive. There is in Eliot's writings an immediate critical sense which is expert and infallible, but it consists with a theoretical innocence. Behind it is no great philosophical habit, nor philosophical will, to push through it to definition.

He rarely cares to theorize in set passages about poetry. He is not what we call—with a prejudice for the unadulterated article that may go along with our profound greenness—a "thinker." He does not make ultimate generalizations though he makes shrewd ones. They are half-truths, or gnomic truths sometimes. There are enough of them to have stocked the mind of a generation with his wisdom, so that young men speak up and quote Eliot pertinently on nearly any literary occasion. They give him the character of a prophet rather than the character of a philosopher.

Eliot might be said to be a practitioner of Arnold's "touchstone" method of judging poetry, though with infinite refinements; he cites, not the same handful of resounding lines for every purpose, but lines similar to the given lines, with an easy perception of which lines are best. No critic proceeds so regularly by the technique of comparative quotation, and no critic can ever have been so apt in electing the lines to quote.

That is the practical value of knowing all about your tradition.

But there is something more in Eliot, something doubtful, though it probably does no harm. A historical critic in this sense is a man with touchstones, and a man who quotes; but if he has a certain strain of piety in him he may easily expend upon some inaccessible entity which he calls "the tradition" a degree of feeling that is luxurious, and cannot be translated practically into criticism. Historical sense as Eliot talks about it seems to be what makes you see your own little effort of poetry, if you are a poet, as the moment when you had the happiness of being the mouthpiece of The Great Tradition. Perhaps you have in you an excess of reverent feeling looking for what Eliot in another connection calls its "objective correlative," and what it finds is the mystery called the tradition. Some modern social thinkers seem often to be in the same relation to their own ineffable reality, which is universal Human Society. The two objects are quite distinct, but they may be equally mystical and impracticable.

I think Eliot is a traditionalist of this latter sort up to a certain point; up to the point where it would obscure and dull his critical judgment of a given poem. Then he reverts simply to the good critic, with much resourcefulness in the historic documents of his art. No mischief is done. But there are great difficulties when Eliot leaves the documents in order to theorize about the function of the ever-living tradition at the moment when actual new poetry is being written.

Though a traditionalist, Eliot is obliged to concede that circumstances must alter cases, and that each new poet must after all compose a new poem which cannot be exactly what any previous poem has been. His notion of dealing with this insuperable fact is, in effect, though the action seems incredible when put in terms, to represent the tradition as looking over the new circumstances and writing its own poem, while the poet depersonalizes himself and operates in the capacity of a private secretary to the tradition. This is to pay almost superstitious honors to tradition. But I can quote a strange extended passage in which Eliot tries to show how the poetic operates. It is in "Tradition and the Individual Talent." The essay was written in 1917, when Eliot was establishing his critical practice, and presumably thinking his hardest about the principles and definitions; but its argument is referred to and confirmed in "The Function of Criticism" of 1923; and it becomes the first or introductory essay in the *Selected Essays* of 1932, by which time his best critical essays have certainly been written; so that it cannot be said to come out of a critical inexperience. Page 4 of *Selected Essays:* [2]

> No poet, no artist of any art, has his complete meaning alone. His significance, his appreciation is the appreciation of his relation to the dead poets and artists. You cannot value him alone; you must set him, for contrast and comparison, among the dead. I mean this as a principle of aesthetic, not merely historical, criticism. The necessity that he shall conform, that he shall cohere, is not onesided; what happens when a new work of art is created is something that happens simultaneously to all the works of art which preceded it. The existing monuments form an ideal order among themselves, which is modified by the introduction of the new (the really new) work of art among them. The existing order is complete before the new work arrives; for order to persist after the supervention of novelty, the *whole* existing order must be, if ever so slightly, altered; and so the relations, proportions, values of each work of art toward the whole are readjusted; and this is conformity between the old and the new. Whoever has approved this idea of order, of the form of European, of English literature will not find it preposterous that the past should be altered by the present as much as the present is directed by the past. And the poet who is aware of this will be aware of great difficulties and responsibilities.

I interrupt to remark that the poet might ask Mr. Eliot to be more specific about these responsibilities. He was told first that when his new poem stands beside the old poems something "happens" both to them and to it; they alter each other. But now it is indicated that what happens is really his responsibility. I think Eliot is urging him, under a pretty metaphor of a rather theoretical or Hegelian kind, not to make his poem too new; if he will conform closely with the tradition, the tradition in turn will condescend to conform a little with him. What is not suggested to the poet is that he might use his own head and make an aesthetic judgment of the new thing he is doing. It may be a rhetorical plea for "Evolution but not Revolution." But the metaphor lends itself to suggesting to the ingenious revolutionist that his new poem will automatically make an alteration in the tradition, and it might as well be a big one. But presently:

---

[2] All my quotations will come from this volume. The selections include a wide variety of critical masterpieces, and religious essays as well as critical. After its date of publication the critical work declines in purity.

To proceed to a more intelligible exposition of the relation of the poet to the past; he can neither take the past as a lump, an indiscriminate bolus, nor can he form himself wholly on one or two private admirations, nor can he form himself wholly on one preferred period. The first course is inadmissible, the second is an important experience of youth, and the third is a pleasant and highly desirable supplement. The poet must be very conscious of the main current, which does not at all flow invariably through the most distinguished reputations. He must be quite aware of the obvious fact that art never improves, but that the material of art is never quite the same. He must be aware that the mind of Europe—the mind of his own country—a mind which he learns in time to be much more important than his own private mind— is a mind which changes, and that this change is a development which abandons nothing *en route,* which does not superannuate either Shakespeare, or Homer, or the rock drawing of the Magdalenian draughtsman. That this development, refinement perhaps, complication certainly, is not, from the point of view of the artist, any improvement. Perhaps not even an improvement from the point of view of the psychologist or not to the extent which we imagine; perhaps only in the end based upon a complication in economics and machinery. But the difference between the present and the past is that the conscious present is an awareness of the past in a way and to an extent which the past's awareness of itself cannot show.

I cannot tell quite what this passage means, unless possibly that the body of poetry has increased itself in the past by the most deliberate additions in the light of perfect historical consciousness, and that it must continue to do so in the person of the new poet today. We ask, will it do so automatically then? Or is it up to the new poet to decide, and is this merely the appeal of a conservative to his piety? The role assigned him is one of complete abnegation:

> The progress of an artist is a continual self-sacrifice, a continual extinction of personality.

And here Eliot offers his famous chemical metaphor for the poet's act of depersonalization:

> It is in this depersonalization that art may be said to approach the condition of science. I, therefore, invite you to consider, as a suggestive analogy, the action which takes place when a bit of

finely filiated platinum is introduced into a chamber containing oxygen and sulphur dioxide. . . . When the two gases previously mentioned are mixed in the presence of a filament of platinum, they form sulphurous acid. This combination takes place only if the platinum is present; nevertheless the newly formed acid contains no trace of platinum, and the platinum itself is apparently unaffected; has remained inert, neutral, and unchanged. The mind of the poet is the shred of platinum.

Eliot does not identify the chemicals in this reaction, other than the catalyst, which is the poet's mind. The precipitate, the sulphurous acid, clearly is poetry. Whatever the poetry is made of, it is made when the poet allows the secret forces to work in the laboratory of his consciousness, yet without his taking personal direction of the process. This is very nearly a doctrine of poetic automatism. I do not understand it on its own terms though I think I see some of the considerations in Eliot's mind. Its rhetorical use would seem to be to persuade the individualist poet not to assert himself too stoutly against the tradition, which is bigger than he; and to persuade the reader not to value the blatant self-assertive sort of poems, or, else, it would be to render a merely formal piety to the tradition, by insisting that even the apparent innovations of poets were really fulfillments of history; which would be a comforting if not very realistic belief.

### 3.

Eliot's argument about tradition is not a theory of poetry. But he is not without a theory of poetry, and he does not write specific criticism without conscientious references to his theory. He states it in the same essay we have been examining, "Tradition and the Individual Talent." I think it is one of the most unmanageable theories that a critic could profess; but it is not an unmodern kind of theory; it is equivalent to some version of Richards' psychologistic theory. I quote from page 8:

The experience, you will notice, the elements which enter the presence of the transforming catalyst, are of two kinds: emotions and feelings.[3] The effect of a work of art upon the person

---

[3] Eliot seems to consider that he is really continuing the chemical metaphor which illustrated the relation of the new poet to the tradition. But there is no connection between that discussion and this one. I have the feeling that the metaphor is not quite apt for illustrating either topic, so that he uses it twice.

who enjoys it is an experience different in kind from any experience not of art. It may be formed out of one emotion, or may be a combination of several; and various feelings, inhering for the writer in particular words or phrases or images, may be added to compose the final result. Or great poetry may be made without the direct use of any emotion whatever: composed out of feelings solely. Canto XV of the *Inferno* (Brunetto Latini) is a working up of the emotion evident in the situation; but the effect, though single as that of any work of art, is obtained by considerable complexity of detail. The last quatrain gives an image, a feeling attaching to an image, which "came," which did not develop simply out of what precedes, but which was probably in suspension in the poet's mind until the proper combination arrived for it to add itself to. The poet's mind is in fact a receptacle for seizing and storing up numberless feelings, phrases, images, which remain there until all the particles which can unite to form a new compound are present together.

If you compare several representative passages of the greatest poetry you see how great is the variety of types of combination, and also how completely any semi-ethical criterion of "sublimity" misses the mark. For it is not the "greatness," the intensity, of the emotions, the components, but the intensity of the artistic process, the pressure, so to speak, under which the fusion takes place, that counts. The episode of Paolo and Francesca employs a definite emotion, but the intensity of the poetry is something quite different from whatever intensity in the supposed experience it may give the impression of. It is no more intense, furthermore, than Canto XXVI, the voyage of Ulysses, which has not the direct dependence upon an emotion. Great variety is possible in the process of transmutation of emotion: the murder of Agamemnon, or the agony of Othello, gives an artistic effect apparently closer to a possible original than the scenes from Dante. In the *Agamemnon,* the artistic emotion approximates to the emotion of an actual spectator; in *Othello* to the emotion of the protagonist himself. But the difference between art and the event is always absolute; the combination which is the murder of Agamemnon is probably as complex as that which is the voyage of Ulysses. In either case there has been a fusion of elements. The ode of Keats contains a number of feelings which have nothing particular to do with the nightingale, but which the nightingale, partly, perhaps, because of its attractive name, and partly because of its reputation, served to bring together.

One of the contributions of this argument to theory is the aesthetic truth that the emotion we have for the artistic object cannot be the same as the emotion we might have had for the natural or original object; we have often received that truth through the doctrine of "psychic distance," or of artistic "detachment," or even of art as "imitation." But in what lies the difference in the emotions? And what is a "transmuted" emotion? I think it is impossible to talk clearly about these matters until we drop the vocabulary of emotions and talk about the respective cognitive objects, or the cognitive situations, which identify them. But to bridge this passage we may observe that the original emotion was the sort of powerful affective glow that attaches to an act of practical consummation. Perhaps we might call it a practical emotion; and then we should distinguish the emotion which attaches to the mere image of the object, when called up for retrospect or put together by inventive imagination, as at best an experimental or tentative emotion, or a self-conscious, philosophical, or speculative emotion; whatever would constitute an *aesthetic* emotion. But probably the most important thing in Eliot's statement is his recognition of *big* emotions as set off against *little* feelings; and I should say the big emotion refers to our reception of the main situation, or situation as a whole, and the little feelings refer to our reception of the heterogeneous detail of the situation. Or, the emotion attaches to the main *structure*, the feelings attach to the local *texture*. These are the terms which seem to me most practical in critical analysis. In action, as opposed to art, the situation as a whole engages us too completely; and I mean that it engages our cognitive attention too completely, just as truly as it engages our emotion. It is when this situation exists for imagination, not for action, that we are freed from its domination and can attend to its texture. But a very great effort of salvage would be required to rewrite this discourse of Eliot's into our terms, or other terms that were articulate.

Compared with Richards' versions of poetry as emotion, Eliot is the more disorderly; Richards, for example, would hardly have talked about a fusion of "feelings, phrases, images," into one compound.

A little further on, Eliot writes:

> It is not in his personal emotions, the emotions provoked by particular events in his life, that the poet is in any way remarkable

or interesting. His particular emotions may be simple, or crude, or flat. The emotion in his poetry will be a very complex thing, but not with the complexity of the emotions in life. One error, in fact, of eccentricity in poetry is to seek for new human emotions to express; and in this search for novelty in the wrong place it discovers the perverse. The business of the poet is not to find new emotions, but to use the ordinary ones and, in working them up into poetry, to express feelings which are not in actual emotions at all. And emotions which he has never experienced will serve his turn as well as those familiar to him. Consequently, we must believe that "emotion recollected in tranquillity" is an inexact formula. For it is neither emotion, nor recollection, nor, without distortion of meaning, tranquillity. It is a concentration of a very great number of experiences which to the practical and active person would not seem to be experiences at all; it is a concentration which does not happen consciously or of deliberation. These experiences are not "recollected," and they finally unite in an atmosphere which is "tranquil" only in that it is a passive attending upon the event. Of course this is not quite the whole story. There is a great deal, in the writing of poetry, which must be conscious and deliberate. In fact, the bad poet is usually unconscious where he ought to be conscious, and conscious where he ought to be unconscious. Both errors tend to make him "personal." Poetry is not a turning loose of emotion, but an escape from emotion; it is not the expression of personality, but an escape from personality. But, of course, only those who have personality and emotions know what it is to want to escape from these things.

I shall try a little salvage here. "Emotion recollected in tranquillity" was a crude locution in which Wordsworth himself tried the psychological version of aesthetic theory; perhaps it was Wordsworth's version of the most "modern" way of thinking in that age. But it might be translated, though rather laboriously, something like this: "a situation of great emotional import remembered afterward, in the impracticable form of image, so that the furious emotion cannot now assert itself." The aesthetic consequence is easy to see. The aesthetic consequence is easy to see. The original emotion blinded us to the texture of the object, but now there is leisure for the texture. Several of Eliot's remarks would support my paraphrase. For example, the one about the "very great number of experiences which to the practical and active person would not seem to be experiences at all"; that is apropos of the texture of the object. And the concluding remarks about the poet's need to escape from emotion; they are apropos of the way the useful aspect of the object loses its monopoly over attention so that the texture may be attended to.

"Feelings" and "emotions" are the jargon of poetic theory with the new critics, and with the best ones it is Eliot's usage which provides the sanction. The half-communication that results is painful to the humble reader, and suggests that there is something esoteric in the vocation of criticism, and that Eliot is initiated but the humble reader is not. . . .

## 6.

The problem of poetry and belief is no great problem for Eliot; he waives the necessity of belief. In his essay on Dante he discusses this at length:

> My point is that you cannot afford to *ignore* Dante's philosophical and theological beliefs, or to skip the passages which express them most clearly; but that on the other hand you are not called upon to believe them yourself. . . . For there is a difference (which here I hardly do more than assert) between philosophical *belief* and poetic *assent*. . . . You are not called upon to believe what Dante believed, for your belief will not give you a groat's worth more of understanding and appreciation; but you are called upon more and more to understand it.

But in religion the problem for Eliot is a very great problem; he insists upon belief. I incline to think that the problem exists in poetry as in religion, and is very nearly the same problem.

In religion, Eliot is aggressively orthodox; and he is a controversialist of great power—he went to school to Babbitt. His religious dialectic is probably not the most engaging aspect of his personality with the contemporary intellectual public, things being as they are; but it is very strong, and its severity is sincerity. "In religion, Anglo-Catholic." And how does one arrive, doctrinally and institutionally, at this decision? It is a public issue. It seems possible that Eliot sought for a standard of religious judgment, and found it in the same place as the one that had served him in his literary judgments. He found it in a tradition, and the tradition (a) was actually operative and (b) was English. But that may not be the fact, or at least all the fact. Upon occasions he invites quite another inference, indicating that he has rational or philosophical supports under his standard. But these he never discusses; and I have not heard it maintained that he is a theologian. He writes a great deal about religion, but not as the philosophical defender of the faith. Eliot has been embarrassed by the arguments of the rationalists, and it seems to make him short and sharp with them, and to breach that magnanimity with which he used to dispense his literary judgments.

I wish to exhibit Eliot both making an argument from tradition and implying but not making an argument from theology. The locus of these exhibits will be the two essays about Humanism, and the essay on Arnold and Pater. We may observe in advance that Eliot's aversion as an orthodox religionist is for the contemporary school of naturalism. It embraces many branches of thinkers, including perhaps most scientists, if they pronounce upon such things; and there are to be reckoned with certainly those protagonists of science, the Positivists; these in their social outlook become doubtless the Humanitarians; and Eliot more than suspects the cult of including even the Humanists, of whom Mr. Babbitt used to be the leader and now Mr. Foerster is his inheritor.

Mr. Babbitt's naturalistic tendencies came to their most revealing expression in his late book, *Democracy and Leadership,* and Eliot writes, on page 384, as follows:

> The problem of humanism is undoubtedly related to the problem of religion. Mr. Babbitt makes it very clear, here and there throughout the book, that he is unable to take the religious view —that is to say that he cannot accept any dogma or revelation; and that humanism is the *alternative* to religion. And this brings up the question: is this alternative any more than a *substitute?* and if a substitute, does it not bear the same relation to religion that "humanitarianism" bears to humanism? Is it, in the end, a view of life that will work by itself, or is it a derivative of religion which will work only for a short time in history, and only for a few highly cultivated persons like Mr. Babbitt—whose ancestral traditions, furthermore, are Christian, and who is, like many people, at the distance of a generation or so from definite Christian belief? Is it, in other words, durable beyond one or two generations?

That is a pragmatic argument. Humanism is derivative, without its own vitality, and will pass with the passing of religion. What is defective in humanism is that it cannot accept any dogma, or revelation; and one moment after the above passage it is said that humanism suppresses "the divine." But in the following passage the argument changes direction:

> Mr. Babbitt is a stout upholder of tradition and continuity, and he knows, with his immense and encyclopedic information, that the Christian religion is an essential part of the history of our race. Humanism and religion are thus, as historical facts, by no means parallel; humanism has been sporadic, but Christianity continuous. It is quite irrelevant to conjecture the possible development of the European races without Christianity—to imagine, that is, a tradition of humanism equivalent to the actual tradition of Christianity. For all we can say is that we should have been very different creatures, whether better or worse. Our problem being to form the future, we can only form it on the materials of the past; we must *use* our heredity, instead of denying it. The religious habits of the race are still very strong, in all places, at all times, and for all people. There is no humanistic habit; humanism is, I think, merely the state of mind of a few persons in a few places at a few times. To exist at all, it is dependent upon some other attitude, for it is essentially critical—I would even say parasitical. It has been, and still can be, of great value; but it will never provide showers of partridges or abundance of manna for the chosen peoples.

This is the pure argument from tradition. Eliot is saying that it should be unnecessary to tell a member of his own race, generation, and class why we need a religion; let him look at the common history. This is not a position without dignity, and it will be supposed that religionists must many times have taken it effectively. But it did not prove effective with Mr. Babbitt, in the sequel; nor is its effectiveness very considerable with many able minds who are not now so religiously inclined by heredity and training as they might be, but tainted with naturalistic aversions and positivistic hopes; and calling for everybody to put his cards upon the table so that everything may be settled on its merits. In the pack with which they are playing is no card named the religious tradition. With this hard breed of thinkers, laying out a new world, the argument from tradition does not rate as a philosophic argument.

The fact is that Eliot did not make his point with Mr. Babbitt, so that shortly afterwards he is resuming the argument; but this time with Mr. Foerster, who has just edited a Symposium of humanistic essays. Eliot begins gently by announcing himself as a Humanist anxious to check the prejudice of the school against religion before it is committed irretrievably. Page 394:

> Now I have no desire to undermine the humanist position. But I fear that it may take on more and more of the character of a positive philosophy—and any philosophy, in our time, is likely to take on the character of a substitute for religious dogma. It is Humanism's positivistic tendencies that are alarming.

For Mr. Foerster had written such things as this:

> This centre to which humanism refers everything, this centripetal energy which counteracts the multifarious centrifugal impulses, this magnetic will which draws the flux of our sensations toward it while itself remaining at rest, is the reality which gives rise to religion. Pure humanism is content to describe it thus in physical terms, as an observed fact of experience; it hesitates to pass beyond its experimental knowledge to the dogmatic affirmations of any of the great religions. It cannot bring itself to accept a formal theology (any more than it can accept a romantic idealism) that has been set up in defiance of reason, for it holds that the value of supernatural intuition must be tested by the intellect.

This is the kernel of a passage which Eliot attacks as "a composition of ignorance, prejudice, confused thinking and bad writing." But the part of the reply which interests us here is very slight:

> When he proceeds to distinguish Humanism from religion by saying that Humanism "holds that the value of supernatural intuition must be tested by the intellect," one wonders with what sort of religion he is contrasting it: for this kind of test was held by the Church long before the word Humanism was coined.

We understand the limitations of any essay, yet Eliot might have had more to say to Mr. Foerster than this; he might have assumed that Mr. Foerster had himself done some thinking, and even informed himself about the test made by the Church before he and his group of philosophers were born, but was not satisfied with it. He continues the essay by ridiculing Humanists as mere literary men; they think of religion as somewhere included among literary values; of literature as fair exchange for religion. Eliot removes this possibility expressly in one of the eight listed principles which he lays down for the guidance of a proper Humanism:

> V. Humanism can have no positive theories about philosophy or theology. All that it can ask, in the most tolerant spirit, is: Is this particular philosophy or religion civilized, or is it not?

But at the end he returns for an instant to Mr. Foerster's real difficulty. The intellectual acceptance of the dogma is much easier than Mr. Foerster supposes:

> Most people suppose that some people, because they enjoy the luxury of Christian sentiments and the excitement of Christian ritual, swallow or pretend to swallow incredible dogma. For some the process is exactly opposite. Rational assent may arrive late, intellectual conviction may come slowly, but they come inevitably without violence to honesty and nature. To put the sentiments in order is a later and an immensely difficult task: intellectual freedom is earlier and easier than complete spiritual freedom.

The intellectual conviction that somehow just "comes" is not a counter that Mr. Foerster is likely to accept.

The "coming" of intellectual conviction in the manner just mentioned may be again, if we could fully analyse our sense of the phrase, the argument from tradition, meaning: "This is the way it happens with men of good will who entrust themselves to organized religion; they do not have to philosophize their decision; the understanding of the thing comes with the practice, the continuance in the traditional discipline; and that is what a tradition is for." Once more, I think it a good argument if it will work. But I suggest that the argument from tradition will not work now as it used to; that we are dealing with a revolutionary party which happens to comprise a large proportion of the intellectuals of our age; and that a more explicit and philosophical argument is necessary if we propose to have any effect. The question would be whether the policy of traditionary piety is altogether eligible now. I confess incidentally, and since I do not mean to seem to assume that I have any advantages over Mr. Eliot, that the difficulties faced by the religious establishments are difficulties which I feel equally in the sense that I deplore them, and that I cannot solve them. But

I am not quite so mistrustful of the naturalists and positivists as he is.

Eliot is one of the foci of a distinguished group of literary men with whose sentiments I have always had complete sympathy; I am convinced of their rightness, but not of what I should call their righteousness; for they do not propose to have commerce with the world. Mr. Allen Tate begins a recent essay by remarking:

> It has been frequently remarked that the moral and intellectual confusion of our age is such that communication among certain points of view is impossible. All that remains to do is to state our positions and to let them stand upon the record of our time. The point of view that this essay assumes has been proved in the past generation to be incommunicable to the positivist attitude that has captured the modern world. Historicism, psychologism, scientism, in general the confident application of the scientific vocabularies to the spiritual realm, has created a spiritual disorder that may be briefly described in terms of a dilemma. . . .

I have said probably nearly as much, and more than once; but increasingly now I feel that such a policy is too luxurious for my blood. The forces that have captured the world are trying to found a new civilization, and I imagine about that, first, that it is going to be much harder than they suppose to get everything into it, and, second, that when they have got a new civilization it may turn out to be oddly like the old one. There might be something in having one's own civilization, anyhow. But I am often impressed by their honesty, and also by the sense that they are making some headway. Almost every day they find evidences which they cannot deal with so nicely as they expected. Perhaps a good index to their progress, certainly a favorable index, could be read in the strange involutions of Mr. John Dewey's experience as an honest thinker; the essential facts that Eliot would insist on, whether in his capacity of man of letters, or moralist, or religionist, have all had their curious appearance in Dewey's thought. Perhaps his school can make the disposition of them eventually. But tradition means very little to these thinkers; they have renounced their heritage of tradition. That may not be such a monstrous villainy, and perhaps not even such a monstrous folly, unless Mr. Eliot insists on being very stiff, and declining for himself any gesture of participation in what they are obliged to regard as an inevitable undertaking.

How is all this a topic for the literary critic? That is coming now. In the essay, "Arnold and Pater," 1930, Eliot attacks Arnold for subtracting from religion its intellectual affirmations. And Arnold is the very best name available on which to make out the case of the great apostasy. Arnold knew everything, and lacked intellectual decision. To me the most resonant and tragic version of the decline of institutional religion has been Arnold's perfect statement, pointing to the vulnerable spot in the defense of the establishment by its guardians: "Our religion has materialized itself in the fact, in the supposed fact; it has attached its emotion to the fact, and now the fact is failing it." The Old Testament they regarded as history, till upset by their own "liberal theologians" a short while ago; and the damage spread, much more than inferentially, to the reputation of the New Testament. Eliot quotes and comments a remark of Arnold's:

"The *Guardian* proclaims 'the miracle of the incarnation' to be the 'fundamental truth' for Christians. How strange that on me should devolve the office of instructing the *Guardian* that the fundamental thing for Christians is not the Incarnation but the imitation of Christ!"

While wondering whether Arnold's own "imitation" is even a good piece of mimicry, we notice that he employs *truth* and *thing* as interchangeable: and a very slight knowledge of the field in which he was skirmishing should have told him that a "fundamental truth" in theology and a "fundamental thing" in his own loose jargon have nothing comparable about them.

But we shall not find in Eliot's writings much about the fundamental truths of the theologians. I should consider that he proposes to keep religion quite tightly tied to its "fact." I have felt annoyance with Arnold for not discussing the issue of the "fact." But as between Arnold and Eliot, we have one thinker rejecting the fact, and the other affirming it, and neither contributing philosophically to the discussion.

The issue of the fact is as much a problem for poetic criticism as it is for religion, and in the two contexts it is the same issue. The kind of fact in question is the "supernatural" fact; it appears constitutionally in every religious discipline, but it appears luridly and with the greatest frequency in poetry. I am in sympathy with Arnold's perception of something like a common cause between religion and poetry. But everything depends on what we propose to say, how we propose to think, about the supernatural fact. A hard philosophical labor is involved, presumably one so fair and patient that it could make itself intelligible to naturalists and positivists; and it comes under aesthetics as under religion.

An issue of fact rather than emotion. Not only Arnold but Richards, and not only Richards but Eliot himself, are agreed that poetry in some manner is exempted from having to furnish a real factuality for its so-called facts or objects, since it only wants to offer emotional experiences, and these can feed on fictions and fancies as well as on facts. Arnold, and Richards too, though he has not advertised his religious difficulties, consider that the general formula will do for religion as well; that religion is a special kind of emotional experience, indifferent to the standing of its facts. Eliot does not draw the line much more than they between fact and fiction in poetry, but he draws it firmly in religion; he requires the fact. He says of Arnold:

> Arnold's prose writings fall into two parts; those on Culture and those on Religion; and the books about Christianity seem only to say again and again—merely that the Christian faith is of course impossible to the man of culture. They are tediously negative. But they are negative in a peculiar fashion: their aim is to affirm that the emotions of Christianity can and must be preserved without the belief. From this proposition two different types of man can extract two different types of conclusion: (1) that Religion is Morals, (2) that Religion is Art. The effect of Arnold's religious campaign is to divorce religion from thought.

In my view, Eliot is right about the concern of religion with the fact and Arnold is wrong; and both are wrong about the concern of poetry.

I should approve both the conclusions that Eliot finds men drawing from their own experience of religion: "(1) that Religion is Morals, (2) that Religion is Art." Orthodox religious dogma is closely comparable with some body of Platonic or poetic "myth"; it is poetry, or at least it once was poetry; and again and again it is poetically experienced afresh, in the official pageantry and ritual of the public occasions. But it differs radically from the merely poetic myth in the hard and systematic practical use intended for it: it supports the popular morality, which is the general economy of the will impelling people to realize the destinies held out to them in the high dogma.

To Eliot dogma is just dogma, and it is unarguable. It is "revealed" or "divine" truth. Now the hypotheses of science also are "mythical" on the structural side, and "supernatural" in the sense that they cannot be directly evidenced within our inspection of nature; and there are probably scientists, and certainly camp-followers of science, who swear by them blindly, or use them with complete dogmatism. But there is a difference between saying "hypothesis" and saying "revelation." Probably the better thing we have gained from our progress in science has not been some substantive or material benefit, but a methodological one. We know how we are thinking when we think; we can think critically, self-consciously, and with the intent not to deceive ourselves. Science, at its not too rare best, can do its thinking with complete awareness of when it resorts to hypothesis. And another name for hypothesis is speculation. But religion is reluctant to concede that its "revealed truth" is speculation. The history of that reluctance must be an interesting one if we could recover it.

The sorts of "truth" to which religion aspires are not susceptible of precise treatment; the mathematical, physical, chemical elements in them cannot be isolated and calculated. But it would not follow that they cannot be approached in the scientific method. Aristotle regarded any branch of study as a kind of science if pursued hard and intelligently, but knew all about the absurdity of expecting a science to yield more precise knowledge than accorded with the nature of its content. Religionists, we may imagine, have been keenly aware of (1) the practical importance of their speculations for the whole population, and (2) the impossibility of arguing them with the brilliant precision which so much impresses the public in favor of the natural sciences. These two considerations might well have persuaded religionists to propose the artificial sanction of "revelation." The speculations become sacrosanct. But the history of thought would indicate that this is a status which cannot perpetuate itself.

Our institutionalized religion—or religions, to use the plural, for we are not all "in religion Anglo-Catholic"—are in an uncomfortable and indeed desperate position, perhaps proportionately to the degree of arrogance with which they cite their mandatory revela-

tions, against a generation which is acutely conscious of methodological standards in its thinking. If they do not abandon dogmatism,
I have the fear that they will be abandoned. And yet I think our
ruling religious dogmas can be substantively grounded. (If Mr.
Eliot does not think that he is of lesser faith than I am.) I suppose
everybody has his own speculative generalizations which have
religious significance; and whether, and at what stage, they are to
be institutionalized is a problem both scientific and aesthetic.

But I am being very brief; I do not presume to have the solution
of the difficulties. This is a word of personal testimony for what it is
worth. And I bring it back in conclusion to the poetic topic.

Had Mr. Eliot only served his "literature" with half the zeal he
served his "religion"! He believes in believing the religious dogmas,
not the affirmations of poetry. I can see no necessity for waiving the
intellectual standards on behalf of poets. If Dante's beliefs cannot be
accepted by his reader, it is the worse for Dante with that reader, not
a matter of indifference as Eliot has argued. If Shelley's argument
is foolish, it makes his poetry foolish. In my mind Dante's beliefs are
very bold speculations at which the accusing finger has pointed
steadily for a long time now, but substantively are better grounded,
and methodologically far more consistent, than Shelley's beliefs. That
consideration would enter into my preference of Dante over Shelley.

Other considerations would enter in, which can easily be sur-
mised; they would not be far from Eliot's own considerations. Thus,
the two poetries, technically regarded; that is, the provisions of texture, and not only the speculative structures; the propriety of the
structural-textural relations. All such considerations would be for the
more specific and professional act of criticism.

# YVOR WINTERS *

T. S. ELIOT is probably the most widely respected literary figure of our time; he is known primarily as the leader of the intellectual reaction against the romanticism of which he began his career as a disciple. It is my purpose to show that his intellectualism and his reactionary position are alike an illusion. It is perhaps needless to say that I use the word *reactionary* in no emotional or pejorative sense, but in a simple and literal one; I regard myself as a reactionary.

Eliot is a theorist who has repeatedly contradicted himself on every important issue that he has touched, and he has dealt in some fashion with most of the important literary issues of our time. Between some of his contradictory statements there is a greater or less lapse of time, and one might account for them by a change of view if he showed any consciousness of contradiction; but many of them occur within the same book or even within the same essay. In this connection, however, the year 1928 should be held in mind as a crucial one if any important change is to be demonstrated, for it was in this year, in his book of essays *For Lancelot Andrewes,* that he announced his conversion to Catholicism and to classicism.

The first aim of this essay will be to demonstrate the existence of these contradictions; the second will be to determine as far as possible the main tendency in his theories; and the last will be to show the effect of this tendency upon his poetry and to indicate the effect upon his disciples.

Eliot's critical discussion deals with a fairly definite number of topics, and in the interests of clarity I shall do my best to treat each topic separately, though a certain amount of overlapping will be inevitable.

## I. AUTOTELIC ART

In *The Function of Criticism* [1] Eliot writes:

* *T. S. Eliot or The Illusion of Reaction,* from THE ANATOMY OF NONSENSE, pp. 120–167, Copyright, 1943, by New Directions, Norfolk, Connecticut.
[1] Selected Essays, by T. S. Eliot. Harcourt, Brace & Co. P. 13. (1932).

No exponent of criticism . . . has, I presume, ever made the preposterous assumption that criticism is an autotelic activity. I do not deny that art may be affirmed to serve ends beyond itself; but art is not required to be aware of these ends, and indeed performs its functions, whatever they may be, according to various theories of value, much better by indifference to them. Criticism, on the other hand, must always profess an end in view, which, roughly speaking, appears to be the elucidation of works of art and the correction of taste.

One is confronted here with several problems. How, for example, can an artist perform a function better for not knowing what it is? Is Eliot assuming an automatic, or unconscious art, an art which is an extreme form of romantic mysticism? Where also is the line between prose which is art and prose which is not art? Are we to assume that there is no art in expository prose, let us say in Johnson's Introduction to his dictionary? Or merely that there is no art in that branch of expository prose which we call literary criticism? And if there is no art in expository prose, then what shall we say about expository verse? What shall we do, let us wonder in passing, with the first of Donne's *Holy Sonnets,* with the *Epistle to Dr. Arbuthnot,* or with much of *The Divine Comedy?* In the same essay he adds: [2]

I have assumed as axiomatic that a creation, a work of art, is autotelic; and that criticism is about something other than itself.

Art, then is about itself, but this information does not help me to answer my questions, for I do not understand it. What, for example, would Pope or Dante have understood if this statement had been made to them regarding the poems which I have just mentioned? Or what can we understand with regard to these poems? About all we can deduce from such a passage is that the artist does not really know what he is doing; a doctrine which we shall find suggested and elucidated elsewhere, and which leads directly to the plainest kind of determinism.

Yet every poem appears to the unpracticed eye to say something about some aspect of human experience. What are we to make of this? In one of his earliest and most famous essays, Eliot deals with this problem by way of a figure of speech: [3]

---

[2] Ibid., p. 19.

[3] *Tradition and the Individual Talent,* Ibid., p. 7 and thereafter.

The analogy was that of the catalyst. When the two gases previously mentioned are mixed in the presence of a filament of platinum, they form sulphurous acid. This combination takes place only if the platinum is present; nevertheless the newly formed acid contains no trace of platinum, and the platinum itself is apparently unaffected: has remained inert, neutral, and unchanged. The mind of the poet is the shred of platinum. It may partly or exclusively operate upon the experience of the man himself; but the more perfect the artist, the more completely separate in him will be the man who suffers and the mind which creates; the more perfectly will the mind digest and transmute the passions which are its material.

The experience, you will notice, the elements which enter the presence of the transforming catalyst, are of two kinds: emotions and feelings. The effect of a work of art upon the person who enjoys it is an experience different in kind from any experience not of art. It may be formed out of one emotion, or may be a combination of several; and various feelings, inhering for the writer in particular words or phrases or images, may be added to compose the final result. Or great poetry may be made without the direct use of any emotion whatever: composed out of feelings solely. Canto XV of the *Inferno* (Brunetto Latini) is a working up of the emotion evident in the situation; but the effect, though single as that of any work of art, is obtained by a considerable complexity of detail. The last quatrain gives an image, a feeling attaching to an image, which "came," which did not develop simply out of what precedes, but which was probably in suspension in the poet's mind until the proper combination arrived for it to add itself to. The poet's mind is in fact a receptacle for seizing and storing up numberless feelings, phrases, images, which remain there until all the particles which can unite to form a new compound are present together.

If you compare several representative passages of the greatest poetry you see how great is the variety of the types of combination, and also how completely any semi-ethical criterion of sublimity misses the mark. For it is not the "greatness," the intensity, of the emotions, the components, but the intensity of the artistic process, the pressure, so to speak, under which the fusion takes place, that counts. The episode of Paolo and Francesca employs a definite emotion, but the intensity of the poetry is something quite different from whatever intensity in the supposed experience it may give the impression of . . . the murder of Agamem-

non, or the agony of Othello, gives an artistic effect apparently
closer to a possible original than the scenes from Dante. In the
*Agamemnon,* the artistic emotion approximates to the emotion
of an actual spectator; in *Othello* to the emotion of the protagonist himself. But the difference between art and the event is always
absolute.

This passage requires a good deal of comment. In the first place,
one should note the words *emotion* and *feeling:* the first refers to
an emotion, as we commonly use the term, which arises from an experience outside of literature; the second to an emotion stirred by a
work or a fragment of literature. Emotion and feeling are the in-
gredients of literary art; there is no reference to rational understanding. Emotion, moreover, in Eliot's sense of the word, is transformed
by the artistic process into something which differs absolutely from
that which it was originally, so that semi-ethical criteria are irrelevant
to our judgment of the work of art. Art appears to be in this passage,
as in Poe, a matter of the novel combination of materials; and there
is no question of the artist's understanding what he is saying: the
criterion, as in Poe, is one of *effect.* This is interesting, for in reading
Eliot, one cannot avoid the conclusion that he has absorbed much
from Poe, but through early or fragmentary or otherwise uncritical
reading: many of Eliot's theories resemble those of Poe without Eliot
apparently knowing it, and his references to Poe are almost invariably
inaccurate.[4]
There is further evidence in this passage that Eliot regards the
poet as passive: he refers to him as "inert, neutral, unchanged," during and after the act of creation. Yet the figure is not developed consistently, for later Eliot asserts that it is "the intensity of the artistic
process, the pressure, so to speak, under which the fusion takes place
that counts." He does not say whether this intensity is a function of
the inert mind of the poet or an accident affecting the mind from
without. Nor, if we try to interpret the figure, to translate it into

---

[4] In the essay on Marvell (Selected Essays, New York, p. 259), for example,
Eliot writes: "There is here the element of *surprise,* as when Villon says: Neces-
sité faict gens mesprendre Et faim saillir le loup des bois, the surprise which Poe
considered of the highest importance." But it was *originality* not *surprise,* about
which Poe theorized, and he conceived it as a more or less arbitrary effect of
scenery or meter, not as simple precision of comparison. See my essay on Poe in
*Maule's Curse,* New Directions, 1938, or in American Literature VIII-4, p. 379.

plain language, can we determine what is meant either by inertness or by intensity; nor can we guess what occurs when the poet writes: the entire process is a mystery, and if the critic can say no more about it than he has said, he would have done well to employ less and simpler language.

If I may be pardoned for insisting, for a moment, on my own view of these matters, I should like to suggest that it describes more accurately the facts which Eliot appears to have in mind than does the theory of Eliot himself. According to my view, the artistic process is one of moral evaluation of human experience, by means of a technique which renders possible an evaluation more precise than any other. The poet tries to understand his experience in rational terms, to state his understanding, and simultaneously to state, by means of the feelings which we attach to words, the kind and degree of emotion that should properly be motivated by this understanding. The artistic result differs from the crude experience mainly in its refinement of judgment: the difference in really good art is enormous, but the difference is of degree rather than of kind. The "intensity" of the work of art, which is different from the intensity of the crude experience, lies in this: that what we call intensity in a work of art is a combination of the importance of the original subject and the precision of the judgment; whereas that which we call intensity in life is most often the confused and therefore frightening emotion resulting from a situation which we have not yet had time to meet and understand, and our feeling toward which, as it approaches clarity and control, approaches, though from a considerable distance, the condition of art.

I must ask the reader to bear carefully in mind not only the passage just quoted from Eliot but my statement of my own point of view, while he is considering the following passage from the essay called *The Metaphysical Poets:* [5]

> In the seventeenth century a dissociation of sensibility set in, from which we have never recovered; and this dissociation, as is natural, was aggravated by the two most powerful poets of the century, Milton and Dryden. Each of these men performed certain poetic functions so magnificently well that the magnitude of the effect concealed the absence of others. The language went

---

[5] Op. Cit., p. 247.

on and in some respects improved; the best verse of Collins, Gray, Johnson, and even Goldsmith satisfies some of our fastidious demands better than that of Donne or Marvell or King. But while the language became more refined, the feeling became more crude. The feeling, the sensibility, expressed in the *Country Churchyard* (to say nothing of Tennyson and Browning) is cruder than in the *Coy Mistress.*

The significance of this passage is not quite clear, but Eliot returns to the subject and elucidates it in his essay on Marvell: [6]

> When we come to Gray and Collins, the sophistication remains only in the language, and has disappeared from the feeling. Gray and Collins were masters, but they had lost that hold on human values, that firm grasp of human experience, which is a formidable achievement of the Elizabethan and Jacobean poets.

But how does this firm grasp of human values get into an autotelic art, to which ethical criteria are irrelevant? Has Eliot changed his mind radically over a period of years? *The Function of Criticism,* from which the first quotation in this essay is drawn is dated [7] 1923. *Tradition and the Individual Talent,* which provides the second quotation is dated 1917, and first appeared in book-form in *The Sacred Wood,* in 1921. The two other essays, however, are both dated 1921, and the essay on Swinburne, which appears in *The Sacred Wood,* finds Swinburne a poet of very limited value because his poetry was not nourished on human experience, and it ends with the statement: [8]

> . . . the language which is more important to us is that which is struggling to digest and express new objects, new feelings, new aspects, as, for instance, the prose of Mr. James Joyce or the earlier Conrad.

How does the language "digest" these subjects, without being "about" them? This passage and the passage from the essay on Marvell, though carelessly put, are comprehensible in my terms but not in the terms of the other essays cited. Eliot has not changed his mind over a given period, for the dates of the essays forbid such a view. The fact of the matter is that at any given time he can speak with

---

[6] Ibid., p. 256.

[7] Ibid. see list of dates in table of contents.

[8] Ibid., p. 285.

equal firmness and dignity on both sides of almost any question, and with no realization of the difficulties in which he is involved.

## II. THE THEORY OF THE OBJECTIVE CORRELATIVE

My own view of poetry, which I have already indicated, is a simple one: I believe that the feeling expressed by the work is, or should be, motivated by the artist's comprehension of his subject, which is drawn from human experience; and that the value of the work depends upon the justness of the motivation, in whole and in detail. Eliot sometimes adopts this view, but in the main he prefers to assume the emotion as initial: the result is his famous and widely influential theory of the objective correlative. In his essay on Hamlet [9] he writes:

> The only way of expressing emotion in the form of art is by finding an "objective correlative"; in other words, a set of objects, a situation, a chain of events which shall be the formula for that *particular* emotion; such that when the external facts, which must terminate in sensory experience, are given, the emotion is immediately evoked.

This seems to me, I confess, a reversal of the normal processes of understanding human experience, and a dangerous reversal. Mario Praz traces this concept to Pound: [10]

> Pound's idea of poetry as "a sort of inspired mathematics which gives us equations, not for abstract figures, triangles, spheres, and the like, but for the human emotions," may be said to be the starting point for Eliot's theory of the "Objective correlative."

Praz continues:

> That influence is closely connected with Eliot's interpretation of Dante's allegory along the lines suggested by Ezra Pound —as we have seen above. Clear visual images, a concise and luminous language: these are the two qualities of Dante Eliot has in mind. The former is the "objective correlative" of the emotions they intend to suggest, the latter appeals to the auditory

[9] Ibid., p. 124.
[10] Southern Review, Vol. II, No. 3, pp. 525–548. The passage from Pound occurs on p. 5, *The Spirit of Romance*.

imagination: there is an element of extreme precision and extreme vagueness in both . . . The pattern of images in *Ash Wednesday* seems thus suggested by Dante, but in a peculiar way. It is as if Eliot had been reading Dante without giving much heed to the meaning, but letting himself be impressed by a few clear visual images.

Praz is unquestionably correct in his claims for the extensive influence of Pound upon Eliot's critical theories. Nevertheless, this particular theory is at least as old as Poe and is more than likely older, and Poe states it much more nearly in Eliot's terms. Poe writes in his essay on Hawthorne:[11]

> . . . having conceived, with deliberate care, a certain unique or single *effect* to be wrought out, he [the skillful literary artist] then invents such incidents—he then combines such events as may best aid him in establishing this preconceived effect.

One will find the same procedure elaborated in *The Philosophy of Composition.*

Eliot, however, is unable to adhere to his position. In the same essay—indeed on the same page—he writes:

> Hamlet is up against the difficulty that his disgust is occasioned by his mother, but that his mother is not an adequate equivalent for it; his disgust envelops and exceeds her. It is thus a feeling which he cannot understand . . .

And the play as a whole is found at fault in the end for the same reason with relation to Shakespeare: the events of the play are not an adequate equivalent for the disgust which Shakespeare, in Eliot's opinion, was trying to express. Now finding an "objective correlative" for an emotion is not the same thing as understanding it: to understand it we must know and correctly judge its motive. There seems to be a suggestion here that Eliot's theory is inadequate to his feeling about the play. There is a similar suggestion in this passage from the essay on Cyril Tourneur:[12]

---

[11] Stedman and Woodberry edition, p. 31 of the second of the three volumes of Poe's criticism. For further comment see my essay on Poe, already mentioned.

[12] Op. cit., p. 166.

The cynicism, the loathing and disgust of humanity, expressed consummately in *The Revenger's Tragedy,* are immature in the respect that they exceed the object.

And a few years earlier he is even more explicit. In the essay on Lancelot Andrewes, he writes: [13]

> Andrewes' emotion is purely contemplative; it is not personal, it is wholly evoked by the object of contemplation, to which it is adequate; his emotion is wholly contained in and explained by its object. But with Donne there is always something else, the "baffling" of which Mr. Pearsall Smith speaks in his introduction. Donne is a "personality" in a sense in which Andrewes is not: his sermons, one feels, are a "means of self-expression." He is constantly finding an object which shall be adequate to his feelings: Andrewes is wholly absorbed in the object and therefore responds with the adequate emotion. Andrewes has the *goût pour la vie spirituelle,* which is not native to Donne.

Now it is immaterial with respect to my present purposes whether this comparison of the two men is a just one; the point which interests me is this: that Andrewes is praised because he adheres to my principles, whereas Donne is blamed because he adheres to those of Eliot. Eliot does not explain his self-contradiction, nor does he give any evidence that he is aware of it.

### III. THOUGHT AND EMOTION IN POETRY

The theory of the "objective correlative" rests, as Eliot says in discussing Andrewes, on the assumption that the poet is trying to express an emotion, not on the theory that he is trying to understand it. It is as good a fundamental principle as one is likely to find to serve as a justification for the sort of confused motivation which I have discussed under the name of pseudo-reference in an earlier collection of essays called *Primitivism and Decadence.* I should like to reiterate what I shall be able to show in great detail later, that this primacy which Eliot gives to the emotions leads directly to a thorough determinism of the most dangerous sort: if we are bound to express our emotions without understanding them, we obviously

---

[13] Ibid., p. 298. The last three essays mentioned are dated 1919, 1931, and 1926 respectively.

have no way of judging or controlling them, but must take them as they come. Eliot deals with the general subject of the relation of thought to emotion in a great many passages, of which I must confine myself to a relatively small number for comment.

In the essay on *Shakespeare and the Stoicism of Seneca* [14] he says:

> The poet who "thinks" is merely the poet who can express the emotional equivalent of thought. But he is not necessarily interested in the thought itself. We talk as if thought was precise and emotion was vague. In reality there is precise emotion and there is vague emotion. To express precise emotion requires as great intellectual power as to express precise thought.

This passage is a startling one. What, for example, is the emotional equivalent of thought, unless it is the emotion motivated by thought? We are not concerned, here, with the objective correlative of an emotion, but with the emotional correlative of a thought, which must then be expressed by means, I presume, of an objective correlative. What is the nature of the extraordinary sequence of relationships here implied? And if the emotion is to be considered as motivated by the thought, what are we to think of the poet who can express such emotion when he is not "interested in the thought itself"? Furthermore, how can such emotion be expressed except in terms of the motivating thought unless we are to falsify it utterly? And how can it be precise unless the motivating thought is precise?

In the same essay and on the next page Eliot writes:

> The difference between Shakespeare and Dante is that Dante had one coherent system of thought behind him; but that was just his luck, and from the point of view of poetry is an irrelevant accident. It happened that at Dante's time thought was orderly and strong and beautiful, and that it was concentrated in one man of the greatest genius; Dante's poetry receives a boost which in a sense it does not merit, from the fact that the thought behind it is the thought of a man as great and lovely as Dante himself: St. Thomas . . . In truth, neither Shakespeare nor Dante did any real thinking—that was not their job; and the relative value of the thought current at their time, the material enforced upon each to use as the vehicle of his feeling, is of no importance.

---

[14] Ibid., p. 115.

Now Eliot, as we shall see elsewhere, is usually of the opinion that Shakespeare was the inhabitant of a very inferior intellectual milieu, so that this passage is in effect a comparison of two very great poets one of whom is supposed to have inherited (without much effort) the clearest and most intricate philosophy of all time and the other a ragbag of disparate philosophical fragments. But what, then, is the meaning of the passage? In what sense does Dante's poetry "receive a boost," irrespective of the question of merit? Is Dante's poetry better for the clarity of its thought, or is it not? If it is better, in what sense is the clarity of its thought an irrelevant accident? It is not Dante's personal merit with which we are concerned, but the quality of his poetry. The last sentence, however, is emphatic, and it is emphatically anti-intellectual and deterministic at the same time: "the relative value of the thought current at their time, the material enforced upon each to use as the vehicle of his feeling, is of no importance." We may observe from this that the quality of a writer's thought is at once enforced upon him and is irrelevant to the quality of his work.

Much the same view is expressed more fully a little later: [15]

> What every poet starts from is his own emotions. . . . The great poet, in writing himself, writes his time. Thus Dante, hardly knowing it, became the voice of the thirteenth century; Shakespeare, hardly knowing it, became the representative of the end of the sixteenth century, of a turning point in history. But you can hardly say that Dante believed, or did not believe, the Thomist philosophy: you can hardly say that Shakespeare believed, or did not believe, the mixed and muddled scepticism of the Renaissance. If Shakespeare had written according to a better philosophy, he would have written worse poetry; it was his business to express the greatest emotional intensity of his time, based on whatever his time happened to think. Poetry is not a substitute for philosophy or theology or religion, as Mr. Lewis and Mr. Murry sometimes seem to think; it has its own function. But as this function is not intellectual but emotional, it cannot be defined adequately in intellectual terms. We can say that it provides "consolation": strange consolation, which is provided equally by writers so different as Dante and Shakespeare. . . .
>
> I doubt whether belief proper enters into the activity of a great poet, qua poet. That is, Dante, qua poet, did not believe or

---

[15] Ibid., p. 117.

disbelieve the Thomist cosmology or theory of the soul: he merely
made use of it, or a fusion took place between his initial emotional impulses and a theory, for the purpose of making poetry.
The poet makes poetry, the metaphysician makes metaphysics,
the bee makes honey, the spider secretes a filament; you can hardly
say that any of these agents believes: he merely does.

This passage also is curious in a great many ways. In the first
place we have no authority for Shakespeare's intellectual equipment
save Eliot's unsupported impression; and Eliot's impression even of
so monumental a subject as this, as we shall ultimately have occasion
to see, is not incapable of sudden and unpremeditated reversal; but
let us suppose Shakespeare to be what Eliot here says he is. Eliot displays a knowledge of the personal beliefs and motives of two poets
of distant ages that can be matched for its clairvoyance, I imagine,
only by the perceptions of certain characters of Henry James; and he
refines upon this clairvoyance in the case of Dante by distinguishing
between Dante *qua* Dante and Dante *qua* poet. Anyone who can
take this sort of thing seriously is welcome to do so. These points
are all trivial, however, as compared to another; namely a kind of
mystical determinism which has seldom been stated with such naive
emphasis except by Emerson himself. Eliot writes: "Thus Dante,
hardly knowing it, became the voice of the thirteenth century . . ."
And Emerson: "Great men have always confided themselves childlike to the genius of their age . . ." And again:

> The hand that rounded Peter's dome,
> And groined the aisles of Christian Rome,
> Wrought in a sad sincerity;
> Himself from God he could not free.

A passage in which God, the universe, and the period are conceived
to be one. And it is worth noting in passing that Eliot's belief that
only intellectual matter may be treated by the intellect introduces
a new complication, with really extraordinary irradiations, into the
practice of philosophy and of criticism.

Eliot is not without his hesitations, however. In writing elsewhere of Dante,[16] he says:

> And clear visual images are given much more intensity by
> having a meaning—we do not need to know what the meaning

---

[16] Ibid., p. 204.

is, but in our awareness of the image we must be aware that the meaning is there too. Allegory is only one poetic method, but it is a method which has very great advantages.

Dante's is a *visual* imagination. It is a visual imagination in a different sense from that of a modern painter of still life: it is visual in the sense that he lived in an age in which men still saw visions. It was a psychological habit, the trick of which we have forgotten, but as good as any of our own. We have nothing but dreams, and we have forgotten that seeing visions—a practice now relegated to the aberrant and uneducated—was once a more significant, interesting, and disciplined kind of dreaming. We take it for granted that our dreams spring from below: possibly the quality of our dreams suffers in consequence.

It is possible, of course, as Eliot somewhere else remarks, to admire a poem deeply without wholly understanding it; but such admiration must rest on an understanding at least imperfect, and the idea that this admiration is adequate as compared with that which comes with full understanding is mere nonsense. Dante's visions, with their meaning obscured, are dreams, as Praz points out; though in Dante, at least, and in part by virtue of the meaning which helped Dante to see them, they may be dreams of unusual clarity. If the meaning is important in the creation of the poem, at any rate, it is foolish to suppose that one can dispense with it in reading the poem or that the poet did not take his meaning seriously. Only the frailest barrier exists between the idea of this passage and Poe's theory that the poet should lay claim to a meaning when he is aware of none.

Eliot goes still farther, in his essay on Marvell, in the direction of admitting the importance of thought in the poem, but the passage is merely an undeveloped hint, and one does not really know what he meant by it: [17]

> These verses have the suggestiveness of true poetry; and the verses of Morris, which are nothing if not an attempt to suggest, really suggest nothing; and we are inclined to infer that the suggestiveness is the aura around a bright clear center, that you cannot have the aura alone.

And in writing of Dryden, he says likewise: [18]

---

[17] Ibid., p. 259.
[18] Ibid., p. 273.

88 T. S. ELIOT

> Swinburne was also a master of words, but Swinburne's words are all suggestions and no denotation; if they suggest nothing, it is because they suggest too much.

This is a good statement, but there is small reason to believe that Eliot knows what it means. He concludes his essay on the Metaphysical poets, for example,—an essay, which, incidentally, comments with a certain penetration on some of the qualities of metaphysical poetry—with this remarkable judgment: [19]

> It is not a permanent necessity that poets should be interested in philosophy, or in any other subject. We can only say that it appears likely that poets in our civilization, as it exists at present, must be *difficult* . . . The poet must become more and more comprehensive, more allusive, more indirect, in order to force, to dislocate if necessary, language into his meaning . . . Hence we get something which looks very much like the conceit—we get, in fact, a method curiously similar to that of the metaphysical poets . . . .

The idea is illustrated by a passage of fragmentary and weakly allusive French symbolism. This statement by Eliot has been often quoted, and is probably one of the main reasons why so many of the young and decadent romantics of our own period are convinced that they are in the tradition of Donne. If one cannot be profound, it is always fairly easy to be difficult.

Only one deduction is possible from Eliot's many comments upon this subject: namely that he believes that a poet who merely pretends to be saying something may be as successful as one who succeeds in saying something, that, as he said clearly in the passages quoted earlier in this section, the intellectual content of a poem is irrelevant to its value. That the intellectual content of a poem, whether good, bad, or fraudulent is an inseparable part of the poem and is inextricably involved in the emotion, simply by virtue of the fact that the poem is composed of words, he does not seem to consider.

### IV. POETRY AND BELIEF

The subject of poetry and belief is little more than a subsidiary topic under the preceding head; for this reason, I shall consider only one

---

[19] Ibid., p. 248.

passage from Eliot, a characteristic one, and shall try to make a few elementary distinctions of my own. This may seem presumptuous, but the problem of poetry and belief does not seem to be nearly so difficult as more learned authorities than myself have apparently thought it. In writing of Dante, Eliot comments as follows on certain ideas of I. A. Richards:[20]

> We may raise the question whether "literature" exists; but for certain purposes, such as the purpose of this essay on Dante, we must assume that there is literature and literary appreciation; we must assume that the reader can obtain the full "literary" or (if you will) "aesthetic" enjoyment without sharing the beliefs of the author . . .
>
> I deny, in short, that the reader must share the beliefs of the poet in order to enjoy the poetry fully. I have also asserted that we can distinguish between Dante's beliefs as a man and his beliefs as a poet. But we are forced to believe that there is a particular relation between the two, and that the poet "means what he says." If we learned, for instance, that *De Rerum Natura* was a Latin exercise which Dante had composed for relaxation after completing *The Divine Comedy,* and published under the name of one Lucretius, I am sure that our capacity for enjoying either poem would be mutilated . . .
>
> And I confess to considerable difficulty in analyzing my own feelings, a difficulty which makes me hesitate to accept Mr. Richards' theories of "pseudo-statements." On reading the line which he uses,

> Beauty is truth, truth beauty . . .

> I am at first inclined to agree with him, because this statement of equivalence means nothing to me. But on rereading the whole Ode, this line strikes me as a serious blemish on a beautiful poem; and the reason must be either that I fail to understand it, or that it is a statement which is untrue . . .

Like Eliot, I find the statement of Keats a blemish, and for the reason given, a reason which, however, Eliot has no right to give, for the general theories which we have been examining will not support it. What "particular relation" can there be between the beliefs of the two Dantes, or how can the poet "mean what he says" if he is "not necessarily interested in the thought itself"? Eliot is not making

---

[20] Ibid., p. 229.

fine distinctions when he writes thus; he is indulging in unpardonable confusion.

The difficulty in the statement by Keats, however, is not the same difficulty that Dante might be supposed to encounter in Lucretius or Lucretius in Dante; the difficulty is one of simple incomprehensibility. Beauty and Truth are abstract terms with distinct meanings; to say that they are interchangeable without explaining oneself leads to confusion. The non-Christian, however, might easily share a wide community of belief with Dante. The portraits of the damned are portraits of human beings, represented in Hell as they might be seen in life, suffering for sins most of which are acknowledged to be sins by intelligent men, whether Christian or not. As we proceed, however, toward the final vision of beatitude, we find ourselves dealing with concepts which are more and more purely Christian, and it is more than likely that only the convinced Christian can feel the poetry at something like its full value: for the rest of us, the poetry offers a theoretic projection of the imagination, a representation more or less dramatic. Not purely, however: for such poetry will of necessity be colored by feelings, desires, and ideas common to all men, and this alloy renders easier our entrance into the Christian state of feeling.

Let us consider another case. One of the few great poems of the twentieth century in America, I imagine, is *Sunday Morning,* by Wallace Stevens. The poem is a meditative composition, discreetly didactic in form; and its doctrine is one of more or less Paterian hedonism. Now I am not, myself, a hedonist of any variety; my dislike for the philosophy is profound, and I believe that it has, in the long run, done serious damage to the style of Wallace Stevens. But I know that hedonists exist, and the state of mind portrayed in the poem seems proper to them, and moreover it seems beautifully portrayed. It is no more necessary that one be a hedonist in order to enjoy this particular poem than that one be a murderer in order to enjoy Macbeth. Furthermore, in my own case, various subsidiary themes facilitate my entrance into the dominant theme: the theme of twentieth century scepticism, of doubt of immortality, the vision of the world as an infinitesimal island floating in infinite space. These themes, however, might merely increase the difficulty for Dante; but allowing Dante the same opportunity for the historical study of our period that we enjoy in the study of his, we may reasonably guess that he would be able to understand the poem fairly well. My chief objection to a hedonistic philosophy is not that it contradicts my own view of human experience, but that it offers a very small portion of it in place of the whole, and that the error of mistaking that portion for the whole may prove very serious; that portion, however, may be truly described. On the other hand, Emerson, I believe, contradicts the most elementary and obvious facts of experience, and his poems may offer a problem of considerable difficulty. Emerson believes that all good comes from surrender to instinct and emotion; all evil from the functioning of the rational faculty. Emerson's ideal man would be, it appears to me certain, an automaton, a madman; it is simply impossible to envisage human experience in these terms, for the terms are a negation of everything that we know. When Emerson, therefore, preaches his doctrine directly, in purely didactic terms, and with intentions purely to explain and convince, as in *The Problem,* he achieves a kind of incomprehensibility comparable to that in the passage from Keats. His language is very general, with the result that certain passages, if found in isolation, might be given a significance anything but Emersonian, as, for instance, could this passage about Michael Angelo:

> The hand that rounded Peter's dome,
> And groined the aisles of Christian Rome,
> Wrought in a sad sincerity;
> Himself from God he could not free.

Standing alone, these lines offer an impressive portrait of the devout Christian artist. But if we take them in the entire poem, we find that they mean something the reverse of Christian: we find that the God in question is the God of the Pantheist, and that the artist could not free himself from Him, simply because he wrought automatically as a determined and inseparable portion of the whole. If we could force ourselves to see what Emerson meant, and refuse to be misled by the traditional associations of the language when it is considered fragmentarily, then the poem, it seems to me, would be damaged past remedy. Of course we can never quite do this; the traditional associations are there, and they keep the poem alive in a marginal and unsatisfactory way, but nevertheless alive, and this is true of much similar poetry.

And one might find a poem stated throughout in terms so general that alternative interpretations might be possible. Consider, for example, Blake's *Introduction* to the *Songs of Experience*. Blake's philosophy resembles that of Emerson, except that it is not pantheistic; it contradicts the common observation of human nature in much the same fashion. The *Introduction* is, in fact, an invitation to humanity to throw off the shackles of intellect and law, and thus to free the true God, who was overthrown by Lucifer and bound in Hell: it rests on a precise inversion not only of Christian mythology, which perhaps does not matter, but of Christian morality as well. Yet we know this only by examining Blake as a whole; the poem as an isolated invocation might as well be Christian. What then are we to do with such a poem? Are we to read it with an attempt to accept for the moment Blake's full meaning, even if that meaning appears to be nonsense? If we do that, we shall have the same difficulty as in the poem by Emerson. Are we to read it with a resolute determination to give it as much of our own private meaning as the nature of the statement permits, even while realizing that Blake's meaning was the reverse of this? Such a procedure would be justified, so far as it might be possible, I believe, if it were necessary. In this poem, however, the abstract statement is very general: the poem is an invocation to humanity to free itself from evil and to enter the good life; the feeling of the poem is a feeling proper to that very general statement, and we may reasonably take the poem in that condition of generality and not trouble ourselves about the difficulties of Blake's philosophy until we actually trip on them.

These speculations, however, all derive from the conviction that the thought of a poem must be in some sense acceptable; that the thought is of the greatest importance as a part of the poem itself. Eliot, in the last passage quoted, would like, it appears, to make some such admission, but is hampered by the contrary trend of his general theory; and he once more takes refuge in mystery. But the believer in pure poetry will probably demand to know what there will be in pre-romantic poetry for the reader who believes with Emerson. The question in one form or another is constantly raised, and is mildly interesting. One may reply at the outset that the romantic theorist is by his nature either an untalented or an untrained theorist, and is therefore, like Emerson, practically certain to be inconsistent. His inconsistencies will probably rescue a good deal of the poetry in question for him. However, his understanding of such poetry, like Emerson's, is likely to be a very imperfect affair. If we could find a truly consistent Emersonian, it is certain that he would understand nothing of pre-romantic poetry or of anything else; furthermore he would have no particular rights in the matter. One might as well demand poetic rights for those who cannot read or speak, or poetic rights for idiots. Poetry is for the intelligent.

### V. TRADITION

Much of what has been thus far discussed verges on the question of tradition. The question is one that has fascinated Eliot from the beginning, and on which he has made some of his most interesting comments. In the early essay, *Tradition and the Individual Talent*, he writes: [21]

> We dwell with satisfaction upon the poet's difference from his predecessors, especially his immediate predecessors; we endeavor to find something that can be isolated in order to be enjoyed. Whereas if we approach a poet without this prejudice we shall often find that not only the best but the most individual parts of his work may be those in which the dead poets, his ancestors, assert their immortality most vigorously. And I do not mean the impressionable period of adolescence, but the period of full maturity.

This seems to me admirable as far as it goes, but the relation of the individual contribution to the traditional procedure is not made very clear. One may depart from it in almost any direction, and Eliot in regarding Pound as the greatest modern poet in English, seems to depart somewhat curiously: what, precisely, is Pound's relationship to tradition, and why is it superior to that of Bridges, Hardy, or Robinson? And in what does it resemble the relationship of Valéry, whom Eliot apparently judges, as do I, to be the greatest modern in French? On the face of it Pound and Valéry appear to have almost nothing in common save native talent: Pound's relationship to tradition is that of one who has abandoned its method and pillaged its details—he is merely a barbarian on the loose in a museum; Valéry's relationship to tradition is that of a poet who has mastered and used the best of traditional method, and has used that method to deal

---

[21] Ibid., p. 4.

with original and intelligent matter. Valéry is a living and beautifully functioning mind; Pound is a rich but disordered memory.
Eliot continues in the same essay:

> Yet if the only form of tradition, of handing down, consisted
> in following the ways of the immediate generation before us in a
> blind or timid adherence to its successes, "tradition" should posi-
> tively be discouraged. We have seen many such simple currents
> soon lost in the sand; and novelty is better than repetition  Tradi-
> tion is a matter of much wider significance. It cannot be inherited,
> and if you want it you must obtain it by great labor. It involves in
> the first place, the historical sense, which we may call nearly in-
> dispensable to anyone who would continue to be a poet beyond
> his twenty-fifth year; and the historical sense involves a perception
> not only of the pastness of the past, but of its presence; the his-
> torical sense compels a man to write not merely with his own
> generation in his bones, but with a feeling that the whole of the
> literature of Europe from Homer and within it the whole of
> the literature of his own country has a simultaneous existence
> and composes a simultaneous order. This historical sense, which
> is a sense of the timeless as well as of the temporal, and of the
> timeless and of the temporal together, is what makes a writer
> traditional.

This passage raises much the same questions as the last, and
even more emphatically: and these questions become central to the
whole question of Eliot's influence when we arrive, as we shall arrive later, at the question of the determining effect upon a writer
of his own time. Is Pound, for example, a man who possesses this
historical sense, when he writes a formless revery loaded with quotations and literary reminiscences, but having no other discernible relationship to past literature? And is Eliot another such man, when he
does almost the same thing with less skill? Or is Valéry such a man,
when he brings to bear upon problems of the modern mind and of
the modern sensibility a mode of thinking and of writing, an entire
moral, literary, and philosophical apparatus descended from Greek
antiquity but heavily influenced by the tradition of his own country
from the time of its greatest literary period, that of Racine, to the
present? Eliot has praised both men in equally high terms, but,
though he has pillaged a few lines from Valéry, he has followed the

method of Pound. If the view of tradition offered gives no reason for choice between two men so diverse, it is worthless, and if it leads us to choose Pound, it is vicious.

And finally it is interesting to note that Eliot informs us in this essay that tradition can be obtained only by hard labor, whereas in his later and Christian period he offers a less Christian view: [22]

> I hold . . . that a *tradition* is rather a way of feeling and acting which characterizes a group throughout generations; and that it must largely be, or that many of the elements in it must be, unconscious; whereas the maintenance of *orthodoxy* is a matter which calls for the exercise of all our conscious intelligence. . . . Tradition may be conceived as a by-product of right living, not to be aimed at directly. It is of the blood, so to speak, rather than of the brain.

From which we may deduce that tradition is a way of feeling and orthodoxy the corpus of ideas by which we may criticize it. But in the paragraph preceding, the paragraph in which Eliot justifies his own poetry against the criticism of Paul Elmer More, a paragraph which I shall later have occasion to quote, Eliot informs us that tradition, so conceived, cannot be modified by orthodoxy, that the attempt to modify one's feeling as a result of self-criticism can lead to nothing save pious insincerity. Orthodoxy thus becomes a mere intellectual pastime, like chess, with no spiritual value, and one's feelings, from which poetry and character alike appear to be derived, are determined and beyond the power of self-modification.

Eliot's concept of the relation of the artist to tradition may be illustrated by one more characteristic passage: [23]

> I was dealing then with the artist, and the sense of tradition which, it seemed to me, the artist should have; but it was generally a problem of order; and the function of criticism seems to be essentially a problem of order too. I thought of literature then, as I think of it now, of the literature of the world, of the literature of Europe, of the literature of a single country, not as a collection of the writings of individuals, but as "organic wholes," as systems in relation to which, and only in relation to which, individual works of literary art, and the works of individual

---

[22] *After Strange Gods*, Harcourt, Brace, and Co., 1933. Pp. 31–2.
[23] *The Function of Criticism, Selected Essays*, Harcourt, Brace, p. 12.

artists, have their significance. There is accordingly something outside of the artist to which he owes allegiance, a devotion to which he must surrender and sacrifice himself in order to earn and obtain his unique position. A common inheritance and a common cause unite artists consciously or unconsciously: it must be admitted that the union is mostly unconscious. Between the true artists of any time there is, I believe, an unconscious community. And as our instincts of tidiness imperatively command us not to leave to the haphazard of unconsciousness what we can attempt to do consciously, we are forced to conclude that what happens unconsciously we could bring about and form into a purpose, if we made a conscious attempt.

Such a phrase as "organic whole" in this connection has a deterministic flavor almost as extreme as anything to be found in Taine. Further, if we are to indulge our privilege to be particular, what is the nature of the organic whole which includes and determines Pound and Valéry, Eliot and Robinson? And is it the function of the conscious intellect merely to accelerate and render efficient that which otherwise would happen unconsciously? If so, we have a determinism, which though perhaps not wholly pure, is surely pure enough.

The best possible comment on this kind of theorizing has been made by Eliot himself. In the *Introduction* to *The Use of Poetry and the Use of Criticism* [24] he has written:

> I hold indeed that in an age in which the use of poetry is something agreed upon you are more likely to get that minute and scrupulous examination of felicity and blemish, line by line, which is conspicuously absent from the criticism of our time, a criticism which seems to demand of poetry, not that it shall be well written, but that it shall be "representative of its age."

But it is primarily Eliot and a small handful of his influential disciples, not the rest of us, who demand that our poetry shall be representative of its age; and they appear to have decided consciously that the unconscious tendency of the age is to produce poetry in the manner of Pound and Eliot, except when one of them by some unaccountable atavism occasionally happens to feel a liking for a poet of some other kind.

---

[24] *The Use of Poetry and the Use of Criticism,* by T. S. Eliot. Faber and Faber, London. P. 25.

## VI. DETERMINISM

We have seen that the entire tendency of Eliot's thought is toward a deterministic view of literature. Yet Eliot is very severe in his comments upon deterministic views when he is able to recognize them. In the essay on John Bramhall, he writes as follows: [25]

> Hobbes' philosophy is not so much a philosophy as it is an adumbration of the universe of material atoms regulated by laws of motion which formed the scientific view of the world from Newton to Einstein. Hence there is quite naturally no place in Hobbes's universe for the human will; what he failed to see is that there was no place in it for consciousness either, or for human beings. So his only philosophical theory is a theory of sense perception, and his psychology leaves no place in the world for his theory of government. His theory of government has no philosophic basis: it is merely a collection of discrete opinions, prejudices, and genuine reflections upon experience which are given a spurious unity by a shadowy metaphysic.
>
> The attitude of Hobbes toward moral philosophy has by no means disappeared from human thought; nor has the confusion between moral philosophy and a mechanistic psychology.

In *Catholicism and International Order* [26] he writes:

> The non-Catholic, certainly the non-Christian philosopher, feeling no obligation to alter himself, and therefore no cogent need to understand himself, is apt to be under the sway of his prejudices, his social background, his individual tastes. So, I dare say, are we: but we at least, I hope, admit our duty to try to subdue them.

And on the next page of the same essay:

> Very few people, indeed, want to be better than they are; or, to put it in more consecrated terms, hunger and thirst after righteousness. And what we happen to like as individuals outside of the main current which is the Catholic tradition is apt to be what our own sort of people within a narrow limit of place and time have been happening to like. We are likely to assume

---

[25] *Selected Essays*, p. 303.
[26] *Catholicism and International Order*, in *Essays Ancient and Modern*, Harcourt, Brace and Co., N. Y., p. 118.

as eternal truths things that in fact have only been taken for
granted by a small body of people or for a very short period of
time.

And in *The Function of Criticism:* [27]

> The critic, one would suppose, if he is to justify his existence,
> should endeavor to discipline his personal prejudices and cranks
> —tares to which we are all subject—and compose his differences
> with as many of his fellows as possible, in the common pursuit
> of true judgment.

And three pages farther in the same essay:

> The question is, the first question, *not* what comes natural
> or what comes *easy* to us, but what is right?

The general tendency of all of these passages is to affirm the
power of man to criticize and improve himself, with reference to
an absolute norm, and to affirm the necessity of his doing so. With this
point of view I am in perfect agreement. It is with reference to this
point of view, apparently, that Eliot objects to a passage from Herbert Read. At the end of his volume entitled *After Strange Gods,*
Eliot offers an appendix containing four specimens of modern heresy,
of which Read's statement is the third:

> Character, in short, is an impersonal ideal which the in-
> dividual selects and to which he sacrifices all other claims, espe-
> cially those of the sentiments or emotions. It follows that character
> must be placed in opposition to personality, which is the general
> common denominator of our sentiments and emotions. That is,
> indeed, the opposition I wish to emphasize; and when I have
> said further that all poetry, in which I wish to include all lyrical
> impulses whatever, is the product of the personality, and there-
> fore inhibited in a character, I have stated the main theme of
> my essay.

Briefly, this passage means that poetry is the product of what
we are, and that any attempt to remake ourselves according to an
ideal will damage the poetry, and Eliot objects to it, I should judge,
because it recommends the poet's doing what is natural and easy to
him instead of what is right. Yet Eliot, in defending his own poetry,

---

[27] *Selected Essays,* p. 14.

at the end of the first essay in the same volume, uses Read's argument with no apparent realization of the fact:[28]

> From another aspect also I have a personal interest in the clearing up of the use of the terms with which I have been concerned. My friend Dr. Paul Elmer More is not the first critic to call attention to the apparent incoherence between my verse and my critical prose—though he is the first whose perplexity on this account has caused me any distress. It would appear that while I maintain the most correct opinions in my criticism, I do nothing but violate them in my verse; and thus appear in a double if not double-faced role. I feel no shame in the matter. I am not of course interested by those critics who praise my criticism in order to discredit my verse, or those who praise my verse in order to discredit my opinion in religious or social affairs; I am only interested in answering those critics who, like Dr. More, have paid me the compliment—deserved or not does not here matter—of expressing some approval of both. I should say that in one's prose reflections one may be legitimately occupied with ideals, whereas in the writing of verse one can only deal with actuality. Why, I would ask, is most religious verse so bad; and why does so little religious verse reach the highest levels of poetry? Largely, I think, because of a pious insincerity.

Now if we change Eliot's *ideals* to Read's *character* (an ideal concept), and Eliot's *actuality* to Read's *personality,* and the terms in these two passages are certainly interchangeable, we have exactly the same statement in both men, and it is less excusable in Eliot than in Read because Read has at least the virtue of being roughly consistent with himself. In both men the statement means about this: that our individual natures are determined for us, and our actual way of feeling cannot be changed, though it may be a pious and admirable practice to consider the theoretical characteristics of a better kind of nature—it may be a pious and admirable practice to do so, that is, so long as we do not indulge in the pious insincerity of attempting to conform our own nature to this ideal. The pious sincerity which Eliot has derived from his Christianity in the past thirteen or fourteen years would probably baffle the simpler sort of Christian.

And lest the reader think that I have misrepresented Eliot by

---

[28] *After Strange Gods,* p. 30.

taking a passage unfairly from its context, let me cite another and briefer passage from earlier in the same essay: [29]

> No sensible author, in the midst of something that he is trying to write, can stop to consider whether it is going to be romantic or the opposite. At the moment when one writes, one is what one is, and the damage of a lifetime, and of having been born into an unsettled society, cannot be repaired at the moment of composition.

At the moment when one writes, one is what one is: one has, in other words no power over that moment; one must surrender to one's feelings and one's habits at that moment if one is to achieve sincerity. Yet at what point in a poet's career does this become true? If it were true at the age of sixteen, the poet would develop but little beyond that age; and if the poet at the age of sixteen is to be encouraged to improve his literary habits, why should not the poet at the age of forty-six? Obviously one will not change one's literary habits between moments of composition; one will change them if at all in writing. And if one's conversion to Catholicism and to classicism is worth a flourish of the pen, it is worth risking a few years of unsatisfactory composition in order to form new habits. I am reasonably certain that both Aquinas and Aristotle are on my side in this matter. Eliot's position is one of unmitigated determinism.

The point of view here indicated is, furthermore, related to the Marxist and Fascist view that the individual lacks the private and personal power to achieve goodness in a corrupt society; it is a utopian point of view, not a Christian one. Christianity rests upon the assumption that man can, with God's grace, save himself in a corrupt world; and if Eliot is convinced that the civilization of our period, bad as it may be, offers greater hazards, let us say than the Mediterranean civilization of the time of Augustine, or the British civilization of the time of Bede, he would do well to clarify his opinion.

Eliot appears to have adopted uncritically some such nostalgic historical lyricism as that of the later Henry Adams. Like Adams, he repeatedly contrasts the period of Dante and Aquinas with the twentieth century; and when he refers to the period of Dante and Aquinas, it is obvious that he refers especially to the minds of Dante and Aquinas, not to the vast underworld of sluggishly brutal paganism

---

[29] Ibid., p. 27.

which surrounded them, as it is obvious that in his references to the
twentieth century he has in mind his own confusion, as well as that
of such men as John Dewey and Bertrand Russell, and not such
minds as those of Gilson, Maillol, and Valéry. It is a difficult if not
impossible thing to define the spirit of any age: the age of Pope, the
mind of Pope himself, is a scene of complicated conflict; and nearly
any other age is more complicated still. The inept deism of *The Essay
on Man* was not forced upon Pope by the age: Pope himself, by virtue
of his inability to think and his ability to write as if he thought perfectly, did at least as much as Shaftesbury to impose it on the age,
and had he possessed as sharp a mind as Samuel Johnson the history
of the age might easily have been greatly different from what it was.

The writer bent on finding the spirit of an age is certain to be
the victim of impressions of a very limited kind; and seeking the
spirit of his own age, in order that he may conform to it and thus
be at once sincere and properly determined, he is likely to be the
victim of impressions which merely flatter his weakness. In order to
illustrate this difficulty, let me cite two passages from Eliot describing
the age of Shakespeare. In the essay on John Ford we find the following statement: [30]

> In the work of Shakespeare as a whole, there is to be read
> the profoundest, and indeed one of the most sombre studies of
> humanity that has ever been made in poetry; though it is in
> fact so comprehensive that we cannot qualify it as a whole as
> either glad or sorry. We recognize the same assumption of per-
> manence in his minor fellows. Dante held it also, and the great
> Greek dramatists. In periods of unsettlement and change we do
> not observe this: it was a changing world which met the eyes
> of Lucian or of Petronius.

And in *Shakespeare and the Stoicism of Seneca* [31] we meet this
alternative impression:

> In Elizabethan England we have conditions apparently ut-
> terly different from those of Imperial Rome. But it was a period
> of dissolution and chaos; and in such a period any emotional
> attitude which seems to give a man something firm, even if it
> be only the attitude of "I am myself alone," is eagerly taken up.

[30] *Selected Essays*, p. 179.
[31] Ibid., p. 112.

If the second statement is a true one, then we cannot but cite the cases of Jonson and Shakespeare to prove that art need not be chaotic in a period of chaos; if the first statement is a true one, we must cope with Webster and Fletcher. The two statements taken together, along with the speculations which they inspire, may reasonably lead us to believe that most periods are varied and full of hazards, that the existence of Gilson and Valéry in our own period may be real and not an illusion, and that any attempt to gauge the spirit of the age by a glance of the eye is likely to result in very casual impressionism.

### VII. THE DRAMATIC ELEMENT IN LYRIC POETRY

"It has been said by T. S. Eliot that the best lyric poetry of our time is dramatic, that it is good because it is dramatic." So writes Allen Tate,[32] and though I cannot put my finger on the passage in Eliot in which the statement occurs, there are many passages nearly as explicit.

F. O. Matthiessen writes: [33]

> Perhaps the most important thing that is revealed by applying Eliot's conception of the "objective correlative" to his own work is the essentially dramatic nature of all his poetry. What is said by one of the speakers in his "Dialogue on Dramatic Poetry" certainly seems expressive of one of his own most sustained beliefs:
>
> "What great poetry is not dramatic? Even the minor writers of the Greek Anthology, even Martial, are dramatic. Who is more dramatic than Homer or Dante? We are human beings, and in what are we more interested than in human actions and human attitudes? Even when he assaults, and with supreme mastery, the divine mystery, does not Dante engage us in the question of the human attitude toward this mystery—which is dramatic?"
>
> In the terms of such a description the dramatic element in poetry lies simply in its power to communicate a sense of real

---

[32] *Reactionary Essays on Poetry and Ideas,* by Allen Tate, Scribners, N. Y. P. 200.
[33] *The Achievement of T. S. Eliot,* by F. O. Matthiessen, Houghton Mifflin, Boston and N. Y. P. 66.

life, a sense of *the immediate present*—that is, of the full quality of a moment as it is actually felt to consist.

What Eliot means by the dramatic in lyrical poetry, one can only deduce as best one is able: the combination of Homer and the minor writers of the Greek Anthology, for example, gives one ample opportunity to think at large. The notion, derived by most of his disciples, however, and one of the two upon which they most commonly act, is indicated by the phrase *the immediate present,* which is italicized in Matthiessen's commentary. Poetry is dramatic—and hence good—in so far as it produces the illusion that the experience described is taking place in the immediate present.

Now when Matthiessen suggests that there is any relationship between this concept and the concept of the objective correlative, he is merely indulging in incoherence. The idea of the objective correlative is this: that the poet starts with an emotion and after casting about finds objective data which he believes can be used to embody it; nothing more. Matthiessen's concept seems to place the main emphasis on the data themselves. Matthiessen does not attempt, as I remember, to reconcile this concept of the dramatic with the concept of autotelic art, but it would be well worth his trouble. The idea of an art which is about itself, yet which is successful in so far as it gives a sense of the immediate present in dealing with something other than itself, would provide a worthy foundation for a system of esthetics.

Matthiessen is by no means alone. Theodore Spencer [34] in an essay on Yeats, written more or less in answer to an essay by myself on T. Sturge Moore, has written as follows:

> . . . Mr. Yvor Winters has recently compared the poetry of W. B. Yeats with the poetry of T. Sturge Moore . . . In his opinion, Moore is a greater poet than Yeats . . . To say that Moore is a better poet than Yeats seems to me meaningless. . . . Compare, for example, the opening lines of Moore's sonnet, "Apuleius Meditates," which Mr. Winters praises very highly, with the opening of Yeats's sonnet on Leda and the Swan.

[34] *The Later Poetry of W. B. Yeats,* by Theodore Spencer, Hound and Horn, Vol. VII, p. 164, and *Literary Opinion in America,* ed. by M. D. Zabel, Harpers, N. Y. P. 263. My essay on Moore is in the Hound and Horn, Vol. VI, P. 534.

Spencer then quotes the passages, which the reader may examine if he desires, and proceeds:

> There is an important distinction illustrated here, a distinc-
> tion which applies to other poetry than that of Moore and Yeats.
> It is the distinction between the poetry of revery and the poetry
> of immediacy.

He elaborates upon this distinction in terms which indicate that his concept of immediacy is essentially similar to that of Matthiessen.

Now I agree with Spencer that the lines from Yeats are better than the lines from Moore: the poem by Yeats is one of his two or three best, perhaps his best, and the lines from Moore, as I pointed out in quoting them, are extremely faulty. Spencer in failing to note my criticism of these lines adhered rigidly to a convention of contemporary literary controversy against which it would ill become a very young writer like myself to protest. But whatever the faults of Moore's poem, it is not a poem of revery; it is, like other and better poems by Moore and other men, a poem of meditation. Pound's *Cantos* are poems of revery and so likewise are most of Eliot's poems: revery proceeds by the random association of daydream, and possesses a minimum of rational coherence; in fact, in the form it takes in the stream-of-consciousness novel, it is frequently defended because of the sense of immediacy it produces, the assumption being that this is the way people really think. Spencer is very revealing when he fails to distinguish between revery and meditation.

For what, after all, is a poem, if we approach it in my own innocent state of mind? It is a statement about an experience, real or imagined. The statement must follow the experience in time: Donne, for example, could not have written *The Ecstasy* while engaged in the experience described. The poem is a commentary upon something that has happened or that has been imagined as having happened; it is an act of meditation. The poem is more valuable than the event by virtue of its being an act of meditation: it is the event plus the understanding of the event. Why then should the poet be required to produce the illusion of the immediate experience without intervention of the understanding? Perhaps the understanding is supposed to occur surreptitiously, while the poet is pretending that something else is occurring. But what is the value of such deception?

Is it assumed that understanding itself is not a "real" form of experience? The practical effect of the doctrine of dramatic immediacy is to encourage a more or less melodramatic emotionalism: such melodramatic emotionalism is perhaps the worst fault of Yeats, a poet whom Eliot admires, I should judge, little more than do I, but who is admired uncritically by Eliot's most eminent disciples.

Eliot has given rise, however, to another and in some respects different view of the way in which lyrical poetry may be dramatic. Many of his essays are attempts to define the stylistic qualities of one or another of the Elizabethan dramatists; they quote dramatic passages which he analyzes at length, the same passages being requoted and reanalyzed by many younger writers who appear to be more familiar with Eliot's views of the dramatists than with the dramatists themselves; and his own poetic style, even as early as Prufrock, has been heavily influenced by the style of these dramatists. *Gerontion,* for example, which I believe to be his best poem, is written in a more or less Websterian blank verse, has the texture of dramatic monologue, and seems to imply a dramatic context from which it has been excised. But this texture is the wrong texture for a lyric. Such poetry in a play is intended to exhibit the mannerisms of a character, so that Eliot runs the risk of imitating Bosola rather than Webster, which is a serious risk indeed; and such a passage in a play is likely to be full of allusions to matter within the play but without the passage, so that imitation of the style in a short poem is likely to result in incomprehensible irrelevancies. In the second and third essays in my volume called *Primitivism and Decadence* I endeavored to analyze some of these particular effects in *Gerontion* itself.

It is worth noting that Shakespeare and Jonson, for example, the two greatest dramatists in English and two of the half dozen or so greatest masters of the English lyric, employed dramatic blank verse only when writing drama, and employed the conventions of the lyric in writing the lyric; and further that one will be hard put to find a passage in any of their plays which, as a passage, and clean of its context, will stand serious comparison with any of a dozen short poems by either man.

No matter how the doctrine of dramatic immediacy is understood, it is a doctrine which leads to illegitimate emotionalism; and understood as it appears in Eliot's practice, it leads to irrelevance and to incoherence as well.

### VIII. ELIOT'S POETIC PRACTICE

Before attempting to relate Eliot's poetry to the body of opinion which I have been endeavoring to elucidate, I must summarize very briefly the career of Ezra Pound, who is beyond question the chief influence on Eliot's style. I shall describe the poetry of these men in the most general terms, for I have already dealt with it, and with similar poetry, in greater detail in a volume of criticism called *Primitivism and Decadence*. In that book I dealt with the types of poetic structure employed by these and allied poets, and sought to show the necessary effect of such structures upon the ultimate value of their work. I am concerned now, not with a detailed description of these structures, which I feel that I may reasonably take for granted, but with some of the principal concepts which generated them.

Ezra Pound, Eliot's master in poetry, began his poetic career as a student of the troubadours and of other early Romance poets, and as a disciple of Swinburne, the pre-Raphaelites, and the early Yeats. If we examine such a poem as his *Canzon: Of Incense*, for example, we see a poem written in a difficult Provençal form, but showing a quality of feeling which appears to derive from the late romantics. It is part of an attempt, extending over some years, by a belated disciple of the nineties, to recreate early Romance poetry in the modern world, and with very little explicit reference to the modern world. The attempt was doomed at the outset: the late romantic influences were unsound, and the early Romance models, though admirable in their kind, represented an elaborate development of a very limited state of mind, the elaboration and the limitation equally being the product of a very special social system and philosophy now dead these many hundred years. One might imitate Dante more successfully than Arnaut Daniel, I imagine, as one might imitate Jonson more successfully than Spenser: Dante and Jonson are timeless stylists; Spenser, and I should judge from what little I know of him, Daniel, display—with great beauty, no doubt—the eccentricities of their times, in spite of the fact that there are apparently important differences between the respective eccentricities. The curious thing about it, however, is this: that it came much closer to succeeding than one would have expected. The Pound of this period is not as good as the best Swinburne, but he is better than Dante Rossetti or the early Yeats, and by a comfortable margin.

About 1912 or a little later, however, Pound appears to have turned from his Provençal models except as he continued at times to translate them; he became a modern. Pound's aim appears now to have been no longer the recreation of a past period, but the exploration of the life of his own time as he might be able to understand it. We have as a result the tentative beginnings to be found in his collection called *Lustra:* satirical thumb-nail sketches of people seen in London, and simple but real fragments of life seen more seriously, though very impressionistically, such as *Fish and the Shadow.* This poetry, whether satirical or not, is notable mainly for the effect it gives of charming fragments, as of something valuable shattered, a quality which I have elsewhere described as essentially primitive: aside from differences of subject matter, it greatly resembles the slight but startling observations to be found in much of the poetry of the American Indian. We have a trained and refined sensibility unsupported by a unifying intellect, and employing the brief and annotative method apparently proper to it.

It was at about this stage in Pound's development that the widow of Ernest Fenollosa appears to have been struck with the idea that Pound was the man to put into final literary form the many literal translations left by her husband. According to the story current, she was impressed by the similarity of Pound's poetry to the Chinese, in spirit if not in form. She may well have been impressed by the translations which Pound had already made from other languages: his version of the Anglo-Saxon *Sea-Farer,* and of a certain Provençal alba, alone, are enough to place him among the very few great translators in English. In any event, Pound got the manuscripts and set to work on them. They apparently provided him with material exactly suited to his talents at that stage of his development: the Chinese poets, like Pound, were primitive in their outlook, and dealt with the more obvious and uncomplicated aspects of experience; but their outlook, though primitive, like Pound's, differed from Pound's in a richness and security of feeling within its limits—their subjects, though simple, were nevertheless more rich than any with which Pound had thus far dealt, and, though this may not seem important at first glance, they lent themselves to the composition of

poems longer than most which Pound had thus far attempted, so
that he had an opportunity to explore the possibilities of the free
verse which he had previously begun to employ.

Whether or not the first *Cantos* were begun before the work on
the Fenollosa manuscripts I cannot say; but the first three *Cantos* as
they originally appeared in *Poetry: A Magazine of Verse* were awk-
wardly Browningesque affairs which bear little resemblance to the
later *Cantos* or to their own later forms. The *Cantos* in general come
after the Chinese translations: in length they quite surpass the Chinese
translations, and in meter they show a greater development as well,
for whereas the Chinese translations are written in what is really a
heavily cadenced prose that continually verges on verse without
achieving it, the *Cantos* are written in a slow and heavily accentual
verse, which at its best displays an extraordinary suavity and grace of
movement.

But in the *Cantos* Pound is thrown back on his own subject matter, and although his style has developed enormously since the poems
which preceded the Chinese versions, his general intelligence has
remained about where it was. He is no longer at liberty to borrow
the technical and more or less intellectual framework of the troubadours, and he has none of his own to offer, yet he is bent on fusing
his impressions into some kind of whole, and he seems to desire a
whole which shall not falsify them or violate their essential quality:
only one convention is plausible, the convention of remembered impressions, or revery. Thus we get the *Cantos,* poems in which a poet
remembers his past experience of all kinds, literary, personal, and
imaginative, and moves from recollection to recollection purely and
simply by means of suggestion. We may observe as a brief and fairly
obvious example of the method the passage in the fourth *Canto* which
begins in the second paragraph and extends to the passage beginning
"Thus the light rains." This section takes us through references to a
number of stories, some historical and some mythological, of cannibalism and of transformation, and the two kinds of stories appear solely
because both elements appear in a few of them, so that the transition
from allusion to allusion is easy. The other transitions in this *Canto*
may appear more arbitrary if one merely describes them, but the
feeling inherent in the revery is so constant that one is not troubled
so long as one resigns oneself to the form of revery and asks for no
more.

Pound at maturity, then, sees life primarily as a matter of re-membered impressions, and his art is an art of revery: he is a sensi-bility without a mind, or with as little mind as is well possible. It is this Pound who provides the foundation for the more ambitious work of Eliot.

X   Eliot's earliest poems display various influences if one regard the detail. The influence of Elizabethan dramatic verse is already evident in *Prufrock,* and the influence of Pound's satirical sketches is to be found in some of the short early poems. The principal influence is probably that of Laforgue, whose poetry Pound had begun to cham-pion at least as early as 1917: the influence is seen not only in trans-lated passages, but in the whole attitude of romantic irony in an urban setting, of which Laforgue is perhaps the most interesting exemplar among the French poets of the late nineteenth century. The longer poems in this book already display the structure of revery which is carried farther in Pound's *Cantos* and in the later Eliot. There follow a few poems in rimed quatrains, which display a trace of the influence of Corbière, a strong influence of Gautier, and very little of Pound, except in so far as Corbière and Gautier are two of Pound's favorite poets. In the same original collection with these ap-peared *Gerontion,* the first example of Eliot's later manner and mat-ter, and in my own opinion the most considerable of his poems.

*Gerontion* is the portrait of an individual from whom grace has been withdrawn, and who is dying of spiritual starvation while remembering his past; it is thus a prelude to *The Waste Land,* a por-trait of a society from which grace has been withdrawn and which is dying of its own triviality and ugliness. I should like to deal pri-marily with *The Waste Land,* for its method is that of all the later work and it illustrates very clearly the problems to which I have been leading, and the faults which seriously weaken even a poem of so much strength as *Gerontion.*

The matter of *The Waste Land* is Baudelairian. It is no accident that the last line of the introductory poem of *The Waste Land* is also the last line of the preface of *Les Fleurs du Mal.* That preface details the sins of the modern world as they appeared to Baudelaire, and it names as the most horrible of them all the sin of Ennui. Now Ennui, as it appears in much romantic literature is very much the same sin as the Christian sin of acedia, or spiritual torpor, and it might well be regarded as the most deadly of sins because it leads to all the others and interferes with one's struggling against them: it would be above all other sins the most likely to appear, if we accept Christian postulates, in a man or a society deprived of grace.

Both poets deal with such a society, and both endeavor to judge it from a more or less Christian position. But there is this difference between them, if no other: that Eliot surrenders his form to his subject, whereas Baudelaire does not do so. Henry Adams, whose inflence on Eliot's entire poetic theory is probably greater than has been guessed, worked out in his *Education,* in *Mont Saint Michel and Chartres,* and in certain minor essays the entire theory of modern society and its relationship to the society of the Middle Ages, upon which Eliot's critical theory rests; and near the end of *Mont Saint Michel and Chartres* he offered the now commonplace theory that modern art must be chaotic in order to express chaos [35]—a variant, I suppose, of the earlier romantic doctrine of organic form sponsored by Coleridge; and Eliot was sufficiently moved by him to construct one of the better lines of *Gerontion*—"In depraved May, dogwood and chestnut, flowering judas"—from the first paragraph of the eighteenth chapter of the *Education.*

Now if the modern world is demonstrably chaotic in relationship to the world of past periods, and if we accept the postulate that the poet is formed by the society into which he is born, that this age must give him not merely his subject matter but his entire spiritual shape, as it were, so that the form of his art will be determined by the quality of his age, then the formlessness of Pound's *Cantos* is something determined by forces more important than any in Pound's character: the *Cantos* offer the only form available to the poet who would write honestly and sensitively; this in spite, as I have already suggested, of the awkward presence of such writers as Valéry, Robinson, Bridges, and Hardy. Eliot, in dealing with the chaos of this graceless world, found his form ready to use, and he produced *The Waste Land.*

Baudelaire, however, did something very different. Eliot writes of him as follows: [36]

> To say this is only to say that Baudelaire belongs to a definite place in time. Inevitably the offspring of romanticism, and by his nature the first counter-romantic in poetry, he could, like

---

[35] *Mont Saint Michel and Chartres,* by Henry Adams. Houghton Mifflin Co., Boston and N. Y., p. 375: "Art had to be confused in order to express confusion; but perhaps it was truest, so."

[36] *Selected Essays,* p. 340.

anyone else, only work with the materials which were there. It must not be forgotten that a poet in a romantic age cannot be a "classical" poet except in tendency. If he is sincere, he must express with individual differences the general state of mind— not as a *duty,* but simply because he cannot help participating in it.

This passage should sound remarkably familiar to the reader who has been so patient as to reach it; it contains an element of truth and a larger element of error. What Baudelaire actually accomplished in his best work was a vision and evaluation of evil as it appeared to him in his own time, that is, in the guise of romantic excess. He was not a rigorous thinker, though his thought was often profound, and his judgment was sometimes beguiled by the romanticism which at other times he judged with appalling lucidity. A poet is conditioned by his time to this extent, that it offers him most of his subject matter; but what he does with that subject matter—let me insist at the risk of excommunication—is very largely the result of his own intelligence and talent. A minor talent, or an imperfect talent, may be grievously damaged through the influence of a bad tradition, such as the tradition represented by Pound and Eliot; but a greater talent need not be. To assume that Shakespeare and Jonson possessed no great intellectual power may occasionally be comforting to us, but a study of either man will not support the assumption. As H. B. Parkes has said in another connection, there is nothing inevitable about stupidity.

The subject matter of *The Waste Land* is in general similar to that of *Les Fleurs du Mal*. Yet if one will compare let us say *Le Jeu* with *A Game of Chess,* one may perhaps note what Eliot overlooked. Eliot, in dealing with debased and stupid material, felt himself obliged to seek his form in his matter: the result is confusion and journalistic reproduction of detail. Baudelaire, in dealing with similar matter, sought to evaluate it in terms of eternal verity: he sought his form and his point of view in tradition, and from that point of view and in that form he judged his material, and the result is a profound evaluation of evil. The difference is the difference between triviality and greatness.

The difference is in part, however, merely the difference between a poet with a great native gift for poetic style and a poet with very little gift. Eliot has written in his essay on Massinger: [37]

---

[37] Ibid., p. 182.

One of the surest of tests is the way in which a poet borrows. Immature poets imitate; mature poets steal; bad poets deface what they take, and good poets make it into something better, or at least something different. The good poet welds his theft into a whole of feeling which is unique, utterly different from that from which it was torn; the bad poet throws it into something which has no cohesion.

Such a statement might easily be used in defense of Pound, who, except for Eliot, borrows more extensively than any other poet of our time: Pound's revery has a discernible consistency at its best, and the borrowed material is either selected or reworked so judiciously that it seems in place. And such a statement might be cited in defense of *Gerontion* and even of some of Eliot's earlier work, frail as it is. But the meter of *The Waste Land* is not the suave meter of *The Cantos* or of *Gerontion:* it is a broken blank verse interspersed with bad free verse and rimed doggerel. And what is one to say of the last eight lines of *The Waste Land,* which are composed, as nearly as I can determine with the aid of the notes, of unaltered passages from seven sources? A sequence of such quotations cannot by any stretch of the imagination achieve unity, and its disunity can be justified on no grounds except the Adams-Eliot doctrine of modern art, of which the less said by this time the better. The method is that of a man who is unable to deal with his subject, and resorts to the rough approximation of quotation; it is the method of the New England farmer who meets every situation in life with a saw from *Poor Richard;* it betokens the death of the mind and of the sensibility alike. The last line, in fact, is a classic of its kind. It reads: "Shantih shantih shantih," and in the note at the end of the poem Eliot tells us that " 'The Peace which passeth understanding' is a feeble translation of the content of this word." Surely there was never another great sentiment expressed with such charming simplicity!

Eliot, in brief, has surrendered to the acedia which Baudelaire was able to judge; Eliot suffers from the delusion that he is judging it when he is merely exhibiting it. He has loosely thrown together a collection of disparate and fragmentary principles which fall roughly into two contradictory groups, the romantic on the one hand and on the other the classical and Christian; and being unaware of his own contradictions, he is able to make a virtue of what appears to be private spiritual laziness; he is able to enjoy at one and the same time the pleasures of indulgence and the dignity of disapproval. He is right in confessing that his later work has not appreciably changed, and Mario Praz is right in finding in it more of the nature of dream than of vision. And he is right again in regarding as heretical, that is, as anti-Christian, the ideas which he has used to justify his failure to change when he meets those ideas expressed by another writer; though it is strange that he should fail to recognize the heresy when he employs it himself. When Eliot announced his conversion to Catholicism and to Classicism in 1927, his modernist followers were astonished, and they have never really forgiven him; but they might well have spared themselves so much devout feeling, for the conversion appears to have been merely nominal; at least, so far as one can judge from what Eliot has written, it really meant nothing at all.

There are scattered essays, especially early essays analyzing qualities of style, which are valuable even when one does not agree with them, and his poems display charming or excellent passages here and there as well, and *Gerontion* in fact deserves much higher praise than this. To this side of Eliot I may appear unfair. The fact of the matter is, however, that it has received far more than its due praise from other hands than mine; and the theory and influence of Eliot, with which I am at present dealing, seem to me the most dangerous and nearly the least defensible of our time. They have grown upon our time with all the benumbing energy of a bad habit, till any attempt to analyze the defects of modern poetry in the light of civilized standards is accepted merely as evidence that the critic is not of the elect, is not a recipient of the grace of the Zeitgeist; till the good poetry written in our time is more commonly than not excluded from consideration and even from publication, because it is regarded as insensitive to the realities of the twentieth century. And when one seeks closely to find the features of the divinity, the primal spirit of the age to whose will surrender is required, one may well be appalled; for behind the shadows thrown by veil after veil of indeterminate prose one will find, if one is patient, the face of Ezra Pound in apotheosis.

# VAN WYCK BROOKS *

TO think of literature as merely literary, as something that was derived from literature, struck Allston as utterly frivolous. He certainly enjoyed, no one more so, the play of the critical mind; but not to see vital necessity as the governing law of literature seemed to him the utmost of critical blindness. Writers, to be sure, drew strength from writers, but they drew most of their strength from something else, a consciousness of human needs and longings; and their ultimate value was to be determined by the measure in which they responded to these longings and needs. One did not always have to say this. In times when it was understood, one might affirm the fact by implication; but the great critics had affirmed it, either by statement or implication,—human values underlay their literary values. But was this the time merely to imply it, when one saw literary values floating in a void? Had not the time come to restate it? Mr. Eliot, in his way, recognized that this time had come; but his "well turned compliments to religion," as Mr. E. M. Forster called them, struck Allston as inadequate and meagre. At best, he had seen these values in sectarian terms and not at all in terms that were broadly human; for how many of the great writers would have survived if they had had to fit his bed of Procrustes? Mr. Eliot's judgment of writers according to their "orthodoxy" was a matter of straining at gnats and swallowing camels; and this, in fact, was the nature of his critical procedure. He had denied the primary in the interest of the secondary: was it not by this means that he had effected a "transvaluation of English literature," to quote the phrase of one who admitted this claim? Milton, he said, was "unsatisfactory," *Hamlet* was an "artistic failure," Goethe, in philosophy and poetry, merely "dabbled," and "made no great success of either," Emerson was no "real observer of the moral life," Emerson's essays were an "encumbrance," Byron was "uninteresting," Shelley and Keats were overrated, the genius of Dickens was "decadent," and so on and so on. Meanwhile,

---

* From OPINIONS OF OLIVER ALLSTON, pp. 218–227, Copyright, 1941, by Van Wyck Brooks. E. P. Dutton & Co., Inc., New York.

Dryden, the "great master of contempt," was virtually more important than any of these. Dryden, in any case, with his "art of making
the small great," was one whom Eliot admired beyond these others,
—by virtue of affinity, perhaps; and Eliot made even Dryden smaller
than he was, as one saw by comparing Lowell's magnanimous essay
on Dryden with his treatment of this poet. While, at this Eliotizing
of history, all the mazed world stood by hushed, Ezra Pound too re-
arranged the classics. He admitted Confucius and Homer and two
or three dozen other authors (who did not include Thucydides, the
"journalist"); and, "without the slightest compunction," he "chucked
out" Pindar. There was room in Mr. Pound's list for Rimbaud and
Corbière, but he had not troubled to chuck out the others: he found
them unworthy even of a gesture of contempt. Allston said these
statements were "interesting but tough," as Huck Finn remarked of
*Pilgrim's Progress;* and equally interesting were the statements of
Mr. Yvor Winters, who had taken heart from the boldness of Eliot
and Pound. Mr. Yvor Winters had run through American literature,
in which he had unearthed surprising facts, as that Emerson was a
"fraud at the core," Melville's *Omoo* and *Typee* were trifles, Poe was
a "bad writer, exceptionally bad," and *The House of the Seven Gables*
like *Hamlet,* was a "failure." Now, if ever acts of genius were performed in America, they were these writings, precisely; and Allston
could only say, reading Mr. Winters, "His bread is my cake, and vice
versa." But could one "transvalue" literature in this fashion? Beyond
the exhibition of one's own folly, could one accomplish anything by
such a procedure? "For the law of the gods," Allston said, "they have
set up their own traditions;" or, if not the law of the gods, the traditions of men. No doubt, it was wholesome to challenge tradition,
and perhaps by over-emphasizing aesthetic standards these critics had
served a useful purpose. But was their "hard bright precision" worth
so much?—and were they not floating in a void? Luckily for them,
these critics reached only a handful of readers, among whom they
could say what they chose,—they ran small risk of exposure to the
light of truth; yet how strange, in another decade, it was sure to
seem that a few little men in any circle could have got away with all
these murders. Were they not, in regard to all these writers, in the
position of Henry James, who said that Tolstoy and Dostoievsky did
"not *do* to read any longer"? They did not do to read because they
lacked James's neatness in the sphere of aesthetics; and yet, in James's

own phrase, the "quantity of presenting their genius launches them in" precisely rendered this neatness impossible to them. Well, if one had to make a choice, which should one prefer, the neatness or the quantity of genius? Humanity chose to accept the genius, with as much form as it could get, and, if need were, to sacrifice the form in favour of the genius. It was something quite beyond aesthetics that caused one to read Dostoievsky and Tolstoy and all these other great writers whom the critics "chucked out;" and these critics had given a sorry account of themselves by ignoring what humanity needed and intended to have.

So rose in Allston's mind the question of tradition, which Mr. Eliot especially took under his wing. In one of his essays, Mr. Eliot had given a good account of tradition. "The historical sense," he said, "compels a man to write not merely with his own generation in his bones, but with a feeling that the whole of the literature of Europe from Homer and within it the whole of the literature of his own country has a simultaneous existence and composes a simultaneous order." With this historical sense, precisely, Allston wrote himself, and he admired Eliot's definition: the literature of his own country, the literature of Europe, the literature of all mankind, he said, composed for him a "simultaneous order,"—with the life of mankind, of Europe, of his country behind it. In theory, therefore, he agreed with Eliot, although Eliot seldom spoke of the life of mankind; and he sometimes wondered what Eliot's "own country" was,—it certainly was not America, and was it England? Was not Eliot's vague tradition a Latin tradition? However this might be, and however they agreed in theory, in practice Allston and Eliot were worlds apart. Defining his traditionalism, Eliot quoted a phrase of Remy de Gourmont: "To erect into laws one's personal impressions, this is the great effort of a man if he is sincere." This was the rule that Eliot followed in practice. He had erected into laws his personal impressions; he had made up a tradition to suit himself,—and was not tradition really necessitated? For what had one's personal impressions to do with tradition?—and what was a man who erected his impressions into laws? Was not such a man more truly a destroyer of tradition? Tradition is the sum of all that humankind has kept alive for its own advancement and perfection; it is that which unites mankind in its common struggle and gives it stability and direction. But Eliot had no wish to unite mankind except on his own peculiar sectarian terms; and he had gone far to repudiate the common tradition in favour of his personal impressions and his personal choices. He had plucked out the plums that pleased himself, implying that the rest of the pudding was not worth eating; and was the pudding his to pluck from? Was it not rather, in truth, humanity's pudding?—and was he not like any other little Jack Horner? Like Henry James, for instance, who thought the plum *The Awkward Age* was better than *War and Peace* and *The Brothers Karamazov*? Little Jack Horners always prefer the particular plums that please themselves, and they regard these plums as the big plums; they even insist that their plums are big, for, if these turned out to be little, what light might this not throw on their own dimensions? Meantime, they forget that they are in a corner, while the centre of the room is occupied by someone else. But the someone in the centre sits in the place of humanity, and he has the final word. Eliot's tradition, Allston said, was no real tradition. It was a phantasmal tradition merely, and this phantasmal tradition was a dog in the manger. It would not eat the corn and it blocked the doorway, so that no other creature could get at it and eat it.

Now, Allston had taken tradition for granted ever since he was a boy. He had never thought of explaining or defending it, for the sense of the past was instinctive in him as well as the sense of the future. But his gorge had slowly risen as he saw this false traditionalism assuming such authority in the world of letters, and at last he felt constrained to say with Campanella:

> Do thou, with heart fervent and proudly mild,
> Make war upon these fraud-engendering schools.

Tradition results from vital necessity, he repeated more than once. One cannot make up a tradition, as Eliot does, by leaving out the beef and potatoes that constitute the meal in favour of the sweets and condiments that please one's palate; and to take this tradition for "orthodoxy" is to block the door indeed. There was James Joyce, the sick Irish Jesuit, whom Eliot described as orthodox, and who had done more than Eliot to destroy tradition. Had he not, in *Ulysses*, in his *Oxen of the Sun*, run through the whole of English literature, depreciating with his parodies its greatest authors, deforming every one of them, Gibbon, Burke, Goldsmith, Lamb, De Quincey, Dickens, Ruskin, Newman, Bunyan, Burns and a dozen others? What fools

he made them seem, as he filled his travesties of their styles with
trivial and salacious implications!—and all for the glorification of
James Joyce. For what a big boy he must be to have put all these
authors in their places! The past in all of Joyce's work went out in
a bad smell, while Joyce settled down complacently in his "snot-
green" world; and yet Joyce was represented as defending tradition!
Out upon this nonsense, Allston said. He admitted that all this de-
romanticizing had a minor function, which one might compare to
the insulin treatment for schizophrenia. Its object was to rub down
the mental grooves formed by conventional habits, restoring the mind
to the primitive for a fresh start. But suppose the patient did not
react? Suppose the treatment did not succeed? And was not humanity
rather an important patient? Besides, in literature one had to remember the standard of health, and Joyce was not at all concerned with
this. His falsification of tradition had well-nigh wiped tradition out
in minds that were already divorced from tradition: and it seemed
to Allston that to reaffirm the true tradition was an indispensable
task of the contemporary critic.

Thus Allston returned to Eliot's definition, which Eliot failed to
sustain: the literature of his own country, the literature of Europe,
the literature of all mankind, he said, composed for him a simultaneous order,—with the life of mankind, of Europe, of his country behind it. He began at home, with his own country, as the door through
which to approach the rest; and he said it was time to restore the
American classics, retaining the critical spirit, subjecting them to
the proper tests, but accepting them, where one could, with one's
whole heart. For what was more important than a sense of one's
group-history, if only as a means of entering other groups? What
could be more tonic, if only as a means of understanding the life of
the rest of mankind? It seemed to Allston highly important that we
should possess an American memory, and this had driven him into
historical writing. What could contribute more to the stiffening of
American writers, promoting their maturity and health, giving them
the sense of a group to which they are responsible, affording them
stability and purpose? Yes, the sense of the past behind them is the
tap-root of American writers, the sense of the achievements of their
group; and, behind this, they must have a sense of the life and
achievements of all mankind, a sense of the collective effort of the
human race. What else could so contribute to knit them together, to

give them a line of direction for the future of the race? Such was tradition, Allston repeated, the great sustainer of primary literature, the sum of the literary wisdom which the race has kept, the embodiment of those traits which humanity needs for its survival and perfection.

# FERNER NUHN *

THE teaching of the essays is in keeping with the way taken by the man. The essays, too, mistrust everything local or "home-made." They fear the good judgment of the individual. They continually look for some external authority that has nothing to do with the accidental nature of the individual person, who might, as it were, have been born in St. Louis.

First the essays taught that this external authority might be found in literary tradition. Yet it was soon obvious that the necessity of personal choice or "inner light" is not removed by literary tradition, which has never been codified into a complete external system. The attention of the essays moved, then, from the aesthetic toward the religious, and within the religious, toward authoritarianism. The characteristic words of the essays changed from tradition to dogma and classicism to orthodoxy.

Here lies the real question of the essays, not the question of God or truth or reality, but of dogma, institution, and authority. The critic is fond of quoting Dante's famous line:

la sua voluntade è nostra pace

—thy will is our peace—and nothing could be better Calvinism or better Emerson. But this is not the question raised by the essays. Nor is it the question of the usefulness of institutions in themselves—no one, or few, will deny the place of institutions. The question is whether, at the level of genius where the point is relevant, a man can trust his own vision of truth, or must still trust someone else's —for dogma is other men's visions codified into a system.

The argument of Dante versus Shakespeare, which runs through the essays, turns on this point of primary and secondary authority. Can writers of this stature be trusted to trust their own insight into truth? Eliot's criticism answers double. Dante, it seems, could be

---

* *Orpheus in Hell: T. S. Eliot,* from THE WIND BLEW FROM THE EAST, pp. 205–221, 246–255, Copyright, 1942, by Ferner Nuhn. Harper & Brothers, New York.

trusted to trust his own insight, but Shakespeare could not. But again, the reason Dante could be trusted and Shakespeare not was that Dante lived at a time when everyone, including Dante, had a trustworthy method, rule, and belief already given him. "Dante's advantages" (over Shakespeare, the essay on Dante says) "are not due to greater genius, but to the fact that he wrote when Europe was still more or less one," that is, under the Church at Rome. Consequently, "He not only thought in a way in which every man of his culture thought, but he employed a method which was common and commonly understood throughout Europe."

But again the same essay says that Dante at his best could dispense with all institutional authority. Eliot quotes Dante's Virgil to that effect, in the lines from *The Divine Comedy* in which Virgil, who was not good enough to go with Dante into Paradise, was still good enough to anoint Dante for the heavenly journey:

> No more expect my word or sign, [Virgil to Dante]. Your Will is free, straight and whole, and not to follow it would be sin: wherefore I crown and mitre you (king and bishop) over yourself.

Dante's will is free; Dante is now king and bishop over himself; Dante may now follow his own "inner light," quite as if he were a good Quaker or Unitarian. Or as Eliot puts it: "Dante has now arrived at a condition, for the purpose of the rest of the journey, which is that of the blessed: for political and ecclesiastical organizations are only required because of imperfections of the human will."

So there is something higher than institutional dogma and authority—if you have disciplined yourself to reach this state. Dogma and authority, it seems, are only means to an end. The next question is whether Dante's means are the only possible means.

To come back to Shakespeare, as Eliot always does, the question is whether Shakespeare had not also mastered his own will; whether he was not, perhaps, as reliable as Dante in moral judgment on others; and had not found his way, so to speak, through his own purgatory (of *Hamlet*) to the calm of Prospero's island (*The Tempest*); and if poor Shakespeare did not deserve, quite as much as Dante, to have some Virgil or Ben Jonson crown and mitre him king and bishop over himself.

Though with their high wrongs I am struck to the quick,
Yet, with my nobler reason, 'gainst my fury
Do I take part: the rarer action is
In virtue than vengeance: they being penitent,
The sole drift of my purpose doth extend
Not a frown further. Go, release them, Ariel. . . .

Shakespeare may have been unacquainted with certain modes of religious feeling known to Dante. I think he was. Still anyone may judge whether these lines suggest lack of insight on Shakespeare's part into moral or even Christian truth. Eliot's argument did not come to a conclusion, even on the moral question. But no conclusion is possible upon the secondary grounds (of institutions, authorities, and different modes of thought of different times) taken by Eliot's essays.

Shakespeare haunts the essays, just as Jesus haunts the poems. Again and again the essays find it necessary to assure the reader that Shakespeare is "great," in quotation marks, or "universal," in quotation marks, lest the reader be misled by the essays which again and again tell the reader that Shakespeare could not have been universal or great. Shakespeare had a debased philosophy, which could only lead to something bad. But did it lead to something bad in Shakespeare's case? No, it cannot be said that it did. Shakespeare had an inferior audience, while the little group of aristocrats around the Countess of Pembroke, for instance, had all the advantage over Shakespeare and Marlowe of not having to cater to the general public. But was the Shakespearean drama inferior for that reason? No, it cannot be said that it was.

Then there is the "Dialogue on Dramatic Poetry," which is haunted from beginning to end by the greatest writer of dramatic poetry, William Shakespeare, and yet which twice puts forward the strange proposition, Why does Shakespeare fail us?

No answer. There is never any answer, and Shakespeare's ghost walks through the essays, unlaid, unscathed, and unappeased.

There is no appeasing any great ghost I fear, Dante's any more than Shakespeare's, by the burnt offerings of the essays. They are like a pyramid with the top cut off. They do not allow for the highest, but are addressed rather to the superior, and when not to the superior, then to the exclusive. Their highest value is not greatness or genius, but distinction; and indeed this is the quality of the poet's own work. This is the land divided by lot, as the poet wrote.

Actually, the teaching of the essays leads to the bitter truth of the poems. The poems understand and demonstrate high distinction, technical brilliance hardly surpassed; and the essays too understand technical and poetic distinction, and never praise bad poetry. Poet and critic are both alive to "exquisite modulation of tone" and all that has to do with the sense of the ear. In the realm of the human spirit, the poems understand despair and human bondage; and the essays too understand human bondage and the divided will. Neither the poems nor the essays understand, or at least demonstrate themselves, release and freedom, and it is too bad that they pretend to.

The greatest insight of the essays is into those literary works which do show spiritual division, failure to reach a conclusion, and either conscious or unconscious doubt. This is the literature of suffering, suffering without catharsis, prayer or penitence without purgation. A great example of this is Baudelaire, and Eliot wrote with insight, "He was one of those who have great strength, but the strength merely to suffer. He could not escape suffering and could not transcend it, so he attracted pain to himself. But what he could do, with that immense passive strength and sensibilities which no pain could impair, was to study his suffering."

Donne, in a way, "is such another," and so, strangely enough is the Tennyson of "Maud," of whose curious underground conflict Eliot made an astute analysis. And it is at this point that the essayist, a little gloatingly I think, catches up for once with Shakespeare's ghost. Hamlet, the equivocal and ghost-ridden, provides the chance, and Eliot's study of the Hamlet problem makes its point, just as it is made with the infinitely lesser affair of "Maud." But the point is the same: Hamlet, the seething soliloquist, like the seething monologuist of "Maud," was "dominated by an emotion which is inexpressible, because it was in excess of the facts as they appear." Disgust with his mother does not cover the whole situation. There is something else, something which even Shakespeare, apparently, has not isolated.

The truth is, Hamlet is disgusted with himself, and this self-disgust is prior to everything else. If this is not true (and if I may here add a note) how explain the speech of Hamlet to Ophelia: "I am myself indifferent honest, but yet I could accuse me of such things that it were better my mother had not borne me." What are these things Hamlet might accuse himself of, in terms of actual deeds done—in terms of drama? We do not know. If they are evil deeds, they are probably not of a crudely vicious sort. Nevertheless, they are "offenses," in Hamlet's own eyes, such as lead him to say of himself ". . . with more offenses at my beck than I have thoughts to put them in, imagination to give them shape, or time to act them in." Now, does this not mean that what really weighs on Hamlet is not his mother's offenses, but his own? If so, should they not be "thought, shaped, and acted" in the play, if we are to know Hamlet's tragedy instead of merely his confusion?

*Hamlet,* in any case, is the play of Shakespeare that you might most nearly describe in the terms Eliot uses for Baudelaire: suffering that could not be escaped or transcended, but attracted more pain to itself. They are also the terms that you can use very well to describe "The Waste Land," "The Hollow Men," "Ash Wednesday."

From the humorless and anxious essays it is a relief to turn to the poems, much as one might leave an unseaworthy ship that is continually taking on more water than it can handle, and take to the lifeboats. The water is cold and the going difficult, but at least this medium will support you.

Somewhere Eliot has written that the difference between criticism and poetry is that criticism must point to ideals, while poetry needs only express actuality. Nothing could be further from the truth so far as his own work is concerned. The poems point to all the values which the criticism refuses to acknowledge, and the more actual the poems are, the more they leave a place for the higher values. They know the second best from the best, and if "Ash Wednesday" says:

I no longer strive to strive towards such things

it is not because the poet does not recognize that "such things" are worth striving for.

And whereas the criticism argues for orthodoxy that may be got from outside the individual head and tamped in, like sawdust, the poetry jeers:

We are the hollow men
We are the stuffed men

Leaning together
Headpiece filled with straw. Alas!

If the essays overemphasize measure, control, self-denial, and all
the negative virtues, concerning which the greatest philosopher of
measure, Aristotle, wrote a book to say that too much denial is exactly as bad as too much indulgence (but poor Aristotle, he was
unacquainted with the "genteel tradition" of later New England,
and so could not imagine anyone, as he said, with "a *defect* in respect
of pleasure")—if the essays exaggerate denial, there is the truth about
Prufrock in the poem, who mourns:

I have measured out my life in coffee spoons.

If the essays outline a way that puts the letter above the spirit and
suspects love and all outward movements of the heart, there is the
confession of the unhappy soul in "Animula":

Unable to fare forward or retreat,
Fearing the warm reality, the offered good,
Denying the importunity of the blood,
Shadow of its own shadows, spectre in its own gloom,
Leaving disordered papers in a dusty room. . . .

And so on. What the essays leave out the poems put in, and what
the essays argue for the poems rebel against, according to the best
laws of compensation known to Emerson and Plato. Or as the an-
cients put it, Nature expelled with a pitchfork returns just the same.

Truth and nature, as well as beauty and art, lie with the poems—
no man can sing without somehow singing truly. The poems may
sing the song of the minstrel, like Arnold in Dante's *Purgatory,* who
weeps and goes singing. Again, they may recite the ditties of the
court fool. Hieronymo's mad againe. But in any case, there are qualities and quality in the poems. There is no pleasure, no fun, not even
wit or eloquence in the essays, with their stiff official tone and magisterial stare. No laughter in the courtroom. The poems are full of fun.
No one could be as solemn as the official figure of the criticism, so
there is the unofficial figure of the poetry who continually exposes
solemnity.

Even Prufrock, in the author's first important poem, is aware
of this side of the character:

> At times, indeed, almost ridiculous
> Almost, at times, the Fool.

For a complete picture of the Fool, in all his motley, there is the portrait drawn of him "in demotic French," in the verse called *"Mélange Adultère de Tout"*—Mixture Adulterous of Everything. He is all quick-change disguises: *"En Amerique, professeur; en Angleterre, journaliste,"* and so on through a dozen other masquerades. With long strides and in a sweat you'd scarcely keep up with this terrific fellow. In Yorkshire, a lecturer; in London a small-time banker; really, you'd give your head! In Paris you'll find him wearing the black cap of *jemenfoutiste,* or, I suppose, Dadaism. In Germany he's a transcendental philosopher, transported to the seventh heaven. Hither and yon he flits on his various brilliant triumphs, all the way from Damascus to Omaha. He celebrated his last birthday at a water hole in Africa, disguised in a giraffeskin. They'll be pointing out his monument some day on the burning slopes of Mozambique.

This is not only good fun, it is strength, the power to turn over the other side of the medal of Jove. That is the power the poems continually show, as the essays never really do.

The fun can be much less pleasant than in *"Mélange Adultère de Tout."* The turnabout exposure can be grisly, as in "The Hollow Man," or "Lines for an Old Man." Still, humor is its redeeming grace, even when mordant. The poems provide their own antidote. There is no protection against the magisterial stare of the essays. Your innocent reader, your unformed young person looking for the correct thing, your dull scholar, is outstared and coerced by the essays, quite without conscience. But anyone should know how to take this Old Man of the poems, dreadful as he is. Let the young, the innocent, the dull beware:

> When I lay bare the tooth of wit
> The hissing over the archèd tongue
> Is more affectionate than hate,
> More bitter than the love of youth,
> And inaccessible by the young.
> Reflected from my golden eye
> The dullard knows that he is mad.
> Tell me if I am not glad!

We know where we are, here. It is our own fault if we think we must be mad just because this malicious old fellow's eye looks so sane. Even more, we know that malice self-exposed becomes something a little different from malice.

So we know where we are, on the whole, all through the poems, if we understand them at all, which I admit is another question.

The difficulty of Eliot's poetry follows partly I think from the position outlined by the critic, which in turn followed on the way taken by the man. The way was away from everything native or "home-made." The theory, too, is not to trust the individual nature, integrity, or power of expression, but to look for some external model—that is, somebody else's way of trusting and expressing himself. Hence, everything in Eliot's poetry tends to be at a remove. Hence the myriad disguises and ventriloquisms of the poems, which the young poet of "The Portrait of a Lady" had already said he had to use in order to say anything at all:

> And I must borrow every changing shape
> To find expression . . . dance, dance
> Like a dancing bear,
> Cry like a parrot, chatter like an ape.

Somewhere I believe Eliot has mentioned how many lines in his poetry up to the time were both satisfactory to him and his own —fifty or sixty if I'm not mistaken. At any rate, the phenomenon was extraordinary, extraordinary because the poetry is at once so borrowed and so personal. There is no mistaking an Eliot line; there is hardly an Eliot line that is Eliot.

How can this be? How explain the genuineness so to speak of the forgery? (If forgery sounds like too harsh a word, and it is, I refer you to the backhanded dedication of "The Waste Land": "to Ezra Pound, *il miglior fabbro*"—the better forger—a clearly false accusation however you want to take it!) I think the explanation lies in the one faculty of the poet which keeps its authority so to speak through all the various transformations, the listening faculty. "The eyes are not here, There are no eyes here," so the poet writes in "The Hollow Men." But the ear, the still and unexpressive organ in man, is always there, and is one of the finest in poetry. Wherever the ear's cadence is heard, in other poetry, or in the music hall, or on the street, the poet picks it out. When it reappears in Eliot's verse it is unmistakable; it has the stamp on it and has been subject in turn to a hundred imitations that do not have the stamp.

This is the faculty of the hidden hermit thrush. For the rest, on the side of personal feeling, the answer to Eliot's style is the same one we have been giving. The style is the man; this method of taking at second hand was the choice and life of the person. The man had turned spirit and letter around. Spirit followed on the letter—waited for some other letter to answer its need. What we know (the man and critic had said) is not the same great reality that all the poets and philosophers know, dead or alive, and that God himself is, but the picture of reality other philosophers and poets have made. This means in effect that the poet could recognize his own reality only through other recognitions.

Nevertheless, it is a personal reality the poet waits to recognize, very personal in fact. The touch, through the gloves of other poets, is extremely sensitive. Whatever words of someone else tell the exact position and feeling known to the poet become alive, like a second skin or a third ear drum. The spirit lives as it were in the skin, ear, tongue, heart of other poets.

There is something ghostly about this, and it is no wonder the poet was fascinated with the bodiless voice of Philomel, voices singing out of empty cisterns and exhausted wells, the hidden thrush, and so on. One has to be a ghost to enter into other bodies; likewise one's own body, losing its ghost, loses everything that is breathing, living, and less tangible than dried guts and bones.

> Lady, three white leopards sat under a juniper tree
> In the cool of the day, having fed to satiety
> On my legs my heart my liver and that which had been contained
> In the hollow round of my skull.

Such too, was the lot of Webster and Donne, as the poet supposed:

> Who found no substitute for sense,
> To seize and clutch and penetrate;

and who consequently could find no comfort in thought:

> But our lot crawls between dry ribs
> To keep our metaphysics warm.

But this would be the worst kind of metaphysics, in fact it is not metaphysics at all. It is a form of superstition, or confusion of matter and spirit—the unfortunate feeling that ideas ought to be tangible to be true, while matter ought to be immaterial if it is to be good. It is like saying that one gets the virtue of the doctor's prescription by swallowing the piece of paper he gives it to you on. No wonder the poet was to see only fear, and not life, in a handful of dust. Emerson, with his distinction between the law for things and the law for man, would easily answer the point. But if Emerson were too much a home-made product, one could not do better than hear Thomas Aquinas on the subject, who presumably belonged to the right line of the Fathers. No body can receive the substantial form of another body, said this philosopher, unless it lose its own form by corruption. But intellect is not corrupted, but rather is perfected by receiving the forms of all bodies; since it is perfected by understanding, and understands by having in itself the forms of things understood.

Let us eat real bread or meat—matter going through changes of form—for the sake of the body, but for the sake of the mind, let us imagine all things in their own forms everywhere, wherever we happen to be. In this way one might put the local and the general in their proper places, and grow wise in Omaha. But our poet, who had supposed the ideal life depended on being in the right physical locality, was to find that all appeared local and physical in the ideal one, as we gather from the sorry conclusion in "Ash Wednesday" that:

> . . . time is always time
> And place is always and only place
> And what is actual is actual only for one time
> And only one place. . . .

But the method of the poems, again, is the method of literalism, as if one *could* find the right time and right place, verbally speaking, on the dead dusty rolls of papyrus and ink which have come down from the first cave scribbler. The poet does find the places that corresponded to his own feeling with astonishing, if laborious, aptness. The labor is the reader's too. He must read through Eliot's reading in order to find what the poet found for his writing. Strangely enough, the more one reads of this erudite author's reading, the more personal the poetry becomes. In spite of the quotations in six or seven languages,

the poems are quite the opposite of academic exercises of a library-
filled head, for example, Mr. Pound's literary revivals. They are personal, even private, in extreme.

The method makes for its own peculiar quality and tone, the
tone that echoes twice in the reader's ear—the echo of an echo, the
glass that reflects again. There is always an extra note, a shadow,
between reality and understanding. Listen:

> Because I do not hope to turn again
> Because I do not hope
> Because I do not hope to turn

or

> Here is no water but only rock
> Rock and no water and the sandy road
> The road winding above among the mountains
> Which are mountains of rock without water
> If there were water we should stop and drink
> Amongst the rock one cannot stop or think. . . .

or the brilliant single line:

> Stone, bronze, stone, steel, stone, oakleaves horses' heels

or almost in parody of itself:

> If the lost word is lost, if the spent word is spent
> If the unheard, unspoken
> Word is unspoken, unheard;
> Still is the unspoken word, the Word unheard,
> The Word without a word, the Word within
> The world and for the world;
> And the light shone in darkness and
> Against the Word the unstilled world still whirled
> About the centre of the silent Word.

Beautiful and haunted, listening for the word that is already an
echo, chiming again, gong answering gong across an empty space:
such is the lovely unmistakable quality of Eliot's verse. "The Waste
Land" itself is like a great hollow gong, echoing from beginning to
end, echoing in large units and small, and chiming both with itself
and a hundred smaller and larger units of other works; so that at
two removes, and muffled, reality sounds.

This makes the difficulty, the twice-reflected image, and further, the associational image that depends not on the general associational character of language, but upon some particular association that happened to have been fixed in the poet's mind by his reading. "The Waste Land" is the height of all this complicated cross-reference. There is first an impression, and that may be a good deal in itself, lovely and haunting, but impressionistic: a blur of images of decay and drought and fear. More precise meaning waits on uncovering at least one layer of images, and sometimes three or four. This uncovering process is certainly not an aesthetic act, or aesthetic satisfaction. It is a detective act, if you like mystery stories. The poet has determined his readers to be one part reader and three parts sleuth, if they are to get any general satisfaction out of "The Waste Land." . . .

The reader knows what action, or drama, in a dramatic poem is, for example, the incident of the Ancient Mariner and the sea creatures in Coleridge's fable, which offers comparison with "The Waste Land" in many ways. In both cases you have, apparently, a hero who has committed a fault; you have drought, suffering, and enchantment; you have the severe spiritual testing of the hero. In "The Ancient Mariner," however, unlike "The Waste Land," something happens: the mariner in his suffering becomes aware of the sea creatures, "O happy living things!" and after this unconscious act of sympathy his powers return, he prays, his burden falls. "And when I woke it rained."

That is redemption, or movement in the way of spiritual recovery. It did not rain in "The Waste Land," and there is no reason why it should have. There might be another sort of action, fatal or tragic. Almost any poem, say, of Robinson Jeffers, not to mention Shakespeare or the Greeks, would do to illustrate tragic action, how the chief character because of some fatal flaw of pride or corruptibility moves from error to unrepented error and so to final disaster. There is no "would have" about it; what happened happened and must be accounted for, and with an intractable character, the accounting is finally tragic.

The surprising fact about "The Waste Land," with all its dark threats and horrors, is that it is not tragic: nothing fatal really happens. The reason is that it is not dramatic. The fable, or epic, elements, as I have suggested, fall subordinate in the end to the confessional motive, and that is the note left with us. Hence that last tag end of the poem, which so far I have not mentioned:

> I sat upon the shore
> Fishing, with the arid plain behind me
> Shall I at least set my lands in order?
> London Bridge is falling down falling down falling down
> *Poi s'ascose nel foco che gli affina*
> *Quando fiam uti chelidon*—O swallow swallow
> *Le Prince d'Aquitaine à la tour abolie*
> These fragments I have shored against my ruins
> Why then Ile fit you. Hieronymo's mad againe.
> Datta, Dayadhvam. Damyata.
> Shantih shantih shantih

Even after following through the poem, this passage will no doubt look rather obscure, and lucidity is surely not a merit of "The Waste Land." But we still have, as you see, our ever-resurgent "I character," who now takes his place where he has never really vacated it, as the author commenting on himself. Our poet-hero-commentator sits on the shore fishing, is still casting for the holy fish of truth, as he was at the beginning. The arid plain is behind him—perhaps this means that we have got out of Dante's upper hell and are now only in purgatory. Shall he not set his own lands in order? or in other words, they are not in order yet. As for the old kingdom, there seems to be no hope for that; London Bridge is falling down falling down falling down, my fair lady. Our hero-author-victim asks his good lady to remember him as she climbs toward heaven, while he dives back into the purgatorial fire that refines him.

When shall he be as the swallow, that is the true bird of poetry, favored by Apollo, and with a body as well as a voice? O sister swallow, when shall his spring come? The prospect is not good. Our prince of the sea, wrecked voyageur, misguided knight, blighted god—Ferdinand, Adonis, Phlebas, Palinurus, Gawain, Parsifal, Rishyacringa, Tiresias, T. S. Eliot—came to the broken tower, himself like a tower struck by lightning. He is inconsolable. The only thing he can do is pick up the pieces. Still he is glad to oblige. Like Hieronymo he will amuse the court for an hour or two with his little make-believe tragedy. Hieronymo has these hallucinations when he thinks of his lost son. But as a matter of fact, Hieronymo's never better than when he's mad! And again the warning Sanskrit thunder, and peace, peace where alas there is no peace.

There is one development here however. We have the reversal, or turnabout confession, that you can find in most of Eliot's poems—the author turning on the author. If the Prophet has struck too high a note, the Fool will take down the Prophet. It is Marsyas the rash flute player flaying himself. There is strength in this, and indeed this note of humor and self-mockery has been the strength of the poem throughout. The pathos, if it were pure pathos, would be intolerable. But even in the test of the Dry Mountains, pathos is saved by humor—if there were water we should stop and drink . . . here one can neither stand nor lie nor sit. What we can do is make even the worst situation look slightly ridiculous.

This gives a clue as to what has actually happened to the epic form as used by Eliot in "The Waste Land." Nothing could be more in the grand tradition than the models for Eliot's poem: *The Divine Comedy, The Aeneid,* the great myths of the Grail and the solar cycles, the spiritual epic of Calvary itself. But Eliot has not taken his own subject seriously enough to make an epic of it. He supposes, apparently, that the modern world is not important enough to deserve serious treatment. Dante might think enough of Florence and a local feud between Guelphs and Ghibellines to fit it into cosmic drama. Eliot reduces London and the fate of western Europe to mock tragedy.

As the poem turns from prophecy into confession so far as its spiritual content is concerned, so the form turns from epic to mock-epic. When humanity is not important enough for sympathy, a hero will not be serious enough for sacrifice. He may, however, be a mock hero, and it is a mock hero and mock heroics that actually emerge from "The Waste Land." There has been every appearance of heroics, just as there has been every appearance of disaster and tribulation. Our hero has been buried alive in the underworld, fried in the lava of the burned-over land, tossed sizzling into the deepest sea, struck by a triple thunderbolt from the highest heaven. Still he neither succumbs nor triumphs. The heroics simply won't come off. At the end we still have the hero unchanged, fishing in the same pond, ready for more bolts, burning, burying, and drowning.

Our hero, in short, is a tough character. If he is sensitive and suffering, he is not suffering and sensitive enough either to melt into something better or crack into something worse. He survives as he is, because he is tough—and toughness is a quality that is good for comedy or burlesque, but useless for serious drama. As such, it is a perfectly legitimate quality; only it is not some other quality, such as daring, self-sacrifice, asceticism, humility, wisdom, or love. The tag end of "The Waste Land," with its "Hieronymo's mad againe," loses us our epic hero, but gains as a mock-epic one, and allows us to view the whole poem, in a sense, as a mock-epic or mock-heroic.

In the study of the author as a whole, we are left with the two alternating characters, much as in the case of Henry Adams. There is the prophet, or preacher (like Adams's "witty scholar") who admits no fallibility, and the fool, or errant soul (like Adams's "penitent child") who admits no consistency. The two characters, in various guises, go on and on, the one preaching a gospel that is supposed to be the only salvation (for example, the Witness in "The Rock"), the other telling of doubt and despair that no gospel can touch (for example the harried soul, Harry, in *The Family Reunion*).

Again, as with Henry Adams, there is the turning of the errant soul from the hard justice of the Fathers to the charity of the Sisters and Mothers:

> . . . Will the veiled sister pray
> For children at the gate
> Who will not go away and cannot pray. . . .

Yet I think this takes a somewhat different form from Adams's drastic rebellion from the stern law that he connected with the Fathers. Adams had taken the masculine God as Law without Love, just as he was to take the feminine God as Love without Law. But if there is alienation from a Father-God in Eliot, it is not in failure to have understood love as an attribute of divinity. Everything points to the fact that love and law had once been seen together, and then lost together. Our poet mourns the lost image of his father—full fathom five he lies—and we believe in the earlier vision:

> Looking into the heart of light, the silence.

But:

> I that was near your heart was removed therefrom
> To lose beauty in terror, terror in inquisition.

It is only after the alienation that divinity, or truth, separates into paternal wrath on the one hand and possible maternal charity on the other, and the poet writes, "No place of grace for those who avoid the face."

Everything suggests the case of the son who had inherited the family blessing—and then somehow, through willfulness or pride, forfeited it. If we were to inquire in what manner, I think the Coriolanus story might be of help, the case of the aristocrat contemptuous of the "common people." Actually the missing relation, with Coriolanus, is the one to his fellow men—to the brothers. And it is through this failing that the other relation fails, the relation to truth, or God. Coriolanus, taught overweening pride by his mother, spurns the "voices" or opinion of his fellow citizens. He calls them curs, and says he prizes their love as he would the dead carcasses of unburied men. In fact, he prefers exile to any concession to the people, crying characteristically as he leaves, "Me banished? I banish you!" When his noble friend suggests that he repent and ask for reconciliation Coriolanus says, "For them! I cannot do it to the gods; Must I then do't to them?"

In Eliot's case, the significant point is the continued preoccupation with the lost image of the Father, and the general dissatisfaction with the Mother alone as a spiritual symbol. In terms of Mother Church, this disaffection amounts to a scandal, not only in "The Hollow Men," where she is called the hope only of empty men, but in "Ash Wednesday," where we read this ambiguous homage:

> Grace to the Mother
> For the Garden
> Where all love ends.

According to Dante's religious belief, or any other real faith in this mode of belief, this of course is where love begins. In Dante there is no conflict between a masculine and feminine deity, any more than there is between love and law, history and God, or fate and nature. Eliot, like Henry Adams, separates truth and history; he turns to a past "period of unity" not for the present, or eternal, values in it, but for a historical situation that has actually disappeared. It is precisely what is gone that would have to be present to realize Eliot's demands. The same applies to the aristocratic political and social situation that would have to be conjured back from the past. Nothing is surer than that to value a past age for what belongs to it peculiarly is to miss in it what belongs to all ages. The recognition of this is our poet's despair.

"The Waste Land" is the picture of what is dying in the present, as it is of what is dead of the past. We must take this for its not always clarified truth. It tells of the decay of old modes as it does of the abuse of new ones. It tells of the remnants of the feudal in the commercial, the patriarchal in the agricultural, the imperial in the democratic. It reflects Pre-Raphaelite and Symbolist playing at religion for the color in it, and the effort to substitute the too-strong secular sciences for too-weak morals and religion. It reflects, in short, a society overburdened with traditional forms which are yet impotent to deal with a modern world—which leave, instead, a fatally widened chasm between form and morality, tradition and human needs. Our poet has eaten of this fruit. Henry James had circled around it, been fascinated by it, hinted at the phosphorescent gleams on its beautiful old surfaces. But James had kept himself apart, saved by innocence, to keep a precarious hold on enchantment. The poet of "The Waste Land" is not innocent, has partaken, and the fruit has been bitter.

Hence, from James's ambiguous children, child brides, and wide-eyed young provincials wandering bedazzled in the old palace gardens, you get Eliot's weary middle-aged lovers, lost sailors, haunted souls, bitter and evil old men: Prufrock, Phlebas, Harry, Gerontion, Tiresias. From James's adolescent dreams of union with the enchanted beauty of the past, we come to the nightmares of bondage in Eliot's dark towers of the Waste Land. Still there is no "middle life," no flow and continuity, no generation and reproduction for the sons of a new world committed to the forms of the old. With Eliot all is disenchantment and remorse, folly and despair. "The unread vision in the higher dream" recedes further and further into the mist, while the glittering pageantry of tradition in the mother kingdom has become a funeral procession:

> While jewelled unicorns draw by the gilded hearse.

The virtue of "The Waste Land" and Eliot's mordant and self-mocking verses is that it is knowledge, if partial and bitter. Here are James's blanks filled in—all those hints of evil and treachery, horror and perverted good, that James left so shadowy. For James they were all overlaid by glamour and glimpsed through innocence. With Eliot they are exposed in knowledge and chagrin. Not that we can take Eliot's knowledge whole, any more than we could take James's glamour pure. Eliot's hopelessness on one side is too complete, just as his grievance is unmeasured, his mockery unselected, and his insight undefined. The observer must decide for himself how much territory these states of mind actually cover, for Eliot has not put them in their place. Each one in turn consumes the universe and, most unfortunate of all, the sense of irreparable wrong. The observer knows that all these states must each represent but a limited content of fact and significance. Some knowledge of this, indeed, seems to be present in the author's last work (as this is written), the play, *The Family Reunion.*

It is a Puritan, Calvinist, New England hell that this Orpheus sings: New England in its dry humor, Puritan in its fastidiousness, Calvinist in its introspectiveness and terrible and wrong sense of predestination. It is Calvinist, too, in a certain exclusiveness, as if one should want to keep a conception of the Elect even in Hades. Baudelaire is French, Latin, Catholic in contrast to our poet.

But it is with Baudelaire that we are to compare Eliot and "The Waste Land," rather than with Dante, or Virgil, or Milton. The vision is of the underside, from the underside. This may be called, not a vision of truth itself, but of truth as it looks from a false position. From here, even good appears bad, because it seems inaccessible, and all patient humanity, with its mixed faults and virtues, becomes red faces sneering and snarling. The heavens themselves seem veiled in all aspects except God the Destroyer—who actually is not God, but only, again, a form of the opposed self. We do not praise the failure of reconciliation and integration. We do respect the sensibility to the position.

# D. S. SAVAGE *

## (1)

THE reputation of T. S. Eliot is now so well established that there is little need here for preliminary eulogy or appreciation. Mr. Eliot is certainly one of the most significant poets of the last two decades, and his work has made an indelible impression on the minds of the more sensitive among his contemporaries, while his influence on both the practice and theory of poetry has been enormous. If there is any danger it is not of undervaluing or neglecting Mr. Eliot's achievement, but of allowing it that too static respect which we accord to the conventionally accepted value. It may be almost axiomatic that Eliot's work provides us with an example of modern poetry at its highest level, but there is a need, from time to time, for a critical estimation which disregards axioms and comes to its subject with a fresh vision. Mr. Eliot's considerable reputation was earned first of all by his earlier work, and I may as well begin by saying that I see this writer's development as a poet to fall into two distinct parts. As I see it there is a qualitative difference between his earlier and his later work which, though few critics have thought it worth while to comment on, is surely, granting Eliot's importance, of some considerable significance.

Eliot's poetry and his prose writing have developed side by side. An early poetry of concentrated poetic value was accomplished by a fastidiously tasteful and sometimes slightly precious aesthetic criticism. But as he has grown older, the moralist in Eliot has developed somewhat at the expense of the aesthete. With his conversion to Anglo-Catholicism a pronouncedly religiose strain begins to be heard both in the prose and in the poems. From *The Waste Land* (1922) and *The Hollow Men* (1925) it is something of a jump to the contemplative tones of *Ash Wednesday* (1930) and the succeeding poems. But while Eliot's later verse is interesting up to a point it lacks the in-

* *The Orthodoxy of T. S. Eliot,* from THE PERSONAL PRINCIPLE, pp. 91–112. George Routledge & Sons Ltd., London, 1944.

tegrity and the astringent personal quality of the earlier poems. To put it unequivocally, I see Eliot's poetic career from about 1925 as one of deterioration, if one can thus describe a process so sharply and clearly defined as the break between the one half of his work and the other.

Eliot's early poems, up to and including *The Hollow Men,* are unique in our literature. But besides being in itself a unique and valid achievement, which is of course its central and pivotal importance, his work of this period has meaning for literature as a whole, has meaning in relation to the continuity of the tradition of English poetry. Following the romantic movement of the early nineteenth century, and the enervated neo-romanticism of Tennyson, Browning and Swinburne, the pre-Raphaelites, and the poets of the *fin-de-siècle,* poetry as a whole, the idiom of verse which was shared by all the poets writing at that time, had ebbed to a low-water mark of flaccidity and nervelessness which it would be difficult to parallel from any period of English history. For the injection of a new and invigorating current, the renewal and tautening of this idiom, we are indebted in large measure to Mr. Eliot's practice, following upon that of Ezra Pound; a practice which drew its strength from an acquaintance with contemporary French poetry, which had escaped the English dissolution in large measure, and from a by-passing of the English neo-romantic currents which made possible a fresh contact with English poetry of the most vigorous period. It needed just such a cosmopolitan American poet as Mr. Eliot, with his unique gifts, to do this job of work, a job of work which could only have been done, of course, through actual creative achievement. As an American, Eliot was sufficiently detached from the provincialism into which English poetry had declined, and sufficiently in touch both with alien currents and with the older tradition of English verse, to do what was so badly needed. He brought content and form together to provide contemporary Britain with a new and vivid poetry of what has aptly been called "the modern experience". In these poems the city-world of latterday industrial civilization with its psychological uncertainties and spiritual ennui is given exactly adequate expression. Lacking this idiom and this spiritual outlook, which were Eliot's contributions to poetry, English poets were tending either to revert to balladry and conventionalism, like Watson, Kipling and Bridges, or to evade "the modern experience," to sidetrack it in the manner of Flecker and the Georgians. Eliot rejected both academicism and pomposity, and the quiet, sardonic, penetratingly realistic attitude he took and expressed, at first affronting the literate public, soon captured the imagination of his younger readers and, more than any other single influence, helped to bring poetry back to a serious confrontation of the actual world of daily experience.

This world of Eliot's is sharply and acridly *there*, intensely personal, intensely realized, particular and immediate. His descriptions are vividly unforgettable:

> Among the smoke and fog of a December afternoon
> You have the scene arrange itself—as it will seem to do—
> With "I have saved this afternoon for you";
> And four wax candles in the darkened room,
> Four rings of light upon the ceiling overhead,
> An atmosphere of Juliet's tomb
> Prepared for all the things to be said, or left unsaid.
> We have been, let us say, to hear the latest Pole
> Transmit the Preludes, through his hair and fingertips.
> "So intimate, this Chopin, that I think his soul
> Should be resurrected only among friends
> Some two or three, who will not touch the bloom
> That is rubbed and questioned in the concert room."
> —And so the conversation slips
> Among velleities and carefully caught regrets
> Through attenuated tones of violins
> Mingled with remote cornets
> And begins . . .

So begins *Portrait of a Lady.* And from this and other poems of that period one remembers the recurrent novel and startling phrases and evocations:

> Let us go then, you and I,
> When the evening is spread out against the sky
> Like a patient etherised upon a table . . .
>
> Shall I say, I have gone at dusk through narrow streets
> And watched the smoke that rises from the pipes
> Of lonely men in shirt-sleeves, leaning out of windows? . . .

And if this is "period-poetry", evoking the emotional quality of an unrecapturable past day, it is period-poetry of the most valuable kind, in which the emotional atmosphere is transformed into something permanent.

Superficially, we may say that the difference apparent between the early poems and the later is one of *environment*. Whereas Eliot first became recognized for his uniquely personal presentment of the squalor and decay of the industrial metropolis and its soiled and banal humanity: whereas he was the acutely perceptive poet of "The damp souls of housemaids/ Sprouting despondently at area gates", of "the hands/ That are raising dingy shades/ In a thousand furnished rooms" and the like, in the later poems this environment is passed over, like a disreputable associate of a misspent youth, for the rarer atmosphere of religious meditation and contemplation. But where the world of the early poems carries real and intense conviction, the atmosphere of the later verse, because of its intellectual rather than sensuous nature, fails to impose its reality sharply and definitely upon the reader's perceptions. The later verse, contemplative and refined, is lifted from the graphic presentment of actuality, and the poet's mind begins to work less concretely: in fact, less poetically. From the particular, Eliot passes to the generalized, observation and evocation, and the attempt to grapple this to the concrete actuality of experience, to endow it with authentic life, results in the strained impotence of the generalized image. Where Eliot tries determinedly to achieve concreteness in certain of his poems without this expedient, the attempt will lead him to the employment of archaic or biblical imagery, which is literary rather than actual: as in *A Song for Simeon*:

> Before the time of cords and scourges and lamentations
> Grant us thy peace.
> Before the stations of the mountain of desolation.
> Before the certain hour of maternal sorrow,
> Now at this birth season of decease,
> Let the Infant, the still unspeaking and unspoken Word,
> Grant Israel's consolation
> To one who has eighty years and no to-morrow. . . .

The loss of immediacy apparent in his later work, the substitution of the contemplative abstraction for the evocative imagery, is to be seen in such passages as this from *Ash Wednesday*:

> Because I know that time is always time
> And place is always and only place

And what is actual is actual only for one time
And only for one place
I rejoice that things are as they are and
I renounce the blessed face
And renounce the voice
Because I cannot hope to turn again
Consequently I rejoice, having to construct something
Upon which to rejoice. . . .

But perhaps one may best present Eliot's poetic declension by contrasting the earlier *Preludes* with those short poems of his later period which follow upon the same structural pattern and appear in a certain manner to be their counterpart. The force and economy of phrasing of the brief *Preludes* entitles them to comparison with verse of the order of Shakespeare's songs. But compare this:

The winter evening settles down
With smell of steaks in passageways.
Six o'clock.
The burnt-out ends of smoky days.
And now a gusty shower wraps
The grimy scraps
Of withered leaves about your feet
And newspapers from vacant lots;
The showers beat
On broken blinds and chimney-pots,
And at the corner of the street
A lonely cab-horse steams and stamps.
And then the lighting of the lamps.

with this:

The wind sprang up at four o'clock
The wind sprang up and broke the bells
Swinging between life and death
Here, in death's dream kingdom
The waking echo of confusing strife
Is it a dream or something else
When the surface of the blackened river
Is a face that sweats with tears?
I saw across the blackened river
The camp fire shake with alien spears.
Here, across death's other river
The Tartar horsemen shake their spears.

where the loss of concrete imagery and emotional immediacy is so apparent as to require no comment.

Of the later poems, there remain the Choruses from *The Rock*, lines with a didactic import originally printed in the context of a propagandist pageant-play. Of these one can but say that they admirably serve their purpose; some of them are solemnly impressive; they have not the integral structure of *poems*. And lastly there is the sequence of long poems which begins with *Burnt Norton* and proceeds through *East Coker* and *The Dry Salvages* to *Little Gidding*.

It would be impossible to pretend that these poems are not, in their way, impressive achievements. They bear the marks of deep sincerity, of a mature intelligence and of experienced and conscientious craftsmanship. But despite all that has been claimed for them (and claimed, one finds it impossible not to conjecture, mainly on the strength of Mr. Eliot's formidable reputation) they must be marked down as imperfectly realized summaries of experience, as poetic failures. The dominant emotions conveyed by the early poems are those of weariness, boredom, frustration, self-doubt and dissatisfaction, but these qualities are brought within the crystallizing range of the poet's craftsmanship and are thereby mastered and transformed, made truly significant. The air of aridity, of weariness, which is exhaled by these later poems is marginal, is not part of the substance of the poetry itself, but is unintentional, arising from qualities which the poet has failed to bring in subjection to his inspiration. Morality in Eliot's mind having replaced art as the potential transforming agent of experience, a function which it is quite incapable of performing, the result is that Eliot's career oddly resembles, to make a theological comparison, a fall from the reign of Grace to the rule of Law.

Of these later poems the most memorable, because most concretely conceived, is *East Coker*. But the poems share the common disadvantage of being little more than loosely connected philosophizings about the nature of reality and the value of experience, of which the poetry is ornamental rather than essential. Patches of imagery are stuck on, as it were, from outside, to give poetic verisimilitude to a skeleton of abstract intellectualism. There is a laboured straining after effect, as in the following examples of the generalized image:

His rhythm was present in the nursery bedroom,
In the rank ailanthus of the April dooryard,
In the smell of grapes on the autumn table,
And the evening circle in the winter gaslight. . . .

For most of us, there is only the unattended
Moment, the moment in and out of time,
The distraction fit, lost in a shaft of sunlight,
The wild thyme unseen, or the winter lightning
Or the waterfall, or music heard so deeply
That it is not heard at all . . .

where the catalogue effect would seem to arise from the poet's need
to grope in several vague images after an effect which he has failed
to achieve with one deep, incisive impression. One thinks involun-
tarily of the examples of concrete, particular imagery which were so
admirable a feature of the early poems, of lines such as—

I have seen eyes in the street
Trying to peer through lighted shutters,
And a crab one afternoon in a pool,
An old crab with barnacles on his back,
Gripped the end of a stick which I held him. . . .

where the experience and the resultant image are particular, personal
and definite. Long familiarity, in my own case at least, has not blurred
this image or lessened its excitement.

It is a curiously notable fact that poets seem irresistibly impelled
to give themselves away in their work: are driven, it seems, to make
explicit not merely their inmost thoughts and emotions, which indeed
they may effectively disguise, but their inner and private assessment
of their own achievement. In *East Coker,* two passages are of considerable revelatory interest. The first is an attempted exercise on the
pattern of the *Preludes:*

What is the late November doing
With the disturbance of the spring,
And creatures of the summer heat,
And snowdrops writhing under feet,
And hollyhocks that aim too high
Red into grey and tumble down
Late roses filled with early snow. . . .

The second is the deliberately flat and prosaic commentary upon this passage, in which the poet's dissatisfaction with his craft is directly expressed:

> That was a way of putting it—not very satisfactory:
> A periphrastic study in a worn-out poetical fashion,
> Leaving one still with the intolerable wrestle
> With words and meanings. The poetry does not matter. . . .

And this is amplified, after yet another passage in "a worn-out poetical fashion", in section V of that poem:

> So here I am, in the middle way, having had twenty years—
> Twenty years largely wasted, the years of l'entre deux guerres—
> Trying to learn to use words, and every attempt
> Is a wholly new start, and a different kind of failure
> Because one has only learnt to get the better of words
> For the thing one no longer has to say, or the way in which
> One is no longer disposed to say it. And so each venture
> Is a new beginning, a raid on the inarticulate
> With shabby equipment always deteriorating
> Into the general mess of imprecision of feeling . . .

It is possible to make too much of such "revelatory" passages, but these at least tentatively suggest themselves as providing an enlightening self-commentary upon Eliot's progress as a poet.

## (II)

The prose writings of T. S. Eliot, whatever one thinks of their ultimate importance, are of interest for the sporadic light they cast upon the development of their author's attitude to literature.

The pivotal viewpoint of Eliot the literary critic may be said to be one of "Impersonalism", allied with a devotion to Tradition. Here are some key-passages from an early essay, *Tradition and the Individual Talent:*

> . . . Tradition . . . cannot be inherited, and if you want it you must obtain it by great labour. It involves, in the first place, the historical sense, which we may call nearly indispensable to anyone who would continue to be a poet beyond his twenty-fifth year; and the historical sense involves a perception, not only of the pastness of the past, but of its presence; the his-

torical sense compels a man to write not merely with his own
generation in his bones, but with a feeling that the whole of the
literature of Europe from Homer and within it the whole of the
literature of his own country has a simultaneous existence and
composes a simultaneous order . . .

No poet, nor artist of any art, has his complete meaning
alone. His significance, his appreciation, is the appreciation of
his relation to the dead poets and artists. You cannot value him
alone; you must set him, for contrast and comparison, among
the dead . . .

What is to be insisted upon is that the poet must develop
or procure the consciousness of the past and that he should continue to develop this consciousness throughout his career.

What happens is a continual surrender of himself as he is
at the moment to something which is more valuable. The
progress of an artist is a continual self-sacrifice, a continual extinction of personality.

Eliot then makes his well-known comparison of the mind of the
poet to a catalyst which, remaining unchanged itself, forms new com-
pounds out of disparate elements:

The mind of the poet . . . may partly or exclusively operate
upon the experience of the man himself; but, the more perfect
the artist, the more completely separate in him will be the man
who suffers and the mind which creates . . .

Poetry is not a turning loose of emotion, but an escape from
emotion; it is not the expression of personality, but an escape
from personality. But, of course, only those who have personality
and emotions know what it means to want to escape from these
things . . .

The emotion of art is impersonal. And the poet cannot
reach this impersonality without surrendering himself wholly
to the work to be done. And he is not likely to know what is to
be done unless he lives in what is not merely the present, but the
present moment of the past, unless he is conscious not of what
is dead, but of what is already living.

And, as he expresses it again in a somewhat later essay, *The Function
of Criticism*:

I thought of literature then, as I think of it now . . . not
as a collection of the writings of individuals, but as "organic
wholes", as systems in relation to which, and only in relation

to which, individual works of literary art, and the works of individual artists, have their significance. There is accordingly something outside of the artist to which he owes allegiance, a devotion to which he must surrender and sacrifice himself in order to earn and to obtain his unique position.

In literature this attitude leads Mr. Eliot towards the position of neo-classicism; in religion it leads naturally enough to Catholic Orthodoxy. Since this attitude is grounded upon a certain definitive view of personality it may be as well to clarify that view before proceeding further.

Eliot's view of personality follows very closely indeed upon that of T. E. Hulme, a writer who has evidently had a great influence upon his thought. And since Eliot's Orthodoxy would seem to be very similar to the rationalistic Catholicism of Hulme, it may be worth while to devote some little space to an elucidation of the viewpoint which these two writers hold in common on fundamental questions. Here, then, is Hulme on the nature of man:

> . . . Put shortly, these are the two views then. One, that man is intrinsically good, spoilt by circumstance; and the other that he is intrinsically limited, but disciplined by order and tradition to something fairly decent. To the one party, man's nature is like a well, to the other like a bucket. The view which regards man as a well, a reservoir full of possibilities, I call the romantic; the one which regards him as a very finite and fixed creature, I call the classical.

And this is what Hulme has to say about classicism and religion:

> It would be a mistake to identify the classical view with that of materialism. On the contrary, it is absolutely identical with the normal religious attitude. I should put it this way: that part of the fixed nature of man is the belief in the Deity. This should be as fixed and true for every man as belief in the existence of matter and in the objective world. It is parallel to appetite, the instinct of sex, and all the other fixed qualities. Now at certain times, by the use of either force or rhetoric, these instincts have been suppressed—in Florence under Savonarola, in Geneva under Calvin, and here under the roundheads. The inevitable result of such a process is that the repressed instinct bursts out again in some abnormal direction. Just as in the case of the other instincts, nature has her revenge. The instincts that

find their right and proper outlet in religion must come out in some other way. You do not believe in a God, so you begin to believe that man is a god. You do not believe in Heaven, so you begin to believe in a heaven on earth. In other words, you get romanticism . . . Romanticism then . . . is spilt religion.

Taking the first statement, that upon the nature of man, first, it should not be hard to see that Hulme's antithesis is a false one. Whom or what does Hulme mean by "man?" It should be apparent to one who has thought at all on the question that humanity is not composed of an undifferentiated mass of individuals, all alike as to gifts, capacities and potentialities. The human community is a hierarchy and there is a very considerable difference indeed between those members of it who are near the summit of the hierarchy and those who compose its base. To speak of the human "herd" in such terms as Hulme uses may be relatively correct. But it certainly does not apply to the rare individuals who create values, and are not merely the passive recipients of them in a socialized form. Nor is there such a simple division between only two opposed views of man. One need not believe that man is "intrinsically good and spoilt by circumstances" to see that the best among men have unplumbed potentialities. One can believe that our humanity is corrupt, and that it yet contains creative potentiality. And to speak of man as an extremely limited creature who can be "disciplined by order and tradition to something fairly decent" inevitably leads one to the question, From whence originate the order and tradition by which man can be thus disciplined? Hulme's view of faith also has, I suggest, nothing religious about it. A religious mind would not, for example, say that belief in the Deity is "part of the fixed nature of man," but rather that the existence of God is an ultimate verity, and that man has a mind capable of apprehending this truth. Nor is it correct, as Hulme seems to suggest, that religions (such as Hulme's and Eliot's own Western Catholicism) spring ready-made into being, complete with fixed traditions and dogmas and an elaborate ecclesiastical structure which has only to be passively accepted by man in general. Quite otherwise. The impersonal and social paraphernalia of religious belief are the socialized end-products of what has begun as fluid, living personal faith and zeal. And just as the elaborate, formalized Catholic hierarchy of the Middle Ages was the end-product, so to speak (though still containing living personal force within itself) of the subversive, unofficial, dynamically personal community of Christians who formed the early Church, so those collectivized values which we know as Tradition have their origin in the personal creative acts of original human beings. We do not find Dante, Shakespeare, Michelangelo, Beethoven talking about "relating themselves to tradition" and so on. They make the tradition, giving birth to imperative spiritual urgencies stirring within themselves. And if they are so fortunate as to find a harmony between their own creative attitude and the world-view currently accepted by the society of their time, so much the better. All human values originate from within individual human beings. There is nowhere else for them to come from.

Hulme's decadent, rationalistic Catholicism which has no place for faith is like his art which has no place for creativeness. It is entirely symptomatic that Hulme attributes the "extraordinary efflorescence of verse in the Elizabethan period" to the discovery of the medium of blank verse. "We shall not," he says, "get any new efflorescence of verse until we get a new technique, a new convention, to turn ourselves loose in." This academic attitude towards art which is so extraordinarily dense and unperceptive derives from an inability to admit any spiritual significance to the artist's creative acts. If the medium of blank verse was "discovered" by the Elizabethan poets, and if the efflorescence of verse of that period can be attributed to that discovery, it was discovered not through accident or through poking about impersonally with arid laboratory experiments but out of a superabundance of personal creativeness which violently forced its way into a new form. It is quite parochial and unrealistic to treat of poetry as though it were an activity entirely severed from the complex of personal-social forces in which it is conceived, to speak as though a new movement (Hulme of course wanted a "classical" movement) could arise upon merely a technical impetus, unrelated to the inner life of man. Eliot himself is in this respect a little more perceptive than Hulme, but his own criticism distinctly bears the mark of Hulme's academic and fragmentary approach.

The fragmentariness of Eliot's own outlook, its dislocated aspect, may be guessed at from a reading of his prose works as a whole, but it is in *After Strange Gods* (1934) that the disunity of his approach to life and literature is made glaringly manifest, the more so because one feels that here an attempt is being made, through the association of "tradition" with "orthodoxy," to piece the fragments together.

This little book, which purports to be a study of the diabolical influence in modern literature, is far from being an impressive work. It is a patchwork of notions and prejudices enlivened with those occasional acute observations which we have learned to expect from Mr. Eliot's pen. But so far from being a study of the "diabolical influence", it reveals no more than the most distant nodding acquaintance with the powers of darkness. The whole point and purport of the book is distinctly anomalous. Mr. Eliot's concern seems to be to apply an external rule-of-thumb by which serious literature should be assessed; but then it transpires that he is not concerned with literary evaluations, that he is merely using the works of certain eminent authors to illustrate a moralistic point of view.

Let us briefly consider Mr. Eliot's viewpoint with regard to tradition and orthodoxy as expressed in this book. "I wished simply", he says, "to indicate the connotation which the term *tradition* has for me, before proceeding to associate it with the concept of *orthodoxy,* which seems to me more fundamental (with its opposite, heterodoxy, for which I shall also use the term *heresy*) than the pair *classicism-romanticism* which is frequently used." He then appears to require that writers should be assessed from this point of view; that is, by their conformity or otherwise to orthodoxy and tradition.

Perhaps Mr. Eliot's attitude may be clarified by the quotation of a passage from this book, on Thomas Hardy. "The work of the late Thomas Hardy", he says, "represents an interesting example of a powerful personality uncurbed by an *institutional attachment* or by *submission* to any *objective beliefs"* (my italics). What is the implication? That by an acceptance of Mr. Eliot's panacea on Thomas Hardy's part, his work would have gained enormously in significance and value? Hardly that, perhaps. Yet what other conclusion is to be drawn from Eliot's contentions?

Of a similar character is Eliot's assessment of D. H. Lawrence. What seems to him to be important is not the degree of imaginative insight which any given writer can bring to bear upon experience, but the degree to which he can be said to toe the line of an exterior orthodoxy. It is from this point of view that he condemns Lawrence. Now D. H. Lawrence may quite possibly have been, as I myself do in fact believe, on the wrong track altogether, and Mr. Eliot may ultimately be quite right in his condemnation, but a writer of this quality demands at least something more than the frigid disapprobation of the moralist with his rule of thumb, and one cannot but feel that Eliot simply has not earned the right to his condemnation. He gets it by a short cut. Disapproving strongly of Lawrence, as a moralist Eliot would seem as strongly to approve of James Joyce. "The most ethically orthodox of the more eminent writers of my time is Mr. Joyce." This may, in a sense, be true enough; but what then? And why not G. K. Chesterton or Sheila Kaye-Smith? James Joyce may be "ethically orthodox" (though was he, as a matter of fact, a believer at all?). But for the consciousness of our time it is obviously Lawrence, not Joyce, who is of genuine religious significance. Lawrence was possessed by a fervid religiousness which, to be sure, was chaotic and undirected into any *form* of belief; and Eliot is justified in pointing this last fact out. Yet would Lawrence's significance have been deepened, or destroyed, by a mechanical "acceptance" of Mr. Eliot's objective and institutional orthodoxy? However palpable his faults and errors, Lawrence had the courage and the personal integrity to live out his own personal pattern to the end. His meaning derives from that, and it is a living meaning, though a sad one. But if Lawrence presents us with the phenomenon of religiousness without religion, surely in Joyce we can trace the opposite, the form of Catholicism without the religious spirit. Joyce, who is intellectually correct, a well-turned-out standard product of Catholic orthodoxy, whose intellectual machinery operates in the standard manner, passes Mr. Eliot's muster, while Lawrence, a man filled with prophetic vision, is summarily cast into the outer darkness of his disapproval.

Both Lawrence and Hardy were men with a certain unique insight into reality, however warped or partial, which they pursued with heroic integrity. That is their value for us, and it is a real value, a real *religious* value. For what merit is there in the mechanical acceptance of an objective, i.e. socially approved, fabric of beliefs? If such acceptance is reached integrally and as the completion of a genuinely personal pattern—is reached out of an inner striving for truth—then it is a different matter. But then it is not "orthodoxy" which is attained, but something of which orthodoxy is only the shadow.

Mr. Eliot manoeuvres delicately around this question of or-

152     T. S. ELIOT

thodoxy. ". . . While tradition, being a matter of good habits, is necessarily real only in a social group, orthodoxy exists whether realized in anyone's thought or not . . . as by Athanasius, orthodoxy may be upheld by one man against the world." Now this latter statement can only be defended by identifying *orthodoxy* with *truth*. It may in a certain sense be said that truth exists "whether realized in anyone's thought or not", that it may be "upheld by one man against the world". But this cannot be said of orthodoxy, as such, which is not a personal but a social, collective matter. *Orthodox,* by definition, means "holding *correct* or *currently accepted* opinions especially on religious doctrine, *not heretical or independent-minded or original; generally accepted* as right or true especially in theology, in harmony with what is *authoritatively established, approved, conventional."* (Concise Oxford Dictionary). How, then, can it be upheld by one man against the world? It is then not orthodoxy but something else, again, of which orthodoxy is only the shadow. Orthodoxy can be termed so only by an appeal to the collective opinion, if not of the present, then of the past, or of the future.

Now, the problem which Mr. Eliot here raises and so summarily disposes of is one of supreme importance. The entire question of the position of creativeness and of the artist's responsibility and function is involved. But Mr. Eliot evades the issue.

What was Mr. Eliot's intention in writing *After Strange Gods?* "As for the small number of writers", he admits, "in this or any other period who are worth taking seriously, I am very far from asserting that any of these is wholly 'orthodox', or even that it would be relevant to rank them according to degrees of orthodoxy." If that is so, (as is indisputable), what is the point of his monograph? Is it the writer's first duty to undertake a personal, creative illumination of experienced reality, or is it to be orthodox, to submit to the external imposition of objective authority? This is a question which Mr. Eliot evades, even deliberately evades, though it is fundamental to his outlook. If the writer is held to be a genuine creator of values, then what is the relevance of this dogmatic, moralistic approach to works of literature? It surely cannot be gainsaid that here we touch on a deep-seated equivocation in Eliot's thought. For you cannot have it both ways. You cannot admit the significance of the creative writer as an originator of values and at the same time

demand his subservience to an external authority which claims to be
the sole dispenser of values. And if you deny that it is the function
of the creative writer to create values, you are then driven to the
ultimately sterile position of regarding literature as merely a superior type of entertainment, a view which inevitably precludes it from
being taken seriously, to its own detriment, and would certainly
seem to preclude it from playing a part of any great moment in human affairs.

From this viewpoint, art cannot but be seen as an ornamental
excrescence upon life, something set apart from man's painful and
joyful exploration of his human condition. In which case one might
well ask, in what region of life *is* man's crucial activity to be seen
as taking place? If the reality of such crucial activity be admitted,
wherever it occurs, shall we not expect to see it reflected in every
sphere and especially in the sphere of art, where man is engaged in
the task of presenting to himself a unified and clarified vision of experience? In reality, however, a view which denies creative significance to art is always found to be a view which denies creative
significance to human activity as a whole. It is a view which sees no
inherent meaning in human life and destiny, which ignores the
reality in order to superimpose upon it a "symbolical" pattern whereby
"salvation" becomes one of a series of formal, stereotyped gestures
rather than a living experience. It is not at bottom a religious view
at all. When it takes a religious form, it is religious only in the social,
collective, ecclesiastical sense, a religion without faith. That is why
orthodoxy (as Mr. Eliot propounds it), conformity to an institution,
submission to a system of objective beliefs, is not for the artist, the
creative spirit, at all. It is for the multitude of "copies", for social man,
for the masses: indeed, it is largely their construction. The "original"
human being embraces it, when he does so, by going back on his own
originality: not from faith, but out of doubt and despair.

> We are the hollow men
> We are the stuffed men
> Leaning together
> Headpiece filled with straw. Alas!
> Our dried voices, when
> We whisper together
> Are quiet and meaningless

As wind in dry grass
Or rats' feet over broken glass
In our dry cellar.

Shape without form, shade without colour,
Paralysed force, gesture without motion;

Those who have crossed
With direct eyes, to death's other Kingdom
Remember us—if at all—not as lost
Violent souls, but only
As the hollow men
The stuffed men.


## III

T. S. Eliot is still quite commonly thought of as an individualistic, self-centred lyricist of the "Ivory Tower" genre, isolated from social current and preoccupied with the minutiae of strictly private sensation. This is strange, for it is of course the precise opposite of the truth. Eliot is first and last, in orientation, a man of society, acutely conscious of the social problems of his day, with a pronouncedly democratic bias.

Wyndham Lewis is quite correct in pointing out this democratic bias of Eliot's. His constant emphasis of impersonal values at the expense of personal ones originates from this.

As a poet Eliot has never been very intimately personal—like D. H. Lawrence, for example. While the experience conveyed through the poems is genuine and deeply felt, it is presented nearly always in a social perspective. The experiencing mind of the early poems sees itself in its relationship to a squalid environment devoid of beauty and of spiritual meaning. Prufrock's obscure predicament is obviously a social one. Burbank with his Baedeker confronts the world of Bleistein with his cigar. And so on and so forth. *The Waste Land* (1922) is, structurally, almost completely conceived in social terms. It is true of course that it is the predicament of the individual which makes Eliot concern himself with society, but the fact remains that he sees the individual in perpetual relationship to society, past and present (but particularly past), and that he sees him as dependent upon it, just as he sees, as a critic, the writer's need to relate himself to tradition. This fundamentally collective, numerical, democratic outlook it is which gives him his distrust of "originality" and all the things associated with that term. One remembers his words on the subject: "The artist's concern with originality, certainly, may be considered as largely negative: he wishes only to avoid saying what has already been said as well as it can be . . . To assert that a work is 'original' should be very modest praise: it should be no more than to say that the work is not patently negligible." And associated, of course, with this distrust of originality is his distrust of personality, his inability to conceive of the individual person as a real centre of creativeness, giving birth to real values, and the need to subordinate the individual to some superior collective principle—in the case of the man, to the Church, in the case of the poet, to tradition—and, for all I know to the contrary, in the case of the citizen, to the State.

A suggestive light can be cast upon these attitudes of Eliot's if one disregards his carefully arranged and probably unconscious protective colouring, or camouflage, and considers him against the background of his origin as a clear case of "Americanism." Eliot presents, however, unlike Whitman and Hart Crane, an Americanism in reverse, a reactive Americanism. Eliot is concerned to emphasize all those cultural values which have been left out of account in the American idea of civilization, which appear as mere excrescences upon the surface of American life. (It is not suggested that this in any way invalidates the worth of his achievement or even necessarily the truth of his ideas.) Like Henry James, who also, in the same way, became a naturalized British subject, Eliot has acquired the cosmopolitan view of life: he is more European than the Europeans. (What native British poet of our day would have thought it worth while to declare himself, like Eliot, an Anglo-Catholic in religion, a royalist in politics, and a traditionalist in literature?) Eliot is more scholarly, more self-consciously equipped with all the trappings of "culture," than any contemporary British poet, as one can see from the snobbish multilingual epigraphs to his verse and prose, the literary cross-references and the rest of the apparatus of cultural sophistication. One can think of only one other contemporary poet who resembles Eliot in this respect, and that is—another American—Ezra Pound, *il miglior fabbro*. And indeed, this over-exaggeration of accepted cultural values is a reactive fault to which the sensitive American is particularly prone. For what does it reveal but, essentially, an absence of creative self-confidence? The poet, as the product

of an externalized and spiritually uprooted collective civilization, is
entirely impotent to believe that any good can come out of his own
inward being, as a child of the present age, and therefore he appeals
to the assured, established and certified authority of the culture of
the past. His poetic activity, for which the present-day world has
little patience, he may justify to himself and others by appeal to the
values of the collective of the past. This appeal is at once expressive
of a distrust of the artist's function and, allied to this, of the individual's spiritual validity as a centre of creativeness. From this *distrust of the person* issue, first, Eliot's classicism and then, inevitably,
his Catholicism. For, despite a superficially deceptive appearance of
"minority" snobbishness, these attitudes are, I must repeat, basically
democratic. Their concern is always with the values of the collective, which are inevitably always impersonal ones. A foolproof impersonal system, of religion, social life and culture, is the desire and
the need of the individual whose faith in his own interior validity
and in that of other men is, for whatever reason, weak. A vigorous
and vehement personal creativeness has never been one of Eliot's
notable qualities. As a poet he exhibits, with nervous sensitivity, a
strong negative genius of restraint. As a critic he is sensitive and
appreciative, prevaricative and niggling. As a thinker, while a certain quality of shrewdly perceptive common sense pervades his work,
he shows no profundity and no coherent analytical power whatever.
An admirably disciplined use of creative powers of the second order
it is which has earned him his present deserved eminence.

From the viewpoint which Eliot has adopted and taken his stand
on, the individual person, then, must be perpetually subordinated to
the collective, personal values to impersonal ones. Authority resides
outside the individual, who must not presume to stand alone: in
every case he must form part of a pattern, and he must assess his activities from the point of view of the harmony of the pattern. This
is a viewpoint which places the minimum of responsibility upon the
individual and the minimum emphasis upon the individual's inner
creativity. I would suggest that the effect on the individual who holds
it cannot be other than to inhibit creativeness and induce inner
sterility, if, indeed, the attitude itself does not originate in these very
qualities.

I do not say that the two things which Mr. Eliot desires, that
is, a true sense of cultural continuity and a socially accepted ortho-

doxy, are undesirable things. On the contrary. Within such a framework the original individual should be able to give expression to his creative energies, perhaps more freely than where there is complete outward anarchy of values, while from a purely social point of view the advantage to the community through the enrichment of common life would be considerable. We need hardly fear that personal originality would be overcome or crushed under a socially approved structure of belief, thought and behaviour if that structure is a valid approximation to the structure of reality itself. It is the inverted, regressive, uncreative attitude of Eliot towards these things which is to be condemned, not the things themselves. The creative spirit must be strong enough not to hanker after an external system which will take the load of responsibility from off his shoulders, for the reason that if any such system is to arise it can only be as an outcome, an end-product, of original personal creative effort. The modern artist who longs impotently for a time when he can be released from interior struggle in order to take his values outwardly from external society only reveals his own inner bankruptcy. Authentic human existence depends, at the source, upon those creative "originals" whose task is to be a fountain and source of values for society, that is, for the multitude of echoing "copies." And their concern must be, not with the ultimate social consequence of creativeness, but with the immediate urgencies of creative activity itself.

# KARL SHAPIRO *

ELIOT began with count of eye, but early
    (We hear of his destroying couplets) turned
To more immediate music. One corrective
He introduced, the even step of French,
Opened a window on the Parisian schools
Which at the same time looked upon the English
For an exchange of form; an old artesian
Spring began to flow between these tongues,
Replenishing both. Yet this was incidental
To the main tide of metric. Poets abroad
Were all establishing prose cadences
In rime, some we have seen with ruinous
Effect and Eliot and a skillful few
With revolutionary success. The clean
Conversational voice of the American
Once and for all outlawed the late-Victorian
Lilt. Tennyson, Swinburne and the like
Went down, their age discredited by all
Who scorned the sweet Arthurian melancholy
Of smooth roundel and plaster elegy.

When it appears, the study of the music
Of *Ash Wednesday* should compel the minds of all
Poets; for in a hundred years no poem
Has sung itself so exquisitely well.
The frightened beauty of *The Hound of Heaven*
Is not the sister of this psalm that sings
In the ascendant voice of sad desire; but hear
How every step enjoins the heart to follow
Whether it will or not, or start or stop
Or turn again or kneel and genuflect.

* From ESSAY ON RIME, pp. 16–17, 22, 29, 40, 60–61, Copyright, 1945, by Karl Shapiro. Random House, Inc., New York.

And who will parse the broken measure of
*The Waste Land,* our world-weary masterpiece
In which the very metric tells the tale?
Who will devise the necessary scale
To read this rime as Milton's has been read?

. . . Eliot
Himself in the *Quartets* (in my opinion
His most depressing prosody) makes shift
Of rhythms one thought he had exhausted ten
Or fifteen years before . . .

Suspect the poet who wallows in symbology
And reinforces what he has to say
With "indigestible portions"; who takes phrases,
Sentences, paragraphs and passages
Into the soft gray matter of his brain
And over them secretes his nacreous pearl.
The prominent symbol of our verse is "bone."
How few successes lead our failures on.
In passing, let us mention Eliot
Whose influence on our rhetoric is as small
As his impact on our belief is great.
I cannot guess the cause, unless it is
That English as he uses it in rime
Is personal in the highest and best sense.
One would be rash to imitate a style
Which signs its name at every even pause. . . .

By nineteen twenty the thin ice of belief
Had cracked and given way. The figure-skater
Of rime had sunk beneath the lake, and art
Took on a deep and submarine aspect.
The corpse, the crawling rat, the bones, the wraith
Arrived in sequence; a whole world lay wrecked
And inundated. Prufrock filled with grief
And whimsical mockery walked along the beach,
Envied the crab and heard the mermaid sing.
He toyed with death by drowning, fascinated

Like Arnold by the ebbing Sea of Faith.
Nor did the watcher understand his plight
In its true character, for *The Hollow Men,*
*The Waste Land* and *The Hippopotamus*
All seemed the obituary of the spirit
For whose demise the worldly celebrants
Made this macabre music. What we know
In retrospect is that the prophet's eyes
Were turned toward the cathedral and the past
As toward a promise. But in the interim
Between his deep and masterly despair
And the overt fulfillment of his faith
His word was our poetic law. It is
Ironical that the monsters of his pen,
Sweeney and the young man carbuncular,
Should have enhanced our widespread disbelief
In one another. The younger men who saw
A theological Anglican emerge
From the familiar cracked sarcophagus
Thought it a yogi or a New England witch.
A dirge for him was sounded from the left;
All thought it hollow to pursue the strange
Pied Piper of despair to church. . . .

# T. H. THOMPSON *

A CHANCE remark of a friend of mine sent me back recently to a re-reading of Mr. Eliot's poems. And the re-reading in the light of that remark furnished me with a new interpretation of a certain aspect of his poetic labyrinth—an interpretation, I hope, sufficiently interesting to be included in the corpus of Eliotic criticism.

While out for a walk I had been quoting *Sweeney Among the Nightingales,* and when I came to the line:

> And sang within the bloody wood,

my friend interrupted me. He pointed out that the man who wrote the *Sacred Wood* could not possibly have written "bloody wood" in this poem. "Bloody" was the wrong word. It had no meaning here, even as a transferred epithet. I at once started to doubt my memory, but later on looking up the poem I found I had been right. It was "bloody wood." Eliot had written it, and must have done so purposely. I re-read all the poems, and in doing so made one vital discovery. I think I have solved the Sweeney problem.

Sweeney is a baffling person. He runs in and out poems like a naughty boy; scarcely offers an explanation of his conduct; and generally confounds critics by his bad manners and rude behaviour. Ah, say the critics, he is a symbol, and pass on. That is an easy way of getting over a difficulty, but it is untrue. Sweeney is anything but a symbol, very far from it, as I shall show in a moment.

The reason for the usual misinterpretation is largely due to Mr. Eliot's peculiar methods. He tries to write in three centuries at the same time. That is, he adopts the mind of a seventeenth century metaphysical poet to write twentieth century detective fiction with a romantic nineteenth century pen. The result is confusing. And that is precisely Mr. Eliot's object. By a brilliant piece of literary obfuscation, by skilfully ringing the changes with metaphysical and ro-

---

* *The Bloody Wood,* from *The London Mercury,* Vol. XXIX (January, 1934) pp. 233–239.

mantic, he has managed to embody in his poems a gruesome murder story without anyone being any wiser.

Sweeney of course is the central figure of the story, and the reader is the detective. From scattered hints and clues, from dark sayings and mysterious exclamations, we are left to unfold for ourselves the sordid little tale. What a search it is. It demands the greatest patience. Mr. Eliot plays a subtle game; drawing red herrings across our path; confronting us with quotations in many tongues; and adding notes to lead us astray. He does not try to make it easy for us. His object seems to be to produce a work more intricate and ingenious than the best Crime Club novel.

Let us look at the story: Sweeney, the hero of this murder drama, appears in five poems. Three times in the 1920 volume; in *The Waste Land;* and in the more recently published *Sweeney Agonistes.* These poems must be read as a sequence. He makes his bow in a poem called *Sweeney Erect.* The poem opens with all the Miltonic stops out; a grand piece of rhetoric, rich in subtle allusions so beloved by the Alexandrians. The raging seas of the Aegean are before us, and Ariadne deserted by her lover stands in the gales on her lonely island. This is the text of the poem—woman forsaken. Then follows a fragmentary allusion to Homer: (Nausicaa and Polypheme).

This flickering reference at once suggests to the reader the voyage of Odysseus, man the wanderer. As Theseus' perjured sails hasten from Ariadne, so Odysseus is torn from Nausicaa. Nausicaa and Polypheme, Beauty and the Beast. Man the wanderer encounters both. Every word of the two opening stanzas is overcharged with meaning. But we must not delay. The next line introduces us to Sweeney. It is morning and he is getting out of bed:

> Gesture of orang-outang
> Rises from the sheets in steam

Sweeney, the modern Polyphemus, shakes off sleep in Mrs. Turner's brothel. He is not a beautiful specimen. We see him a gross featured creature, stretching and clawing at the pillow slip. His movements are bestial and his knowledge is circumscribed by sex, for we learn:

> He knows the female temperament.

He appears to be a man for the ladies. (O Ariadne! O Nausicaa!) And this is later confirmed by the dramatically enigmatic conclusion of the poem. The razor; the hysterical woman in bed; the chatter of the ladies in the corridor; Mrs. Turner fussily righteous; and finally Doris, as *dea ex machina,* entering from the bath-room with a glass of brandy. At the end we are left dizzy and bewildered. What exactly did happen? What is it all about? I think we can safely say from the data at our disposal that the Ariadne theme, that of the injured or forsaken woman, has been played in Mrs. Turner's house, and that Sweeney has been responsible. He has brought tragedy to this little world of women, and as Mrs. Turner says, it does the house no sort of good. But the full nature of the tragedy we have yet to discover. And who is Ariadne?

The next reference to Sweeney is surprising. In a poem entitled *Mr. Eliot's Sunday Morning Service* he is introduced in an abrupt and unexpected fashion. While Mr. Eliot is pursuing his devotions, but not, as he himself admits, with absorbed attention, we are told that:

> Sweeney shifts from ham to ham
> Stirring the water in his bath.

Now what can we make of this inappropriate snapshot produced in the middle of a Church Service? The reader blinks, perplexed, and unless he remembers he is reading a detective story, he dismisses the lines as pointless. But notice two things: we are definitely told that Sweeney has a bath on Sunday morning—probably in the very room Doris has just vacated: but more important, we gather that while having his bath he debated some difficult problem with himself. He was in meditative mood. He "shifts from ham to ham"; he "stirs the water." The actions of a man in serious thought. If it were an ordinary bath he would splash the water, not stir it; he would sing, not shift from ham to ham. Yes, he has something on his mind. But the whole sinister significance of the incident is not yet apparent. We shall hear more of that Sunday morning bath.

The last poem in the 1920 volume is devoted to Sweeney. Mr. Eliot does his best to confuse us here. He draws all kinds of red herrings across our path; he disguises Sweeney till he resembles a character from *Alice in Wonderland*—(his ape neck swells into a giraffe)—he talks Greek to us; he introduces Hebrews who wear Spanish capes; he also puts us off the scent by saying that Sweeney is among the nightingales, which of course is fantastically untrue. Our hero is drinking with the cosmopolitan crowd in the inn, and does not worry about nightingales. He is no little St. Francis as the title of the poem would suggest, though Mr. Eliot would have us believe so. No, Sweeney's visit to the Inn near the Convent of the Sacred Heart has nothing to do with nightingales. They are red herrings and are used to throw dust in our eyes. The motive for his visit will be revealed in time.

Mention of the nightingales, however, brings us to our initial problem, the problem of the "bloody wood" in which they sang. What was Mr. Eliot's meaning? The adjective is so precise that it stamps the wood with a distinct identity. To casual readers it may suggest little, but actually it has a deep significance. The "bloody wood" stands on the threshold of that grim poetic vault "The Waste Land." It is a suburb. That is, a place of horror. A suburb of the Waste Land. In this wood, life is found in its rawest, lowest, most lustful state. Here was the home of our primitive ancestors, some of whose fierce blood passions can cut through the trappings of civilization and visit us even today. Here was Agamemnon murdered, and beasts of prey like Sweeney hunt in its thickets and tear their victims with their claws. The "bloody wood" therefore is the dwelling of atavistic recollections, where man the animal prowls, from which man the angel shrinks. Yet while the ape-man hunts, nightingales sing in the branches for those who have ears to hear.

From the "bloody wood" it is a short step into *The Waste Land,* Mr. Eliot's most important poem. Quite unexpectedly Sweeney makes a sudden intrusion as he did on an earlier occasion during a Sunday morning service. In Part 3, *The Fire Sermon* we read:

> But at my back from time to time I hear
> The sound of horns and motors, which shall bring
> Sweeney to Mrs. Porter in the spring.
> O the moon shone bright on Mrs. Porter
> And on her daughter
> They wash their feet in soda water
> Et O ces voix d'enfants, chantant dans la coupole!

And the next lines are startling:

> Twit twit twit
> Jug jug jug jug jug jug
> So rudely forc'd.
> Tereu

It is the chant of the nightingales singing in the "bloody wood" while the children sing in French in the Convent of the Sacred Heart near by. It is a complete echo from the previous poem. Sweeney meanwhile, oblivious of the singing around him, accompanied by the sound of motor horns, hurries on his way to visit a new love, a Mrs. Porter, whose amazing ablutions appear to have won his regard. This is an important development in the Sweeney story. Observe that Mrs. Turner's brothel no longer attracts him. He is a fickle ape. Observe also that Mrs. Porter must be a woman of means if she can afford to use soda water for washing purposes. Lastly observe that Mrs. Porter has a daughter.

The scene for the tragedy is laid. Sweeney arrives in a motor car on a moonlight night in spring at the home of these unsuspecting women. He plays the role of the wealthy lover. The ladies wash their feet. Sweeney prepares his plan. All the most evil passions of "the bloody wood" are aroused. The nightingales wail plaintively. Then:

> So rudely forced.
> Tereu.

That is all. If Mr. Eliot had said no more about it the whole thing would have remained wrapped in mystery for ever, and we should never have known what happened at Mrs. Porter's, or who was rudely forced. But in *Sweeney Agonistes,* a publication which appeared ten years after *The Waste Land,* the details of the crime are revealed to us, and it is Sweeney himself who makes a personal confession. For the first time we hear the genuine accents of a beast of the "bloody wood," and his words are like his physical form, gross, revolting, bestial.

Once more we find ourselves back in Mrs. Turner's brothel. Doris and Dusty, two of the ladies, are entertaining some Americans. Then Sweeney enters. He is apparently very drunk. His first remark to Doris, the woman who had been so helpful with her brandy on his last visit here, is cruel but characteristic:

> I'll carry you off
> To a cannibal isle.

The latent ferocity of the "bloody wood" is in these words, they denote the primitive, the barbaric, the uncivilised. Evidently Doris has annoyed him and he retaliates by showing his claws. He will eat her, he says. A little later he defines life as:

> Birth, and copulation, and death.

This is the orang-outang speaking, the apenecked giraffe, as he shuffles in the stench of the "bloody wood."

Meanwhile the other guests in Maison Turner, inspired by, or resenting Sweeney's morbid talk, strike up a song of an aphrodisiac nature to excite the girls, but Doris remains unmoved. Sweeney breaks in once more. He has altered his definition of life, perhaps the singing of the Americans has upset him. He now asserts, "Life is death." After which profound statement he embarks upon a gloomy recitation of a murder story, shocking the reader and spoiling the merry evening at Mrs. Turner's:

> I knew a man once did a girl in
> Any man might do a girl in
> Any man has to, needs to, wants to
> Once in a lifetime, do a girl in.
> Well he kept her there in a bath.
> With a gallon of lysol in a bath.

At once the attentive reader becomes alert. His memory switches back to a scene at Mrs. Turner's months before: the flashing razor; the shrieking woman in bed; Doris rushing in with the brandy. And also that sinister bathroom incident inserted in the poem on Mr. Eliot's Sunday Morning Service: Sweeney stirring the water in his bath while the poet prayed. And also that visit to Mrs. Porter on a spring night while she and her daughter were washing their feet, probably in their bathroom. This wild story has the appearance of a confession. A chain of clues rises before us.

But to continue: apparently the man having drowned the girl in a bath lived in the same house with the corpse for two months and eventually hounded by the furies of conscience went mad. As Sweeney recites this sorry tale he grows more and more excited and incoherent, and finally drifts into drunken madness:

> We're gona sit here and drink this booze
> We're gona sit here and have a tune
> We're gona stay and we're gona go
> And somebody's gotta pay the rent.

At this point Doris interrupts with three simple but pregnant words:

I know who.

Now obviously this is not the answer to the wild drunken effusions that Sweeney has just belched into the air. No, she conveys very clearly, and Sweeney realises it, that she knows who is the man that did the girl in. He quickly silences her by saying:

That's nothing to me and nothing to you.

He does not wish her to give away any secrets in public. But it is too late. Even if the American guests don't know, we do. We see Sweeney in his true proportions, a self-confessed murderer. Having collected the evidence we are now at liberty to trace the whole story which Mr. Eliot has so cunningly concealed in his poems.

Sweeney, a licentious libertine of Irish-American extraction domiciled in London, had a lady friend, a Miss Ariadne Porter, who was employed at the time of their liaison in a house of ill fame under Mrs. Turner's efficient management. Miss Porter must have acquired an absorbing affection for her lover, which at length became irksome to him; for he threatened to desert her. Hysterics followed, and Sweeney, influenced by the morbid idea that every man in his time should kill a woman, proceeded to threaten his pretty mistress with a razor. Her screams roused the house, and Doris opportunely intervened and prevented his murderous intention, thereby earning his ingratitude. In his bath on Sunday morning Sweeney meditated on possibilities of ridding himself of the tiresome Ariadne, and the bath suggested a solution—he would drown her. Ariadne meanwhile frightened of his rough usage had fled to the home of her mother, Mrs. Porter, where she lay in hiding for awhile. Sweeney in dudgeon withdrew his allegiance from Mrs. Turner and took to frequenting the Inn near the Convent. It was here he met Ariadne again. One gloomy night he saw her conversing indistinctly with the innkeeper at the door. He made inquiries, found out where she lived, and pursued her in his motor car (the whole passage is associated with ideas of pursuit). He found Ariadne and her mother washing themselves with soda water. Note the significance of this episode: the poor girl who washed in soda water by moonlight was soon to have a bath with a gallon of lysol. The moonlight innocence of the soda water is contrasted with the horror of the lysol to follow.

As the nightingales tell us Sweeney "rudely forced" his way in and committed the act he had premeditated. The "rudely forced" passage may refer to the actual immersion of Miss Porter, and the line which immediately precedes it:

Jug jug jug jug jug jug

would then represent onomatopoetically the sound of the lysol being poured into the bath from a jug.

Of Mrs. Porter's reactions to all this we are told nothing. She may have fled for refuge to the Convent of the Sacred Heart, or again she may be that mad woman who appears later in *The Waste Land* using her hair for fiddle strings. There is no direct evidence for either theory, but both are conceivable. We trust the first mentioned is the true one.

After the crime Sweeney established himself in the house. Mrs. Porter, as we have mentioned before, was a woman of comfortable income. Sweeney at once appropriated her money which he used for paying the rent collector and the milkman; milk appears to have been his staple diet during the two months he lived there. But he was unable to dispose of the body in the bath, and this got on his nerves. Probably the first irritation was caused by finding the bath occupied on Sunday morning, his usual time for practising the ritual of cleanliness. But as the weeks passed he grew worse and worse, he began to brood and conscience played havoc with him.

At last overwhelmed by the torment in his mind and lacerated by the whips and scourges of the Furies he crept back, half mad, half drunk, to Mrs. Turner's brothel. The wheel has come full circle. The pink broad-bottomed ape who rose from bed here lustily one morning over two months before, has returned a drivelling lunatic at night to die. We know the rest. How he insulted Doris; how prompted by bravado or despair he gave details of the murder; how Doris at once guessed his meaning, and how in the words "I know who" she passed on the secret to the world at large. Amid the noise of laughter from the brothel and an imperative knocking at the door Sweeney passes out of the poem.

Such is his story. A story which will intrigue all readers of detective fiction by its subtlety, finesse, and cunning air of mystification. Yet the last word may not have been spoken. Sweeney is a wily person and sufficiently elusive to dodge an English hangman. Who knows, he may have returned to New York with Mr. Klipstein and Mr. Krumpacker; he may still live to trouble and delight us with a few more graceful antics, perhaps on Broadway this time or among the whippoorwills.

# EDMUND WILSON *

I HAVE noted the similarity between the English seventeenth-century poets and the French nineteenth-century Symbolists. The poetry of T. S. Eliot has, in our own time, brought together these two traditions, as it is Eliot who, so far as I know, has for the first time called attention to their resemblance. "The form," he says, "in which I began to write, in 1908 or 1909, was directly drawn from the study of Laforgue together with the later Elizabethan drama; and I do not know anyone who started from exactly that point."

I have so far, in discussing the early Symbolists, spoken chiefly of Mallarmé. But T. S. Eliot derived, as he indicates, from a different branch of the Symbolist tradition. In 1873 there had appeared in Paris a book of poems called "Les Amours Jaunes," by a writer who signed himself Tristan Corbière. "Les Amours Jaunes" was received with complete indifference, and scarcely more than a year after it appeared, the author died of consumption. Only thirty at the time of his death, Tristan Corbière had been an eccentric and very maladjusted man: he was the son of a sea captain who had also written sea stories and he had had an excellent education, but he chose for himself the life of an outlaw. In Paris, he slept all day and spent the nights in the cafés or at his verses, greeting at dawn the Paris harlots as they emerged from the station house or the hotel with the same half-harsh, half-tender fellow-feeling for the exile from conventional society which, when he was at home in his native Brittany, caused him to flee the house of his family and seek the company of the customs-men and sailors—living skeleton and invalid as he was, performing prodigies of courage and endurance in the navigation of a little cutter which he sailed by preference in the worst possible weather. He made a pose of his unsociability and of what he considered his physical ugliness, at the same time that he undoubtedly suffered over them. Melancholy, with a feverishly active mind, full of groanings and vulgar jokes, he used to amuse himself by going

* T. S. Eliot, from AXEL'S CASTLE, pp. 93–131, Copyright, 1931,
Copyright, © 1959 by Edmund Wilson

about in convict's clothes and by firing guns and revolvers out the window in protest against the singing of the village choir; and on one occasion, on a visit to Rome, he appeared in the streets in evening dress, with a mitre on his head and two eyes painted on his forehead, leading a pig decorated with ribbons. And Corbière's poetry was a poetry of the outcast: often colloquial and homely, yet with a rhetoric of fantastic slang; often with the manner of slapdash doggerel, yet sure of its own morose artistic effects; full of the parade of romantic personality, yet incessantly humiliating itself with a self-mockery scurrilous and savage, out of which, as Huysmans said, would sometimes rise without warning "a cry of sharp pain like the breaking of a 'cello string"—Corbière's verse brought back into French poetry qualities which had been alien to its spirit since François Villon's day.

So outlandish did Corbière appear even from the point of view of the Romantics that he was dismissed, when he was noticed at all, as not merely unseemly but insane—till Paul Verlaine, in 1883, did him honor in a series of articles, "Les Poètes Maudits," which was one of the important critical events in the development of Symbolism. Verlaine himself, a more accomplished artist, but a less original and interesting personality, had been strongly influenced by "Les Amours Jaunes"—he seems, indeed, to have caught over from Corbière, not only certain artistic effects, but even something of his own poetic personality, his peculiar accent of wistful naïveté: compare Corbière's "Rondels pour Après" with Verlaine's sonnet which begins, "L'espoir luit comme un brin de paille dans l'étable"; or "Paria" with "Casper Hauser."

But another French poet, Jules Laforgue, nineteen years younger than Corbière, had independently developed a tone and technique— poignant-ironic, grandiose-slangy, scurrilous-naïve—which had much in common with Corbière's. Laforgue was the son of a schoolmaster and, for all his nonchalance in handling rudely the conventions of French poetry, much more a professional man of letters than Corbière. Laforgue even errs through preciosity in his fashion; what with Corbière seems a personal and inevitable, if eccentric, manner of speech, in Laforgue sounds self-conscious and deliberate, almost sometimes a literary exercise. He was tubercular, as Corbière was also, and dead at twenty-seven—and his gentleness and sadness are still those of a sick well-cared-for child; his asperities, his surprising images, his coquetries, his cynicism, and his impudence, are still those of a clever schoolboy. Laforgue's friends procured him a post as reader to the Empress Augusta of Germany; and, falling under the spell of German philosophy, he brought its jargon into his verse, contributing thereby to Symbolism perhaps the one element of obscurity which it had lacked.

Yet Laforgue is a very fine poet and one of the most remarkable of the Symbolists. He and Corbière had introduced a new variety of vocabulary and a new flexibility of feeling. With Mallarmé, it may be said that, on the whole, it is the imagery, not the feeling, which is variable: though sometimes playful, he is classical in the sense (as Yeats and Valéry are) that he sustains a certain grandeur of tone. But it is from the conversational-ironic, rather than from the serious-æsthetic, tradition of Symbolism that T. S. Eliot derives. Corbière and Laforgue are almost everywhere in his early work. The emphatic witty quatrains of Corbière, with their sudden lapses into tenderness or pathos, are heard again in the satiric verse of Eliot: a poem like "Mr. Eliot's Sunday Morning Service" would hardly, one imagines, have been written without Corbière's "Rapsodie Foraine." And as "Conversation Galante" derives clearly from certain poems in Laforgue's "Complaintes" and "Imitation de Notre-Dame la Lune," so the more elaborate "Portrait of a Lady" and "The Love Song of J. Alfred Prufrock" follow closely the longer poems of Laforgue. Compare the conclusion of "Mr. Prufrock" with the conclusion of the early version of Laforgue's poem "Légende":

I grow old . . . I grow old . . .
I shall wear the bottoms of my trousers rolled.

Shall I part my hair behind? Do I dare to eat a peach?
I shall wear white flannel trousers, and walk upon the beach.
I have heard the mermaids singing, each to each.

I do not think that they will sing to me.

I have seen them riding seaward on the waves
Combing the white hair of the waves blown back
When the wind blows the water white and black.

We have lingered in the chambers of the sea
By sea-girls wreathed with seaweed red and brown
Till human voices wake us, and we drown.

. . .

Hier l'orchestre attaqua
Sa dernière polka

Oh! L'automme, l'automme!
  Les casinos
  Qu'on abandonne
  Remisent leurs pianos! . . .

Phrases, verroteries,
Caillots de souvenirs.
Oh! comme elle est maigrie!
Que vais-je devenir? . . .

Adieu! Les filles d'ifs dans les grisailles
Ont l'air de pleureuses de funerailles
Sous l'autan noir qui veut que tout s'en aille.

        Assez, assez,
    C'est toi qui as commencé.

Va, ce n'est plus l'odeur de tes fourrures.
Va, vos moindres clins d'yeux sont des parjures.
Tais-toi, avec vous autres rien ne dure.

        Tais-toi, tais-toi,
    On n'aime qu'une fois . . .

Here it will be seen that Eliot has reproduced Laforgue's irregular metrical scheme almost line for line. Furthermore, the subject of Laforgue's poem—the hesitations and constraints of a man either too timid or too disillusioned to make love to a woman who provokes his ironic pity at the same time that she stirs gusts of stifled emotion —has a strong resemblance to the subjects of "Mr. Prufrock" and the "Portrait of a Lady." And in another poem, "La Figlia Che Piange," Eliot has adapted a line of Laforgue's: "Simple et sans foi comme un bonjour"—"Simple and faithless as a smile and shake of the hand." He has even brought over into English some of the unstressed effect of French verse: how different, for example, is the alexandrine of Eliot's just quoted from the classical English alexandrine "which like a wounded snake drags its slow length along" or "with sparkless ashes loads an unlamented urn." (In his exhaustive "Influence du Symbolisme Français sur la Poésie Américaine de 1910 à 1920," M. René Taupin has shown the influence of Gautier also in Eliot's satiric poems: "The Hippopotamus," it appears, is almost a transcript of a hippopotamus by Gautier, and the "Grishkin is nice" passage in

"Whispers of Immortality" repeats a "Carmen est maigre" of Gautier.)

It must not be supposed, however, that Eliot is not original or that he is not the equal of either of his masters. Those longer and more elaborate poems—"Derniers Vers" in the collected edition—which Laforgue was constructing at the time of his death out of more fragmentary and less mature work are certainly his most important performances: through his masterly flexibility of vocabulary and metric, he has here achieved one of the definitive expressions of the pathetic-ironic, wordly-æsthetic moods of the *fin de siècle* temperament. Yet, though Eliot has, in certain obvious respects, applied Laforgue's formula so faithfully, he cannot properly be described as an imitator because he is in some ways a superior artist. He is more mature than Laforgue ever was, and his workmanship is perfect in a way that Corbière's and Laforgue's were rarely. T. S. Eliot's peculiar distinction lies, as Clive Bell has said, in his "phrasing." Laforgue's images are often far-fetched and inappropriately grotesque: his sins in this respect are really very closely akin to those of the English metaphysical poets; but Eliot's taste is absolutely sure—his images always precisely right. And the impression that Eliot leaves, even in these earliest poems, is clear, vivid and unforgettable: we do not subordinate him to his Symbolist predecessors any more than, when we find him, as in "Gerontion," writing in the rhythms of late Elizabethan blank-verse, we associate him with Middleton or Webster.

When we come to examine Eliot's themes, we recognize something which we have found already in Laforgue, but which appears in Eliot in a more intense form. One of the principal preoccupations of Flaubert—a great hero of Eliot's, as of Eliot's fellow-poet, Ezra Pound's—had been the inferiority of the present to the past: the Romantics had discovered the possibilities of the historical imagination; with their thirst for boldness, grandeur, and magnificence, they had located these qualities in past epochs—especially the Middle Ages and the Renaissance. And Flaubert, who shared with the Romantics this appetite for the gorgeous and the untamed, but who constrained himself, also, to confront the actual nineteenth-century world, pursued two parallel lines of fiction which lent significance and relief to each other. On the one hand, he reconstructed, in "Salammbô" and in "La Tentation de Saint-Antoine," the splendid barbarities of the pagan world and the heroic piety of the early Christian; and on the other, he caricatured, in "Madame Bovary," in "L'Education Sentimentale" and in "Bouvard et Pécuchet," the pusillanimity and mediocrity of contemporary bourgeois France. This whole point of view of Flaubert's—summed up, as it were, in "Trois Contes," where the three periods are contrasted in one book—was profoundly to affect modern literature. We shall find it later on in Joyce; but in the meantime we must note its reappearance in the poetry of Eliot. Eliot, like Flaubert, feels at every turn that human life is now ignoble, sordid or tame, and he is haunted and tormented by intimations that it has once been otherwise. In "Burbank with a Baedeker: Bleistein with a Cigar," the young American tourist in Venice, superseded in his affair with the Princess Volupine by a vulgar Austrian Jew, meditates on the clipped wings and pared claws of the Lion of St. Mark's, the symbol of the old arrogant Venice and of the world where such a city was possible. In "A Cooking Egg," the poet demands, after a call upon a very mild, dull spinster: "Where are the eagles and the trumpets?" and himself returns the saddened answer: "Buried beneath some snow-deep Alps." In "Lune de Miel," the Middle Western American travellers, stifled with the summer heat and devoured by the bedbugs of Ravenna, are contrasted with the noble crumbling beauty of the old Byzantine church less than a league away, of which they are totally unaware and to which they have apparently no relation; and in "Mr. Eliot's Sunday Morning Service," the combined grossness and aridity of the modern clergymen is contrasted with the pure and fresh religious feeling of a picture of the baptism of Christ by "a painter of the Umbrian school." In the best and most effective of these poems, "Sweeney Among the Nightingales," the poet, during a drowsy, idiotic and mildly sinister scene in some low dive, where two of the girls are supposed to be plotting against one of the men, remembers, at the sound of nightingales singing, the murder of Agamemnon in Æschylus:

> The host with someone indistinct
> Converses at the door apart,
> The nightingales are singing near
> The Convent of the Sacred Heart,
>
> And sang within the bloody wood
> When Agamemnon cried aloud,
> And let their liquid siftings fall
> To stain the stiff dishonoured shroud.

The present is more timid than the past: the bourgeois are afraid to let themselves go. The French had been preoccupied with this idea ever since the first days of Romanticism; but Eliot was to deal with the theme from a somewhat different point of view, a point of view characteristically American. For T. S. Eliot, though born in St. Louis, comes from a New England family and was educated at Harvard; and he is in some ways a typical product of our New England civilization. He is distinguished by that combination of practical prudence with moral idealism which shows itself in its later developments as an excessive fastidiousness and scrupulousness. One of the principal subjects of Eliot's poetry is really that regret at situations unexplored, that dark rankling of passions inhibited, which has figured so conspicuously in the work of the American writers of New England and New York from Hawthorne to Edith Wharton. T. S. Eliot, in this respect, has much in common with Henry James. Mr. Prufrock and the poet of the "Portrait of a Lady," with their helpless consciousness of having dared too little, correspond exactly to the middle-aged heroes of "The Ambassadors" and "The Beast in the Jungle," realizing sadly too late in life that they have been living too cautiously and too poorly. The fear of life, in Henry James, is closely bound up with the fear of vulgarity. And Eliot, too, fears vulgarity—which he embodies in the symbolic figure of "Apeneck Sweeney"—at the same time that he is fascinated by it. Yet he chafes at the limitations and pretenses of the culture represented by Boston—a society "quite uncivilized," as he says, "but refined beyond the point of civilization." He has some amusing satiric poems about old New England ladies—in one of which he reflects on his way to the house of his Cousin Harriet, how

> . . . evening quickens faintly in the street,
> Wakening the appetites of life in some
> And to others bringing the *Boston Evening Transcript*.

And the "Portrait of a Lady," whether the scene be laid in Boston or in London, is essentially a poem of that New England society "refined beyond the point of civilization": from the Lady, who serves tea among lighted candles—"an atmosphere of Juliet's tomb"—with her dampening efforts at flattery and flirtation through the medium of cultured conversation—her slightly stale and faded gush about Chopin and her memories of Paris in the spring—the poet is seized with an impulse to flee:

I take my hat: how can I make a cowardly amends
For what she has said to me?
You will see me any morning in the park
Reading the comics and the sporting page.
Particularly I remark
An English countess goes upon the stage,
A Greek was murdered at a Polish dance,
Another bank defaulter has confessed.
I keep my countenance,
I remain self-possessed
Except when a street piano, mechanical and tired,
Reiterates some worn-out common song
With the smell of hyacinths across the garden
Recalling things that other people have desired.

But he is always debating things with his conscience: his incurable moral solicitude makes him wonder:

Are these ideas right or wrong?

So Mr. Prufrock in the room where
                . . . women come and go
            Talking of Michelangelo,

wistfully asks himself:

Shall I say, I have gone at dusk through narrow streets
And watched the smoke that rises from the pipes
Of lonely men in shirt-sleeves, leaning out of windows? . . .

And Mr. Prufrock wonders also whether he should not put a question to his lady—but he never gets to the point of putting it.


II

But Eliot's most complete expression of this theme of emotional starvation is to be found in the later and longer poem called "The Waste Land" (1922). The Waste Land of the poem is a symbol borrowed from the myth of the Holy Grail: it is a desolate and sterile country ruled by an impotent king, in which not only have the crops ceased to grow and the animals to reproduce, but the very human inhabitants have become incapable of having children. But this sterility we soon identify as the sterility of the Puritan temperament. On the first pages we find again the theme of the girl with the hyacinths (themselves a symbol for the rearisen god of the fertility rites who will save the rainless country from drouth) which has already figured in "La Figlia Che Piange" and "Dans le Restaurant"—a memory which apparently represents for the poet some fulfillment foregone in youth and now agonizingly desired; and in the last pages it is repeated. We recognize throughout "The Waste Land" the peculiar conflicts of the Puritan turned artist: the horror of vulgarity and the shy sympathy with the common life, the ascetic shrinking from sexual experience and the distress at the drying up of the springs of sexual emotion, with the straining after a religious emotion which may be made to take its place.

Yet though Eliot's spiritual and intellectual roots are still more firmly fixed in New England than is, I believe, ordinarily understood, there is in "The Waste Land" a good deal more than the mere gloomy moods of a New Englander regretting an emotionally undernourished youth. The colonization by the Puritans of New England was merely an incident in that rise of the middle class which has brought a commercial-industrial civilization to the European cities as well as to the American ones. T. S. Eliot now lives in London and has become an English citizen; but the desolation, the æsthetic and spiritual drouth, of Anglo-Saxon middle-class society oppresses London as well as Boston. The terrible dreariness of the great modern cities is the atmosphere in which "The Waste Land" takes place—amidst this dreariness, brief, vivid images emerge, brief pure moments of feeling are distilled; but all about us we are aware of nameless millions performing barren office routines, wearing down their souls in interminable labors of which the products never bring them profit—people whose pleasures are so sordid and so feeble that they seem almost sadder than their pains. And this Waste Land has another aspect: it is a place not merely of desolation, but of anarchy and doubt. In our post-War world of shattered institutions, strained nerves and bankrupt ideals, life no longer seems serious or coherent—we have no belief in the things we do and consequently we have no heart for them.

The poet of "The Waste Land" is living half the time in the real world of contemporary London and half the time in the haunted wilderness of the mediæval legend. The water for which he longs in the twilight desert of his dream is to quench the spiritual thirst which torments him in the London dusk; and as Gerontion, "an old man in a dry month," thought of the young men who had fought in the rain, as Prufrock fancied riding the waves with mermaids and lingering in the chambers of the sea, as Mr. Apollinax has been imagined drawing strength from the deep sea-caves of coral islands —so the poet of "The Waste Land," making water the symbol of all freedom, all fecundity and flowering of the soul, invokes in desperate need the memory of an April shower of his youth, the song of the hermit thrush with its sound of water dripping and the vision of a drowned Phœnician sailor, sunk beyond "the cry of gulls and the deep sea swell," who has at least died by water, not thirst. The poet, who seems now to be travelling in a country cracked by drouth, can only feverishly dream of these things. One's head may be well stored with literature, but the heroic prelude of the Elizabethans has ironic echoes in modern London streets and modern London drawing-rooms: lines remembered from Shakespeare turn to jazz or refer themselves to the sound of phonographs. And now it is one's personal regrets again—the girl in the hyacinth-garden—"the awful daring of a moment's surrender which an age of prudence can never retract" —the key which turned once, and once only, in the prison of inhibition and isolation. Now he stands on the arid plain again, and the dry-rotted world of London seems to be crumbling about him—the poem ends in a medley of quotations from a medley of literatures— like Gérard de Nerval's "Desdichado," the poet is disinherited; like the author of the "Pervigilium Veneris," he laments that his song is mute and asks when the spring will come which will set it free like the swallow's; like Arnaut Daniel, in Dante, as he disappears in the refining fire, he begs the world to raise a prayer for his torment. "These fragments I have shored against my ruins."

"The Waste Land," in method as well as in mood, has left Laforgue far behind. Eliot has developed a new technique, at once laconic, quick, and precise, for representing the transmutations of thought, the interplay of perception and reflection. Dealing with subjects complex in the same way as those of Yeats's poem "Among School-Children" and Valéry's "Cimetière Marin," Eliot has found for them a different language. As May Sinclair has said of Eliot, his "trick of cutting his corners and his curves makes him seem obscure when he is clear as daylight. His thoughts move very rapidly and by astounding cuts. They move not by logical stages and majestic roundings of the full literary curve, but as live thoughts move in live brains." Let us examine, as an illustration, the lovely nightingale passage from "The Waste Land." Eliot is describing a room in London:

> Above the antique mantel was displayed
> As though a window gave upon the sylvan scene
> The change of Philomel, by the barbarous king
> So rudely forced; yet there the nightingale
> Filled all the desert with inviolable voice
> And still she cried, and still the world pursues,
> "Jug Jug" to dirty ears.

That is, the poet sees, above the mantel, a picture of Philomela changed to a nightingale, and it gives his mind a moment's swift release. The picture is like a window opening upon Milton's earthly paradise—the "sylvan scene," as Eliot explains in a note, is a phrase from "Paradise Lost"—and the poet associates his own plight in the modern city, in which some "infinitely gentle, infinitely suffering thing," to quote one of Eliot's earlier poems, is somehow being done to death, with Philomela, raped and mutilated by Tereus. But in the earthly paradise, there had been a nightingale singing: Philomela had wept her woes in song, though the barbarous king had cut out her tongue—her sweet voice had remained inviolable. And with a sudden change of tense, the poet flashes back from the myth to his present situation:

> And still she *cried,* and still the world *pursues,*
> "Jug Jug" to dirty ears.

The song of birds was represented in old English popular poetry by such outlandish syllables as "Jug Jug"—so Philomela's cry sounds to the vulgar. Eliot has here, in seven lines of extraordinary liquidity and beauty, fused the picture, the passage from Milton and the legend from Ovid, into a single moment of vague poignant longing.

"The Waste Land" is dedicated to Ezra Pound, to whom Eliot elsewhere acknowledges a debt; and he has here evidently been influenced by Pound's "Cantos." "The Waste Land," like the "Cantos," is fragmentary in form and packed with literary quotation and allusion. In fact, the passage just discussed above has a resemblance to a passage on the same subject—the Philomela-Procne myth—at the beginning of Pound's Fourth Canto. Eliot and Pound have, in fact, founded a school of poetry which depends on literary quotation and reference to an unprecedented degree. Jules Laforgue had sometimes parodied, in his poems, the great lines of other poets—

> O Nature, donne-moi la force et le courage
> De me croire en âge . . .

And Eliot had, in his early poetry, introduced phrases from Shakespeare and Blake for purposes of ironic effect. He has always, furthermore, been addicted to prefacing his poems with quotations and echoing passages from other poets. But now, in "The Waste Land," he carries this tendency to what one must suppose its extreme possible limit: here, in a poem of only four hundred and three lines (to which are added, however, seven pages of notes), he manages to include quotations from, allusions to, or imitations of, at least thirty-five different writers (some of them, such as Shakespeare and Dante, laid under contribution several times)—as well as several popular songs; and to introduce passages in six foreign languages, including Sanskrit. And we must also take into consideration that the idea of the literary medley itself seems to have been borrowed from still another writer, Pound. We are always being dismayed, in our general reading, to discover that lines among those which we had believed to represent Eliot's residuum of original invention had been taken over or adapted from other writers (sometimes very unexpected ones: thus, it appears now, from Eliot's essay on Bishop Andrewes, that the first five lines of "The Journey of the Magi," as well as the "word within a word, unable to speak a word" of "Gerontion," had been salvaged from Andrewes's sermons; and the "stiff dishonoured shroud" of "Sweeney Among the Nightingales" seems to be an echo of the "dim dishonoured brow" of Whittier's poem about Daniel Webster). One would be inclined *a priori* to assume that all this load of erudition and literature would be enough to sink any writer, and that such a production as "The Waste Land" must be a work of second-hand inspiration. And it is true that, in reading Eliot and Pound, we are sometimes visited by uneasy recollections of Ausonius, in the fourth century, composing Greek-and-Latin macaronics and piecing together poetic mosaics out of verses from Virgil. Yet Eliot manages to be most effective precisely—in "The Waste Land"—where he might be expected to be least original—he succeeds in conveying his meaning, in communicating his emotion, in spite of all his learned or mysterious allusions, and whether we understand them or not.

In this respect, there is a curious contrast between Eliot and Ezra Pound. Pound's work *has* been partially sunk by its cargo of erudition, whereas Eliot, in ten years' time, has left upon English poetry a mark more unmistakable than that of any other poet writing English. It is, in fact, probably true at the present time that Eliot is being praised too extravagantly and Pound, though he has deeply influenced a few, on the whole unfairly neglected. I should explain Eliot's greater popularity by the fact that, for all his fragmentary method, he possesses a complete literary personality in a way that Pound, for all his integrity, does not. Ezra Pound, a fine poet though he is, does not dominate us like a master imagination—he rather delights us like a miscellaneous collection of admirably chosen works of art. It is true that Pound, in spite of his inveterate translating, is a man of genuine originality—but his heterogeneous shorter poems, and the heterogeneous passages which go to make his longer ones, never seem to come together in a whole—as his general prose writing gives scrappy expression to a variety of ideas, a variety of enthusiasms and prejudices, some ridiculous and some valid, some learned and some half-baked, which, though valuable to his generation as polemic, as propaganda and as illuminating casual criticism, do not establish and develop a distinct reasoned point of view as Eliot's prose-writings do. T. S. Eliot has thought persistently and coherently about the relations between the different phases of human experience, and his passion for proportion and order is reflected in his poems. He is, in his way, a complete man, and if it is true, as I believe, that he has accomplished what he has credited Ezra Pound with accomplishing—if he has brought a new personal rhythm into the language—so that he has been able to lend even to the borrowed rhythms, the quoted words, of his great predecessors a new music and a new meaning—it is this intellectual completeness and soundness which has given his rhythm its special prestige.

Another factor which has probably contributed to Eliot's extraordinary success is the essentially dramatic character of his imagination. We may be puzzled by his continual preoccupation with the possibilities of a modern poetic drama—that is to say, of modern drama in verse. Why, we wonder, should he worry about drama in verse—why, after Ibsen, Hauptmann, Shaw and Chekov, should he be dissatisfied with plays in prose? We may put it down to an academic assumption that English drama ended when the blank verse of the Elizabethans ran into the sands, until it occurs to us that Eliot himself is really a dramatic poet. Mr. Prufrock and Sweeney are characters as none of the personages of Pound, Valéry or Yeats is—they have become a part of our modern mythology. And most of the best of Eliot's poems are based on unexpected dramatic contrasts: "The Waste Land" especially, I am sure, owes a large part of its power to its dramatic quality, which makes it peculiarly effective read aloud. Eliot has even tried his hand at writing a play, and the two episodes from "Wanna Go Home, Baby" which he has published in *The Criterion* seem rather promising. They are written in a sort of jazz dramatic metre which suggests certain scenes of John Howard Lawson's "Processional"; and there can be no question that the future of drama in verse, if it has any future, lies in some such direction. "We cannot reinstate," Eliot has written, "either blank verse or the heroic couplet. The next form of drama will have to be a verse drama, but in new verse forms. Perhaps the conditions of modern life (think how large a part is now played in our sensory life by the internal combustion engine!) have altered our perception of rhythms. At any rate, the recognized forms of speech-verse are not as efficient as they should be; probably a new form will be devised out of colloquial speech."

In any case, that first handful of Eliot's poems, brought out in the middle of the War (1917) and generally read, if at all, at the time, as some sort of modern *vers de société,* was soon found, as Wyndham Lewis has said, to have had the effect of a little musk that scents up a whole room. And as for "The Waste Land," it enchanted and devastated a whole generation. Attempts have been made to reproduce it—by Aldington, Nancy Cunard, etc.—at least a dozen times. And as Eliot, lately out of Harvard, assumed the rôle of the middle-aged Prufrock and to-day, at forty, in one of his latest poems, "The Song of Simeon," speaks in the character of an old man "with eighty years and no to-morrow"—so "Gerontion" and "The Waste Land" have made the young poets old before their time. In London, as in New York, and in the universities both here and in England, they for a time took to inhabiting exclusively barren beaches, cactus-grown deserts, and dusty attics overrun with rats—the only properties they allowed themselves to work with were a few fragments of old shattered glass or a sparse sprinkling of broken bones. They had purged themselves of Masefield as of Shelley for dry tongues and rheumatic joints. The dry breath of the Waste Land now blighted the most amiable country landscapes; and the sound of jazz, which had formerly seemed jolly, now inspired only horror and despair. But in this case, we may forgive the young for growing prematurely decrepit: where some of even the finest intelligences of the elder generation read "The Waste Land" with blankness or laughter, the young had recognized a poet.

III

As a critic, Eliot occupies to-day a position of distinction and influence equal in importance to his position as a poet. His writings have been comparatively brief and rare—he has published only four small books of criticism—yet he has probably affected literary opinion, during the period since the War, more profoundly than any other critic writing English. Eliot's prose style has a kind of felicity different from that of his poetic style; it is almost primly precise and sober, yet with a sort of sensitive charm in its austerity—closely reasoned and making its points with the fewest possible words, yet always even, effortless and lucid. In a reaction against the impressionistic criticism which flourished at the end of the century and which has survived into our own time—the sort of criticism which, in dealing with poetry, attempts to reproduce its effect by having recourse to poetic prose—T. S. Eliot has undertaken a kind of scientific study of æsthetic values: avoiding impressionistic rhetoric and *a priori* æsthetic theories alike, he compares works of literature coolly and tries to distinguish between different orders of artistic effects and the different degrees of satisfaction to be derived from them.

And by this method, Eliot has done more than perhaps any other modern critic to effect a revaluation of English literature. We sometimes follow his literary criticism with the same sort of eagerness and excitement with which we follow a philosophical inquiry. Professor Saintsbury has played in literature much the same sort of rôle that he has played as a connoisseur of wines, that of an agreeable and entertaining guide of excellent taste and enormous experience; Edmund Gosse, often intelligent and courageous in dealing with French or Scandinavian writers, could never quite, when it came to English literature, bring himself to drop his official character of Librarian of the House of Lords—his attitude was always a little that of the Beef Eater in the Tower of London, who assumes the transcendent value of the Crown Jewels which he has been set to guard and does not presume to form a personal opinion as to their taste or their respective merits; and the moral passion of Paul Elmer More has ended by paralyzing his æsthetic appreciation. But T. S. Eliot, with an infinitely sensitive apparatus for æsthetic appreciation, approaching English literature as an American, with an American's peculiar combination of avidity and detachment and with more than the ordinary English critic's reading in the literatures, ancient and modern, of the Continent, has been able to succeed as few writers have done in the excessively delicate task of estimating English, Irish and American writers in relation to one another, and writers in English in relation to writers on the Continent. The extent of Eliot's influence is amazing: these short essays, sent out without publicity as mere scattered notes on literature, yet sped with so intense a seriousness and weighted with so wide a learning, have not only had the effect of discrediting the academic clichés of the text-books, but are even by way of establishing in the minds of the generation now in college a new set of literary clichés. With the ascendancy of T. S. Eliot, the Elizabethan dramatists have come back into fashion, and the nineteenth-century poets gone out. Milton's poetic reputation has sunk, and Dryden's and Pope's have risen. It is as much as one's life is worth nowadays, among young people, to say an approving word for Shelley or a dubious one about Donne. And as for the enthusiasm for Dante—to paraphrase the man in Hemingway's novel, there's been nothing like it since the Fratellinis!

Eliot's rôle as a literary critic has been very similar to Valéry's in France: indeed, the ideas of the two men and their ways of stating them have corresponded so closely that one guesses they must influence each other a good deal. Like Valéry, Eliot believes that a work of art is not an oracular outpouring, but an object which has been constructed deliberately with the aim of producing a certain effect. He has brought back to English criticism something of that trenchant rationalism which he admires in the eighteenth century, but with a much more catholic appreciation of different styles and points of view than the eighteenth century allowed. The Romantics, of course, fare badly before this criticism. Vague sentiment vaguely expressed, rhetorical effusion disguising bad art—these Eliot's laconic scorn has nipped. For him, Byron is "a disorderly mind, and an uninteresting one": Keats and Shelley "not nearly such great poets as they are supposed to be"; whereas the powers of Dryden are "wider, but no greater than those of Milton." Just as Valéry lately protested in a lecture that he was unable to understand the well known lines of Alfred de Musset:

> Les plus désespérés sont les chants les plus beaux,
> Et j'en sais d'immortels qui sont de purs sanglots.

so Eliot, in an essay on Crashaw, has confessed, with a certain superciliousness, his inability to understand the following stanza from Shelley's "Skylark":

> Keen as are the arrows
>   Of that silver sphere
> Whose intense lamp narrows
>   In the white dawn clear,
> Until we hardly see, who feel that it is there.

"For the first time, perhaps," says Eliot, "in verse of such eminence, sound exists without sense."

It will be seen that Eliot differs from Valéry in believing that poetry should make "sense." And he elsewhere, in his essay on Dante in "The Sacred Wood," remonstrates with Valéry for asserting that philosophy has no place in poetry. Yet Eliot's point of view, though more intelligently reasoned and expressed, comes down finally to the same sort of thing as Valéry's and seems to me open to the same sort of objection. Eliot's conclusion in respect to the relation of philosophy to poetry is that, though philosphy *has* its place in poetry, it is only as something which we "see" among the other things with which the poet presents us, a set of ideas which penetrate his world, as in the case of the "Divina Commedia": in the case of such a poet as Lucretius, the philosophy sometimes seems antagonistic to the poetry only because it happens to be a philosophy "not rich enough in feeling . . . incapable of complete expansion into pure vision." Furthermore, "the original form of philosophy cannot be poetic": the poet must use a philosophy already invented by somebody else. Now, though we may admire the justice of Eliot's judgments on the various degrees of artistic success achieved by Dante, Lucretius and others, it becomes plainer and plainer, as time goes on, that the real effect of Eliot's, as of Valéry's, literary criticism, is to impose upon us a conception of poetry as some sort of pure and rare æsthetic essence with no relation to any of the practical human uses for which, for some reason never explained, only the technique of prose is appropriate.

Now this point of view, as I have already suggested in writing about Paul Valéry, seems to me absolutely unhistorical—an impossible attempt to make æsthetic values independent of all the other values. Who will agree with Eliot, for example, that a poet cannot be an original thinker and that it is not possible for a poet to be a completely successful artist and yet persuade us to accept his ideas at the same time? There is a good deal in Dante's morality which he never got out of the Scholastics, as, for all we know, there may be a good deal in Lucretius which he never got out of Epicurus. When we read Lucretius and Dante, we are affected by them just as we are by prose writers of eloquence and imagination—we are compelled to take their opinions seriously. And as soon as we admit that prose writing may be considered on the same basis with verse, it becomes evident that we cannot, in the case of Plato, discriminate so finely as to the capacity of his philosophy for being "expanded into pure vision" that we are able to put our finger on the point where the novelist or poet stops and the scientist or metaphysician begins; nor, with Blake any more than with Nietzsche and Emerson, distinguish the poet from the aphorist. The truth is, of course, that, in Lucretius' time, verse was used for all sorts of didactic purposes for which we no longer consider it appropriate—they had agricultural poems, astronomical poems, poems of literary criticism. How can the "Georgics," the "Ars Poetica" and Manilius be dealt with from the point of view of the capacity of their material for being "expanded into pure vision"? To modern readers, the subjects of the "Georgics"—bee-keeping, stock-raising, and so forth—seem unsuitable and sometimes annoying in verse; yet for Virgil's contemporaries, the poem must have been completely successful—as, indeed, granted the subject, it is. Nor does it follow that, because we are coming to use poetry for fewer and fewer literary purposes, our critical taste is becoming more and more refined, so that we are beginning to perceive for the first time the true, pure and exalted function of poetry: that is, simply, as Valéry says, to produce a "state"—as Eliot says, to afford a "superior amusement." It is much more likely that for some reason or other, verse as a technique of

literary expression is being abandoned by humanity altogether—
perhaps because it is a more primitive, and hence a more barbarous
technique than prose. Is it possible to believe, for example, that Eliot's
hope of having verse reinstated on the stage—even verse of the new
kind which he proposes—is likely ever to be realized?

The tendency to keep verse isolated from prose and to confine
it to certain highly specialized functions dates in English at least
from the time of Coleridge, when, in spite of the long narrative poems
which were fashionable, verse was already beginning to fall into dis-
use. Coleridge defined a poem as "that species of composition which
is opposed to works of science by proposing for its *immediate* object
pleasure, not truth; and from all other species (having *this* object
in common with it), it is discriminated by proposing to itself such
delight from the *whole,* as is compatible with a distinct gratification
from each component part." Poe, who had doubtless read Coleridge
on the subject, wrote thirty years later that there was no such thing
as a long poem, that "no very long poem would ever be popular
again," etc. Eliot and Valéry follow Coleridge and Poe in their
theory as well as in their verse, and they seem to me to confuse certain questions by talking as if the whole of literature existed simultaneously in a vacuum, as if Homer's and Shakespeare's situations
had been the same as Mallarmé's and Laforgue's, as if the latter had
been attempting to play the same sort of rôles as the former and
could be judged on the same basis. It is inevitable, of course, that we
should try to arrive at absolute values through the comparison of the
work of different periods—I have just praised Eliot for his success
at this—but it seems to me that in this particular matter a good many
difficulties would be cleared up if certain literary discussions could
be removed from the artificially restricted field of verse—in which it is
assumed that nothing is possible or desirable but a quintessential distillation called "poetry," and that that distillation has nothing in common with anything possible to obtain through prose—to the field of
literature in general. Has not such a great modern novel as "Madame
Bovary," for example, at least as much in common with Virgil and
Dante as with Balzac and Dickens? Is it not comparable from the
point of view of intensity, music and perfection of the parts, with
the best verse of any period? And we shall consider Joyce in this
connection later.

With all gratitude, therefore, for the salutary effect of Eliot's earlier criticism in curbing the carelessness and gush of the aftermath of Romanticism, it seems plain that the anti-Romantic reaction is leading finally into pedantry and into a futile æstheticism. "Poetry," Eliot wrote in "The Sacred Wood," "is not a turning loose of emotion, but an escape from emotion; it is not the expression of personality, but an escape from personality. But, of course, only those who have personality and emotion know what it means to want to escape from them." This was valid, and even noble, in 1920 when "The Sacred Wood" was published; but to-day, aften ten years of depersonalized and over-intellectualized verse, so much of it written in imitation of Eliot, the same sort of thing in the mouths of Eliot's disciples sounds like an excuse for *not* possessing emotion and personality.

Yet, in spite of the weaknesses of Eliot's position as he has sometimes been driven to state it dogmatically, he has himself largely succeeded in escaping the vices which it seems to encourage. The old nineteenth century criticism of Ruskin, Renan, Taine, Sainte-Beuve, was closely allied to history and novel writing, and was also the vehicle for all sorts of ideas about the purpose and destiny of human life in general. The criticism of our own day examines literature, art, ideas and specimens of human society in the past with a detached scientific interest or a detached æsthetic appreciation which seems in either case to lead nowhere. A critic like Herbert Read makes dull discriminations between different kinds of literature; a critic like Albert Thibaudet discovers dull resemblances between the ideas of philosophers and poets; a critic like I. A. Richards writes about poetry from the point of view of a scientist studying the psychological reactions of readers; and such a critic as Clive Bell writes about painting so exclusively and cloyingly from the point of view of the varying degrees of pleasure to be derived from the pictures of different painters that we would willingly have Ruskin and all his sermonizing back. And even Virginia Woolf and Lytton Strachey have this in common with Clive Bell that they seem to feel they have done enough when they have distinguished the kind of pleasure to be derived from one kind of book, the kind of interest to be felt in one kind of personality, from the kind to be found in another. One is supposed to have read everything and enjoyed everything and to understand exactly the reasons for one's enjoyment, but not to enjoy anything excessively nor to raise an issue of one kind of thing against another. Each of the essays of Strachey or Mrs. Woolf, so compact yet so beautifully rounded out, is completely self-contained and does not lead to anything beyond itself; and finally, for all their brilliance, we begin to find them tiresome.

Now there is a good deal in T. S. Eliot of this pedantry and sterility of his age. He is very much given, for example, to becoming involved in literary Houses-that-Jack-Built: "We find this quality occasionally in Wordsworth," he will write, "but it is a quality which Wordsworth shares with Shenstone rather than with Collins and Gray. And for the right sort of enjoyment of Shenstone, we must read his prose as well as his verse. The 'Essays on Men and Manners' are in the tradition of the great French aphorists of the seventeenth century, and should be read with the full sense of their relation to Vauvenargues, La Rochefoucauld and (with his wider range) La Bruyère. We shall do well to read enough of Theophrastus to understand the kind of effect at which La Bruyère aimed. (Professor Somebody-or-other's book on 'Theophrastus and the Peripatetics' gives us the clew to the intellectual atmosphere in which Theophrastus wrote and enables us to gauge the influences on his work—very different from each other—of Plato and Aristotle.)" At this rate (though I have parodied Eliot), we should have to read the whole of literature in order to appreciate a single book, and Eliot fails to supply us with a reason why we should go to the trouble of doing so. Yet against the background of the criticism of his time, Eliot has stood out unmistakably as a man passionately interested in literature. The real intensity of his enthusiasm makes us forget the primness of his tone; and his occasional dogmatism is redeemed by his ability to see beyond his own ideas, his willingness to admit the relative character of his conclusions.

IV

But if Eliot, in spite of the meagreness of his production, has become for his generation a leader, it is also because his career has been a progress, because he has evidently been on his way somewhere, when many of his contemporaries, more prolific and equally gifted, have been fixed in their hedonism or despair. The poet of "The Waste Land" was too serious to continue with the same complacence as some of his contemporaries inhabiting that godforsaken desert. It was certain he would not stick at that point, and one watched him to see what he would do.

This destination has now, however, become plain. In the preface to the new 1928 edition of "The Sacred Wood," poetry is still regarded as a "superior amusement," but Eliot reports on his part "an expansion or development of interests." Poetry is now perceived to have "something to do with morals, and with religion, and even with politics perhaps, though we cannot say what." In "For Lancelot Andrewes," published in the same year, Eliot declares himself a classicist in literature, an Anglo-Catholic in religion and a royalist in politics, and announces that he has in preparation "three small books" treating of these subjects and to be called respectively "The School of Donne," "The Principles of Modern Heresy," and "The Outline of Royalism." There follows a slender selection of essays, which hint quietly at what may be expected.

We must await the further exposition of Eliot's new body of doctrine before it will be possible to discuss it properly. In the meantime, we can only applaud his desire to formulate a consistent central position, at the same time that we may regret the unpromising character of the ideals and institutions which he invokes. One cannot but recognize in Eliot's recent writings a kind of reactionary point of view which had already been becoming fashionable among certain sorts of literary people—a point of view which has much in common with that of the neo-Thomists in France and that of the Humanists in America. "Unless by civilization," writes Eliot, "you mean material progress, cleanliness, etc. . . . if you mean a spiritual co-ordination on a high level, then it is doubtful whether civilization can endure without religion, and religion without a church." Yet you can hardly have an effective church without a cult of Christ as the son of God; and you cannot have such a cult without more willingness to accept the supernatural than most of us to-day are able to muster. We feel in contemporary writers like Eliot a desire to believe in religious revelation, a belief that it would be a good thing to believe, rather than a genuine belief. The faith of the modern convert seems to burn only with a low blue flame. "Our literature," Eliot has himself recently made a character in a dialogue say, "is a substitute for religion, and so is our religion." From such a faith, uninspired by hope, unequipped with zeal or force, what guidance for the future can we expect?

One cannot, however, doubt the reality of the experience to which Eliot testifies in his recent writings—though it seems to us less an Anglo-Catholic conversion than a reawakening of the New

Englander's conscience, of the never quite exorcised conviction of the ineradicable sinfulness of man. Eliot admires Machiavelli because Machiavelli assumes the baseness of human nature as an unalterable fact; and he looks for light to the theologians who offer salvation, not through economic readjustment, political reform, education or biological and psychological study, but solely through "grace." Eliot apparently to-day regards "Evil" as some sort of ultimate reality, which it is impossible either to correct or to analyze. His moral principles seem to me stronger and more authentic than his religious mysticism—and his relation to the Anglo-Catholic Church appears largely artificial. The English seventeenth century divines whose poetry and sermons he admires so much, upon whom he seems so much to depend for nourishment, exist in a richer, a more mysterious, a more heavily saturated atmosphere, in which even monumental outlines are blurred; Eliot himself is stiffer and cooler, more intent, more relentless, more clear. He has his own sort of graciousness, but he seems, as the phrase is, a little thin-lipped. His religious tradition has reached him by way of Boston.

In any case, Eliot's new phase of piety has brought with it a new humility. He apologizes in his 1928 preface for the "assumption of pontifical solemnity" which he now detects in "The Sacred Wood," and his recent little book on Dante (a most admirable introduction) not merely surprises but almost embarrasses us by the modesty with which Eliot professes to desire nothing but to be of use to beginners and to tell us of a few of the beautiful things which he has found in the great poet. I will not say that this humility has enfeebled his poetry. The three devout little poems which he has published as Christmas cards since "The Hollow Men" announced the nadir of the phase of sterility and despair given such effective expression in "The Waste Land," seem comparatively uninspired; but the long poem or group of poems, "Ash-Wednesday" (1930), which follows a scheme somewhat similar to that of "The Waste Land," is a not unworthy successor to it.

The poet begins with the confession of his bankruptcy:

> Because I do not hope to turn again
> Because I do not hope
> Because I do not hope to turn
> Desiring this man's gift and that man's scope
> I no longer strive to strive towards such things

(Why should the agèd eagle stretch its wings?)
Why should I mourn
The vanished power of the usual reign? . . .

Because these wings are no longer wings to fly
But merely vans to beat the air
The air which is now thoroughly small and dry
Smaller and dryer than the will
Teach us to care and not to care
Teach us to sit still.

Pray for us sinners now and at the hour of our death
Pray for us now and at the hour of our death.

There follow passages in which the prayer is apparently answered: the
poet's contrition and pious resignation are rewarded by a series of
visions which first console then lighten his heart. We find an imagery
new for Eliot, a symbolism semi-ecclesiastical and not without a
Pre-Raphaelite flavor: white leopards, a Lady gowned in white, juni-
pers and yews, "The Rose" and "The Garden," and jewelled unicorns
drawing a gilded hearse: these are varied by an interlude which returns to the imagery and mood of "The Waste Land," and a swirling
churning anguished passage which suggests certain things of Gertrude Stein's. At last the themes of the first section recur: the impotent wings of the agèd eagle seem to revive, as,

From the wide window towards the granite shore
The white sails still fly seaward, seaward flying
Unbroken wings.
And the lost heart stiffens and rejoices
In the lost lilac and the lost sea voices
And the weak spirit quickens to rebel
For the bent golden-rod and the lost sea smell
Quickens to recover
The cry of quail and the whirling plover
And the blind eye creates
The empty forms between the ivory gates
And smell renews the salt savour of the sandy earth . . .

The broken prayer, at once childlike and mystically subtle, with
which the poem ends seems to imply that the poet has come closer to
the strength and revelation he craves: grace is about to descend.

Blessèd sister, holy mother, spirit of the fountain, spirit of the garden,
Suffer us not to mock ourselves with falsehood

> Teach us to care and not to care
> Teach us to sit still
> Even among these rocks,
> Our peace in His will
> And even among these rocks
> Sister, mother
> And spirit of the river, spirit of the sea,
> Suffer me not to be separated
>
> And let my cry come unto Thee.

The literary and conventional imagery upon which "Ash-Wednesday" so largely relies and which is less vivid because more artificial than that of Eliot's earlier poems, seems to me a definite feature of inferiority; the "devil of the stairs" and the "shape twisted on the banister," which are in Eliot's familiar and unmistakable personal vein, somehow come off better than the jewelled unicorn, which incongruously suggests Yeats. And I am made a little tired at hearing Eliot, only in his early forties, present himself as an "agèd eagle" who asks why he should make the effort to stretch his wings. Yet "Ash-Wednesday," though less brilliant and intense than Eliot at his very best, is distinguished by most of the qualities which made his other poems remarkable: the exquisite phrasing in which we feel that every word is in its place and that there is not a word too much; the metrical mastery which catches so naturally, yet with so true a modulation, the faltering accents of the supplicant, blending the cadences of the liturgy with those of perplexed brooding thought; and, above all, that "peculiar honesty" in "exhibiting the essential sickness or strength of the human soul" of which Eliot has written in connection with Blake and which, in his own case, even at the moment when his psychological plight seems most depressing and his ways of rescuing himself from it least sympathetic, still gives him a place among those upon whose words we reflect with most interest and whose tones we remember longest.

# F. R. LEAVIS *

THE situation upon which Mr. Eliot impinged has now been fairly described. The magnitude of the impact may be said to have been registered with the publication of *Poems* 1909–1925; but the contents of that volume had appeared at various times earlier. *Prufrock*, the earliest section, which is dated 1917, itself constitutes an important event in the history of English poetry. The title poem, *The Love Song of J. Alfred Prufrock*, which is printed at the beginning of *Poems* 1909–1925, represents a complete break with the nineteenth-century tradition, and a new start. It must indeed have been difficult to take seriously in 1917, for it defies the traditional canon of seriousness:

> I grow old . . . I grow old . . .
> I shall wear the bottoms of my trousers rolled.

Can this be poetry? And yet there are passages that, for all their oddness of imagery and tone, do not immediately condemn themselves as 'unpoetical' even by anthological standards:

> The yellow fog that rubs its back upon the windowpanes,
> The yellow smoke that rubs its muzzle on the windowpanes
> Licked its tongue into the corners of the evening,
> Lingered upon the pools that stand in drains,
> Let fall upon its back the soot that falls from chimneys,
> Slipped by the terrace, made a sudden leap,
> And seeing that it was a soft October night,
> Curled once about the house, and fell asleep.

—Indeed, it is as necessary to revise the traditional idea of the distinction between seriousness and levity in approaching this poetry as in approaching the Metaphysical poetry of the seventeenth century. And as striking as this subtlety and flexibility of tone, this complexity of attitude, is the nature (exemplified in the passage just quoted) of

* *T. S. Eliot*, from NEW BEARINGS IN ENGLISH POETRY, pp. 75–91, 112–132. Chatto & Windus, London, 1932.

the imagery. The canons of the poetical are forgotten; the poet assumes the right to make use of any materials that seem to him significant. We have here, in short, poetry that expresses freely a modern sensibility, the ways of feeling, the modes of experience, of one fully alive in his own age. Already the technical achievement is such as to be rich in promise of development and application.

Yet it must be admitted that if *The Love Song of J. Alfred Prufrock* stood alone there would be some excuse for unreadiness to recognize in it this kind of significance. A certain heaviness about the gestures ('heavy' in the sense of caricature)—

> Do I dare
> Disturb the universe?

and

> Though I have seen my head (grown slightly bald)
> brought in upon a platter

—emphasizes the touch of conscious elegance in the disillusion, and makes 'clever' seem a more adequate description than it ought:

> I have seen the moment of my greatness flicker,
> And I have seen the eternal Footman hold my coat, and snicker,
> And in short, I was afraid.

But in *Portrait of a Lady* the poise is more subtle, and it is maintained with sure and exquisite delicacy. The poet's command both of his experience and of his technique (if we can distinguish) is perfect. Without any limiting suggestion of caricature he can write:

> And I must borrow every changing shape
> To find expression . . . dance, dance
> Like a dancing bear,
> Cry like a parrot, chatter like an ape.
> Let us take the air, in a tobacco trance—
> Well! and what if she should die some afternoon,
> Afternoon grey and smoky, evening yellow and rose;
> Should die and leave me sitting pen in hand
> With the smoke coming down above the housetops . . .

The flexibility and the control of this are maintained throughout the poem. The utterances of the lady are in the idiom and cadence of modern speech, and they go perfectly with the movement of the verse, which, for all its freedom and variety, is nevertheless very strict and precise. The poet is as close to the contemporary world as any novelist could be, and his formal verse medium makes possible a concentration and a directness, audacities of transition and psychological notation, such as are forbidden to the novelist. Only a very strong originality could so have triumphed over traditional habits, and only very strong preconceptions could hinder the poem's being recognized as the work of a major poet.

Portrait of a Lady is the most remarkable thing in the Prufrock section. Preludes and Rhapsody on a Windy Night develop that imagery of urban disillusion which has since done so much service in the verse of adolescent romantic pessimists. The use of this imagery relates him to Baudelaire, and the occasion now arises to note his debt to certain later French poets. To a young practitioner faced with Mr. Eliot's problems Tristan Corbière and Jules Laforgue offered starting points such as were not to be found in English poetry of the nineteenth century. How closely he studied French verse may be gathered from the verse, retained in Poems 1909–1925, that he himself wrote in French. He learnt, by his own account, from Jules Laforgue in particular, and the evidence is apparent in his early work. The evidence lies not so much in a Laforguian exercise like Conversation Galante as in The Love Song of J. Alfred Prufrock and Portrait of a Lady. It is difficult to distinguish between attitude and technique: he was able to derive means of expression from Laforgue because of a certain community with him in situation and sensibility. The self-ironical, self-distrustful attitudes of Prufrock owe their definition largely to Laforgue, and there the technical debt shows itself; it shows itself in the ironical transitions, and also in the handling of the verse. But this last head has been made too much of by some critics: French moves so differently from English that to learn from French verse an English poet must be original. And to learn as Mr. Eliot learnt in general from Laforgue is to be original to the point of genius. Already in the collection of 1917 he is himself as only a major poet can be.

The other derivation he assigns to his verse—'the form in which I began to write, in 1908 or 1909, was directly drawn from the study of Laforgue together with the later Elizabethan drama'—manifests itself plainly in the first poem of the section following Prufrock, that dated 1920. It is not for nothing that in Gerontion he alludes to one of the finest passages of Middleton:

I that was near your heart was removed therefrom
To lose beauty in terror, terror in inquisition.
I have lost my passion: why should I need to keep it
Since what is kept must be adulterated?

*Geronion.*

I that am of your blood was taken from you
For your better health; look no more upon it,
But cast it to the ground regardlessly.
Let the common sewer take it from distinction.

*The Changeling,* v. iii.

The comparison would be worth making at greater length in order
to bring out, not only the likeness in movement of Mr. Eliot's verse
to mature Elizabethan dramatic verse, but also Mr. Eliot's astonishing
power. Nowhere in Middleton, or, for that matter, Webster, Tourneur, or anywhere outside Shakespeare, can we find a passage so
sustained in quality as *Geronion.* In his essay on Massinger he says:
'with the end of Chapman, Middleton, Webster, Tourneur, Donne
we end a period when the intellect was immediately at the tips of
the senses. Sensation became word and word sensation.' *Geronion*
answers to this description as well as anything by any of the authors
enumerated: it expresses psychological subtleties and complexities
in imagery of varied richness and marvellously sure realization. The
whole body of the words seems to be used. Qualities that (if we ignore
Hopkins as he was ignored) have been absent from English poetry
since the period that Mr. Eliot describes (his critical preoccupation
with it is significant) reappear with him.

The effect of his few and brief critical references to Milton is
notorious. The effect upon Miltonic influence of his practice is likely
to be even more radical. If we look at the first *Hyperion* of Keats we
see that it points forward to Tennyson and backward to Milton. This
simple reminder (a safe generalization would call for more qualifying
than is in place here) serves to bring home the prevalence of certain
limitations in the way in which English has been used in poetry since
Milton. Milton and Tennyson are very different, but when Tennyson,
or any other poet of the nineteenth century (which saw a rough first
draft in the revised *Hyperion*), wrote blank verse, even when he
intended it to be dramatic, it followed Milton rather than Shake-

speare—a Milton who could be associated with Spenser. Even when Shakespeare was consciously the model, it was a Shakespeare felt through Milton. Language was used in a generally Miltonic way even in unMiltonic verse. To justify the phrase, 'a generally Miltonic way,' a difficult and varying analysis would be necessary; but I have in mind Milton's habit of exploiting language as a kind of musical medium outside himself, as it were. There is no pressure in his verse of any complex and varying current of feeling and sensation; the words have little substance or muscular quality: Milton is using only a small part of the resources of the English language. The remoteness of his poetic idiom from his own speech is to be considered here. ('English must be kept up,' said Keats, explaining his abandonment of the Miltonic first *Hyperion*). A man's most vivid emotional and sensuous experience is inevitably bound up with the language that he actually speaks.

The brief account given above of the relation of *Gerontion* to Middleton and his contemporaries must not be allowed to suggest that Mr. Eliot's verse has anything in it of pastiche. For all its richness and variety and power of assimilating odds and ends from Lancelot Andrewes (for instance), its staple idiom and movement derive immediately from modern speech.

These considerations have been put too briefly to be critically impregnable: no simple formula will cover poetic practice in the nineteenth century. That they can be put so briefly and yet serve their purpose, that one can take so much for understood, is due to Mr. Eliot. That young practitioners are now using words very differently from the poets of the last age is also due mainly to him.

The dramatic derivation of the verse is not all that there is dramatic about *Gerontion*: it has a really dramatic detachment. In this respect it represents a great advance upon anything printed earlier in *Poems* 1909-1925. *Prufrock* and *Portrait of a Lady* are concerned with the directly personal embarrassments, disillusions and distresses of a sophisticated young man. It is not a superficial difference that *Gerontion* has for *persona* an old man, embodying a situation remote from that of the poet. From a position far above his immediate concerns as a particular individual, projecting himself, as it were, into a comprehensive and representative human consciousness, the poet contemplates human life and asks what it all comes to. The introductory quotation gives the hint:

> *Thou hast nor youth nor age*
> *But as it were an after dinner sleep*
> *Dreaming of both.*

—*Gerontion* has the impersonality of great poetry.

In method, too, *Gerontion* represents a development. Since the method is that, or a large part of that, of *The Waste Land,* it seems better to risk some elementary observations upon it, for *The Waste Land* has been found difficult. Instructions how to read the poem (should anything more than the title and the epigraph be necessary) are given in the last line:

> Tenants of the house,
> Thoughts of a dry brain in a dry season.

It has neither narrative nor logical continuity, and the only theatre in which the characters mentioned come together, or could, is the mind of the old man. The Jew who squats on the window-sill could not hear the old man even if he spoke his thoughts aloud, and the field overhead in which the goat coughs has no geographical relation to the house. All the persons, incidents and images are there to evoke the immediate consciousness of the old man as he broods over a life lived through and asks what is the outcome, what the meaning, what the residue. This seems simple enough, and the transitions and associations are not obscure.

The poem opens with what is to be a recurrent theme of Mr. Eliot's: the mixing of 'memory and desire' in present barrenness. The old man in his 'dry month,' waiting for the life-giving 'rain' that he knows will never come, is stirred to envy, then to poignant recollection, by the story of hot-blooded vitality, which contrasts with the squalor of his actual surroundings. Youthful desire mingles in memory with the most exalted emotions, those associated with the mysteries of religion:

> The word within a word, unable to speak a word,
> Swaddled with darkness. In the juvescence of the year
> Came Christ the tiger.
>
> In depraved May . . .

Here, in the last two phrases, Mr. Eliot does in concentration what he does by his notorious transitions from theme to theme: widely different emotions and feelings are contrasted and fused. It is the kind of effect that Shakespeare gets in such a line as

> Lilies that fester smell far worse than weeds,

where the associations that cluster round 'lilies'—fragrant flowers and emblems of purity—are contrasted and fused with those attaching to 'fester,' which applies to rotting flesh.

In *Gerontion* the contrast is developed: the emotional intensities evoked by the reference to the Sacrament are contrasted with the stale cosmopolitan depravity evoked by the names and by the suggested incidents and associations:

> To be eaten, to be divided, to be drunk
> Among whispers; by Mr. Silvero
> With caressing hands, at Limoges
> Who walked all night in the next room;
>
> By Hakagawa, bowing among the Titians;
> By Madame de Tournquist, in the dark room
> Shifting the candles; Fräulein von Kulp
> Who turned in the hall, one hand on the door.

'Among whispers' may be pointed to as a characteristic transition. They are first the whispers of religious awe; then, in the new context, they become clandestine and sinister, the whispers of intrigue. The reference to 'the Titians' brings in art: art and religion, the two refuges from time and the sordid actuality, suffer the same staling depravation. Fräulein von Kulp is seen vividly, a precise particular figure in a precise particular posture, but far in the past; she serves only to emphasize the present vacancy:

> Vacant shuttles
> Weave the wind. I have no ghosts,
> An old man in a draughty house
> Under a windy knob.

But this kind of elucidation is perhaps insulting. At any rate, no more can be needed: more than enough has been done to illustrate the method. And only an analysis on Mr. Empson's lines could be anything like fair to the subtleties of the poem; for Mr. Eliot's effects depend a great deal upon ambiguity. One of the most obvious instances occurs near the end:

> . . . De Bailhache, Fresca, Mrs. Cammel, whirled
> Beyond the circuit of the shuddering Bear
> In fractured atoms. Gull against the wind, in the windy straits
> Of Belle Isle, or running on the Horn,
> White feathers in the snow, the Gulf claims,
> And an old man driven by the Trades
> To a sleepy corner.

The gull following upon those names that evoke *The News of the World* enforces partly the inevitable end, the common reduction to 'fractured atoms.' A bunch of feathers blown in the gale, it brings home poignantly the puny helplessness of the individual life. But also, in its clean, swift vitality, it contrasts with the frowsy squalor of finance, crime and divorce. Similarly with respect to the old man: it stands to him for inevitable death and dissolution; but it also stands for the strength and ardour that he has lost.

There would seem to be little to impede the recognition of *Gerontion* as great poetry. But *Burbank with a Baedeker: Bleistein with a Cigar* and certain other of the poems that follow develop (giving definition at the same time to a characteristic preoccupation of the poet) a technical device that seems to have been responsible for some of the recalcitrance shown towards *The Waste Land*. They use as essential means quotation and allusion. The references in *Burbank* to *Antony and Cleopatra* are obvious, and their purpose is plainly a kind of ironical contrast: heroic love, lust in the grand style and the pitiful modern instance. The characteristic preoccupation which I have mentioned some critics see as a tendency to condemn the present by the standards of an ideal past. This is too simple an account. In *Sweeney Among the Nightingales,* for example, the contrast is clearly something more than that between the sordid incident in a modern brothel and the murder of Agamemnon:

> The circles of the stormy moon
> Slide westward towards the River Plate,
> Death and the Raven drift above
> And Sweeney guards the hornèd gate.
>
> Gloomy Orion and the Dog
> Are veiled; and hushed the shrunken seas;
> The person in the Spanish cape
> Tries to sit on Sweeney's knees,

> Slips and pulls the table cloth
> Overturns a coffee-cup . . .

Moreover, the number of allusions in *Burbank* has not yet been taken account of. There is no need to enumerate them: they refer to half-a-dozen or more authors. The best commentary on them, perhaps, is *A Cooking Egg,* which does not represent Mr. Eliot at his best, but exhibits his *procédé* with especial plainness. It is not merely as foils ✓ to the mean actuality that these varied references are there. The wide culture, the familiarity with various cultures, that they represent has a closer bearing upon the sense of stale disillusion. This point✓ will be made clear when we come to *The Waste Land.*

I have been a good deal embarrassed by the fear of dwelling on the obvious to the extent of insulting the reader. But where Mr. Eliot's poetry is concerned it still seems necessary to say elementary things. It is still possible for a critic belonging to a younger generation than Mr. Eliot's to remark of one of those ironical contrasts that we have been considering:

> In regard to the pretty-pretty element, it seems evident that the names Nausicaa and Polypheme, while not to be regarded merely as pretty-pretty (because the poem contains sordid phrases too), are, to a certain extent, conversely, to be looked on as jam to help us take the bitter sordid powder.

The essay to which this is a footnote appears in the second volume of *Scrutinies,* and itself deserves a brief scrutiny, since that volume makes some pretension to represent the young advance-guard of criticism, and the essayist is in intelligent company. The misgiving aroused by the title—*The Lyric Impulse in the Poetry of T. S. Eliot*—finds unexpectedly thorough confirmation. Mr. Eliot's 'lyric impulse,' we discover, is 'his poetic, Shelleyan impulse.' When, in spite of his resistant sophistication, he yields to it he breaks into 'pure English lyric style.' The third part of *The Waste Land* is judged to be more unified than the rest 'perhaps because the subject, sensual love, is naturally more close to Mr. Eliot's heart (as to the heart of a lyric poet) than the more abstract considerations with which the other parts of the poem wish to deal. . . .' We find propounded as a theme for critical treatment 'the poetisation of the unpoetical.' In short, what the critic, in the latest idiom and accent, is applying to the diagnosis of Mr. Eliot is the familiar idea of the intrinsically poetical.

Some elementary observation, then, is not unwarranted. And, immediately, it may be noted that this testimony to the strength of the 'poetical' tradition brings out the greatness of Mr. Eliot's achievement: in his work by 1920 English poetry had made a new start.

It was *The Waste Land* that compelled recognition for the achievement. The poem appeared first in the opening numbers of *The Criterion* (October 1922 and January 1923). The title, we know, comes from Miss J. L. Weston's book, *From Ritual to Romance,* the theme of which is anthropological: the Waste Land there has a significance in terms of Fertility Ritual. What is the significance of the modern Waste Land? The answer may be read in what appears as the rich disorganization of the poem. The seeming disjointedness is intimately related to the erudition that has annoyed so many readers and to the wealth of literary borrowings and allusions. These characteristics reflect the present state of civilization. The traditions and cultures have mingled, and the historical imagination makes the past contemporary; no one tradition can digest so great a variety of materials, and the result is a break-down of forms and the irrevocable loss of that sense of absoluteness which seems necessary to a robust culture. The bearing of this on the technique developed in *Burbank* and *A Cooking Egg* does not need enlarging upon. . . .

*The Waste Land,* then, whatever its difficulty, is, or should be, obviously a poem. It is self-subsistent poem. Indeed, though it would lose if the notes could be suppressed and forgotten, yet the more important criticism might be said to be, not that it depends upon them too much, but rather that without them, and without the support of *From Ritual to Romance,* it would not lose more. It has, that is, certain limitations in any case; limitations inherent in the conditions that produced it. Comprehensiveness, in the very nature of the undertaking, must be in some sense at the cost of structure: absence of direction, of organizing principle, in life could hardly be made to subserve the highest kind of organization in art.

But when all qualifications have been urged, *The Waste Land* remains a great positive achievement, and one of the first importance for English poetry. In it a mind fully alive in the age compels a poetic triumph out of the peculiar difficulties facing a poet in the age. And in solving his own problem as a poet Mr. Eliot did more than solve the problem for himself. Even if *The Waste Land* had been, as used to be said, a 'dead end' for him, it would still have been a new start for English poetry.

But, of course, to judge it a 'dead end' was shallow. It was to ignore the implications of the effort that alone could have availed to express formlessness itself as form. So complete and vigorous a statement of the Waste Land could hardly (to risk being both crude and impertinent) forecast an exhausted, hopeless sojourn there. As for the nature of the effort, the intimacy with Dante that the poem betrays has its significance. There is no great distance in time and no gulf of any kind between the poet of *The Waste Land* and the critic who associates himself later with 'a tendency—discernible even in art— toward a higher and clearer conception of Reason, and a more severe and serene control of the emotions by Reason'; and who writes of Proust 'as a point of demarcation between a generation for whom the dissolution of value had in itself a positive value, and the generation which is beginning to turn its attention to an athleticism, a *training,* of the soul as severe and ascetic as the training of the body of a runner.'

Nevertheless, the poem succeeding *The Waste Land* in *Poems* 1909-1925, and bringing that collection to a close, gave some plausibility to the superficial verdict. The epigraph of *The Hollow Men*— '*Mistah Kurtz—he dead*'—coming from *The Heart of Darkness,* suggests a dissolution of all the sanctions of life; and the tailing off of the poem into

> *This is the way the world ends*
> *Not with a bang but a whimper*

so completely justifies itself that it does not appear the audacity it is: 'audacity' suggests too much vigour. The poem develops certain elements of *The Waste Land* in a kind of neurasthenic agony. Yet this evocation of

> Shape without form, shade without colour,
> Paralysed force, gesture without motion

is a marvellous positive achievement, and if we should be tempted to relate too crudely the 'mind that created' with 'the man who suffered' we have the various drafts to remind us that it is after all a poem that we are dealing with. The terrible closing section, with its nightmare poise over the grotesque, is a triumph of aplomb. The three middle sections begin that exploration of 'the dreamcrossed twilight' which (in a different spirit) is to be pursued in *Ash Wednesday*.

Between *The Hollow Men* and *Ash Wednesday* come three poems published separately in the *Ariel* series. These show a curious change. We find in them, instead of the fevered torment of *The Hollow Men,* a kind of inert resignation. The movements are tired and nerveless; they suggest marvellously the failure of rhythm. If the extreme agony of consciousness has passed, so has the extraordinary vitality that went with it. But the change has another aspect. These three poems reveal a significant preoccupation; they have a direction, and they all point the same way. *Journey of the Magi* and *A Song for Simeon* deal dramatically with their religious theme, the promise of salvation, but the dramatic form amounts to little more than delicacy in the presentment of intimate personal issues:

> . . . were we led all that way for
> Birth or Death? There was a Birth, certainly,
> We had evidence and no doubt. I had seen birth and death,
> But had thought they were different; this Birth was
> Hard and bitter agony for us, like Death, our death.
> We returned to our places, these Kingdoms,
> But no longer at ease here, in the old dispensation,
> With an alien people clutching their gods.
> I should be glad of another death.

The queer, essential equivocalness of this is the poet's, and the dramatic theme, it becomes clear, is a means to the expression of it. The ambivalence comes out still more strikingly in the end of *A Song for Simeon:*

> I am tired with my own life and the lives of those after me,
> I am dying in my own death and the deaths of those after me.
> Let thy servant depart,
> Having seen thy salvation.

It is something very different from an affirmation that so transforms the original theme: the air is 'thoroughly small and dry.' And yet there is something positive present, if only a direction of feeling and contemplation—something specifically religious. At the end of *Animula,* the third *Ariel* poem, the liturgical note characteristic of *Ash Wednesday* appears.

What seemed most to distinguish the first poem of *Ash Wednes-*

*day,* when, as *Perch' io non spero,* it appeared in *Commerce,* from the *Ariel* poems was the rhythm. The rhythm varies within the sequence from part to part, but it is in general very much more nerved and positive than that of the *Ariel* poems. In the comparison it is not extravagant to speak of it as having certain qualities of ritual; it produces in a high degree the frame-effect, establishing apart from the world a special order of experience, dedicated to spiritual exercises. To discuss *Ash Wednesday,* then, is a delicate business, incurring danger both of crudity and impertinence. We remind ourselves of Mr. Eliot's precept and practice in criticism: the sequence is poetry, and highly formal poetry. Yet it is impossible not to see in it a process of self-scrutiny, of self-exploration; or not to feel that the poetical problem at any point was a spiritual problem, a problem in the attainment of a difficult sincerity. The poetry belongs to

> . . . the time of tension between dying and birth
> The place of solitude where three dreams cross

and is a striving after a spiritual state based upon a reality elusive and yet ultimate.

We cannot help recalling Mr. Eliot's various observations about the problem of belief. This, for instance, seems germane:

> I cannot see that poetry can ever be separated from something which I should call belief, and to which I cannot see any reason for refusing the name of belief, unless we are to reshuffle names together. It should hardly be needful to say that it will not inevitably be orthodox Christian belief, although that possibility can be entertained, since Christianity will probably continue to modify itself, as in the past, into something that can be believed in (I do not mean *conscious* modifications like modernism, etc., which always have the opposite effect). The majority of people live below the level of belief or doubt. It takes application, and a kind of genius, to believe anything, and to believe *anything* (I do *not* mean merely to believe in some 'religion') will probably become more and more difficult as time goes on.

Mr. Eliot's concern is specifically religious. Certain qualities of genius he indubitably has, and *Ash Wednesday* is a disciplined application of them to the realizing of a spiritual state conceived as depending upon belief—belief in something outside himself. The result is a most subtle poetry of great technical interest; and it is on the technical aspect that critical attention must in any case focus.

For the poet 'technique' was the problem of sincerity. He had to achieve a paradoxical precision-in-vagueness; to persuade the elusive intuition to define itself, without any forcing, among the equivocations of 'the dreamcrossed twilight.' The warning against crude interpretation, against trying to elicit anything in the nature of prose statement, is there in the unexpected absences of punctuation; and in the repetitive effects, which suggest a kind of delicate tentativeness. The poetry itself is an effort at resolving diverse impulsions, recognitions and needs.

*Ash Wednesday* is a whole. Faced with *Perch' io non spero* as a separate poem, one might pardonably, perhaps, see an odd affectation in

Why should the agèd eagle stretch its wings?

But (though the criticism is still made) in a reading of the whole sequence the ironical function of this self-dramatization becomes obvious. It is an insurance against the pride of humility; a self-admonition against the subtle treasons, the refinements, of egotism that beset the quest of sincerity in these regions. Again,

And I pray that I may forget
These matters that with myself I too much discuss
Too much explain

intimates a capacity for a critical attitude towards the 'discussing' that the poetry is.

To take fragments separately at their face value is to misunderstand this poetry, which works by compensations, resolutions, residuums and convergences. What, we ask, does the poet resign and renounce in the first poem, and what is the nature of his renunciation? The line from the Shakespeare sonnet suggests that it is worldly ambition, personal glory, that he renounces. This becomes

The infirm glory of the positive hour;

and

The one veritable transitory power

together with the next lines—

Because I cannot drink
There, where trees flower, and springs flow, for there is nothing again

—seems to identify it with the vital illusion of youth. But, it next appears, what we have here is the sensory evocation of a spiritual state:

Because I know that time is always time
And place is always and only place
And what is actual is actual only for one time
And only for one place
I rejoice that things are as they are and
I renounce the blessed face
And renounce the voice.

—This, with its bare prose statement, has the effect of a complete renunciation of supernatural assurance. And the general effect of the poem is negative. Yet the formula of renunciation—

Teach us to care and not to care
Teach us to sit still

—registers a positive religious impulse, which is confirmed by the liturgical close. And the positive element comes out more significantly in

Consequently I rejoice, having to construct something
Upon which to rejoice

—if the air is 'thoroughly small and dry' it is 'smaller and dryer than the will.' Not for nothing have the rhythms of *Ash Wednesday* so much more life than those of the *Ariel* poems. After this introduction, then, we know what are to be the themes of the following poetry, and what the mode of debate.

It is common to ask of the second poem, 'Who is the Lady, and what do the three white leopards stand for?' As for the first question, Mr. Eliot in his *Dante* writes: 'In the Earthly Paradise Dante encounters a lady named Matilda, whose identity need not at first bother us'; the identity of the Lady in this poem need not bother us at all. She reminds us not only of Matilda but of Beatrice and Piccarda too, and helps to define a mode of religious contemplation that characterizes the poem. The theme of the poem is death, and death is evoked as complete extinction:

End of the endless
Journey to no end
Conclusion of all that
Is inconclusible . . .

—But the effect has extraordinarily little in common with that of the same theme in *The Hollow Men* or *Journey of the Magi* or *A Song for Simeon*. The desire for extinction (ἀποθανεῖν θέλω)—

> I should be glad of another death

and

> I am tired with my own life and the lives of those after me

—becomes curiously transmuted by association with something positive:

> As I am forgotten
> And would be forgotten, so I would forget
> Thus devoted, concentrated in purpose.

The devotion and the concentration are represented by the Lady, who serves to intimate the poet's recourse, in his effort 'to construct something upon which to rejoice,' to a specific religious tradition, and they manifest themselves throughout in rhythm and tone. The 'burden of the grasshopper' (a fine instance, this, of Mr. Eliot's genius in borrowing), though a burden, potently evoked, of annihilation, has nevertheless its share of the religious emotion that pervades the poem. The 'garden where all love ends' is associated with the garden in which God walked 'in the cool of the day.' A religious sense of awe, an apprehension of the supernatural, seems to inform the desert where the bones are scattered.

As for the 'three white leopards,' they are not symbols needing interpretation; they act directly, reinforcing the effect of ritual that we have noted in the verse and suggesting the mode of experience, the kind of spiritual exercise, to which *Ash Wednesday* is devoted. They belong with the 'jewelled unicorns' that have bothered some critics in the fourth poem:

> Redeem
> The unread vision in the higher dream
> While jewelled unicorns draw by the gilded hearse.

Perhaps in this last passage Mr. Eliot has been too helpful and 'the higher dream' is too like explicit elucidation. But it at any rate reminds us conveniently of certain things that he says in his *Dante*. He remarks of the 'pageantry' of the *Paradise*:

It belongs to the world of what I call the *high dream*, and the modern world seems capable only of the low dream.

And he says elsewhere:

> Dante's is a *visual* imagination. It is a visual imagination in a different sense from that of a modern painter of still life: it is visual in the sense that he lived in an age in which men still saw visions. It was a psychological habit, the trick of which we have forgotten, but as good as any of our own. We have nothing but dreams, and we have forgotten that seeing visions—a practice now relegated to the aberrant and the uneducated—was once a more significant, interesting, and disciplined kind of dreaming.

When Mr. Eliot says that we have forgotten the trick he means it. He no more supposes that Dante's mode of vision can be recaptured than that Dante's belief can. But his frequentation of Dante has its place in that effort 'to construct something' and that 'training of the soul' which he speaks of. And his leopards and unicorns seem to insist on the peculiar kind of 'disciplined dreaming' that he strives to attain in 'the dreamcrossed twilight' of *Ash Wednesday*. They go with the formal quality of the verse, in which we have already noted a suggestion of ritual, and with the liturgical element, to define the plane at which this poetry works. The spiritual discipline is one with the poetical.

The third poem of the sequence offers an admirable example of the way in which Mr. Eliot blends the reminiscent (literary or conventional) in imagery with the immediately evocative. The 'stairs' of this poem (they have a 'banister') have their effect for a reader who recognizes no reminiscence. They concentrate the suggestion of directed effort that distinguishes this poetry from the earlier, and they define the nature of the effect. The poem epitomizes, as it were, a spiritual history, and records a sense of an advance and a hardly-dared hope of attainment (qualified by the humility that becomes explicit at the end). But the stairs also recall the stairs of the *Purgatorio*—a reminiscence that is picked up again in the next poem, in a further quotation from that Provençal passage of Canto XXVI which Mr. Eliot has used so much:

> Ara vos prec, per aquella valor
> que vos guida al som de l'escalina,
> sovegna vos a temps de ma dolor.

This, in a new spirit, is the art that he practised in *The Waste Land*.

The opening of the fourth poem recalls a passage of the third,-that giving the view through the 'slotted window':

> . . . beyond the hawthorn blossom and a pasture scene
> The broadbacked figure drest in blue and green
> Enchanted the maytime with an antique flute.
> Blown hair is sweet, brown hair over the mouth blown,
> Lilac and brown hair . . .

This backward glimpse of youth 'where trees flower and springs flow' seems to be dismissed here as 'distraction.' But the sense of refreshment that distinguishes the fourth poem seems to owe something to the same source. The 'violet,' the 'larkspur' and the 'varied green' have an effect like that of 'lilac,' and she 'who walked' may well have had brown hair. But this imagery, which is directly evocative, also lends itself to symbolic associations—

> Going in white and blue, in Mary's colour

and

> In blue of larkspur, blue of Mary's colour

—and she who 'made strong the fountains and made fresh the springs' takes on a specifically religious significance. Is the poet remembering an actual religious experience, or is he using the memory of the time when the springs were fresh as a symbol? The case is subtler. The unspecified 'who' and the indeterminate syntax, together with the element of 'higher dream' that we have already discussed, and the

> White light folded, sheathed about her, folded,

intimate that the process here is analogous to that represented by Dante's Beatrice. The 'yews' again are directly evocative: they have current values; beneath them

> > ghostly shapes
> May meet at noontide; Fear and trembling Hope,
> Silence and Foresight; Death the Skeleton
> And Time the Shadow

—though these yews, owing to the context, suggest a particular religious tradition.

A process analogous to Dante's: but the modern poet can make no pretence to Dante's certitude—to his firm possession of his vision. The ambiguity that constructs a precarious base for rejoicing in the fourth poem brings doubt and fear of inner treachery in the fifth. The breathless, circling, desperately pursuing movement of the opening, with its repetitions and its play upon 'word,' 'Word,' 'world' and 'whirled,' suggests both the agonized effort to seize the unseizable, and the elusive equivocations of the thing grasped. The doubts and self-questionings are developed, and the poem ends with a despairing recognition of the equivocal that recalls, in a significant way, the second poem:

> In the last desert between the last blue rocks
> The desert in the garden the garden in the desert
> Of drouth, spitting from the mouth the withered apple-seed.
>
> O my people.

In the earlier poem the desert that the bones inherit—the 'garden where all love ends'—is associated with the garden in which God walked 'in the cool of the day.' The ambiguity is the condition of a poise between widely divergent impulses and emotions that produces a strange serenity. But here, in the fifth poem, we have instead an equivocation of experience that produces agonizing doubt: which is garden and which is desert?

In the last poem of the sequence the doubt becomes an adjuvant of spiritual discipline, ministering to humility. But an essential ambiguity remains, an ambiguity inescapable

> In this brief transit where the dreams cross.

To symbolize, to conceive for himself, the spiritual order that he aspires towards, the poet inevitably has recourse to his most vital mundane experience. But the memories of this present themselves also as temptation, as incitement to subtle treacheries:

> . . . though I do not wish to wish these things
> From the wide window towards the granite shore
> The white sails still fly seaward, seaward flying
> Unbroken wings
>
> And the lost heart stiffens and rejoices
> In the lost lilac and the lost sea voices
> And the weak spirit quickens to rebel
> For the bent golden-rod and the lost sea smell. . . .

—The 'lost heart' is itself ambiguous: the heart is 'lost' because it succumbs to temptation and 'rebels'; but 'lost' also records a pang of regret, a rebellious questioning of the renunciation: the heart is 'lost' because it has lost the lilac and the sea voices. With 'merely vans to beat the air' the poet looks enviously at the unbroken wings that fly seaward, and prays:

> Suffer us not to mock ourselves with falsehood.

In the *Ariel* poem that appeared after *Ash Wednesday* it is Marina, who was lost and found again, who becomes the symbol for the new realization striven after. But this is to simplify too much. *Marina* belongs, like *Ash Wednesday* to 'the time of tension between dying and birth,' and exhibits an even more subtle ambiguity than anything in the sequence. The liturgical note is absent, and one may indicate the change in rhythm by saying that it has about it nothing of ritual; yet the poem expresses something approaching nearer to assurance than anything in *Ash Wednesday*. Images like the things that the poet 'did not wish to wish' now 'return,' bringing with them a sense of ineffable peace.

The coming of 'this grace' by which the various forms of death

> Are become unsubstantial, reduced by a wind,
> A breath of pine, and the woodsong fog

is associated with the approach of a ship to 'granite islands.' The 'white sails' and the 'granite shore' of *Ash Wednesday* have taken another value here. The ship—'I made this'—represents the effort 'to construct something upon which to rejoice.' Marina, the daughter lost and recovered, evokes the peculiar sense of victory over death that attends upon 'this grace':

> This form, this face, this life
> Living to live in a world of time beyond me; let me
> Resign my life for this life, my speech for that unspoken,
> The awakened, lips parted, the hope, the new ships.

Just what is the nature of the new life we cannot say. It is an elusive apprehension, conveyed poignantly, but in essential ambiguities. The poem is the resultant of diverse suggestions and orientations. The imagery belongs to the 'higher dream':

What is this face, less clear and clearer
The pulse in the arm, less strong and stronger—
Given or lent? more distant than stars and nearer
    than the eye . . .

The indeterminate syntax intimates the kind of relation that exists
between the various elements of the poem: one would not, to put it
crudely, think of trying to relate Marina, her father, the ship and the
islands in a story. And the elusiveness of the relations suggests at the
same time the felt transcendence of the vision and its precariousness.

The poetry of the last phase may lack the charged richness and
the range of *Gerontion* and *The Waste Land*. But it is, perhaps, still
more remarkable by reason of the strange and difficult regions of
experience that it explores. Its association with Mr. Eliot's explicit
Anglo-Catholicism has encouraged, in the guise of criticism, an extraordinarily crude and superficial approach. Critics speak of 'Pre-
Raphaelite imagery' and a 'Pre-Raphaelite flavour' and deplore (or
applaud) the return to the fold. But this poetry is more disconcert-
ingly modern than *The Waste Land*: the preoccupation with traditional Christianity, the use of the Prayer Book, and the devotion to
spiritual discipline should not hinder the reader from seeing that the
modes of feeling, apprehension and expression are such as we can
find nowhere earlier. If it is likely to be significant for young poets,
that is not because of the intellectual fashions that attribute so much
importance to T. E. Hulme, but because contemporary poets are likely
to find that the kind of consciousness represented by *Ash Wednesday*
and *Marina* has a close bearing upon certain problems of their own.
It is not for nothing that in the field of critical thought—in the consideration of those general problems that literary criticism nowadays
cannot ignore—Mr. Eliot remains a directing influence.

# I. A. RICHARDS *

WE too readily forget that, unless something is very wrong with our civilisation, we should be producing three equal poets at least for every poet of high rank in our great-great-grandfathers' day. Something must indeed be wrong; and since Mr. Eliot is one of the very few poets that current conditions have not overcome, the difficulties which he has faced, and the cognate difficulties which his readers encounter, repay study.

Mr. Eliot's poetry has occasioned an unusual amount of irritated or enthusiastic bewilderment. The bewilderment has several sources. The most formidable is the unobtrusiveness, in some cases the absence, of any coherent intellectual thread upon which the items of the poem are strung. A reader of 'Gerontion,' of 'Preludes,' or of 'The Waste Land,' may, if he will, after repeated readings, introduce such a thread. Another reader after much effort may fail to contrive one. But in either case energy will have been misapplied. For the items are united by the accord, contrast, and interaction of their emotional effects, not by an intellectual scheme that analysis must work out. The value lies in the unified response which this interaction creates in the right reader. The only intellectual activity required takes place in the realisation of the separate items. We can, of course, make a 'rationalisation' of the whole experience, as we can of any experience. If we do, we are adding something which does not belong to the poem. Such a logical scheme is, at best, a scaffolding that vanishes when the poem is constructed. But we have so built into our nervous systems a demand for intellectual coherence, even in poetry, that we find a difficulty in doing without it.

This point may be misunderstood, for the charge most usually brought against Mr. Eliot's poetry is that it is overintellectualised. One reason for this is his use of allusion. A reader who in one short poem picks up allusions to *The Aspern Papers, Othello,* 'A Toccata of

* *The Poetry of T. S. Eliot,* from PRINCIPLES OF LITERARY CRITICISM, pp. 289–295. Harcourt, Brace & World, Inc.    New York, and George Routledge & Sons, Ltd., London, 1934.

Galuppi's,' Marston, *The Phoenix and the Turtle, Antony and Cleopatra* (twice), 'The Extasie,' *Macbeth, The Merchant of Venice,* and Ruskin, feels that his wits are being unusually well exercised. He may easily leap to the conclusion that the basis of the poem is in wit also. But this would be a mistake. These things come in, not that the reader may be ingenious or admire the writer's erudition (this last accusation has tempted several critics to disgrace themselves), but for the sake of the emotional aura which they bring and the attitudes they incite. Allusion in Mr. Eliot's hands is a technical device for compression. 'The Waste Land' is the equivalent in content to an epic. Without this device twelve books would have been needed. But these allusions and the notes in which some of them are elucidated have made many a petulant reader turn down his thumb at once. Such a reader has not begun to understand what it is all about.

This objection is connected with another, that of obscurity. To quote a recent pronouncement upon 'The Waste Land' from Mr. Middleton Murry: 'The reader is compelled, in the mere effort to understand, to adopt an attitude of intellectual suspicion, which makes impossible the communication of feeling. The work offends against the most elementary canon of good writing: that the immediate effect should be unambiguous.' Consider first this 'canon.' What would happen, if we pressed it, to Shakespeare's greatest sonnets or to *Hamlet?* The truth is that very much of the best poetry is necessarily ambiguous in its immediate effect. Even the most careful and responsive reader must reread and do hard work before the poem forms itself clearly and unambiguously in his mind. An original poem, as much as a new branch of mathematics, compels the mind which receives it to grow, and this takes time. Anyone who upon reflection asserts the contrary for his own case must be either a demigod or dishonest; probably Mr. Murry was in haste. His remarks show that he has failed in his attempt to read the poem, and they reveal, in part, the reason for his failure—namely, his own over-intellectual approach. To read it successfully he would have to discontinue his present self-mystifications.

The critical question in all cases is whether the poem is worth the trouble it entails. For 'The Waste Land' this is considerable. There is Miss Weston's *From Ritual to Romance* to read, and its 'astral' trimmings to be discarded—they have nothing to do with Mr. Eliot's poem. There is Canto XXVI of the *Purgatorio* to be studied—the relevance of the close of that canto to the whole of Mr. Eliot's work must be insisted upon. It illuminates his persistent concern with sex, the problem of our generation, as religion was the problem of the last. There is the central position of Tiresias in the poem to be puzzled out—the cryptic form of the note which Mr. Eliot writes on this point is just a little tiresome. It is a way of underlining the fact that the poem is concerned with many aspects of the one fact of sex, a hint that is perhaps neither indispensable nor entirely successful.

When all this has been done by the reader, when the materials with which the words are to clothe themselves have been collected, the poem still remains to be read. And it is easy to fail in this undertaking. An 'attitude of intellectual suspicion' must certainly be abandoned. But this is not difficult to those who still know how to give their feelings precedence to their thoughts, who can accept and unify an experience without trying to catch it in an intellectual net or to squeeze out a doctrine. One form of this attempt must be mentioned. Some, misled no doubt by its origin in a Mystery, have endeavoured to give the poem a symbolical reading. But its symbols are not mystical, but emotional. They stand, that is, not for ineffable objects, but for normal human experience. The poem, in fact, is radically naturalistic; only its compression makes it appear otherwise. And in this it probably comes nearer to the original Mystery which it perpetuates than transcendentalism does.

If it were desired to label in three words the most characteristic feature of Mr. Eliot's technique, this might be done by calling his poetry a 'music of ideas.' The ideas are of all kinds, abstract and concrete, general and particular, and, like the musician's phrases, they are arranged, not that they may tell us something, but that their effects in us may combine into a coherent whole of feeling and attitude and produce a peculiar liberation of the will. They are to be responded to, not to be pondered or worked out. This is, of course, a method used intermittently in very much poetry, and only an accentuation and isolation of one of its normal resources. The peculiarity of Mr. Eliot's later, more puzzling, work is his deliberate and almost exclusive employment of it. In the earlier poems this logical freedom appears only occasionally. In 'The Love Song of J. Alfred Prufrock,' for example, there is a patch at the beginning and another at the end, but the rest of the poem is quite straightforward. In 'Gerontion,' the first long poem in this manner, the air of monologue, of a stream of associations, is a kind of disguise, and the last two lines,

Tenants of the house,
Thoughts of a dry brain in a dry season,

are almost an excuse. The close of 'A Cooking Egg' is perhaps the passage in which the technique shows itself most clearly. The reader who appreciates the emotional relevance of the title has the key to the later poems in his hand. I take Pipit to be the retired nurse of the hero of the poem, and *Views of the Oxford Colleges* to be the, still treasured, present which he sent her when he went up to the University. The middle section of the poem I read as a specimen of the rather withered pleasantry in which contemporary culture has culminated and beyond which it finds much difficulty in passing. The final section gives the contrast which is pressed home by the title. Even the most mature egg was new laid once. The only other title of equal significance that I can recall is Mrs. Wharton's *The Age of Innocence,* which might well be studied in this connection. 'The Waste Land' and 'The Hollow Men' (the most beautiful of Mr. Eliot's poems, and in the last section a new development) are purely a 'music of ideas,' and the pretence of a continuous thread of associations is dropped.

How this technique lends itself to misunderstandings we have seen. But many readers who have failed in the end to escape bewilderment have begun by finding on almost every line that Mr. Eliot has written—if we except certain youthful poems on American topics—that personal stamp which is the hardest thing for the craftsman to imitate and perhaps the most certain sign that the experience, good or bad, rendered in the poem is authentic. Only those unfortunate persons who are incapable of reading poetry can resist Mr. Eliot's rhythms. The poem as a whole may elude us while every fragment, as a fragment, comes victoriously home. It is difficult to believe that this is Mr. Eliot's fault rather than the reader's, because a parallel case of a poet who so constantly achieves the hardest part of his task and yet fails in the easier is not to be found. It is much more likely that we have been trying to put the fragments together on a wrong principle.

Another doubt has been expressed. Mr. Eliot repeats himself in two ways. The nightingale, Cleopatra's barge, the rats, and the

smoky candle-end, recur and recur. Is this a sign of a poverty of inspiration? A more plausible explanation is that this repetition is in
part a consequence of the technique above described, and in part
something which many writers who are not accused of poverty also
show. Shelley, with his rivers, towers, and stars, Conrad, Hardy, Walt
Whitman, and Dostoevski spring to mind. When a writer has found
a theme or image which fixes a point of relative stability in the drift
of experience, it is not to be expected that he will avoid it. Such
themes are a means of orientation. And it is quite true that the central
process in all Mr. Eliot's best poems is the same; the conjunction of
feelings which, though superficially opposed,—as squalor, for example,
is opposed to grandeur,—yet tend as they develop to change places
and even to unite. If they do not develop far enough the intention of
the poet is missed. Mr. Eliot is neither sighing after vanished glories
nor holding contemporary experience up to scorn.

Both bitterness and desolation are superficial aspects of his poetry.
There are those who think that he merely takes his readers into the
Waste Land and leaves them there, that in his last poem he confesses
his impotence to release the healing waters. The reply is that some
readers find in his poetry not only a clearer, fuller realisation of their
plight, the plight of a whole generation, than they find elsewhere, but
also through the very energies set free in that realisation a return of
the saving passion.

# F. O. MATTHIESSEN *

My opinion is this: that deep thinking is attainable only by a man of deep feeling, and all truth is a species of revelation. . . . It is *insolent* to *differ* from the public *opinion* in *opinion,* if it be only *opinion.* It is sticking up little *i by itself,* i against the whole alphabet. But one *word* with *meaning* in it is worth the whole alphabet together. Such is a sound argument, an incontrovertible fact.—*Coleridge.*

EVEN sympathetic readers of *Ash Wednesday* and *Triumphal March* may feel that they show a decline from *The Waste Land* in that they do not give expression to so fully packed a range of experience. But, unfortunately for sociological critics, an artist's career cannot be regarded as a continual 'progress', nor plotted on a steadily rising curve. *The Love Song of J. Alfred Prufrock* brought into union Eliot's ironic attitude with all the stimulus that he had received from his initial reading of Laforgue. As a result it possesses a finished mastery both of the material and of the form into which it is cast that puts it far beyond any of the other poems in his first volume of 1917—with the exception of *Portrait of a Lady*—though they were written during the following five years. In like manner, 'Gerontion', in 1919, marks a second crystallization and synthesis which lifts it entirely above the rank of the poems composed at about that time, such as *The Hippopotamus* or *Mr. Eliot's Sunday Morning Service* which read as though they were the work of a much younger, less mature man. Eliot himself, while commenting on Pound, has described the only way in which a poet's curve can be charted: his

> work may proceed along two lines on an imaginary graph; one of the lines being his conscious and continuous effort in technical excellence, that is, in continually developing his medium for the moment when he really has something to say. The other line is just his normal human course of development, his accumulation

* *The Sense of His Own Age,* from THE ACHIEVEMENT OF T. S. ELIOT, Revised Edition, pp. 132–149, Copyright, 1947, by Oxford University Press, New York.

and digestion of experience (experience is not sought for, it is merely accepted in consequence of doing what we really want to do), and by experience I mean the results of reading and reflection, varied interests of all sorts, contacts and acquaintances, as well as passion and adventure. Now and then the two lines may converge at a high peak, so that we get a masterpiece. That is to say, an accumulation of experience has crystallized to form material of art, and years of work in technique have prepared an adequate medium; and something results in which medium and material, form and content, are indistinguishable.

The very completeness of this union may cause confusion for the first readers of a new work: it may make them find difficulties that don't exist; mistake perfection for simpleness or slightness; or underestimate the force of what is being communicated. We tend too easily to pride ourselves on our superiority to the initial stupid reviewers of Wordsworth and Keats, and to forget that new art, a fresh way of interpreting life, has always to make its own audience. When Eliot's first poems appeared during the War, they were read, if at all, as an odd kind of *vers de société;* only gradually was it discovered that this slender volume was to have the effect, as Wyndham Lewis described it, of the little musk that scents a whole room.

In similar fashion, an impression of the comparative tenuousness of Eliot's later poems may prove illusory. It was probably impossible for him to strive towards a focused clarity of expression for his developing religious and political convictions without sacrificing part of his earlier complexity. But if there is loss in quickening surprise through the lessening of his sudden contrasts, there is in compensation a pervading, if less conspicuous quality: a sureness of accent and a quiet depth of tone. The one constant element through all the stages of his work has been his exact fitting of means to end, his rarely failing ability to perfect in each case the very kind of form he wanted for the particular content. The relative slimness of his production has tended to obscure his remarkable range in style. Indeed, as you read through his poems chronologically, he seems to have become expert in one mode of presentation only to move on to something else. After the 1917 volume the re-echoing manner of Laforgue diminishes, and such loosely flowing experiments as *Rhapsody on a Windy Night* disappear altogether. Then, having carried his study of French versification to the point of writing some poems in that language, he mastered his handling of the quatrain of Gautier and thereafter has used it no more. Likewise his meeting of the late Elizabethan dramatists so completely on their own ground has never been repeated since *Gerontion*. Both *The Waste Land* and *Ash Wednesday* are notable for the great variety of original verse forms that they employ within a short space; but the difference between these forms in the two poems is almost total.

Such versatility in style should in no degree be mistaken for mere technical virtuosity. Eliot is simply an example of the type of artist— and Joyce is another—whose motivating desire is to bring his expression to the greatest excellence he can, and then not to repeat it. Certain social implications can assuredly be drawn from the fact that not only Joyce and Eliot, but such other representative artists as Stravinsky and Picasso, have all felt within the past three decades a common urgency not to rest in the development of one manner, but to press on from each discovery to another. In the case of both the novelist and the poet their unwillingness to be confined long to any given method of presentation is obviously owing in part to their extraordinary historical consciousness, to their knowledge of so many possible techniques that they cannot remain satisfied with the limitations of any one. Probing beneath considerations of technique to the reasons for such a period of widespread experimentation in all the arts, one can undoubtedly link it with our contemporary sense of chaotic change and upheaval, of disequilibrium and insecurity. At the same time it is too easily forgotten in the current generalizations about the collapse of our culture that experiment, the trial of new possibilities, is a sign of life and not of death. And the ominous feeling that the fluctuation of the arts furnishes only one of many evidences that we are witnessing the final breakdown of all tradition often fails to take into consideration similar instability in other ages. Perhaps too much has been made of the fact that Donne's experiments, when seen against the background of his day, are even more radical than Eliot's; yet his restless invention of more than forty stanzaic forms is one indelible mark of his unsatisfied quest for certainty. But to take a seemingly far more traditional artist: it should not be obscured by time that Milton's whole career, his unending search for truth that rejected in turn the Anglican and Presbyterian creeds to pass to more and more independent definitions, is paralleled by the remarkably different stages in his development as a poet. Approached without preconceptions

*Arcades* and *Paradise Regained* would scarcely seem to be the work of the same man any more than *Chamber Music* and *Ulysses*. This juxtaposition may seem less incongruous the more one reflects on a remark that I heard Eliot make in conversation, that Joyce is the greatest master of the English language since Milton.

To return from this excursus: the test of the value of any experiment in art lies in the length to which it is carried, whether it is merely the by-product of erratic or undisciplined fancy, or whether it has built up into a completed masterwork. Throughout Eliot's variety persists the enduring sameness that I have already noted, a result of the unusual degree to which he has composed all his work around certain focal centres that possess for him a special symbolical value. He has revealed other long preoccupations of a significance comparable to his persistent return to the twenty-sixth canto of the *Purgatorio*. A pattern could be made of his recurring images: of how often a sudden release of the spirit is expressed through sea-imagery which, with its exact notation of gulls and granite rocks and the details of sailing, seems always to spring from his own boyhood experience off the New England coast, just as his city-imagery belongs to Boston and London; of the equally numerous times when certain spring flowers, lilacs and hyacinths, appear in passages which express the stirring of desire warring against the memory of previous failure; of the widely varied occasions when he presents a moment of beauty and its loss by a glimpse of a girl, 'her hair over her arms and her arms full of flowers'; of how, in such different poems as *Prufrock* and *Ash Wednesday,* a sudden ecstatic loveliness is caught in 'blown hair':

> . . . brown hair over the mouth blown,
> Lilac and brown hair;
> Distraction . . .

The drama of *The Waste Land* is built upon the contrast of repeated and varying symbols of drought and rain; much of its unified effect depends upon the frequent return of the theme of the Unreal City, with its 'trams and dusty trees', its murky streets 'under the brown fog of a winter noon', its dull canal made suddenly horrible by the slimy belly of a rat. In such repulsive images, in his insistent use of the sordid and disgusting to picture disintegration and decay, Eliot is again comparable to Webster. But, in considering Eliot's relatively narrow stock of repeated images, it is gradually discovered that what enables them to embrace a wider range of experience than would at first appear is the fact that they release markedly different shades of feeling according to their contexts. The desert rocks and dry bones of *The Waste Land* and the soaring gull at the close of *Gerontion* carry very different implications from similar objects in *Ash Wednesday*. The subtly differing connotations of the chief symbols within the course of *The Waste Land* itself are one of the strongest means by which the poet conveys the complexity of the existence that confronts him. The life-giving element of water alone can restore the kingdom (water is one of the most ancient symbols of sexual fertility); but in order to break the drought the hero must give himself up to the perilous quest. The necessity of self-sacrifice and the instinctive revulsion from it, the inability to commit himself to belief and the mounting fear that makes him recoil even from the vital forces of life in his dread of defeat and failure—such elements form the situation in which the hero, as unable as Hamlet to come to a resolution, is haunted by the thought of 'death by water'. The doubt that paralyses his desire to give himself is rendered concrete by the way in which water itself so often in the poem is made to appear anything but life-giving, as the squalid Thames instead of the 'damp gust bringing rain' that is longed for. In like manner, the basic symbol of fire is employed in a double sense. In 'The Fire Sermon' it stands for the destroyer, for the sterile lusts of the city, for the desire that burns without any definite object; it is only in the closing lines of the final section that fire, seen under a different aspect, represents the purifier, the purgatorial flame. Thus, purely in terms of Eliot's dominant images, can be discerned the way in which both their repetition and divergence help to bind together his various observations into a unified vision.

Particularly in view of emerging contours in his most recent work, one of the most significant of Eliot's symbols is what he finds in the figure of Coriolanus. The statement in one of his earlier essays that '*Coriolanus* may not be as "interesting" as *Hamlet*, but it is, with *Antony and Cleopatra*, Shakespeare's most assured artistic success,' might have prepared us for the realization that the meaning of this play is deeply implanted in Eliot's consciousness. In *A Cooking Egg* Coriolanus is linked with Sir Philip Sidney as a type of the hero; in *The Waste Land* he appears in the reflections of the poet on the second of the three commands heard in the rumbling of the thunder—*Give, Sympathize, Control*:

> *I have heard the key*
> *Turn in the door once and turn once only*
> *We think of the key, each in his prison*
> *Thinking of the key, each confirms a prison*
> *Only at nightfall, aethereal rumours*
> *Revive for a moment a broken Coriolanus*

The individual locked in his solitary identity can escape from this obsession only by self-surrender and by sympathy with others. Calling him 'a broken Coriolanus' at first seems only another instance of Eliot's manner of contrasting the present and the past: the historic splendour of the great individual is gone; in the modern world the aristocrat has been crushed by the mob—again we are not far from the dilemma voice by Flaubert. But as a relevant undertone here, it must not be forgotten that, in spite of all his noble strength and his gifts of leadership, Coriolanus at least in part deserved his tragedy; pride alienated him from his people and brought him to his destruction, pride which is the worst of sins in Dante's theology (as well as in the view of life which lies behind *Ethan Brand* and *The Scarlet Letter*), since, being at the opposite pole from humility, it cuts the individual off both from man and from God.

Further extension is given to such implications in *Triumphal March*. Coriolanus is not specifically suggested as the hero there; but Eliot subsequently grouped this poem and its sequel under the title *Coriolan*, thus possibly reminiscent of Beethoven's overture as well. And in the second poem, *Difficulties of a Statesman*, there is mention of the Volscians, and words directly borrowed from Shakespeare's play. I suppose *Triumphal March* would be described by Michael Gold as a Fascist poem; but it was written before Hitler's advent to power and none of the qualities of its hero glimpsed for a moment by the waiting crowd suggest either his or Mussolini's:

> *Look*
> *There he is now, look:*
> *There is no interrogation in his eyes*
> *Or in the hands, quiet over the horse's neck,*
> *And the eyes watchful, waiting, perceiving, indifferent.*
> *O hidden under the dove's wing, hidden in the turtle's breast,*
> *Under the palmtree at noon, under the running water*
> *At the still point of the turning world. O hidden.*

In fact the weave of this poem is so intricate, as a result of Eliot's desire to suggest the dense pattern of reality, that the isolation of any one strand into a prose statement runs the risk of oversimplifying its meaning. There is an observed beauty in the heavy processional movement:

> Stone, bronze, stone, steel, stone, oakleaves, horses' heels
> Over the paving.

But there is likewise a full recognition of both the horror and futility of war as it sweeps by in the prolonged inhuman enumeration of its millions of rifles and machine-guns. What is being portrayed is not just one procession; it takes place not only in post-War London or Paris, since there are eagles and trumpets and sacrifice at the temple. The crowd in the streets is both a Roman crowd waiting with its stools and sausages, and a modern crowd in the final fragments of conversation:

> (And Easter Day, we didn't get to the country,
> So we took young Cyril to church. And they rang a bell
> And he said right out loud, *crumpets*.)
>               Don't throw away that sausage,
> It'll come in handy. He's artful. Please, will you
> Give us a light?
> Light
> Light
> Et les soldats faisaient la haie? ILS LA FAISAIENT.

What is to be the symbol for spiritual reality to a world that goes to church only when it can't get to the country, which recognizes in the sign commemorating the presence of the Host simply a bell that reminds young Cyril of the crumpet-man in the street? In the shadow of that question, the casual 'Please, will you give us a light?' suddenly reverberates. What flashes forth from the reiterated word 'light' is not merely the flicker of a match, but searching speculation as to the source from which the light for our age is to come.

In such a context the central figure of the poem is seen to be neither Coriolanus nor a modern statesman alone, no more an Elizabethan than a Roman general; not even a symbol for leadership so much as the embodiment of qualities of spiritual perception and mastery that are integral to any deep apprehension of the meaning of life, and thus also to the existence of any adequate society. The hidden sources of inner life, the reserved balance, which sustain this individual and mark him off from the shallow chaotic flux of mere externalized rootless existence, make him almost a symbol for the harmonious union of emotion and thought that Eliot has so frequently stressed as characteristic of a 'firm grasp of human experience'; these qualities likewise demand a sustained equilibrium in the relations between the individual and the social structure. The ripely developed human being has gained the integrity that comes from self-knowledge, and he therefore understands that no wholeness exists in isolation, that the individual cannot find fulfilment except through also giving of himself to society—a truth none the less implied in *Difficulties of a Statesman* by the fact that what is presented there is the break-down of the relation between the leader and the state in the hopeless confusion of bureaucracy.

These reflections perhaps disclose some of the reasons why Shakespeare's *Coriolanus* has appealed to Eliot with a special urgency. A feeling that this play has an immediate closeness to our own age owing to the particular problem of life with which it deals has not been limited to Eliot. A brilliant younger critic, Harry Levin, wrote during the winter of his impressions of the recent performances of a new translation of *Coriolan* at the Comédie Française, which was done with full 'grandeur and stateliness,' with 'a ghastly Breughelesque mob'; and 'the audience cheered fervently at any slightest political implication. . . . Surely, if certain of Shakespeare's great tragedies have a special significance for certain periods (*Antony and Cleopatra* for the Restoration, *Hamlet* for the romantic movement), *Coriolanus* is the play that should have the richest meaning in our time.'

*Triumphal March* is not a Fascist poem any more than Shakespeare's play, but it points to the problem of the relation of the individual to the social organism, the imperfect solution of which has led directly into the ruthless brutality of the Fascist movement. It is worth calling attention to Eliot's growing interest in politics which forms the background for the appearance of this poem in 1931; especially since he has articulated, in his introduction to Pound, the gradual way in which a poet gathers his material by a process 'largely unconscious, subterranean, so that we cannot gauge its progress except once in every five or ten years,' when all the amassed experience 'accumulates to form a new whole and finds its appropriate expression.' (It must be noted, if only in passing, that this description of the poetic process emphasizes once more Eliot's fundamental belief that a poem is not to be the overflowing of the mood of a moment, but the blending into a concentrated unity the dominant thoughts and feelings of several years.) The part of Eliot's experience which was to crystallize into *Triumphal March* and *Difficulties of a Statesman* began to be evident in his preoccupation with political subjects in several of the essays in *For Lancelot Andrewes,* the composition of which stretched from 1925 to 1928. In addition, the Commentary in *The Criterion* for those years was increasingly taken up with contemporary politics, with the problem in the huge modern state caused by the heavy apathy of all elements in society to the responsibilities of intelligent representative government. The right to vote having been won by all men and women in democratic England and America, regard for its individual value seemed steadily dwindling. In the confused welter of modern society, the mass of mankind, unable to believe in anything very strongly or to understand any situation very well, was in constant danger of being led astray by any show of power in the streets, unable to distinguish between wise leadership and "the golf club Captains," liable to be swept away by any bread and circuses.

In line with such thought, Eliot noted in the spring of 1929: 'If, as we believe, the indifference to politics as actually conducted is growing, then we must prepare a state of mind towards something other than the facile alternative of communist or fascist dictatorship.' In the summer of that same year, in rejoinder to two essays in *The Criterion* defining the philosophic positions of those alternatives, he indicated more exactly what he meant when, in connection with the philosophy behind the Action Française, he spoke of 'the reintroduction of the idea of loyalty to a King, who incarnates the idea of the Nation. And in this idea is, I think, the *alternative* to Nationalism. Fascism seems to me rather (in the form in which it has succeeded up to date) to represent the Napoleonic idea. The latter, in contrast to the idea of Monarchy, is a familiar conventional modern idea: it is the doctrine of success.' The connection of this thought with the Action Française will damn it instantly with many readers, to whom no political group could seem more useless for the needs of England or America. I am not here concerned with the direct applicability of

Eliot's political ideas; indeed, he frequently confesses himself an amateur in such matters, and yet defends the valid and valuable distinction between political ideas and actual politics, a distinction particularly necessary in a time of social disruption, when practice lags behind theory, when, indeed, the only way of clarifying the chaotic jungle of events is by subjecting them to the scrutiny of an articulated theory. But what is important to understand in the present context is that the strain of thought which characterizes Eliot's conception of the ideal state also runs throughout his conception of the nature of art.

He objects to the modern worship of success, the journalistic 'great man complex', which sets up alike a Henry Ford or a Hitler and which, in glorifying alike the office-boy-to-millionaire or the corporal-to-dictator ideal, acclaims as necessary an unscrupulous directness of action. What seems to Eliot most false in such an ideal is that by exalting man's petty triumph it loses all view of anything more important than the individual, of the individual's inevitable limitations and his finding his completion only in something greater than himself, of the ruler's responsibility to his people, of the nation's to other parts of the world. The view of man symbolized in the comparative myths which Eliot drew upon for *The Waste Land* and the view of man lying behind *Ash Wednesday* emphasize in common the doctrine of incarnation, of the word made flesh. As Miss Weston summarized it in her chapter on *The Secret of the Grail* (though Eliot would long since have found a more authoritative statement): 'The end of all the Mystery institutions was the revelation of the Mystery of Man. The central doctrine is that of the Man, the Heavenly Man, the Son of God who . . . though originally endowed with all power, descends into weakness and bondage, and has to win his own freedom, and regain his original state.' But the heart of the story lies in the fact that he does not win salvation for himself, but only through the giving of himself in sacrifice; and thus it symbolizes the mystery which discloses also the way of Everyman's redemption from Hades. Such a view of man, in contrast to the deification of the Hero, does not exalt man at the expense of society. In recognizing man's potentiality for salvation, it does not confuse the perfection of the idea with his inescapable imperfection. In perceiving the divinity in man, it does not set up an overweening worship of individual power, but stresses the likeness of men, their common aspiration and fallibility, their one basis for brotherhood, not in a sentimental humanitarianism, but in their humility before God.

Throughout his life Eliot has been in reaction against the centrifugal individualism which characterized the America into which he was born. His deep-seated desire to link himself with a living tradition grew directly out of his revulsion against the lawless exploitation by which late nineteenth-century American individuals made any coherent society impossible. He was equally dissatisfied with the undefined spirituality of Emerson or Arnold: neither *Self-Reliance* nor *The Buried Life* was adequate. The tenets of the one led logically to an inhuman extreme of individualism, those of the other to a blurring of fundamental distinctions. Neither was restrained by the controlling anchor of dogma. The kind of control Eliot wanted was suggested in Hulme's condensed notes on 'the religious attitude', a fact which reveals the fertility of that thinker's *Speculations* not only in demanding the qualities of poetry for which Pound and Eliot were to strive, but likewise in foreshadowing many of the bases of Eliot's maturing religious and political thought. What Hulme insisted on was the fundamental confusion that had been brought about 'by the failure to recognize the *gap* between the regions of vital and human thought and things, and that of the *absolute* values of ethics and religion. We introduce into human things the Perfection that properly belongs only to the divine, and thus confuse both human and divine things by not clearly separating them.' Hulme might have been thinking of either Emerson or Arnold when he wrote those sentences, although any other nineteenth-century 'prophet' would have served him as well. The religious attitude, as Hulme defines it, consists in its view of man 'as essentially limited and imperfect. He is endowed with Original Sin. While he can occasionally accomplish acts which partake of perfection, he can never himself *be* perfect. Certain secondary results in regard to ordinary human action in society follow from this. A man is essentially bad, he can only accomplish anything of value by discipline—ethical and political. Order is thus not merely negative, but creative and liberating. Institutions are necessary.' Eliot quoted this last passage in his essay on Baudelaire. One could not find a more compact expression of the gradually hardening lines of his own thought, as he has moved from and yet retained so many elements of the Puritan strain.

But as Eliot's mind has reached towards the Catholic position,

he has been acutely conscious of the new violent extreme which
threatens society to-day, the overwhelming of valuable impulses in
the individual life by the narrow iron standardization of dictatorship.
Not that he holds any brief whatsoever for the value of the expansive
expression of an uncontrolled 'personality', for the impure artist who,
like Rousseau or Byron, exploits his idiosyncratic temperament at the
expense of society instead of finding its fulfilment in the impersonal
structure of a work of art. Nevertheless Eliot knows well that art can
come into existence only through the free play of impulses; that it
is worthless to try to demonstrate that 'if Milton had held more
normal doctrines he would have written a better poem', since the
source of Milton's inspiration was bound up with his passionate desire to express those very doctrines. What, however, Eliot insists to be
disastrous 'is that the writer should deliberately give rein to his "individuality," that he should even cultivate his differences from others;
and that his readers should cherish the author of genius, not in spite
of his deviations from the inherited wisdom of the race, but because
of them.' For Eliot understands that the greatest art 'is impersonal, in
the sense that personal emotion, personal experience is extended and
completed in something impersonal, not in the sense of something
divorced from personal experience and passion.'

The very title *Tradition and the Individual Talent* indicates the
stress he has continued to put on the fact that a poem is not a turning
loose of personal emotion, that 'no artist produces great art by a
deliberate attempt to express his personality. He expresses his personality indirectly through concentrating upon a task which is a task
in the same sense as the making of an efficient engine or the turning
of a jug or a table-leg.' There is the voice of the craftsman in that
remark, of the man who has admired Dryden's skill and Pound's
technical expertness, who understands the selfcontained quality of a
finished masterpiece. But there is more than that: the realization that
nothing great has ever been created by a human being without the
creator's 'surrendering himself wholly to the work to be done,' without a continual self-sacrifice 'of himself as he is at the moment to
something which is more valuable.'

In *The Sacred Wood* such views were restricted to observations
on the writing of poetry, in the elaboration of Eliot's belief that the
artist 'must be aware that the mind of Europe, the mind of his own
country . . . is much more important than his own private mind.'

But during the intervening years, as we have seen, Eliot has widened his quest, and become deeply concerned with both religion and politics. In *After Strange Gods* he attempted a description of what he means by orthodoxy to put beside his conception of tradition, itself now extended to a wider context:

> I hold—in summing up—that a *tradition* is rather a way of feeling and acting which characterizes a group throughout generations; and that it must largely be, or that many of the elements in it must be, unconscious; whereas the maintenance of *orthodoxy* is a matter which calls for the exercise of all our conscious intelligence. The two will therefore considerably complement each other.

His conception of the differences between these two elements, and his understanding of the intricate counteraction and interplay between them in a complex civilization, demonstrate his opposition to the falseness of any over-simplified pattern of the social structure. Eliot is careful to make clear that he is not using orthodoxy in the strict theological sense of the term (although, in his own experience, the significance that would now attach itself to his belief in the creative act as consisting in the individual's sacrifice 'of himself as he is at the moment to something which is more valuable' would connect integrally with his growing belief in dogma). What he stresses in his account of the importance of orthodoxy is 'the inherited wisdom of the race,' the carefully sifted central values of human experience that are always at war with extreme individualism in any form. Exactly what he means is disclosed when he states that in examining contemporary literature he is 'not concerned with the authors' *beliefs,* but with orthodoxy of sensibility and with the sense of tradition'; and that in such light D. H. Lawrence is 'an almost perfect example of the heretic. And the most ethically orthodox of the more eminent writers of my time is Mr. Joyce.'

Eliot developed further the contrast between these two writers (in the unpublished lecture already referred to): that Lawrence is always concerned merely with the relations between two individuals and their failure, 'always looking for the perfect relationship and of course never finding it'; that Joyce, on the contrary, is 'concerned with the relation of man to God.' Joyce's scepticism may have carried him beyond the point where he can believe in anything; yet his understanding of the sense of sin is the key to Stephen Dedalus's behaviour in both *The Portrait of the Artist as a Young Man* and in *Ulysses*. And throughout the sordid picture of contemporary Dublin, you still have 'the Catholic idea, the sense that society is more important than the happiness of the individual, hence none of the sentimentality you find in *Sons and Lovers*. In the latter you find only individuals, in the former you find society.' That is to say, in Joyce you have 'a sense of history'; in Lawrence only 'of the moment'— though Eliot's strictures on the inadequacy of Lawrence's interpretation of life did not blind him to the extraordinary sensibility that enabled Lawrence to describe, in a way that Joyce could not, the pain and ecstasy of individual relationships, and to communicate, in visionary flashes, the sensuous fullness of 'the moment.'

In a further reflection on Joyce, Eliot expressed as searching a comment as he has yet made on the relation of the individual to society: 'the Catholic paradox: society is for the salvation of the individual and the individual must be sacrificed to society. Communism is merely a heresy, but a heresy is better than nothing.'

The reason why Eliot is a poet-critic of the first order is that, like Dryden or Arnold, he has not been content to be merely that. Like the author of *Absolom and Achitophel* and *The Hind and the Panther* his mind has wrestled increasingly with some of the main problems of his day. But unlike the author of *Literature and Dogma,* and aided in part by his mistakes, the increased sphere of Eliot's interests has not caused him to confuse their different functions. Eliot is hardly more qualified for metaphysical speculation than Arnold was—he himself has spoken of his 'incapacity for abstruse reasoning'; in spite of his long training in philosophy, his mind is too heavily concrete, his insight too purely intuitive, to qualify him for sustained flight in the realm of pure logic. Nor, in all probability, will either his political or religious thought build up into a wholly adequate system. But his consistent concern with these spheres of thought and action has yielded him a much deeper understanding of the nature of art and its value for society than was possessed by the author of *Tradition and the Individual Talent*. For now, as he says, he conceives of tradition as being of the blood, as 'the means by which the vitality of the past enriches the life of the present.' Orthodoxy is of the brain, and is not unrelated to the quality which he previously discovered in the philosopher Bradley (the author of *Appearance and Reality* and perhaps Eliot's chief master in prose style): the quality of wisdom which 'consists largely of scepticism and uncynical disillusion.' In comparison, however, orthodoxy would probably appear as something 'older, more patient, more supple and more wise.'

In the co-operation between tradition and orthodoxy 'is the reconciliation of thought and feeling.' And that brings us once more to the very heart of Eliot's most fundamental belief as an artist: the necessary union of intellect and emotion. He finds it in 'the consummate art' of the finest philosophic prose style in our language, 'in which acute intellect and passionate feeling preserve a classic balance.' Such union, in which words are 'so close to the object' that the two become identified, as surely in Eliot as in Donne or Baudelaire, is the chief attribute of great poetry as well.

# R. P. BLACKMUR *

IF you want a text to head and animate a discussion of Mr. Eliot's work from *Ash Wednesday* to *Murder in the Cathedral,* there is none better—for exactness, for ambiguity, and for a capacity to irritate those unlikely otherwise to respond—than the following sentence drawn from *After Strange Gods,* which summarises Mr. Eliot's answer to the charge of incoherence between his verse and his critical prose. "I should say that in one's prose reflexions one may be legitimately occupied with ideals, whereas in the writing of verse one can only deal with actuality." Here Mr. Eliot shows his characteristic talent for making statements of position which mislead some, drive others to laboured exegesis, but end by seeming self-evident and a piece with the body of his work. In this instance what is misleading is not in the words but in the common and not always tacit assumption that poetry aims to transcend or idealise the actual; which may be so of some poetry, of official poetry for example, but cannot well be so without vitiating it, of poetry like Mr. Eliot's which has a dramatic or moral cast. Conflict of character, mixture of motive, and the declaration of human purpose and being, cannot be presented (however much they may be argued) except in terms of good and evil, which makes the most actual realm we know.

It is the criterion of the actual, of the important orders among it, and the means of approach that differ; and if we call the differences verbal, intending to belittle them, it is because we wish to escape the pressure of imaginative labour inherent in any genuine picture of the actual—as if the actual were free and ascertainable to all comers at the turn of a tap, instead of being, as it is, a remaining mystery even when long ardour has won·knowledge of it. The actual, for poetry, or for Mr. Eliot's poetry, resides perhaps among "the deeper, unnamed feelings which form the substratum of our being, to which we rarely penetrate"; a notion, and Mr. Eliot's phrasing of it, to which this essay will return. Now, you might say that for the realm of the actual so

---

conceived the psychoanalysts have a means of approach but no criterion, and the Nazis have a criterion which for their purpose makes
means of approach superfluous. Mr. Eliot has a criterion and a means
which may be disentangled but which cannot be separated. But it is
not a criterion that many can adopt to-day. As it happens, the three
major adequate criteria of the actual—the Church of the great Christians, philosophy as it includes Plato, Montaigne, and Spinoza, and,
third, that nameless tradition of the supernatural in daily life which
includes folk-magic and extra-Christian religion; as it happens all
three are in our day either taken as modes of escape or their animating
influence is ignored. This is because of the tireless human genius for
evasion and the inexhaustible human appetite for facts of the kinds
that have use but cannot declare meaning: the statistical facts of
science; it has nothing to do with the adequacy of the criteria themselves. Which indicates only that a man must achieve his own criterion individually and that it may appear disguised.

Mr. Eliot's criterion is the Christianity of the Church of England;
and he is in the process of achieving it for himself. He provides us
with an example of a powerful poetic imagination feeding on a corpus
of insight either foreign or stultifying to the imaginative habit of
most of us, and sustained by an active and inclusive discipline beyond
our conscious needs. He is as far from us as Mr. Yeats, our one in-
dubitable major poet, is with his fairies and lunar phases; and as
close, in his best work, as Mr. Yeats in his, in an immitigable grasp
of reality. It is a question which is the outsider. Mr. Yeats finds Christianity as unsatisfying for himself, finally, as any Huxley; [1] and Mr.
Eliot has emphasised, with reference to Mr. Yeats, that you cannot
take heaven by magic, has argued in several places recently that you
cannot substitute a private for an institutional religion or philosophy.
Both men write verse with the authority and the application of an
orthodoxy. It may be that both are outsiders, if we conceive, as it
may be fruitful to do, that the prevailing essences of English and

---

[1] I hope to consider in another place the extraordinary strength in representing reality which Mr. Yeats derives from his own resort to the supernatural;
a strength so great that it corrects every *material* extravagance of his doctrine.
Here I merely quote three lines addressed to a modern Catholic.

Homer is my example and his unchristened heart.
The lion and the honeycomb, what has Scripture said?
So get you gone, Von Hügel, though with blessings on your head.

American civilisation are heterodox—when the mere sight of any orthodoxy, of any whole view, may be entertained as dramatic and profoundly tragic. Some such notion was perhaps tacitly present in Mr. Eliot's mind when he wrote the following sentence. "At the moment when one writes, one is what one is, and the damage of a lifetime, and of having been born into an unsettled society, cannot be repaired at the moment of composition." At least it is in terms derived from such notion that the spectator can see the tragedy in the lives of such writers as D. H. Lawrence and Hart Crane—perhaps no less in the life of Dante—though the writers themselves may have seen only the pursuit of a task.[2]

Here two interesting and fundamental problems are raised—that of the truth of an orthodoxy and that of the tragedy of an orthodox mind in a heterodox world; one is for theology and the other for imaginative representation; but neither can be here our concern. Our own problem is no less interesting and I think no less fundamental; the problem of the moral and technical validity of Mr. Eliot's Christianity as it labours to seize the actual for representation in his poetry. Validity is not truth in an ascertainable sense, but amounts to truth in a patent sense. We are faced in Mr. Eliot's recent verse with a new and rising strength patently connected with his Christianity; and the Christian discipline is dominant and elemental in the two plays, *The Rock* and *Murder in the Cathedral*. It might formerly have been thought odd to call attention to a writer's religion as still earlier his religious conformity would have been the final test of his value. Now a man's religion is the last thing we can take for granted about him, which is as it should be; and when a writer shows the animating presence of religion in his work, and to the advantage of his work, the nature of that presence and its linkage deserve at least once our earnest examination. Interest will be clearly seen if the statement can be accepted that there has hardly been a poet of similar magnitude in English whose work, not devotional in character, shows the operative, dramatic presence of Christianity. Many poets have relied, like Wordsworth, upon a religion to which they did not adhere, and many have

---

[2] It is notable that from another point of view Henry James saw the artist as an interesting theme for fiction only in his guise as a failure; his success was wholly in his work. See the Prefaces to *The Tragic Muse*, *The Author of Beltraffio*, and *The Lesson of the Master*.

used such a religion provisionally as a foil from the rack; but there are only rarely examples of poets or poems where deliberate affirmative use is made of religion for dramatic purposes. It is true, after the middle age, in the ages of Faith muddled with reason, the Church would not have tolerated such a use at lay hands. There is Milton unarguably; but I should like to submit that Milton's religious dramatisations are theological in an age of theology and that what I am anxious to discriminate in Mr. Eliot is in the dramatisation of the turbulent feelings and the voids beneath the theology. Then there is Blake, whose religion was not Christian and often not religion at all but whose religious convictions permeated his prophetic books; but Blake's religion was self-manufactured as well as self-achieved, with the consequence that it as frequently clogged as freed his insight. Here we are concerned with the operative advantage of an objective religion on the material of dramatic poetry.

That is, the great interest, here as in any domain of criticism, is in the facts that can be stated about the relation between Mr. Eliot's poetry and his religion. No fact requires so much emphasis as the fact that, just as Mr. Yeats' poetry is not magic, Mr. Eliot's poetry is not religion. Religion and magic are backgrounds, and the actual (which may include the experience of magic and religion) is so to speak the foreground for each; the poet is in the area between, and in the light of the one operates upon the other. But there is no way in which, say, the mystery and magic of the Mass can enter directly into the material of poetry; nor on the other hand can poetry alone satisfy the legitimate aspirations of religion. For all I know the Church may hold differently; these propositions are meant to apply from the point of view of poetry alone, which we may think of here as looking for light upon its subject matter. The Church, which is religion embodied, articulated, and groomed, concentrates and spurs the sensibility, directing it with an engine for the judgment of good and evil upon the real world; but it does not alter, it only shapes and guides the apprehension and feeling of the real world. The facts of religion enlighten the facts of the actual, from which they are believed to spring.[3]

---

[3] The facts of science may similarly enlighten, providing there is a medium of poetic imagination; this although Mr. Eliot finds, correctly, the falsely poetic astronomy of our day quite vitiated. It was, says Mr. Eliot, the eternal *silence* of the immense spaces that terrified Pascal.

The act of enlightening or of being enlightened cannot, except for the great mystic, amount to identification of the object with the light in which it was seen; and in poetry it is only the devotional order which would desire such identification. Mr. Eliot's poetry is not devotional, unless we accept the notion that the love of God is best exercised in the knowledge of his works; a notion which would include Shakespeare as above all a devotional poet since he mirrored more of the actual man than any poet we know. But that is not what we mean by devotional poetry and it is ruining the heart of a word to sustain the pretence that we do. We mean as a rule poetry that constructs, or as we say expresses, a personal emotion about God, and I think it requires something approaching a saint to be very often successful in such constructions; and a saint, as Mr. Eliot observes, would limit himself if he undertook much devotional poetry. Otherwise, whatever the sincerity, private devotions are likely to go by rote and intention rather than rise to a represented state; there enters too much the question of what ought to be felt to the denigration (and I should say to God's eye) of what is actually felt—and it is this characteristic predicament of the devout which cripples the development of poets like Hopkins and Crashaw so that we value them most in other, hindered qualities than the devout. It is perhaps indicative in this context of devotional poetry considered as poetry to remember how few from twenty Christian centuries are the great prayers. It would seem that an earnest repetition of the General Confession is a more devout if less emotional act than the composition of a poem.

Mr. Eliot's poetry is not devotional in any sense of which we have been speaking, but, for the outsider—and we are all outsiders when we speak of poetry—it is the more religious for that. It is religious in the sense that Mr. Eliot believes the poetry of Villon and Baudelaire to be religious—only an educated Villon and a healthy Baudelaire: it is penetrated and animated and its significance is determined by Christian feeling, and especially by the Christian distinction of Good and Evil. This feeling and this distinction have in his prose reflexions led him to certain extravagances—I remember as superlative a paper contributed to a Unitarian Monthly attacking the liberal element, which ended magnificently: "They are right. They are damned."—but in his verse, where he has limited himself, if sometimes obscurely, to the actual, there is no resulting extravagance, but the liberation of increased scope and that strength of charitable understanding which is apparently most often possible through Christian judgment.[4]

That is, the Church is in Mr. Eliot's poetry his view of life; it recognises and points the issues and shapes their poetic course; it is the rationale of his drama and the witness of its fate; it is, in short, a way of handling poetic material to its best advantage. It may be much more—as there is always life itself beyond the poetry that declares it; here nothing but the poetry is in question. If we consider the series of poems united in *Ash Wednesday* apart from the influence of that view of life we shall be left in as much of a muddle as if we consider them apart from the influence which Mr. Eliot's merely poetic habits exert upon their Christianity. We should have, in the one case, an emotional elegy without much point but human weakness; and in the other, if we recognised the Christianity and nothing else, we should have only a collection of ritual trappings and reminiscences.

I do not know if there have been efforts to appreciate the Christian tags alone; but I know that so intelligent a critic as Mr. Edmund Wilson (in *Axel's Castle*) missed the Christian *significance* in the poem and saw only a revelation of human weakness and an escapist's despair. Mr. Wilson had a non-literary axe to grind. Mr. I. A. Richards, who had, as Mr. Eliot would say, more nearly the benefits of a Christian education, saw, even if he did not share, the Christian light, although that is not what he calls it. Mr. Richards saw what the poem was about; that it was not a revelation of human weakness and an attempt at escape but a summoning of human strength and an effort to extinguish both hope and despair in the face of death. The poem is neither the devotion of a weary soul nor an emotional elegy; it is, like almost all of Mr. Eliot's poetry, a dramatised projection of experience. As it happens the experience has a religious bias; which means that it calls on specific Christian beliefs to make the projection actual.

That the poem relies on other devices of the poetic imagination is obvious, and that these in their turn make the Christian beliefs actual for the poem—as Shakespeare's devices made Othello's jealousy actual—should be equally obvious. Here I want to emphasise that the abnegation in the first section of the poem is Christian abnegation

[4] The least charity is moral indifference, and Mr. Eliot's attacks upon it (in *After Strange Gods*) are just, whether you share his Christianity or not; but his principles are not the only ones to secure the end in view.

(it is introduced, after all, by the governing title *Ash Wednesday,* which begins the forty days of fast and penance before the resurrection, and which also commemorates the temptation and triumph in the wilderness); and Christian abnegation is an act of strength not weakness, whereby you give up what you can of the evil of the flesh for the good of the soul. The conception is certainly not limited to Christianity; as an ethical myth it is common to most philosophies and religions; but its most dramatic because most specifically familiar form is certainly that rehearsed by the Christian Church. That Mr. Eliot should make serious use of it, aside from his private religion, is natural; and it ought to have helped rather than hindered the understanding of the fundamental human feelings his poem dramatised. Mr. Wilson should have recognised its presence, and had he done so could not have mistaken the intent of the poem, however much for other reasons he might have judged it inadequate, for many persons, to its theme.

Similarly—if there is need for a further example—in the quoted words of Arnaut Daniel in the fourth section, we should, to gain anything like their full significance, not only be aware of their literary origin in the *Purgatorio,* not only feel the weight of Dante at our backs, but also should feel the force of the Christian teaching which made the words poignant for Dante—and so for Mr. Eliot. This or its equivalent. Knowing such matters for poetry is not so hard as it seems when the process is described; perhaps in this case, if the mind strikes instinctively at all the right attitude, the context of the poem will force the right meaning into the reader's mind once the literal meaning is understood. *Sovegna vos:* Be mindful of me, remember my pain. Arnaut wishes Dante to remember him in the wilfully accepted, refining fires of purgatory. It is characteristic of the meaning and integral to the association from which it springs that the words appear in Dante's Provençal. Had Mr. Eliot translated them they would have lost their identity and their air of specific origin; their being a quotation, and the reader knowing them so, commits them to a certain life and excludes other lives; nor could they have brought with them, in bare English, the very Christian context we wish to emphasise.

A different, but associated, effect is secured by the fact that the line which, with variations, opens the first and the last of these poems, appears in Mr. Eliot's English rather than in Guido Cavalcanti's

Italian: at least I assume the line would own its source. Cavalcanti's line reads: "Perch'io non spero di tornar già mai"; Mr. Eliot's first version reads: "Because I do not hope to turn again," and his second: "Although I do not hope to turn again." The difference between "Because" and "Although" is deliberate and for the attentive reader will add much to the meaning. Mr. I. A. Richards has commented on the distinction in *On Imagination*. But the point I wish to make here is not about the general influence of either form of the line; the unwary reader can determine that for himself. My point is smaller, at least initially, and consists in stating two or three facts, and the first fact is very small indeed. "Perche" may be rendered either "because" or "although," depending on the context, here supplied by Mr. Eliot. The second fact is a little larger; although Mr. Eliot may greatly admire the Ballata from which the line was taken, it was not its import in that poem which concerned him in his own, so that to have quoted it in the original would either have given a wrong impression of import or have prefaced a serious work with a meretricious literary ornament. The Italian line (with its overtones about turning and renunciation of many orders) gave him material to remodel for his own purposes in his own poem—with yet a sediment, perhaps, of objective source to act as a mooring. As it happens, which is why the line is discussed here at all, it is indissolubly associated in both its forms with the "great" lines in the poem: the prayer—

> Teach us to care and not to care
> Teach us to sit still

This is a Christian prayer (not, as I gather Mr. Wilson would have it, at all mystical) and represents in an ultimate form for poetry one of the great aspects of the Church—its humility. That it also represents, in another interpretation, a great aspect of Confucianism is immaterial; as it is immaterial that by still another interpretation it represents the heart of Roman stoicism. Mr. Eliot came to it through the Church, or his poem did, and he brought Guido's line with him; [5] and the line as used has a dominant Christian flavour which cannot be expunged. There is thus a transformation of tone in this quotation quite different but to be associated with the quotation of Arnaut's phrase. As materials in the poem, one exerted Christian feeling in its

---

[5] It is amusing but not inconsistent to reflect that Mr. Eliot has noted that Guido was a heretic.

own right, and the other was made to carry Christian feeling by the context—and feeling of the deep and nameless order which is the reality of Mr. Eliot's poetry.

The reader may rightly wonder if he is expected to get at Mr. Eliot's reality so indirectly and through the coils of such close-wound ellipsis; and especially will he wonder if he has read Mr. Eliot's assertion that he would like an audience that could neither read nor write, and this because, as he says, "it is the half-educated and ill-educated, rather than the uneducated, who stand" in the poet's way. Well, the uneducated hardly exist with relation to Mr. Eliot's poetry; and very few of his audience can be said to be rightly educated for it—certainly not this writer; most of us come to his poetry very ill-educated indeed. If modern readers did not as a class have to make up for the defects of their education in the lost cause of Christianity—if we did not find Christianity fascinating because strange, and dramatic because full of a hubris we could no more emulate than that of Oedipus—there would be neither occasion nor point for this particular essay. We have a special work of imaginative recovery to do before we can use Mr. Eliot's poetry to the full. However a later day may see it in perspective, to us Mr. Eliot must be of our time less because he seems to spring from it than because he imposes upon us a deep reminder of a part of our heritage which we have lost except for the stereotypes of spiritual manners. These stereotypes form our natural nexus with the impetus or drive of his poetry; and it is as we see them filled out, refreshed, re-embodied, that his poems become actual for us. Mr. Eliot is perhaps not himself in a position to sympathise with this operation of imaginative recovery; at any rate he rejected the to us plausible statement of Mr. Richards that *The Waste Land* was poetry devoid of beliefs. Mr. Eliot would prefer the advantage of a literal to that of an imaginative faith, immersion to empathy; and he has very much doubted, in his moral judgment of Thomas Hardy, whether what he says could "convey very much to anyone for whom the doctrine of Original Sin is not a very real and tremendous thing." The answer to that is that we do need to know that the doctrine of Original Sin is a reality for Mr. Eliot, and how much so, in order to determine both what light it sheds on Hardy and how to combine it with other insights into Hardy; but we do not need to share Mr. Eliot's conviction of literal application. Indeed, many of us would feel that we had impoverished our belief by making it too easy if we

did share the conviction. Here is the crux of the whole situation between Mr. Eliot and those outside the Faith. The literal believer takes
his myths, which he does not call myths, as supernatural archetypes of
reality; the imaginative believer, who is not a "believer" at all, takes
his myths for the meaning there is in their changing application. The
practical consequences may be similar, since experience and interest
are limited for data to the natural world, but the labour of understanding and the value assigned will be different for each. Thus Mr.
Eliot and Mr. Richards are both correct—although neither would accept my way of saying so. *The Waste Land* is full of beliefs (especially,
for this essay, a belief in the myth of Gethsemane) and is not limited
by them but freed once they are understood to be imaginative. Only
Mr. Eliot is correct for himself alone, while Mr. Richards is correct
for others as well. Our labour is to recapture the imaginative burden
and to avoid the literal like death.

If Mr. Eliot could not accept this notion in the abstract, he employs something very like it in his practical view of poetry, and by
doing so he suggests an admirable solution for the reader's difficulties
with his own poems and especially the difficulty with their Christian
elements. This is the notion of different levels of significance and
response. "In a play of Shakespeare," says Mr. Eliot, "you get several
levels of significance. For the simplest auditors there is the plot, for
the more thoughtful the character and the conflict of character, for
the more literary the words and phrasing, for the more musically
sensitive the rhythm, and for auditors of greater sensitiveness and
understanding a meaning which reveals itself gradually. And I do
not believe that the classification of audience is so clear-cut as this;
but rather that the sensitiveness of every auditor is acted upon by all
these elements at once, though in different degrees of consciousness.
At none of these levels is the auditor bothered by the presence of what
he does not understand, or by the presence of that in which he is not
interested."

I propose to apply a little later the burden of these sentences where
they properly belong: to the two plays, *The Rock* and *Murder in the
Cathedral*. Meanwhile let us twist the reference slightly and apply it to
our present problem: the reader's relation to the Christian element
among other elements in such poems as *Ash Wednesday,* merely
substituting within the quotation the word readers for audience or
auditors. Clearly there are different levels of significance at which the

poem can be read; there are the levels responded to by Mr. Richards and Mr. Wilson; and there is the simplest level where there is "only" the poem to consider. But if the formula is applicable with any justice it is because Mr. Eliot's contention is correct that "the sensitiveness of every reader is acted upon by all these elements at once," and because, further, "at none of these levels is the reader bothered by the presence of what he does not understand, or the presence of that in which he is not interested." In that case we must admit that most readers do not count for more than the simplest form of excitement and vicarious mewing; which is the truth—and it is upon that class that the existence of poetry relies. Then there is a class a little higher in the scale, the class that propagates poetry without understanding it in any conscious sense; this is the class Mr. Wilson describes, the class of young poets who, after _The Waste Land_ began to sink in, "took to inhabiting exclusively barren beaches, cactus-grown deserts, and dusty attics over-run with rats." Possibly these classes are unconsciously affected by all or almost all the possible levels of significance, including those of which the author was unaware; which makes occasion both for pride and prospective humiliation in the poet. I think the notion has something Christian in it; something that smells of grace; and has very little to do with any conception of popular poetry addressed to an audience that can neither read nor write. However that may be, there remains the class that preserves and supports poetry, a class the members of which unfortunately cannot stop short on the level of their unconscious appreciation but necessarily go on, risking any sort of error and ultimate mistake, until they are satisfied as to what a poem means. This may not be the class for which Mr. Eliot or any poet writes; but it includes that very small sub-class of readers of "greater sensitiveness and understanding" for whom the meaning of a poem reveals itself gradually. It is the class for and by both the good and bad members of which honest literary criticism is written.

And it is this class which, confronted by a sensibility so powerful and so foreign as Mr. Eliot's, is determined to get at the means as well as the meaning. It is in that sense that Mr. Eliot's poetry may be a spiritual exercise of great scope. This class, then, apprehending the dominant presence of Christian doctrine and feeling in Mr. Eliot's work, must reach something like the following conclusions as representing provisional truths. The Church is the vehicle through which human purpose is to be seen and its teachings prod and vitalise the poetic sensibility engaged with the actual and with the substrata of the actual. Furthermore, and directly for poetry, the Church presents a gift of moral and philosophical form of a pre-logical character; and it is a great advantage for a poet to find his material fitting into a form whose reason is in mystery rather than logic, and no less reason for that. It is perhaps this insight into the nature of the Church's authority that brought Mr. Eliot to his most magnificent statement about poetry. "The essential advantage for a poet is not to have a beautiful world with which to deal: it is to be able to see beneath both beauty and ugliness; to see the boredom, and the horror, and the glory."

But since this class of reader is not itself Christian—any more than poetry is itself Christian—it will be to our advantage and to that of poetry to remind ourselves emphatically of what Mr. Eliot has himself several times insisted, that the presence of Christianity does not make a poem good. It is the poetry that must be good. Good Christianity will be a very watery thing adulterated with bad poetry, and good poetry can overcome a good deal of defection in a Christian poet's Christianity—as it does in Dante's hate. In admitting and enforcing the advantage of the Church, we commit ourselves, and before measuring our appreciation, to define the limits, both moral and operative, contained in our admission. There are some orders of charity in moral judgment which the doctrines of the Church cannot encompass; there are some experiences, that is, that the Church cannot faithfully mirror because it has no clues or has not the right clues to the reality involved. Thus we find Mr. Eliot refusing to understand Shelley and *Lady Chatterley's Lover;* and we find him also complaining of Irving Babbitt, whom he admired, that he made too much use of the Eastern Philosophies. I doubt, too, if the Church would be the right docent for an inspection of the drama of personality unfolded by Freudian psychology; it would see a different drama. . . . And we have, too, to decide provisionally what the Church, as a supernatural reference, makes up for, and what—whether we miss it or not—it fails to make up for; which is not at all easy to do. Perhaps we may say that the doctrines of the Church (we are not concerned, in poetry, with ritual worship) idealise a pretty complete set of human aspirations, and do this by appealing to a supernatural order. That is a great deal; but for poetry the Church does more. As these ideals are applied for judgment and light, all human action, struggle, and conflict, and all human feelings, too, gain a special significance. For us, as outsiders, the significance becomes greater if we remember that it is a special, a predicted significance, and that other ideals, and no ideals, would give a different significance or none at all. Taken as a whole, the Church, by insisting on being right, became one of the great heresies of the human mind.

Our final obligation with respect to the Church is our smallest but most specific: to deal with it as an element of metric, only to be understood in composition with the other elements. We shall have emphasised and exaggerated in order to accomplish a reduction. But as the Church is not itself logical neither are the other elements in the composition. We have collections of elements, of qualities, which appear side by side, engaged, or entangled, or separate, of which the product is a whole varying with each combination. And a mind, too, such as we wish to think of as whole, is subject to the "damage of a lifetime," and we must think of the pressure and stress of that damage, omnipresent, agonising, even though we cannot and would not wish to say what at the moment it is: unless we say vaguely that it is the personality.

To put together indications of the qualities of a mind and of its suffusing personality is a labour for which there are models but no principles; there is no logical structure; and the more plausible the picture made the more likely it is to be untrustworthy. Mr. Eliot's mind, let us say, is a mind of contrasts which sharpen rather than soften the longer they are weighed. It is the last mind which, in this century, one would have expected to enter the Church in a lay capacity. The worldliness of its prose weapons, its security of posture, its wit, its ability for penetrating doubt and destructive definition, its eye for startling fact and talent for nailing it down in flight, hardly go with what we think of to-day as English or American religious feeling. We are accustomed to emotionalism and fanaticism in religious thought and looseness in religious feeling; the very qualities which are the natural targets of Mr. Eliot's weapons. Possibly it may be that we are unfamiliar with good contemporary Christian writers; they could hardly infect the popular press. Possibly, or even probably, it was these very qualities which, after the demolition of the pretence of value in post-war society, drove him into the Church as the one institution unaffected by the pretence or its demolition. Perhaps the teaching of Irving Babbitt, less by its preliminary richness than by its final inadequacy, was an important influence: we see in Mr. Eliot at least one of the virtues which Babbittt inculcated—Mr. Eliot is never expansive, either in verse or in prose, and expansiveness was a bugaboo to Babbitt.

However that may be, within the Church or not, Mr. Eliot's mind has preserved its worldly qualities. His prose reflexions remain elegant, hard (and in a sense easy—as in manners), controlled, urbane (without the dissimulation associated with ecclesiastical urbanity), and fool-proof. One would say that the mind was self-assured and might pontificate; but there is a redeeming quality of reserve about the assurance of his rare dogmatic extravagances, a reserve which may be taken as the accompaniment of scrupulous emotion and humility. This is—except the reserve—the shell which a mind must needs wear in order to get along without being victimised, and in order to deal, without escape, with things as they are on the surface. It is the part of a mind which is educable from outside, without regard to its inner bias.

Beneath the shell is a body of feeling and a group of convictions. Mr. Eliot is one of the few persons to whom convictions may be ascribed without also the ascription of fanaticism. Prejudice, which he has, is only a by-product of conviction and need be raised as an issue only when the conviction goes wrong; and intolerance, which he condones, is in the intellectual field only the expected consequence of conviction. With a little skill one learns to allow for prejudice and intolerance in Mr. Eliot's mind as we do for any convicted mind. His convictions are those which stem from the Church, from the history of Christian peoples, and from the classical cultures: including the convictions which represent Sophocles, Dante, and Shakespeare, as well as those which represent Original Sin, the Resurrection, and the sin of Spiritual Pride. However complexly arrived at, and with whatever, as the outsider must think them, tactful evasions in application, his convictions are directly and nobly held. If they enhance narrowness and put some human problems on too simple a plane they yet unflaggingly enforce depth. The mind reaches down until it touches bottom. Its weakness is that it does not always take in what it passes.

But a mind furnished only with convictions would be like a room furnished only with light; the brighter the more barren. Mr. Eliot's convictions light a sensibility stocked with feelings and observations and able to go on feeling and observing, where the feelings are more important than the observations. It is this body of feelings, and not

any intermediately necessary intellectualisations of them, which are
his ultimate concern; and ours, when we can bear on them. We may
note here the frequency in his work of physiological images to sym-
bolise the ways of knowing and the quality of things known; the
roots and tentacles and all the anatomical details. Concerned with the
material of life actually lived, his convictions only confirm a form for
the material, make it available, release contact with it; as I suppose, in
the other direction, convictions only confirm a form for the feeling of
faith. And for these operations all learning is only a waiting, a reminiscence, and a key. It is the presence of this material, living and seen,
if underneath, that makes Mr. Eliot master of the big words which,
when directly charged, are our only names for its manifestations as
emotion. Both in his poetry when he needs to and in his prose when
he cares to, Mr. Eliot is free to use all those large emotional words with
absolute precision of contact which your ordinary writer has to avoid
as mere omnibuses of dead emotion.

It is natural then, in connection with these remarks, that in his
prose writing, whether early or late, whether in essays or controversy,
appreciation or judgment, Mr. Eliot is master of the compressed insight, the sudden illumination, the felt comparison, the seminal suggestion, and a stable point of view; and it is equally in course that we
should find him master of persuasive and decimating rhetoric rather
than of sustained argument and exhaustive analysis. He sees and his
words persuade us of the fact that he has seen and of the living aspect
of what he saw; but his words hardly touch, directly, the objective
validity of what he saw. This explains the scope of his influence. There
is no question that he has seen what he asserts; in the field of literature his eye for facts is extraordinarily keen, though like a sharp-
shooter's it hits only what it is looking for. There is no question,
either, if you share his point of view even provisionally, that his
weapons of attack penetrate if they do not dispatch their victims. That
there is more to be seen, his scruples make him admit. But as for the
objects of his attack, not his scruples but his methods leave some of
them alive. You cannot kill an idea unless you have first embraced it,
and Mr. Eliot is chary of embraces. This explains, too, why some of
his followers have turned against him and why others are content to
parrot him. He has an air of authority in his prose, an air of having
said or implied to the point of proof everything that could be said;
when as a matter of fact he has merely said what he felt and demon-

strated his own conviction. Conviction in the end is opinion and personality, which however greatly valuable cannot satisfy those who
wrongly expect more. Those who parrot Mr. Eliot think they share
his conviction but do not understand or possess his personality. Those
who have, dissatisfied, turned against him have merely for the most
part expected too much. The rest of us, if we regard his prose argument as we do his poetry—as a personal edifice—will be content with
what he is.

To argue that the poetry is written by the same mind and intellectually in much the same way as the prose is to show, in this order,
all we need to know. It explains what he leaves out and gives a right
emphasis to what he puts in; and if we add, once again, that his
mind runs almost instinctively to dramatic projections, we understand what kind of organisation his work has—and it has one, deeply
innervated. And I do not mean to beg the question when I say, as
Mr. Eliot said of Shakespeare, that he is himself the unity of his work;
that is the only kind of unity, the only circulating energy which we
call organisation, that we are ever likely to find in the mass of a
man's work. We need to remember only that this unity, this effect
of organisation, will appear differently in works of criticism and
works of poetry, and that it will be more manifest, though less arguable, in the poetry than in the criticism. The poetry is the concrete
—as concrete as the poet can make it—presentation of experience as
emotion. If it is successful it is self-evident; it is subject neither to
denial nor modification but only to the greater labour of recognition.
To say again what we have been saying all along, that is why we can
assent to matters in poetry the intellectual formulation of which
would leave us cold or in opposition. Poetry can use all ideas; argument only the logically consistent. Mr. Eliot put it very well for
readers of his own verse when he wrote for readers of Dante that you
may distinguish understanding from belief. "I will not deny," he
says, "that it may be in practice easier for a Catholic to grasp the
meaning, in many places, than for the ordinary agnostic; but that is
not because the Catholic believes, but because he has been instructed.
It is a matter of knowledge and ignorance, not of belief or scepticism."
And a little later he puts the advantage for readers of poetry "of a
coherent traditional system of dogma and morals like the Catholic:
it stands apart, for understanding and assent even without belief,
from the single individual who propounds it." That is why in our

own context we can understand Mr. Eliot and cannot understand Mr. Pound. The unity that is Mr. Eliot has an objective intellectual version in his Christianity. The unity of Mr. Pound—if there is one —is in a confusion of incoherent, if often too explicitly declared, beliefs.

Christianity, then, is the emphatic form his sensibility fills; it is an artificial question which comes first. It is what happens to the sensibility that counts; the life lived and the death seen. That is the substantial preoccupation of the poet and the reader's gain. The emotion leans for expression on anything it can. Mr. Eliot's sensibility is typical of the poet's, as that of many poets is not. There is no wastage, little thinning out, and the least possible resort to dead form, form without motion. It is a sensibility that cannot deal with the merely surface report—what we used to call naturalism—and be content, but must deal with centres, surds, insights, illuminations, witnessed in chosen, obsessive images. These, as presented, seize enough of the life lived, the death seen, to give the emotion of the actuality of the rest. These we use as poetry; some will keep and some will wear out, as they continue or fail to strike reality as we can bear to know it.[6]

For opposite reasons, this essay can present texts for study neither of the apposite Christian form nor of the private sensibility that fills it; it merely emphasises—with as much repetition as the reader is likely to put up with—that knowledge is better than ignorance for the one, and that the other exists to implement the first. There is the Church for inspection and there are the poems to read. There remains the common labour of literary criticism: the collection of facts about literary works, and comment on the management, the craft or technique, of those works; and this labour, in so far as it leaves the reader in the works themselves, is the only one in itself worth doing. All

---

[6] It is perhaps relevant to quote here part of Mr. Eliot's comment on Arnold's "Poetry is at bottom a criticism of life," in the essay on Arnold in *The Use of Poetry.* "At bottom: that is a great way down; the bottom is the bottom. At the bottom of the abyss is what few ever see, and what those cannot bear to look at for long; and it is not a 'criticism of life.' If we mean life as a whole—not that Arnold ever saw life as a whole—from top to bottom, can anything that we can say of it ultimately, of that awful mystery, be called criticism?" Here Mr. Eliot, as he commonly does at important junctures, which are never arguable, resorts to the emotional version of the actual concerned. The "abyss" is one of his obsessive images.

that has been said so far is conditional and preliminary and also a postscript to reading. The modern reader is not fitted to appreciate either a mind or its works conceived in relation to Christianity as a living discipline; and the effort to appreciate as dead manners what is live blood is as vain as it is likely to prove repulsive. If I have shown to what degree the reader must perform an imaginative resurrection, I have so far done enough.

For Mr. Eliot does spill blood for ink and his discipline does live. It is a commonplace assertion that Mr. Eliot has shaped both his Christianity and his technique to forward the expressive needs of his mind. Here let us keep to the technique; it involves the other; and say that he has deliberately shaped and annealed and alloyed and purified it: the object being a medium of language to enhold the terms of feeling and the sign of the substance felt so as to arouse, sustain, and transform interest at different levels of response; and that he has done so, besides, under the severest of disciplines, adherence to the standards of the good writing that has interested him. I do not say that he has succeeded altogether. Such a technique is the greatest *practical* ambition possible to secure; it takes long to come by and is slow to direct, since if it is to be adequate it must include the craft of presenting everything that is valuable. Very young poets confuse technique either with tricks, dodges, and devices, which are only a part of it, or with doodabs.

> Ambition comes when early force is spent
> And when we find no longer all things possible.

Perhaps I twist a little Mr. Eliot's implications, but it seems to me that the great temptations to which a poet's technique are exposed are the early temptation of the adventitious—the nearest weapon and the neatest subject—, and the temptation of repetition, which comes later, and of which it is the sin that the result is bound to be meretricious. These are fundamentals for all techniques and there are modifications for each; the whole technique of any one poem can never be the whole technique of any other poem, since, such is the limitation of human experience, a new poem is more likely to represent a growth of technique than a *growth* (I do not say change) of subject matter.

Nor will such a technique, for all readers or perhaps for any, ever be completely achieved except in the sum of the greatest poets. There are too many expectations, just enough in their sincerity, that can neither be gratified nor eradicated. There are those, for an extreme example, who expect an art of happiness. But the fact is that the rest of us, whose expectations are less gross, can hardly ever at a given time get over expecting a technique to show us what is not there; nor can we invariably "let" ourselves see what is there.

Confronted by *The Rock* and *Murder in the Cathedral,* it is at once clear, first, that it is Mr. Eliot's technique rather than his subject matter that has grown, and, second, that this technique, new or old, radically limits the number and kind of our expectations. The scope of his poetry, its final magnitude, is a different matter, and the impurity or bloom of the contemporaneous must be rubbed away before it can be determined. What I mean here is that we get neither the kind nor variety of emotional satisfaction from either of his plays that we get from Noel Coward or Congreve or Shakespeare. We are not tittivated or stroked; we do not see society brushed with the pure light of its manners; there is no broad display of human passion and purpose; we get the drama of the Church struggling against society towards God, which is something new (for those who like newness) in English drama; we get the way of the Church against the way of the World. And we get the awful harm as well as the good done men and women in the course of the struggle. It is this harm and this good, this sense of irreparable damage and intransigent glory, as it is in contact with this struggle, that makes the drama actual. It is not spiritual drama; it is not like Dante the drama of damnation, penance, and beatitude; it is the drama of human emotions actualised in the light of spiritual drama. The spirit is there, and intellect, and theology; but all these through actualised emotions of the experience of good and evil, of fraud and ambition, self-deceit and nobility, and the communal humility of the poor—which is a humility beneath Christian humility. This is what we get most in *Murder in the Cathedral,* and what we crucially fail to get in *The Rock.*

It is the substance of this (the same utter view of life) that we get in another way in "Mr. Eliot's Sunday Morning Service" and "The Hippopotamus"—these the tough anti-clerical way; and in still other ways it is the same substance in "Prufrock," "Gerontion," and *The Waste Land.* The substance is permanent; the flux representative. If we take all the poems together with this substance in mind one charge that has been made against them should disappear—that they resent the present and fly into some paradise of the past. On the contrary, they measure the present by living standards which most people relegate to the past. The distinction is sharp; it is between poetry that would have been a shell of mere disillusion and poetry that is alive, and beyond disillusion. As Mr. Eliot himself remarked, *The Waste Land* only showed certain people their own illusion of disillusionment. It is this fundamental identity of substance which marks the unity of his work; that a variety of subjects and diverse approaches conspire to complete, to develop, a single judgment.

The changes—and no one would confuse or wrongly date two of Mr. Eliot's poems—are in the changes and growth of technique. The deliberate principle of growth has been in the direction of appealing to more levels of response, of reaching, finally, the widest possible audience, by attempting to secure in the poetry a base level of significance to which any mind might be expected to respond, without loss or injury to any other level of significance. It is in the light of this re-interpretation that Mr. Eliot's desire for an illiterate audience should be considered. That it is obvious does not make it any less telling, or any less inspiring to work towards, or—remembering the tacit dogma of difficulty held by so many poets—any less refreshing for the prospective reader. That this direction is not a guess on my own part and that he meant his notion of levels of significance in Shakespeare to apply to his own poetry, Mr. Eliot provides a candid text to show. It is at the very end of *The Use of Poetry*. With the great model of Shakespeare, the modern poet would like to write plays. "He would like to be something of a popular entertainer, and be able to think his own thoughts behind a tragic or a comic mask. He would like to convey the pleasures of poetry, not only to a larger audience, but to larger groups of people collectively; and the theatre is the best place to do it. . . . Furthermore, the theatre, by the technical exactions which it makes and limitations which it imposes upon the author, by the obligation to keep for a definite length of time the sustained interest of a large and unprepared and not wholly perceptive group of people, by its problems which have constantly to be solved, has enough to keep the poet's *conscious* mind fully occupied."

The best of Mr. Eliot's paragraph I have omitted: sentences that give the emotion of being a poet. What I have quoted is that part of his prose reflexions concerned with the ideal behind the two plays. It is extraordinary how much of what we want to know these three sentences can be made to explain. The only emphasis needed is this:

that the obligation to keep an audience interested is only indirectly connected with the real interest of the plays. It is primarily a technical obligation; it points to and prepares for the real interest by seeming to be connected with it; and the great liability or technical danger is that the two interests may be confused without being identified, as the great gain is when the two interests are, in crisis, actually identified.

I do not think that in his two plays Mr. Eliot has realised either the radical limitations of his substance or the insuperable limitations of the theatre. The two do not always cooperate and they sometimes overlap. Perhaps it is better so; the comparative failure which says most, like Hamlet, is better than the relative success, like *The Coward*, that says least. The elements of failure must be nevertheless pointed out both when they spread rot and when they are surpassed. *The Rock* gives us an example of failure by confusion of interest which is nearly fatal, and *Murder in the Cathedral* gives us an example of success by fusion of interests.

Contrary to custom in English drama, it is the objective, the witnessing, the only indirectly participating, passages in these plays that are the finest poetry and that do the most work. These are the Choruses, in *The Rock* the chorus that represents the voice of the Church, and, in *Murder in the Cathedral,* the chorus of the women of Canterbury. In *The Rock* there are also choruses of the unemployed, of workmen, and some songs used as ritual chorus. In *Murder in the Cathedral* there is a kind of grand chorus of Priests, Tempters, and Chorus proper, which is used once, in the crisis of the first part. Whereas the traditional uses of the chorus are to comment on and to integrate action, here they are the integrity of the action itself, its actuality. Their relation to the "ordinary" version of the action, the rest of the play, is different in the two plays; and the quality of the work they do is different. It is these differences, in the light of the notion of levels of significance and response and in connection with the effort to maintain interest of both orders, that I wish to lay down the bare bones of. They carry the flesh.

*The Rock* is a pageant play, superficially about the difficulties, the necessity, and the justification of building a church in modern London. The pageant is a loose form and condones the introduction of a great variety of material; and so we are shown, upon the recurring focal scene of a church foundation actually in progress, a variety

of episodes in the history of London churches. The theme and much
of the incident were no doubt set; it is not a promising theme in which
to expand a substance as concentrated as Mr. Eliot's, it is too generous
and like the form chosen too loose, and too inherently facile of execu-
tion. Where almost anything will do passably there is nothing that
will do well. The resulting text is not as drama very promising either.
It is the sort of thing that, as a whole, depends on lushness of production and the personality of performance. At Sadler's Wells it may
have been magnificent, but not because of Mr. Eliot's poetry; and as
it is now, a reader's text, what was important and the very life of
the performance—the incident, the fun, the church-supper social
comment, and the good-humoured satire—reduce the effect of the
poetry because it points away from the poetry instead of towards it.
Bad verse cannot point to good poetry, and there is here the first bad
verse Mr. Eliot has allowed himself to print, as well as his first bad
jokes. The whole play has an air of following the counsel of the
Chorus to the worshippers.

> Be not too curious of Good and Evil;
> Seek not to count the future waves of Time;
> But be ye satisfied that you have light
> Enough to take your step and find your foothold.

It is all satisfied and nearly all spelt in capital letters. Whether the
expected nature of the audience was responsible, the form chosen, or
whether Mr. Eliot was mistaken about both, the fact is that the level
of interest appealed to by the whole play is too low to make passage
to the higher levels natural. The general level lacks emotional probability and therefore lacks actuality. It is dead level writing. The
reader satisfied with the dead level can hardly be expected to perceive, even unconsciously, the higher levels; and the reader interested
in the higher levels cannot but find his interest vitiated by finding it
constantly let down. Take the episode of the Crusades. The conversation between the man and his betrothed is one thing, a flat appeal
to stereotyped emotion; the taking of the Cross, with its sonorous
Latin dressing, is another, an appeal by the direct use of ritual, on
another plane, to the stereotype of the conversation; neither is actualised. The actuality is in the Chorus; but the Chorus is not the
same thing in a different form, it is another thing altogether. There
is a gap between, which is not crossed, and the relations between the

three are disproportional. We hear a distinct voice from another world, which is the real world, and which is the real poem; the actuality of which the other voices are only the substitute and the sham. And the Chorus, in this instance, perhaps loses some of its effect because it comes first, prefacing what it does not perform, and because its phrasing depends on the statements it makes rather than makes the statements.

> Not avarice, lechery, treachery,
> Envy, sloth, gluttony, jealousy, pride:
> It was not these that made the Crusades,
> But these that unmade them.
>
>          .     .     .     .     .
>
> Our age is an age of moderate virtue
> And of moderate vice
> When men will not lay down the Cross
> Because they will never assume it.

Mr. Eliot has not here levied enough upon that other actuality, the actuality bred in the fitting of words together; which is not the same thing as fitting notions together. These strictures apply throughout the episodes of the play and to most of the Choruses to the episodes. It is only rarely, in some of the songs and parts of the general choruses, that we get lines like these, when the poetry escapes the Oppressor.

> Our gaze is submarine, our eyes look upward
> And see the light that fractures through unquiet water.
> We see the light but see not whence it comes.

The Oppressor was the misconceived need of expressing the Church at the level of general interest, instead of intensifying the actuality envisaged by the Church in terms of a represented interest.

This last is what Mr. Eliot has done in his second play, *Murder in the Cathedral,* and I think that the play could not have been better constructed with a view to representing in a self-contained form the mutually interrelated play of different levels of significance, from the lowest to the highest. I do not expect to have exhausted anything but its general interests for a long time to come and I do expect that its actual significance—its revelation of essential human strength and weakness—to grow the whole time. Yet it deals with an emotion I can hardly expect to share, which very few can ever expect to share, except as a last possibility, and which is certainly not an emotion of general interest at all; it deals with the special emotion of Christian martyrdom. Martyrdom is as far removed from common experience as the state of beatitude to which it leads; and it is much further removed, too, from ordinary interests than is the episodic material of *The Rock*. The view of life is as seriously held in either play, and the emotion is in itself as valid in one as in the other; they are in fact substantially the same. The whole difference between the failure of the first and the success of the second play depends on the lowest level of poetic intensity employed. If anything, the lowest level of signif icance (that is, the broadest, appealing to more, and more varied minds) is lower in the second play than the first; and this fact is in itself an element of formal strength and a verification of Mr. Eliot's ideal theory. It almost seems as if in *The Rock* Mr. Eliot had confused conventional significance with basic significance, but in his second play had clarified the confusion.

Applying Mr. Eliot's sentences about levels of significance, we can say that there is for everyone the expectation (we can hardly call it a plot) and ominous atmosphere of murder and death; for others there are the strong rhythms, the pounding alliterations, and the emphatic rhymes; for others the conflict, not of character, but of forces characterised in individual types; for others the tragedy or triumph of faith at the hands of the world; and for others the gradually unfolding meaning in the profound and ambiguous revelation of the expense of martyrdom in good *and* evil as seen in certain speeches of Thomas and in the choruses of the old women of Canterbury. It is the *expense* of martyrdom as a supreme form of human greatness, its expense for the martyr himself and for those less great but bound with it, its expense of good and evil and suffering, rather than its mere glory or its mere tragedy, that seems to me a major part of the play's meaning. Greatness of any kind forces to a crisis the fundamental life and the fundamental death in life both for the great themselves and for those who are affected by it. Martyrdom is the Christian form of personal greatness, and as with other forms of greatness, no human judgment or representation of it can fail of a terrible humility and a terrifying ambiguity. It is the limit of actuality in what Mr. Eliot calls the abyss.

I do not expect to prove that the emotional substance of which these remarks are a reformulation may be found in *Murder in the*

*Cathedral.* There is no proof of the actual but the experience. But if the reader will first realise that the predicament of Thomas Becket is the predicament of human greatness, and that its example affects him, the reader, by reading over the dialogue between Thomas and the Fourth Tempter and Thomas' final speech in Part One, he will at least have put himself in the frame of mind to perceive the higher levels of significance, and the identification of all levels in the six long choruses and the play as a whole. It may be impertinent to point out as a clue or indication, that the Fourth Tempter's last speech repeats, as addressed to Thomas, Thomas' speech on his first appearance in the play, where the words are applied to the Chorus:

> You know and do not know, what it is to act or suffer.
> You know and do not know, that acting is suffering,
> And suffering action. Neither does the actor suffer
> Nor the patient act. But both are fixed
> In an eternal action, an eternal patience
> To which all must consent that it may be willed
> And which all must suffer that they may will it,
> That the pattern may subsist, that the wheel may turn and still
> Be forever still.

And it may be superfluous to note that in the last of Thomas' speech at the end of Part One, he addresses you, the reader, you, the audience. Impertinent or superfluous the emphasis will not be amiss.

The Choruses, which flow from the expression of the common necessities of the poor up to, and in the same language, the expression of Christian dogma, may be said to exist by themselves, but their instance is the greatness of Thomas, as the death in them is Thomas death. Thomas exists by himself, too, and his particular struggle, but both are made actual in relation to the Choruses. They are separate but related; they combine and produce a new thing not in the elements themselves. But the Choruses themselves have interrelated parts which work together by fate because they were rightly chosen and not because, in any ordinary sense, they have natural affinity for each other. The kinds of parts and their proportional bulk are not fixed but vary with the purpose of the particular Chorus; but the predominant elements are the concrete immanence of death and death in life, and the rudimentary, the simple, the inescapable conditions of living, and there is besides the concrete emotion of the hell on earth which is the absence or the losing of God. It is the death and the coming of it, of the Archbishop which measures and instigates all the Chorus has to say; but neither that death, nor its coming, nor its Christian greatness creates its words; rather what it says is the actual experience from which the Christian greatness springs. That is why the chorus is composed of poor women, ordinary women, with ordinary lives and fates and desires, women with a fundamental turbulence of resentment at the expense of greatness.

> What is woven on the loom of fate
> What is woven in the councils of princes
> Is woven also in our veins, our brains,
> Is woven like a pattern of living worms
> In the guts of the women of Canterbury.

It is against this, the common denominator of all experience, that the extraordinary experience of Thomas is seen, and by it made real.

It is shameful to quote for illustration when half the virtue is lost without the context, but I nevertheless quote two passages, one for concreteness of sensual image and as an example of internal rhyme, and the other to show how actual an emotion the expectation of death can be, and how dramatic.

> I have eaten
> Smooth creatures still living, with the strong salt taste of living
>     things under sea; I have tasted
> The living lobster, the crab, the oyster, the whelk and the prawn;
>     and they live and spawn in my bowels, and my bowels dissolve in the light of dawn.

> *Chorus, Priests and Tempters alternately*
> C. Is it the owl that calls, or a signal between the tree?
> P. Is the window-bar made fast, is the door under lock and bolt?
> T. Is it rain that taps at the window, is it wind that pokes at the
>     door?
> C. Does the torch flame in the hall, the candle in the room?
> P. Does the watchman walk by the wall?
> T. Does the mastiff prowl by the gate?
> C. Death has a hundred hands and walks by a thousand ways.
> P. He may come in the sight of all, he may pass unseen unheard.
> T. Come whispering through the ear, or a sudden shock on the
>     skull.

    C. A man may walk with a lamp at night, and yet be drowned in
       a ditch.
    P. A man may climb the stair in the day, and slip on a broken
       step.
    T. A man may sit at meat, and feel the cold in his groin.

These are the easy things that come first; but without them, the
other meaning that comes gradually would not come at all; they are
its basis, in poetry as in life. "The world," says Mr. Eliot, "is trying
the experiment of attempting to form a civilised but non-Christian
mentality." He believes the experiment will fail; and I think we may
be sure it will fail unless it includes in itself the insight, in Christian
terms or not, of which Mr. Eliot gives an actual representation. Meanwhile he redeems the time.

# STEPHEN SPENDER *

### I. T. S. ELIOT IN HIS POETRY

T S. ELIOT is, like Henry James, a naturalized New Englander, who, as a writer, rebels against the English lack of a consistent literary tradition. Unprecedented as his poetry seems in English, it is really a sharp corrective to contemporary writing, rather than a powerful and originating force. A great many of his effects, which seem at first most startling, are transfusions from the French: with him from Baudelaire and, especially, the French Symbolists. His earlier poetry is influenced by Laforgue.

But, unlike James, Eliot does not succeed completely as an original artist, whose work is the source flowing into a whole school of modern writing. In spite of the most extraordinary efforts to reconcile himself with tradition, and yet remain a poet living in the modern world, he has not succeeded in forming the kind of synthesis which one finds in James's work, which makes the later novels creatively imaginative, and yet psychologically more true to their time than the naturalistic books of the earlier period. Eliot seems anxious [1] to make nonsense of someone's calling *The Waste Land* the 'poem of a generation.' Yet it is easy to see in what sense this was meant, and in what sense it contains a truth. For in Eliot, as in a dozen other modern artists—as in Joyce, in Proust, in Baudelaire, in Rilke even—one never is far removed from connotation: from the trick of the object, or the psychological symptom, or the historic parallel, or the apt quotation quickly observed and noted down; always the one particular thing uniquely expressed and treated as a *symptom*. One notices further that there is a tendency in the work of all these artists to regard life as an illness, and themselves (although they, too, are very seriously ill) as doctors or nurses or spiritual fathers, or mere affectionate holders of fading hands.

* From THE DESTRUCTIVE ELEMENT, pp. 132–149, 153–167. Houghton Mifflin Company, Boston, and Jonathan Cape Limited, London, 1936.
[1] In *After Strange Gods*.

Eliot has not only the gift of connotation, but also a genius for describing a particular situation. In *The Waste Land* he seems, more than in any other poem, and more than any other artist, to describe the contemporary post-war situation of a certain very small class of intellectuals in Europe and America. Here, in expressing the situation of a small class, he goes much further than in any other earlier or later poem. For this longer poem seems to form a climax to all that he has as yet written, and the other poems, on the one side, ascend to that position, and on the other hand fall away from it. What one sees in the earlier, as in the later, poems is the experience of a purely isolated sensibility. Although he goes much further than James, in accepting the modern world, his subject-matter is even more limited than that of James: James at least describes a whole aristocratic class in terms that most people could, with a certain amount of application, understand; Eliot indicates the whole modern world, but in a subjective way. A pub-crawling prostitute could understand very well what Henry James meant by the prince and Mr. Verver; they are well within the range of her experience. But no charwoman or prostitute in London would recognize herself in the second part of the *A Game of Chess* section of *The Waste Land,* although it reports almost realistically the conversation of these ladies in a London pub. This passage does not objectively present the people it describes; it merely exists in the mind of the reader, who is made to imagine that he is sharing the life of the people. But what he is really seeing and hearing is a part of his own mind.

Eliot's poetry is full of these fragmentary, intellectualized sense-impressions. They are romantically stimulating, because they suggest some very important private association. The key to modern romanticism is in the private poem, that is, the poetry of public appearances, which are, by the use of language, made full of private significance. Such is the *poésie de départs,* the poetry of the week-end visit to the country, the private jokes in Auden's work. The best example is the suggestion of Baudelaire in his *Intimate Journal,* that perhaps the ships which he observes anchored in the harbour are really pointing towards happiness.

The true descendant of Baudelaire is discovering not an outward reality, but, in external symbols, his own spiritual individuality. It follows that the objects outside himself have an added poignancy, because, in themselves, deprived of the poet's inventive genius, they are fragmentary and devoid of meaning. Modern life is a kind of Hell, but even that view has to be modified; it is, as it were, a fragmentary Hell, a Hell devoid of consistency, too stupid to punish anyone, and without moral severity. It is as impossible, according to the values of the modern world, to be damned as to be saved. In poems like the *Preludes,* the *Rhapsody on a Windy Night,* and *Morning at the Window,* Eliot extends this view of a world where

> Midnight shakes the memory
> As a madman shakes a dead geranium.

The peculiar horror of this world is that the people in it are as much *things* as the gutter, the street, the cats, the pipes, etc. They are spiritually dead, and there is a dead sameness about all their activities:

> And short square fingers stuffing pipes,
> And evening newspapers, and eyes
> Assured of certain certainties,
> The conscience of a blackened street
> Impatient to assume the world.

The only sign of life is that pity is still possible:

> I am moved by fancies that are curled
> Around these images, and cling:
> The notion of some infinitely gentle
> Infinitely suffering thing.

It is not altogether the same pity for human suffering as one finds in James, and that in Wilfred Owen's poetry is so all-sufficient that he could write of them 'the poetry is in the pity.' It is an extension of this pity; humanity is not pitied because it suffers, but because it exists at all, and resembles, in its totality, this gentle and suffering thing. The pity is in the notion of a humanity without humanity.

Eliot, being an extremely moral writer, is also an extremely isolated writer. He is not concerned with saving the world: reformers seem to him as irrelevant as anything else in the objects that surround him. His poetry simply develops from an original position in which it questions the possibility even of damnation, to a firm belief, in his most recent poetry, in the possibility of personal salvation.

The original position is made clear enough in the opening lines of *The Love Song of J. Alfred Prufrock:*

> Let us go then, you and I
> When the evening is spread out against the sky
> Like a patient etherised upon a table;
> Let us go, through certain half-deserted streets,
> The muttering retreats
> Of restless nights in one-night cheap hotels
> And sawdust restaurants with oyster-shells:
> Streets that follow like a tedious argument
> Of insidious intent
> To lead you to an overwhelming question . . .
> Oh, do not ask, "What is it?"
> Let us go and make our visit.

This stanza admirably conveys the poet's situation. In the second and third lines nature is sacrificed by the mind, and the evening becomes a patient. Moreover, if one examines the form of the stanza one sees that it is simply and beautifully adequate to the mood and music of what is expressed, but that it has neither the freedom of so-called free verse, nor any architectural strength and cohesion of its own which extends beyond the purpose of the poem. A new stanza has been contrived but not invented. The clever line of 'Of insidious intent,' which seems so very effective, shows how completely the form will flop, if flopping suits Eliot's purpose. Yet the verse is musically arranged: what is happening in it is that architecture is being sacrificed to expression by a parallel that exactly corresponds to the etherisation of the evening.

We turn over the page, and we meet the inmates of Hell:

> In the room the women come and go
> Talking of Michelangelo.

After a description of the fog, we are made aware of Mr. Prufrock's feeling of social apprehension:

> There will be time, there will be time
> To prepare a face to meet the faces that you meet.

Again:

> And indeed there will be time
> To wonder, "Do I dare?" and, "Do I dare?"
> Time to turn back and descend the stair,
> With a bald spot in the middle of my hair—

From an account of his clothes and his thoughts, we realize that Prufrock is not, as he at first seemed, a rebel to his surroundings. He is really completely a part of them, and his ambition seems to be, as he grows older, more and more ostensibly to 'fit in.' Yet a doubt arises in the reader's mind, because as he reads on he becomes convinced that Mr. Prufrock's policy of conforming is really an ingenious method of saving himself. However, the matter is not quite so simple as that, because it becomes quite certain that Mr. Prufrock has not the courage to make his proposal: this is important because the proposal is not merely a proposal. It has become identified with some statement, some assertion about life or the nature of the Universe, which, one becomes convinced, would, if it were made (and at the same time one feels quite sure it could not be made), settle the question of Mr. Prufrock's salvation:

> And would it have been worth it, after all,
>  After the cups, the marmalade, the tea,
>  Among the porcelain, among some talk of you and me,
>  Would it have been worth while,
>  To have bitten off the matter with a smile,
>  To have squeezed the universe into a ball
>  To roll it toward some overwhelming question,
>  To say: 'I am Lazarus, come from the dead,
>  Come back to tell you all, I shall tell you all'—
>  If one, settling a pillow by her head,
>      Should say: 'That is not what I mean at all;
>      That is not it, at all.'

There is no question in *Prufrock* of anyone else being saved; the others are part of the world of *things,* which is beyond damnation: the question is whether Mr. Prufrock himself is capable of getting out of it, of being alive.

In the second poem in the book, *The Portrait of a Lady,* the question is whether the narrator feels himself essentially and in kind different from the lady whose life he knows to be false and decadent. The difficulty is that she herself (like everyone else belonging to a certain 'set') seems equally aware of the falsity of her surroundings, and she embarrasses her guest by understanding his attitude of considered superiority, and by translating her understanding into behavior which ought to suit his superior moral situation, but which does not happen to be true to him. She accepts him at his own estima-

tion, and then shocks him out of complacency by making an apprais-
ing remark which too palpably does not fit:

> 'You are invulnerable, you have no Achilles' heel.
> You will go on, and when you have prevailed
> You can say: at this point many a one has failed.'

But the truth is very far from this:

> I take my hat: how can I make a cowardly amends
> For what she has said to me?
> You will see me any morning in the park
> Reading the comics and the sporting page.

Again, the problem we are left with is to consider whether the
narrator is capable of personal salvation:

> Well! and what if she should die some afternoon,
> Afternoon grey and smoky, evening yellow and rose;
> Should die and leave me sitting pen in hand
> With the smoke coming down above the housetops:
> Doubtful, for a while
> Not knowing what to feel or if I understand
> Or whether wise or foolish, tardy or too soon . . .
> Would she not have the advantage, after all?
> This music is successful with a 'dying fall'
> Now that we talk of dying—
> And should I have the right to smile?

This poem is particularly interesting because it is one of Eliot's
few attempts to enter into the position of another person in the
modern Inferno. But even here the lady is only interesting because
of the question about the narrator himself which she suggests in his
mind. And her situation is only compared with his because the
thought has occurred to him that it may be possible to identify it
completely with his own. The seriousness of Eliot's earlier poetry is
conveyed by the impression it forces that there is indeed only one
problem: is the soul of the individual capable of being saved, damned
or in any way morally judged? It is a question that applies to individuals, so it is no egotism of the author's that makes him search
deeply for the answer in himself: the answer will be found in him as
much as in anyone. His is the one soul that it is his responsibility to
save.

In the light of his later poetry it is evident that just as Baudelaire was out to be damned, Eliot, perhaps more modestly, is out to be saved. But at this stage the Church is only one of the humours of Hades:

> The hippopotamus's day
> Is passed in sleep; at night he hunts;
> God works in a mysterious way—
> The Church can sleep and feed at once.

In 1920, when he wrote *Gerontion,* the picture of decay was transformed and took on the German features of a *Weltanschauung.* Perhaps T. S. Eliot had already read Hermann Hesse's *Blick ins Chaos,* which is quoted in the notes at the end of *The Waste Land;* or perhaps it was Oswald Spengler, whose *Decline of the West* was more influential outside Germany at that time than it is to-day. Gerontion is an old man, empty of desire, and whose activities are over, save for the 'thoughts of a dry brain in a dry season.' He corresponds to Tiresias in *The Waste Land.* His age, in the life of a single man, is as old as Western Civilization in the life of Civilizations (between seventy and eighty), so he is particularly well qualified to be a sympathetic observer. Like some of the more sensitive intelligences of our own age, he dreams of the more potent events of the past, and his past is identified with the past of Christian culture:

> . . . in the juvescence of the year
> Came Christ the tiger.

The period of most heroic and eloquent activity in our history was the time of the Elizabethans. The motif of this poem is repeated, as it were, on another plane, by a passage written in a style plainly derived from Tourneur, in whom the energy and credulity of Elizabethan poetry had turned, in a last display of wild action and magnificent fireworks, into cynicism, despair, and a strong moral indignation. The passage in *Gerontion* beginning:

> After such knowledge what forgiveness? Think now
> History has many cunning passages, contrived corridors
> And issues, deceives with whispering ambitions,
> Guides us by vanities,

is reminiscent of some favourite lines of Eliot's from *The Revenger's Tragedy:*

Does the silkworm expend her yellow labours
For thee? For thee does she undo herself?
Are lordships sold to maintain ladyships,
For the poor benefit of a bewildering [2] minute?
Why does yon fellow falsify highways,
And put his life between the judge's lips
To refine such a thing—keeps horse and men
To beat their valours for her?

The diction, with its suggestion that what was once simple—the faith in which the age started, and the moral rules obvious to all—is now complicated and mysterious, is essentially alike. And Eliot, by his use of such language, which he adopts again in *The Waste Land,* not only gives the form of his verse an architectural strength which it had previously lacked, but he also achieves a striking historical comparison of the late Elizabethan and early Jacobean writers with those of our own time. We think too often of the late Elizabethans as a group of writers who were overshadowed by the genius of Shakespeare, and of their writing as being a form that was breaking up, even if it was not actually decadent. What we never think enough of is the subject-matter of their writing, or of how far their attention and hence their creativeness was affected by the *outward scene.* Their attention was directed towards Italy—though this is often almost discounted: they are so English, we are told—and they were seeing and hearing, not the fabulous Renaissance and the revival of classicism, but the other side of the Renaissance: the political intrigues, the murders, the violence of cardinals, princes and politicians. Eliot, feeling himself in a Europe of cultural decay, unbelief, mass-murder, torture, political intrigue, usury and faithlessness, made the discovery that the late Elizabethans were describing a world which had much in common with our own.

*Gerontion* is an objective poem. It is in complete contrast to the preceding subjective poems. It no longer expresses the disgust and horror of one man at symptoms which one might after all believe to be purely subjective. It is written in the belief that the decline of civilization is real, that history is, as it were, now senile.

The same objectivity is observed in *The Waste Land,* for which one may take *Gerontion* almost as a study. *The Waste Land* is a restatement of the position which Eliot had reached in 1922; it forms a

[2] In some editions, 'bewitching.'

summary of the situations of the other poems, and besides this, it contains an objective element which the other poems had never expressed.

All the figures of the earlier poems are here. Most important of all, there is Gerontion, grown into Tiresias, a more universal figure, because, not only is he old, and a wise spectator, but in him meet both the sexes. A lady, reminding us of her in *The Portrait of a Lady*, has collapsed completely; is nervous and conscious of failure. And Prufrock, now only a voice, is at last able to answer her questions:

> 'Speak to me. Why do you never speak? Speak.
>   'What are you thinking of? What thinking? What?
> 'I never know what you are thinking. Think.'
> I think we are in rats' alley
> Where the dead men lost their bones.

Sweeney is here, and the company with which we associate him:

> He, the young man carbuncular, arrives,
> A small house agent's clerk, with one bold stare,
> One of the low on whom assurance sits
> As a silk hat on a Bradford millionaire.

Secondly, Eliot has further extended the pastiche method of *Gerontion*. His fragmentary but extraordinary literary sensibility resembles his sensibility to a fragmentary world which surrounds him. As a poet, he is impressed in exactly the same way by lilac, say, as by a line of poetry, such as *'Et O ces voix d'enfants, chantant dans la coupole!'* and in the same way as the imagery of lilac is brought into juxtaposition with the cruelty of youth and the Waste Land, so the line from Verlaine is brought up against a tag from an Australian ballad:

> O the moon shone bright on Mrs. Porter
> And on her daughter;
> They wash their feet in soda water.

Eliot's method is justified, because he is entirely a literary writer, so there is no great contrast between his literary sensibility when it reacts to literature and when it reacts to real phenomena. Indeed, the two uses are sometimes combined, and even in his observation of real phenomena he will put his finger on the description in some book.

For example, 'Simple and faithless as a smile and shake of the hand,' from 'Simple et sans foi comme un bonjour.'

Eliot is the very opposite of everything that is meant by a 'nature poet.' He is never, like Lawrence (who is a genuine nature poet, as revolutionary in his power of invoking an objective world as Wordsworth) describing nature with his mind fixed on some object described, making the reader re-experience all the sensations aroused by that object. His mind is always on the poem, on what is created by the mind, and he picks out the phenomena observed by the mind, to suit the poem. He never appeals to a material reality outside the mind: only, in his most recent poems, to a world of belief that is external to the individual mind.

I. A. Richards has said that in *The Waste Land* T. S. Eliot has effected a 'severance between his poetry and *all* beliefs.' . . . ' "In the destructive element immerse. That is the way." '

I think that the last lines of *The First Sermon* section, 'O Lord thou pluckest me out' are not 'severed' from all belief. But what Eliot most certainly has done is to immerse himself in the destructive element. In *The Waste Land* he has made an artistic whole out of fragments. The poem is not built on the blank verse or free verse meters which are the basis of its separate parts. The meter, so far from being architectural, helps to convey the sense of fragmentariness in the poem. For example, a few lines of the last section of *What the Thunder Said*:

> Here is no water but only rock
> Rock and no water and the sandy road
> The road winding above among the mountains
> Which are mountains of rock without water
> If there were water we should stop and drink,

are not sequentially related to the mood and rhythm of *A Game of Chess*. The lines I have quoted read like some fragment of rhetorical poetic drama: *A Game of Chess* surprises us by its sensual, romantic mood, and *Death by Water* may take the reader to the Greek Anthology. These fragments are not related to each other, but to the whole poem; they only contribute to each other in falling apart, and always suggesting to us that they are parts of something larger than their surroundings. We are reminded of a ruined city in which the parts are all disintegrated, yet still together form a whole. What remains in our minds is the whole poem, which is related to a series of fragments, not a series of fragments which are collected together to construct a whole poem.

Instead of a basis of accepted belief, the whole structure of Eliot's poem is based on certain primitive rituals and myths, which, he seems to feel, must be psychological certainties, being a part of what psychologists call our 'race memory.' He is appealing to scientific legend, where Yeats appeals to poetic legend. The authority behind *The Waste Land* is not the Catholic Church, nor romantic lore, but anthropology from the volumes of Sir James Frazer's *The Golden Bough*. Eliot has tried to indicate, beneath the very ephemeral and violent movements of our own civilization, the gradual and magical contours of man's earliest religious beliefs. The effect he sets out to achieve is illustrated by Freud's remark in *Civilization and its Discontents* that the growth of the individual mind resembles the growth of Rome, supposing that modern Rome, as it is to-day, were coexistent with the buildings of Rome at every period in her history; and that beneath the modern architecture was found the architecture of every earlier period, in a perfect state of preservation.

The method of *The Waste Land* is justified in so far as it fulfils the psychological truth observed by Freud. But Eliot's way of doing this is perhaps a little too studied. The poem seems to lean rather too heavily on Sir James Frazer, and *The Golden Bough* tends to form a private poem concealed in the real poem, in the same way as Joyce's private poem about the Odyssey is enshrined in *Ulysses*. The work is very slightly tainted by the learning of the Cambridge don. Perhaps the main reason for this is that, although Eliot's attitude is much more objective and generalized in *The Waste Land* than in any earlier poem, the psychology of his people is just as crude. His ladies, his bank clerks, his Sweeneys, his Mrs. Porters, his pub conversationalists, are all part of the world of *things*. Psychologically they are far cruder than the Babbitts and other creations of Sinclair Lewis. One of the most astonishing things about Eliot is that a poet with such a strong dramatic style should seem so blinded to the existence of people outside himself. Yet the effect of his poetry depends very largely on this blindness.

Eliot seems to think, quite rightly, that what makes people living is their beliefs. But to him it seems impossible to accept any belief that is not a religious belief: one either rejects all belief, as I. A.

Richards finds he has done in *The Waste Land,* or else one accepts a religious belief in salvation and damnation. Those who do not accept this belief are not even damned, but eternally dead. For that reason, the people about whom he writes in his poems are dead, because they are not allowed to hold with any conviction the small private beliefs which are as many as people's separate occupations. There is a whole list of such beliefs in St. J. Perse's *Anabase,* a poem which Eliot himself has translated: 'He who sees his soul reflected in a blade; the man learned in sciences, in anomastic; the well thought of in councils, he who names fountains,' etc. These are the living: yet they seem to be shut out of Eliot's poetry, because 'to see his soul reflected in a blade' puts a man outside the pale even of the damned.

In front of *Sweeney Agonistes* there is a quotation from St. John of the Cross: 'Hence the soul cannot be possessed of the divine union, until it has divested itself of the love of created beings.' This coupled with a quotation from the *Choephoroe* of Æschylus, where Orestes says, speaking of the Furies, 'You don't see them, you don't—but I see them: they are hunting me down, I must move on.'

These two fragments give a final picture of the haunted world of Eliot's early poetry, and of *The Waste Land.* The characters, the prostitutes and their American pals, are the dead. Their lives are automatic, their only emotions are fear, and a primitive kind of superstition, which occupies them with dealing and cutting packs of cards. The interruption of the telephone with its repeated 'Ting a ling ling' does not break the jazz rhythm of their talk.

Here Eliot's verse is bare of its beautiful effects, and of all poetry. It is intricate, dramatic and ingenious. Only in its organization is it superior to the thing it parodies. Eventually, in the poetry of disillusion, the parody becomes the thing parodied, in the same way as in Auden's *Dance of Death* the jazz songs are exactly like real jazz songs by Noel Coward. The parody no longer exists in the words, but in the dramatic presentation of the characters who speak the words.

Here, in Sweeney's lines, the poeticism is deliberately a falsified poetry:

> Nothing to eat but the fruit as it grows.
> Nothing to see but the palm-trees one way
> And the sea the other way,

Nothing to hear but the sound of the surf.
Nothing at all but three things.

The verse only rises to poetry in the next lines:

DORIS:                         What things?
SWEENEY: Birth, and copulation, and death.
              That's all, that's all, that's all, that's all,
              Birth, and copulation, and death.
DORIS:       I'd be bored.
SWEENEY:                        You'd be bored.
              Birth and copulation and death.

Here the poetry rises to a kind of fierce, destructive emphasis, the expression of a mechanism which is destroying itself.

The mood of *The Waste Land* could not go further than in this poem, for here the bareness and dryness is such that poetry would be poetically false. It is a kind of *reductio ad absurdum*. We have reached a stage when poetry refuses to be poetry.

In the spirit of the terrible quotation from St. John of the Cross, all the possibilities of a human poetry are exhausted. With the exception of Sweeney, haunted by the Furies, the characters in these two fragments are non-human, they are bones.

## 2. T. S. ELIOT IN HIS CRITICISM

In *After Strange Gods,* Eliot alludes to the apparent discrepancy which critics have found between his poetry and his critical prose. 'It would appear that while I maintain the most correct opinions in my criticism, I do nothing but violate them in my verse; and thus appear in a double, if not a double-faced rôle.'

This, and the alternative view that his poetry is to be admired and his prose lamented, are usual opinions. The assumption always is that his verse and prose are quite unrelated to each other.

Actually, they are very closely related. If one reads through the whole of the prose and the whole of the verse, one finds that the same process, the same search for a Tradition and for orthodox principles, combined with the same sensitivity to contemporary life, is developed through both of them. In the essays there are frequent references (they grow more open as time goes on) to problems in which the writer himself is involved in his creative work. A certain light relief is provided, if the reader is curious enough to wonder whether there be any connexion between the following two passages. The first is a discussion of the way in which a poet may select his imagery.[1]

> And this selection probably runs through the whole of his sensitive life. There might be the experience of a child of ten, a small boy peering through sea-water in a rock-pool, and finding a sea-anemone for the first time: the simple experience (not so simple, for an exceptional child, as it looks) might be dormant in his mind for twenty years, and reappear transformed in some verse-context charged with great imaginative pressure.

The second is from the *Rhapsody on a Windy Night:*

> I could see nothing behind that child's eye.
> I have seen eyes in the street
> Trying to peer through lighted shutters,
> And a crab one afternoon in a pool,
> An old crab with barnacles on his back,
> Gripped the end of a stick which I held him.

In its relation to the philosophy which forms the background of his poetry, some of the criticism is most illuminating. Particularly the essays on Baudelaire and Dante, for Dante is the poet whose writing and attitude fulfil most of the conditions which Eliot, in his last essays, has come to impose on the artist. He is Christian, moral, orthodox and traditional. Without Dante, as the supreme example of an orthodox writer, *After Strange Gods* could hardly have been written. Baudeliare, on the other hand, provides the machinery of the modern *Inferno*: and he is also to Eliot an example of the Christian writer. The Introduction to Baudelaire's *Intimate Journal* [2] shows how, unless Baudelaire had decided to be damned, it would have been more difficult for Eliot to set out on the path of salvation. Lastly, there are the critical writings of T. E. Hulme. The paragraph which Eliot quotes at the end of this same Introduction needs no comment:

> In the light of these absolute values, man himself is judged to be essentially limited and imperfect. He is endowed with Original Sin. While he can occasionally accomplish acts which partake of perfection, he can never himself *be* perfect. Certain secondary

---

[1] *The Use of Poetry and the Use of Criticism*, p. 78.
[2] This essay is now published in the volume of *Selected Essays*.

results in regard to ordinary human action in society follow from this. A man is essentially bad, he can only accomplish anything of value by discipline—ethical and political. Order is thus not merely negative, but creative and liberating. Institutions are necessary.

Thus in Dante, Baudelaire, T. E. Hulme, Ezra Pound, the Elizabethans, and a half-dozen other influences, one sees the background of Eliot's poetry in Eliot's prose. The poetry and the prose together form a whole: the poetry is strengthened and given its ideals by the prose, the prose is illustrated and given foundation by the poetry. Perhaps this explains a puzzling sentence in *After Strange Gods:* 'I should say that in one's prose reflexions one may be legitimately occupied with ideals, whereas in the writing of verse one can only deal with actuality.'

His prose is not confined to criticism, and perhaps some of the most important parts of his criticism occur in his poetry. For his poetry is literary and full of quotation, and his use of the passages which he quotes implies a critical attitude. We look in the essays for criticism of the Elizabethans which concerns their ideals: in *Gerontion* and *The Waste Land* for the criticism which emphasizes their historic actuality.

The pervading weakness of Eliot's writing is a certain fragmentariness: 'These fragments I have shored against my ruins,' in *The Waste Land,* and:

> Because I cannot hope to turn again
> Consequently I rejoice, having to construct something
> Upon which to rejoice,

from *Ash Wednesday,* are lines which, without any weakness, yet 'give him away,' because they are so true. In his poetry he is an inhibited writer, exploiting in himself a tendency in his own work to break off just when the reader is expecting him to become most lucid, and making of this tendency a technical device. His prose, in spite of its logical precision, its dryness, and its fine organization, is, in its context, uneven: occasionally there are remarks of brilliant observation, of violent prejudice, or whole paragraphs of sententiousness.

The poetry and the prose to some extent bolster each other up, and are interdependent. The thought that has led the poetry on from stage to stage has been developed in the prose. The prose itself, though,

has weakness: for Eliot is not very good at argument or at abstract discussion, and it is the poetry that illuminates and justifies his ideas.
Without his poetry, the religious and social opinions in his last two
critical works would seem ineffective, and perhaps unimportant.

Both poetry and prose combine to produce the impression of an
extraordinarily conscientious writer, who is prepared to work out all
the ideas which form the background of his poetry, and risk applying this 'ideology' to Church, politics and social life. He and Yeats
are the first English poets of this century who seem to have realized
that if the beliefs which govern a poet when he is writing, are hope-
lessly removed from the beliefs on which contemporary society and
the law are based, then his poetry will seem remote from the life
around him. The poet is driven either into an attitude of eccentric
and defiant individualism, or else he must try and work out his ideas
and relate them to society. Eliot has therefore explained his position
very carefully, and any criticism of that position is relevant to his
poetry.

Unfortunately, though, his explanations are not quite simple. His
conscience seems to have driven him to work out every step in his
development, but it has not enabled him to overcome a certain ambiguity. To take a very obvious example, it is difficult for a writer who
hates an age of usefulness, of birth-control, hygiene, and business, to
recommend efficient institutions and forms of behaviour: when he
recommends the advice on Birth Control of the Lambeth Conference,
or that the censorship should be directed from Lambeth Palace, one
has to remember that such remedies may appeal to him simply because he is reacting from an utilitarian age.

The very first essay in *The Sacred Wood,* on Tradition and the
Individual Talent, might lead one to think that Eliot was to live con-
tentedly among the apostles of 'art for art's sake,' brought up to date
by Bloomsbury, and called 'significant form.' For he offers a neat
formula to illustrate the creation of poetry: 'Consider, as a suggestive
analogy, the action which takes place when a bit of finely filiated
platinum is introduced into a chamber containing oxygen and sulphur
dioxide.'

Michael Roberts has shown that what we are led to suppose happens in this experiment does not really happen at all: T. S. Eliot
also darkly hints in a later passage that there is 'at least one doubtful
analogy' in this essay: but nevertheless, if one has faith, in the mind's

eye such scientific experiments come off. 'When the two gases previously mentioned are mixed in the presence of a filament of platinum, they form sulphurous acid. The mind of the poet is the shred of platinum. It may partly or exclusively operate upon the experience of the man himself; but the more perfect the artist, the more completely separate in him will be the man who suffers and the mind which creates; the more perfectly will the mind digest and transmute the passions which are its material.'

The essay is in fact a vigorous attack on critics who maintain that poetry is the expression of personality, and at the same time it is a defence of tradition. Although the essay is convincingly argued there is a certain doubt left as to its intention.

Firstly, it is rather difficult to understand why Eliot is so much on the defensive about tradition. For, if he is on the defensive, if his purpose is, like Henry James's, to hold up a Continental example to the English, he over-proves his case. Because he proves that, without tradition as an element in the chemical formula, poetry cannot exist. Therefore tradition is a *sine qua non,* and it is difficult to see how some poetry can be 'more traditional' than other poetry, except in the sense that it is better or worse, which is, in fact, the sense in which Eliot uses the word traditional. But he does not seem quite happy at letting the reader know he is doing this.

Now, if good poetry is more traditional than bad poetry, the use of the word traditional immediately becomes very dubious, because many of the best poets are obviously not learned. This so worries Eliot that he immediately adopts the tone, on the one hand mystifying, on the other hand almost sneering, which is typical of him in moments when he is least certain of himself. The reader is sneered at for thinking that tradition is something which a really great poet, like Shakespeare, has to acquire: in case he should dispute this, he is then heavily snubbed by a remark to the effect that less great poets have to work hard to gain a sense of the traditional. 'Tradition . . . cannot be inherited, and if you want it you must obtain it by great labour. It involves, in the first place, the historical sense, which we may call nearly indispensable to anyone who would continue to be a poet beyond his twenty-fifth year.' Don't dare to dispute this, he might have added, unless your name is Shakespeare.

This happens to be very true, but the fact remains that Eliot has altered his position. He is not, like Henry James, making a criticism of the whole of English literature, although he leaves plenty of room for one to think that perhaps he is doing so. What he is really saying is simply that bad poetry is not traditional, and that good poetry is traditional. Further, since he admits that there is no way by which one can examine a poet and discover him to be untraditional, 'untraditional' becomes simply a term of abuse which one reserves for generally accepted poetry which one doesn't happen to like, such as Shelley. It seems rather an elaborate way of bolstering up one's dislikes.

Later on we are told: 'The point of view which I am struggling to attach is perhaps related to the metaphysical theory of the substantial unity of the soul: for the meaning is that the poet has, not a "personality" to express, but a particular medium, which is only a medium and not a personality, in which impressions and experiences combine in peculiar and unexpected ways.'

This is very striking, and it seems to answer satisfactorily the point of view which Eliot opposes, because it refutes altogether the conception of an expressed personality, and reduces it to meaninglessness. Yet two pages further on he says: 'Poetry is not a turning loose of emotion, but an escape from emotion; it is not the expression of personality, but an escape from personality.' [3]

But an escape from personality, which is an escape from emotion, *is* an expression of personality. It is evident that Eliot is saying in other words what a great many people mean when they speak of an 'expression of personality': a fairly impersonal state of mind in which one is able to regard the emotions of one's personality objectively: but this is only a degree of introspection.

A significant aspect of this essay is the omission of all discussion of the part played by either nature or the objective world in poetry. Eliot's view of aesthetic creation seems to be purely cerebral: the outer world of reality is viewed either as digested experience, or else as 'impressions': impressions that only seem important for what they impress on the mind, without regard for the reality which is doing the impressing. We may well wonder how this formula suits Whitman, or the D. H. Lawrence of *Birds, Beasts and Flowers*. It certainly does not fit Lawrence's poetry at all, and Whitman only after a straining which renders the meaning of the word 'traditional' very vague. The fact is that Eliot has quite ignored the kind of artist

---

[3] *Selected Essays*, p. 20.

whose creativeness is stimulated by a perpetual tension between the objective world, the world of nature, and his own inner world: and this consciousness of the world outside is the only real impersonality. To Eliot, as to most modern writers, nature, except in the sense of Georgian nature poetry, does not seem to exist. When one notices this, one also begins to understand certain of Eliot's dislikes. His dislike of Lawrence seems inevitable, but his dislike even of Goethe becomes a little clearer when one considers how unsympathetic to the cerebral writer must be such lines as the following from *Faust*:

> Vom Eise befreit sind Strom und Bäche
> Durch des Frühlings holden, belebenden Blick;
> Im Thale grünet Hoffnungs-Glück;
> Der alte Winter, in seiner Schwäche,
> Zog sich in rauhe Berge zurück.
> Von dorther sendet er fliehend nur
> Ohnmächtige Schauer körnigen Eises
> In Streifen über die grünende Flur;
> Aber die Sonne duldet kein Weisses,
> Überall regt sich Bildung und Streben,
> Alles will sie mit Farben beleben;
> Doch an Blumen fehlt's im Revier,
> Sie nimmt geputzte Menschen dafür.

In Eliot's essay there seems to be little feeling that a sense of tradition can be derived from the conditions of life round the poet; that his audience, or his potential audience, is, as it were, the carrier of tradition, and that he is the one infected. Nor is there, as yet, any feeling that tradition may be found in the Church, or, as we find it in Henry James, amongst an aristocracy. It is to be found in books.

In later essays, he endeavours always to trace the line of tradition in literature, and this, of course, leads him eventually away from books, to the contemporary social environment of the writers whom he is discussing, to morals, and lastly, to theology. A more critical and less analytic attitude to English literature is adopted. One of his exponents in the *Dialogue on Dramatic Poetry* even hints at the possibility that Shakespeare is not traditional enough, because of his lack of an ordered social background. 'Restoration Comedy is a comedy of social manners. It presupposes the existence of a society, therefore of social and moral laws. . . . It laughs at the members of society who transgress its laws. The tragedy of Shakespeare goes much deeper and yet it tells us only that weakness of character leads to disaster. There is no such background of social order such as you perceive behind Corneille and Sophocles.' Then, again: 'So far as I can isolate Shakespeare, I prefer him to all other dramatists of every time. But I cannot do that altogether; and I find the age of Shakespeare moved in a steady current, with back-eddies certainly, towards anarchy and chaos.' [4] And lastly: 'You can never draw the line between aesthetic criticism and moral and social criticism; you cannot draw a line between criticism and metaphysics; you start with literary criticism, and however rigorous an aesthete you may be, you are over the frontier into something else sooner or later.' [5] After this, it is clear that Eliot himself is over the frontier: it becomes a question of the sense in which he is a moralist and a metaphysician.

The best and most renowned of Eliot's essays are those on the Elizabethans. It is when we come to the essay on Blake that we notice suddenly the sharp division of his opinion. For whilst we are told that Blake benefited from his lack of systematic education, and that *The Marriage of Heaven and Hell* is 'naked philosophy, presented,' we are told later that 'we have the same respect for Blake's philosophy (and perhaps for that of Samuel Butler) that we have for an ingenious piece of home-made furniture: we admire the man who has put it together out of the odds and ends about the house.' Now Samuel Butler is certainly not 'naked philosophy, presented,' and his conjunction with Blake, is absurd: it is a tentative effort to disparage Blake, to 'take him down a peg,' and the reason for Eliot's annoyance soon becomes clear, when he adds censoriously: 'We are not really so remote from the Continent, or from our own past, as to be deprived of the advantages of culture, if we wish them.' He ignores the fact that Blake had excellent reasons for not 'wishing them.'

The remark that Blake's philosophy resembles a piece of home-made furniture is ingenious and unjust, nor does it explain why he was not as great an artist as Beethoven, for instance, whose philosophy was also 'home-made.' As so often happens with Eliot, he seems to diagnose with great acuteness, and then is anxious to suggest some cure: but the cure has no relation to the illness. He goes on to say: 'Blake was endowed with a capacity for considerable understanding of human nature, with a remarkable and original sense of language

---

[4] *Selected Essays*, p. 53.
[5] *Ibid.*, p. 55.

and the music of language, and a gift of hallucinated vision. Had these been controlled by a respect for impersonal vision, for common sense, for the objectivity of science, it would have been better for him.' This is the suggested cure. It is more than a cure, in fact, it is a panacea. Blake, Shelley, Goethe, D. H. Lawrence, all of them lacked that little something which Eliot expresses in different ways, but which in the servants' hall would be described as 'knowing one's place.'

The fault with Blake is that he is 'up to twenty, decidedly a traditional.' But after twenty things started to go wrong. Here we encounter the oddest and most personal note in Eliot's criticism. This is a note of almost personal irritation with the writers whom he is criticizing, so strongly does he feel that they oughtn't to be doing something which they do, but something quite different. The great Victorians oughtn't (as we all know) to have written so much. Goethe oughtn't to have written poetry at all: 'his true role was that of the man of the world and sage—a La Rochefoucauld, a La Bruyère, a Vanvenargues.' [6] One feels that he is never quite satisfied with any English writer, except some of the metaphysical poets, and Pope and Dryden. The others never quite obey all the rules, and, of course, they are never 'traditional' enough.

The search for principles, the perpetual sacrifice of what he calls personality, and the study of tradition, led Eliot to the conclusion that one could make no aesthetic judgment which did not imply a moral judgment: and this same path was one perhaps of many that led him finally to theology.

His conclusions attempt to refute the charge that they are themselves home-made, or that they are individualistic, by being rigidly orthodox, and they attempt also to be practical. That is to say they broaden into a social philosophy, and in his more recent criticism he has applied that philosophy to questions outside literary criticism.

It is these practical conclusions that form the test of his traditionalism: for it is evident that no tradition is wholly valid that is not rooted in contemporary life as much as in the life of the past. In one of his recently published American lectures, Eliot very rightly disputes the commonly held view that Wordworth's opinions are unimportant and unrelated to his poetry: 'I am not sure that this critical eclecticism cannot go too far: that we can judge and enjoy a man's poetry while leaving wholly out of account all of the things for which

[6] *The Use of Poetry and the Use of Criticism*, p. 99.

he cared deeply, and on behalf of which he turned his poetry to account.'[7]

Eliot's own opinions are not merely related to his poetry. They qualify his whole critical attitude, and they make him to some extent a preacher. His aim as a writer has been to be a traditionalist: the tradition which he has adopted, being derived from the Church, has also sociological and educative implications. It is his object to show that the application of these principles in social life is as just as it is correct to apply them to literature. He seems to feel that unless he can prove this, he is, in his work, an individualist: not a traditionalist radically connected with the historic process: but isolated, original, personal, in the sense that he is writing about his own beliefs which are 'home-made,' and so make him eccentric, and different from the people around him.

Whereas the Marxist tries to accomplish the same sacrifice of individualist traits in order to achieve the fulfilment of a more united and wider humanity, by an historic act of the will which makes him reach forward and forcibly impose on the present the visualized, completed social system of the future, Eliot looks to the Church, and finds it the single enduring building which survives in the chaos of our civilization. If it is not as powerful in a worldly sense as it was, that is only regrettable in the view of those who are concerned for civilization in this world: for its teachings and its sacraments survive, and their real emphasis lies not on life but on death: moreover, it does offer the only surviving hope for our civilization: 'The world is trying the experiment of attempting to form a civilized but non-Christian mentality. The experiment will fail; but we must be very patient in awaiting its collapse; meanwhile redeeming the time: so that the Faith may be preserved alive through the dark ages before us: to renew and rebuild civilization, and save the World from suicide.'[8]

Sometimes, however, he seems to despair of civilization: 'Perhaps he (Matthew Arnold) cared too much for civilization, forgetting that Heaven and Earth shall pass away, and Mr. Arnold with them, and there is only one stay.'[9] So that he is not so sure about civilization, after all.

This is a doctrine of Death. The implication is that probably

---

[7] *The Use of Poetry and the Use of Criticism*, p. 81.

[8] *Selected Essays*, p. 363.

[9] *The Use of Poetry and the Use of Criticism*, p. 119.

civilization is at an end, but there is still the Church. The Church, though, is a ruin, and is probably incapable of saving the world even if the world wants to be saved, and Mr. Arnold is reproached for seeming to want salvation on earth; the strength of the Church lies in the fact that it has another life to offer.

Meanwhile, there are certain remedies and palliatives that Eliot shows. For example, that married couples should take the advice of priests as to the exercise of Birth Control. 'Here, if anywhere, is definitely a matter upon which the Individual Conscience is no reliable guide; spiritual guidance should be imperative; and it should be clearly placed above medical advice—where also, opinions and theories vary indefinitely.' [10] As though the uncertainty of medicine were a motive for putting the matter in the care of those who may know nothing whatever about it. He proposes that the censorship, if it exist at all, should be at Lambeth Palace. A certain vindictive Puritanism is revealed in these lines: 'Thought, study, mortification, sacrifice: it is such notions as these that should be impressed upon the young.' [11]

It is for such opinions that Eliot will be judged by those who read his prose, and who, perhaps seeking guides, live in the belief that there is only one thing now which is worth doing, and that is to create a new and better civilization.

In *After Strange Gods*, Eliot has restated his traditional faith, extending it considerably beyond the world of literature. 'What I mean by tradition involves all those habitual actions, habits and customs, from the most significant religious rite to our conventional way of greeting a stranger, which represent the blood kinship of the 'same people living in the same place.' Certain conclusions are drawn from this. 'The population should be homogeneous; where two or more cultures exist in the same place they are likely either to become fiercely self-conscious or both to become adulterate. What is still more important is unity of religious background; and reasons of race and religion combine to make any large number of free-thinking Jews undesirable. There must be a proper balance between urban and rural, industrial and agricultural development. And a spirit of excessive tolerance is to be deprecated.' [12]

So much for Internationalism. It is hardly necessary to point out

[10] *Selected Essays*, p. 351.
[11] *Ibid.*, p. 349.
[12] *After Strange Gods*, p. 20.

that although Eliot is not a fascist, there is no sentence in this paragraph with which Mussolini, Hitler, and Mosley would not thoroughly agree. They would probably tolerate even the mild amount of ragging they get in *The Rock* from such an ally; just as they are prepared to tolerate a certain amount from the Church. The doctrine is not Catholic or Protestant. It has no echo in Renaissance Italy or in the teachings of the Church which claimed to stand above all cultures and local characteristics, and to unite all peoples. Nor does it apply to our own history since the Reformation. It is in fact an Old Testament doctrine suited to the intense nationalism and racial self-sufficiency of the Chosen People. There is nothing in the New Testament to correspond to it.

# WILLIAM BUTLER YEATS *

ELIOT has produced his great effect upon his generation because he has described men and women that get out of bed or into it from mere habit; in describing this life that has lost heart his own art seems grey, cold, dry. He is an Alexander Pope, working without apparent imagination, producing his effects by a rejection of all rhythms and metaphors used by the more popular romantics rather than by the discovery of his own, this rejection giving his work an unexaggerated plainness that has the effect of novelty. He has the rhythmical flatness of *The Essay on Man*—despite Miss Sitwell's advocacy I see Pope as Blake and Keats saw him—later, in *The Waste Land,* amid much that is moving in symbol and imagery there is much monotony of accent:

> When lovely woman stoops to folly and
> Paces about her room again, alone,
> She smooths her hair with automatic hand,
> And puts a record on the gramophone.

I was affected, as I am by these lines, when I saw for the first time a painting by Manet. I longed for the vivid colour and light of Rousseau and Courbet, I could not endure the grey middle-tint—and even to-day Manet gives me an incomplete pleasure; he had left the procession. Nor can I put the Eliot of these poems among those that descend from Shakespeare and the translators of the Bible. I think of him as satirist rather than poet. Once only does that early work speak in the great manner:

> The host with someone indistinct
> Converses at the door apart,
> The nightingales are singing near
> The Convent of the Sacred Heart,
>
> And sang within the bloody wood
> When Agamemnon cried aloud,

* From THE OXFORD BOOK OF MODERN VERSE, pp. xxi–xxiii, Oxford University Press, New York, and The Clarendon Press, Oxford, 1936.

> And let their liquid siftings fall
> To stain the stiff dishonoured shroud.

Not until *The Hollow Men* and *Ash Wednesday,* where he is helped by the short lines, and in the dramatic poems where his remarkable sense of actor, chanter, scene, sweeps him away, is there rhythmical animation. Two or three of my friends attribute the change to an emotional enrichment from religion, but his religion compared to that of John Gray, Francis Thompson, Lionel Johnson in *The Dark Angel,* lacks all strong emotion; a New England Protestant by descent, there is little self-surrender in his personal relation to God and the soul. *Murder in the Cathedral* is a powerful stage play because the actor, the monkish habit, certain repeated words, symbolize what we know, not what the author knows. Nowhere has the author explained how Becket and the King differ in aim; Becket's people have been robbed and persecuted in his absence; like the King he demands strong government. Speaking through Becket's mouth Eliot confronts a world growing always more terrible with a religion like that of some great statesman, a pity not less poignant because it tempers the prayer book with the results of mathematical philosophy.

> Peace. And let them be, in their exaltation.
> They speak better than they know, and beyond your understanding.
> They know and do not know, what it is to act or suffer.
> They know and do not know, that acting is suffering
> And suffering is action. Neither does the actor suffer
> Nor the patient act. But both are fixed
> In an eternal action, an eternal patience
> To which all must consent that it may be willed
> And which all must suffer that they may will it,
> That the pattern may subsist, for the pattern is the action
> And the suffering, that the wheel may turn and still
> Be forever still.

# ALLEN TATE *

---

E VERY age, as it sees itself, is peculiarly distracted: its chroniclers notoriously make too much of the variety before their own eyes. We see the variety of the past as mere turbulence within a fixed unity, and our own uniformity of the surface as the sign of a profound disunity of impulse. We have discovered that the ideas that men lived by from about the twelfth to the seventeenth century were absolute and unquestioned. The social turmoil of European history, so this argument runs, was shortsighted disagreement as to the best ways of making these deep assumptions morally good.

Although writers were judged morally, poets purveyed readymade moralities, and no critic expected the poet to give him a brandnew system. A poem was a piece of enjoyment for minds mature enough—that is, convinced enough of a satisfactory destiny—not to demand of every scribbler a way of life.

It is beyond the scope of this discussion, and of my own competence, to attempt an appraisal of any of the more common guides to salvation, including the uncommon one of the Thirty-nine Articles, lately subscribed to by Mr. T. S. Eliot, whose six poems published under the title *Ash Wednesday* are the occasion of this review. For it is my belief that, in a discussion of Eliot's poetry, his religious doctrines in themselves have little that commands interest. Yet it appears that his poetry, notwithstanding the amount of space it gets in critical journals, receives less discussion each year. The moral and religious attitude implicit in it has been related to the Thirty-nine Articles, and to a general intellectual position that Eliot has defended in his essays. The poetry and the prose are taken together as evidence that the author has made an inefficient adaptation to the modern environment; or at least he doesn't say anything very helpful to the American critics in their struggles to adapt themselves. It is an astonishing fact that, near as we are to a decade obsessed by "aesthetic standards," there is less discussion of poetry in a typical modern essay

* From COLLECTED ESSAYS, pp. 210-220, Copyright, 1960, by Allen Tate
Tate

on that fine art than there is in Johnson's essay on Denham. Johnson's judgment is frankly moralistic; he is revolted by unsound morals; but he seldom capitulates to a moral sentiment because it flatters his own moral sense. He requires the qualities of generality, copiousness, perspicuity. He hates Milton for a regicide; but his judgment of *Paradise Lost* is as disinterested as any judgment we should find today; certainly no more crippled by historical prejudice than Mr. Eliot's own views of Milton. Yet Eliot's critics are a little less able each year to see the poetry for Westminster Abbey; the wood is all trees.

I do not pretend to know how far our social and philosophical needs justify a prejudice which may be put somewhat summarily as follows: all forms of human action, economics, politics, even poetry, and certainly industry, are legitimate modes of salvation, but the historic religious mode is illegitimate. It is sufficient here to point out that the man who expects to find salvation in the latest lyric or a well-managed factory will not only not find it there; he is not likely to find it anywhere else. If a young mind is incapable of moral philosophy, a mind without moral philosophy is incapable of understanding poetry. For poetry, of all the arts, demands a serenity of view and a settled temper of the mind, and most of all the power to detach one's own needs from the experience set forth in the poem. A moral sense so organized sets limits to human nature, and is content to observe them. But if the reader lack this moral sense, the poem will be only a body of abstractions either useful or irrelevant to that body of abstractions already forming, but of uncertain direction, in the reader's mind. This reader will see the poem chiefly as biography, and he will proceed to deduce from it a history of the poet's case, to which he will attach himself if his own case resembles it; if it doesn't, he will look for a more useful case. Either way, the poem as a specific object is ignored.

The reasoning that is being brought to bear upon Mr. Eliot's recent verse is as follows: Anglo-Catholicism would not at all satisfy me; therefore, his poetry declines under its influence. Moreover, the poetry is not "contemporary"; it doesn't solve any labor problems; it is special, personal; and it can do us no good. Now the poetry *is* special and personal in quality, which is one of its merits, but what the critics are really saying is this—that Eliot's case-history is not special at all, that it is a general scheme of possible conduct that will not do for them. To accept the poetry seems to amount to accepting an invitation to join the Anglican Church. For the assumption is that the poetry and the religious position are identical.

If this were so, why should not the excellence of the poetry induce writers to join the Church, in the hope of writing as well as Eliot, since the irrelevance of the Church to their own needs makes them reject the poetry? The answer is, of course, that both parts of this fallacy are common. There is an aesthetic Catholicism, and there is a communist-economic rejection of art because it is involved with the tabooed mode of salvation.

The belief is that Eliot's poetry—all other poetry—is a simple record of the responses of a personality to an environment. The belief witnesses the modern desire to judge an art scientifically, practically, industrially; according to how it works. The poetry is viewed first as a pragmatic result; neither stage of the approach gives us "useful" knowledge.

Now a different heredity-environment combination would give us, of mechanical necessity, a different result, a different quantity of power to do a different and perhaps better social work. Doubtless that is true. But there is something disconcerting in this simple solution to the problem when it is looked at more closely. Two vastly different records or case-histories might give us, qualitatively speaking, very similar results: Baudelaire and Eliot have in common many *qualities* but *no history*. Their "results" have at least the common features of irony, humility, introspection, reverence—qualities fit only for contemplation and not for judgment according to their utility in our own conduct.

It is in this, the qualitative sense, that Eliot's recent poetry has been misunderstood. In this sense, the poetry is special, personal, of no use, and highly distinguished. But it is held to be a general formula, not distinct from the general formula that Eliot repeated when he went into the Church.

The form of the poems in *Ash Wednesday* is lyrical and solitary, and there is almost none of the elaborate natural description and allusion that gave to *The Waste Land* a partly realistic and partly symbolic character. These six poems are a brief moment of religious experience in an age that believes religion to be a kind of defeatism and puts all its hope for man in finding the right secular order. The mixed realism and symbolism of *The Waste Land* issued in irony. The direct and lyrical method of the new poems is based upon the simpler quality of humility. The latter quality comes directly out of the former, and there is an even continuity in Eliot's work.

In *The Waste Land* the prestige of our secular faith gave to the style its special character. This faith was the hard, coherent medium through which the discredited forms of the historic cultures emerged only to be stifled; the poem is at once their vindication and the recognition of their defeat. They are defeated in fact, as a politician may be defeated by the popular vote, but their vindication consists in the critical irony that their subordinate position casts upon the modern world.

The typical scene is the seduction of the stenographer by the clerk, in *The Fire Sermon*. Perhaps Mr. J. W. Krutch has not discussed this scene, but a whole generation of critics has, and from a viewpoint that Mr. Krutch has recently made popular: the seduction betrays the disillusion of the poet. The mechanical, brutal scene shows what love really is—that is to say, what it is scientifically, since science is truth: it is only an act of practical necessity, for procreation. The telling of the story by the Greek seer, Tiresias, who is chosen from a past of illusion and ignorance, permits the scene to become *a satire on the unscientific values of the past*. It was all pretense to think that love was anything but a biological necessity. The values of the past were pretty, absurd, and false; the scientific truth is both true and bitter. This is the familiar romantic dilemma, and the critics have read it into the scene from their own romantic despair.

There is no despair in the scene itself. The critics, who being in the state of mind I have described are necessarily blind to an effect of irony, have mistaken the symbols of an ironic contrast for the terms of a philosophic dilemma. It is the kind of metaphorical "logic" typical of romantic criticism since Walter Pater. Mr. Eliot knows too much about classical irony to be overwhelmed by a popular dogma in literary biology. For the seduction scene shows, not what man is, but what *for a moment* he thinks he is. In other words, the clerk stands for the secularization of the religious and qualitative values in the modern world. And the meaning of the contrast between Tiresias and the clerk is not disillusion, but irony. The scene is a masterpiece, perhaps the most profound vision that we have of modern man.

The importance of this scene as a key to the intention of *Ash Wednesday,* lies in the moral identity of humility and irony and in an important difference between them aesthetically. Humility is subjective, a quality of the moral character: it is thus general, invisible, and can only be inferred, not seen. *Irony is the visible, particular, and objective instance of humility.* Irony is the objective quality of an event or situation which stimulates our capacity for humility. It is that arrangement of experience, either premeditated by art or accidentally appearing in the affairs of men, which permits to the spectator an insight superior to that of the actor; it shows him that the practical program, the special ambition, of the actor at that moment is bound to fail. The humility thus derived is the self-respect proceeding from a sense of the folly of men in their desire to dominate a natural force or a situation. The seduction scene is the picture of modern and dominating man. The arrogance and pride of conquest of the "small house agent's clerk" are the badge of science, bumptious practicality, overweening secular faith. The very success of his conquest witnesses its aimless character; it succeeds as a wheel succeeds in turning: he can only conquer again.

His own failure to understand his position is irony, and the poet's insight into it is humility. But for the grace of God, says the poet in effect, there go I. This is essentially the poetic attitude, an attitude that Eliot has been approaching with increasing purity. It is not that his recent verse is better than that of the period ending with *The Waste Land*. Actually it is less spectacular and less complex in subject-matter; for Eliot less frequently objectifies his leading emotion, humility, into irony. His new form is simple, expressive, homogeneous, and direct, and without the early elements of violent contrast.

There is a single ironic passage in *Ash Wednesday,* and significantly enough it is the first stanza of the first poem. This passage presents objectively the poet *as he thinks himself for the moment to be*. It establishes that humility towards his own merit which fixes the tone of the poems that follow. And the irony has been overlooked by the critics because they take the stanza as a literal exposition of the latest phase of the Eliot *case-history*—at a time when, in the words of Mr. Edmund Wilson, "his psychological plight seems most depressing." Thus, here is the vain pose of a Titan too young to be weary of strife, but weary of it nevertheless.

> Because I do not hope to turn again
> Because I do not hope

Because I do not hope to turn
Desiring this man's gift and that man's scope
I no longer strive to strive towards such things
(Why should the agèd eagle stretch its wings?)
Why should I mourn
The vanished power of the usual reign?

If the six poems are taken together as the focus of a specific religious emotion, the opening stanza, instead of being a naive personal "confession," appears in the less lurid light of a highly effective technical performance. This stanza has two features that are necessary to the development of the unique imagery which distinguishes the religious emotion of *Ash Wednesday* from any other religious poetry of our time. It is possibly the only kind of imagery that is valid for religious verse today.

The first feature is the regular yet halting rhythm, the smooth uncertainty of movement which may either proceed to greater regularity or fall away into improvisation. The second feature is the imagery itself. It is trite; it echoes two familiar passages from English poetry. But the quality to be observed is this: it is secular imagery. It sets forth a special ironic situation, but the emotion is not identified with any specific experience. The imagery is thus perfectly suited to the broken rhythm. The stanza is a device for getting the poem under way, starting from a known and general emotion, in a monotonous rhythm, for a direction which, to the reader, is unknown. The ease, the absence of surprise, with which Eliot proceeds to bring out the subject of his meditation is admirable. After some further and ironic deprecation of his worldly powers, he goes on:

And pray to God to have mercy upon us
And pray that I may forget
These matters that with myself I too much discuss,
Too much explain.

We are being told, of course, that there is to be some kind of discourse on God, or a meditation; yet the emotion is still general. The imagery is even flatter than before; it is "poetical" at all only in that special context; for it is the diction of prose. And yet, subtly and imperceptibly, the rhythm has changed; it is irregular and labored. We are being prepared for a new and sudden effect, and it comes in the first lines of the second poem:

Lady, three white leopards sat under a juniper-tree
In the cool of the day, having fed to satiety
On my legs my heart my liver and that which had been contained
In the hollow round of my skull. And God said
Shall these bones live? shall these
Bones live?

From here on, in all the poems, there is constant and sudden change
of rhythm, and there is a corresponding alternation of two kinds of
imagery—the visual and tactile imagery common to all poetry, without significance in itself for any kind of experience, and the traditional religious symbols. The two orders are inextricably fused.

It is evident that Eliot has hit upon the only method now available of using the conventional religious image in poetry. He has re-
duced it from symbol to image, from abstraction to the plane of sensation. And corresponding to this process, there are images of his own
invention which he almost pushes over the boundary of sensation
into abstractions, where they have the appearance of conventional
symbols. The passage I have quoted above is an example of this: for
the "Lady" may be a nun, or even the Virgin, or again she may be
a beautiful woman; but she is presented, through the serious tone of
the invocation, with all the solemnity of a religious figure. The fifth
poem exhibits the reverse of the process; it begins with a series of
plays on the Logos, the most rarefied of all the Christian abstractions;
and it succeeds in creating the effect of immediate experience by
means of a broken and distracted rhythm:

> If the lost word is lost, if the spent word is spent
> If the unheard, unspoken
> Word is unspoken, unheard;
> Still is the unspoken word, the Word unheard,
> The Word without a word, the Word within
> The world and for the world. . . .

# MARIO PRAZ *

IT is curious to look at Eliot's relation to Dante from an Italian point of view, for, while there is an established tradition of Dante worship to which all, both Italians and foreigners, more or less conform—a tradition that affords little variety of manifestations—T. S. Eliot's tribute could not easily be disposed of in a supplement to Paget Toynbee's monumental collection of references and allusions (*Britain's Tribute to Dante in Literature and Art*). Eliot's relation to Dante is too intimate for that, and the fact of this intimacy, and the way in which it was brought about, have in them something entirely novel and, as I have hinted in what I hope may not seem a light-hearted beginning—curious.

Mr. Matthiessen, in his penetrating study of Eliot, *The Achievement of T. S. Eliot,* has established a connection between him and the line of Dante scholarship at Harvard (from Longfellow through Charles Eliot Norton, Santayana, and Charles Grandgent); and since Eliot himself in the Preface to his *Dante* acknowledges his debt to Grandgent's *Dante* and to Santayana's essay in *Three Philosophical Poets,* there is no reason to minimize the part played by traditional scholarship in the formation of Eliot's estimate of Dante. However, it is not through the quiet ways of the schoolroom and the library that Eliot learnt to admire Dante. As in other fields (the metaphysical poets, the Elizabethan dramatists), he may owe much to scholars for broadening his knowledge, but his discoveries have been made, thanks to nonacademic critics, to free lances of culture. Arthur Symons revealed to him Laforgue; Ezra Pound, through his book on *The Spirit of Romance* (1910), and still more through his table-talk, made him aware of the greatness of Dante, gave him that shock of surprise that no recognized authority on the poet could have communicated. Before he knew *The Spirit of Romance* and had opportunities of intercourse with Pound in London, Eliot had read a smattering of the early Italian poets, especially the two Guidos and Cino,

* T. S. Eliot and Dante, from *The Southern Review,* Vol. II, No. 4, pp. 525–548, Copyright, 1937, by Louisiana State University.

but it was Pound who sharpened his interest in these people, who made them alive to him.[1]

No matter how much serious scholars may laugh at Pound's amateurishness and inaccuracy (and whoever has seen his pretentious and futile edition of Cavalcanti, published in Genoa in 1932, is likely to underrate Pound's merits), he had the power of bringing to life the Provençal and early Italian poets, of seeing them "as contemporary with himself." "Any scholar," says Eliot in his "Introduction" to the *Poems* of Ezra Pound, "can see Arnaut Daniel or Guido Cavalcanti as literary figures; only Pound can see them as living beings." Pound could give to his Dante that flavor of experience for which one would vainly seek in the pages of orthodox scholars. Not the least reason why Eliot's relation to Dante is out of the beaten track of Dante-worship lies, no doubt, in the manner in which he discovered him through Pound. The deep resonance throughout Eliot's work of the "superb verses of Arnaut Daniel in his Provençal tongue" (Pound draws attention to these lines: "Arnaut speaks, not in Italian, but in his own tongue; an honor paid to no one else in the *Commedia*.")—

> Ara vos prec, per aquella valor
> que vos guida al som de l'escalina,
> sovenga vos a temps de ma dolor!
> Poi s'ascose nel foco che gli affina—

bears witness to that origin, points to a strong appeal to the "auditory imagination" of Eliot,[2] an appeal infinitely deeper than the bare meaning of the passage would have made. One may doubt whether, without the stimulus of the actual delivery of those lines on the part of such a *gourmet* of pure sounds as Pound, Eliot's imagination would ever have crystallized round them. For, I think, one may trace to Pound that aspect of Eliot which consists in investing a quotation in a foreign language with a significance infinitely more potent than its verbal import, a significance which in Eliot achieves an emblematical pregnancy.

---

[1] Private letter.

[2] The last line appears in *The Waste Land* among the "fragments shored against the poet's ruins" (line 427); *Ara Vos Prec* is the title of the 1919 book of verse; the words "Sovegna vos" appear in *Ash-Wednesday;* the third section of this poem was at first published separately under the title *Som de l'Escalina;* etc. See Matthiessen, p. 101, and the whole IVth Chapter for the "auditory imagination."

Traces of initiation by Pound are to be seen not only in this peculiar attitude to the musical spell of the verse, but also in the critical ideas Eliot has been ex*pound*ing (this was not an intentional pun!) on Dante in his early essay in *The Sacred Wood* (1920), in his lecture on *Shakespeare and the Stoicism of Seneca* (1927), and in his *Dante* (1929).

The aim of this last work, "to persuade the reader first of the importance of Dante as a master—I may even say, *the* master—for a poet writing today in any language," coincides with the climax of *The Spirit of Romance,* whose Chapter VI, ushered by the solemn "Advenit Magister" at the end of Chapter V, deals with *Il Maestro.* At the outset Pound declares: "This book is not a philological work . . . I am interested in poetry," and proceeds with an onslaught at the stupidity of philologists. Nothing could be more alien to Eliot than such a slapdash manner; his way of approach is more modest and subtle, but his essay is shown, in conclusion, to possess the same characteristics as Pound's book: "If my task had been to produce another brief 'introduction to the study of Dante' I should have been incompetent to perform it. But in a series of essays of 'Poets on Poets' the undertaking, as I understand it, is quite a different one . . . I am no Dante scholar, etc." Pound makes dramatically a solemn oath to speak only with firsthand acquaintance of the texts, more plainly he declares that "throughout the book all critical statements are based on a direct study of the texts themselves and not upon commentaries," and apropos of early Italian poems (p. 98): "After a few hours with the originals, criticism becomes a vain thing." Eliot's advice is to the same effect, though couched in a more guarded manner (p. 68): "Read in this way it [the *Vita Nuova*] can be more useful than a dozen commentaries [on the *Comedy*]. The effect of many books about Dante is to give the impression that it is more necessary to read about him than to read what he has written, etc." In either case, then, the author emphasizes the fact that he is a poet, that his chief concern is with the texts themselves, that commentaries are apt to obscure one's appreciation, that the way of approach of the philologist is not his own (Pound goes a step further, and shows the utmost contempt for academic critics).

Pound's idea of poetry (p. 5) as of "a sort of inspired mathematics, which gives us equations, not for abstract figures, triangles, spheres, and the like, but equations for the human emotions," may be said to be the starting-point of Eliot's theory of the "objective correlative" ("Hamlet and His Problems"): "The only way of expressing emotion in the form of art is by finding an 'objective correlative'; in other words, a set of objects, a situation, a chain of events which shall be the formula of that *particular* emotion; such that when the external facts, which must terminate in sensory experience, are given, the emotion is immediately evoked." Pound's statements are not so clear-cut as Eliot's, but I think that, by reading the following passages, in the light of the definition of poetry quoted above, we have the chief elements of Eliot's theory of the "objective correlative," as well as of his interpretation of Dante's vision:

> The cult of Provençe had been a cult of the emotions; and with it there had been some, hardly conscious, study of emotional psychology. In Tuscany the cult is a cult of the harmonies of the mind. If one is in sympathy with this form of *objective imagination* [*italics mine*] and this quality of vision, there is no poetry which has such enduring, such, if I may say so, indestructible charm (p. 103).

Apropos of Guinizelli's sonnet *Vedut'ho la lucente stella diana,* Pound writes (p. 92):

> Here the preciseness of the description denotes, I think, a clarity of imaginative vision. In more sophisticated poetry an epithet would suffice, the picture would be suggested. The dawn would be "rosy-fingered" or "in russet clad." The Tuscan poetry is, however, of a time when the seeing of visions was considered respectable, and the poet takes delight in definite portrayal of his vision. The use of epithet is an advance on this method only when it suggests a vision not less clear, and its danger is obvious. In Milton or Swinburne, for example, it is too often merely a high-sounding word, and not a swift symbol of vanished beauty.

In general, on Tuscan poetry (p. 104):

> Faults this poetry may have . . . . this virtue it ever has, it is not rhetorical, it aims to be what it is, and never pretends to be something which it is not.

And on the *Vita Nuova* in particular (p. 114):

> Anyone who has in any degree the faculty of vision will know that the so-called personifications are real and not artificial.

Dante's precision both in the *Vita Nuova* and in the *Commedia* comes from the attempt to reproduce exactly the thing which has been clearly seen. The "Lord of terrible aspect" is no abstraction, no figure of speech. There are some who can not or will not understand these things.

This passage must be read in connection with what Pound says of allegory (p. 85):

> With the Romaunt of the Rose we come to a third thing . . . we get the allegory, a sort of extension of the fable . . . In the romances he [the medieval author] has told of actions and speech and has generalized about the emotions. In the allegory he learns to separate himself, not yet from complete moods, but from simple qualities and passions, and to visualize them.

These are, then, the points made by Pound in *The Spirit of Romance:* allegory is a means for the poet to separate himself from the emotions, to visualize them; this kind of vision is not a pretence; there is nothing rhetorical about it; in the Middle Ages the seeing of visions was considered respectable; the attempt of the poet to reproduce exactly the thing he has *actually* seen makes for clarity.

If now we read what Eliot says on the same subject in his *Dante* we will easily perceive the affinities:

> The simplicity of Dante has another detailed reason . . . What is important for my purpose is the fact that the allegorical method was a definite method not confined to Italy; and the fact, apparently paradoxical, that the allegorical method makes for simplicity and intelligibility. We incline to think of allegory as a tiresome crossword puzzle. We incline to associate it with dull poems (at best, *The Romance of the Rose*), and in a great poem to ignore it as irrelevant. What we ignore is, in a case like Dante's, its particular effect towards lucidity of style . . . We have to consider the type of mind which by nature and *practice* tended to express itself in allegory; and for a competent poet, allegory means *clear visual images* . . . Allegory is only one poetic method, but it is a method which has very great advantages. Dante's is a *visual* imagination . . . it is visual in the sense that he lived in an age in which men still saw visions . . . We have nothing but dreams, and we have forgotten that seeing visions . . . was once a more significant, interesting, and disciplined kind of dreaming . . . All I ask of the reader, at this point, is to clear his mind, if he can, of every prejudice against allegory, and

to admit at least that it was not a device to enable the uninspired
to write verses, but really a mental habit, which when raised to
the point of genius can make a great poet as well as a great
mystic or saint. And it is the allegory which makes it possible for
the reader who is not even a good Italian scholar to enjoy Dante.
Speech varies, but our eyes are all the same . . . Dante's attempt
is to make us see what he saw.

This passage (*Dante,* pp. 22–23) is closer to *The Spirit of Romance*
than the passage on allegory in the short essay in *The Sacred Wood,*
but the conclusion is the same. In the short essay Eliot justifies the
usefulness of allegory in a poem of so vast an ambit as the *Commedia,*
but he calls it an artificial and mechanical framework, whose intelligence is not necessary: "the emotional structure within the scaffold
is what must be understood, the structure made possible by the scaffold. This structure is an ordered scale of human emotions . . .
Dante's is the most comprehensive, and the most *ordered* presentation of emotions that has ever been made."

Of Dante's use of elaborate imagery such as that of the figure of
the Eagle composed by the spirits of the just in the Paradise (XVIII
and following cantos), Eliot says (p. 54): "Such figures are not merely
antiquated rhetorical devices, but serious and practical means of making the spiritual visible."

Another passage of Pound (p. 117) illustrates for the *Commedia*
the point of view which is in everything but in name Eliot's theory
of the "objective correlative":

> There is little doubt that Dante conceived the real Hell,
> Purgatory, and Paradise as states, and not places. Richard St.
> Victor had, somewhile before, voiced this belief, and it is, more-
> over, a part of the esoteric and mystic dogma. *For the purposes of
> art* and popular religion it is more convenient to deal with such
> matters *objectively;* this also was most natural in an age wherein
> it was the poetic convention to personify abstractions, thoughts,
> and the spirits of the eyes and senses, and indeed nearly every-
> thing that could be regarded as an object, an essence, or a quality.
> It is therefore expedient in reading the *Commedia* to regard
> Dante's descriptions of the actions and conditions of the shades
> as descriptions of men's mental states in life, in which they are,
> after death, compelled to continue: that is to say, *men's inner
> selves stand visibly before the eyes of Dante's intellect* [*italics
> mine*].

We shall see how Eliot as a poet has tried to revive this practice chiefly in *Ash Wednesday:* to find clear images, or rather symbols, appealing to the senses, apt to evoke the emotions of which they are the "objective correlative."

It may be noted incidentally that Pound's definition of the nature of an image in such a way as to stress the union of sense and thought, the presence of the idea *in* the image ("An 'Image' is that which presents an intellectual and emotional complex in an instant of time") [3]—a definition intimately connected with Pound's knowl-edge of Dante's practice—was capable of establishing at once a link between the poetry of Dante and his circle and that of the English metaphysical poets of the Seventeenth Century of whom Eliot was to write [4] that they felt "their thought as immediately as the odor of a rose. A thought to Donne was an experience, it modified his sensibility." [5]

In the brief comparisons of Dante with Milton and Shakespeare, Eliot is also sharing Pound's viewpoint. His slighting allusion to Milton's Satan as "the curly-haired Byronic hero of Milton" (p. 33) agrees with Pound's *"Paradise Lost* is conventional melodrama, and later critics have decided that the devil is intended for the hero, which interpretation leaves the whole without significance" (p. 165). [6] As for Shakespeare, Pound says: "Shakespear alone of the English poets en-

---

[3] Pound's essay reprinted in *Pavannes and Divisions,* 1918. See Matthiessen, pp. 60 and 72.

[4] Essay on "The Metaphysical Poets," in *Homage to John Dryden,* 1924. This essay was originally a review of Prof. Grierson's *Metaphysical Lyrics and Poems of the Seventeenth Century,* Oxford, 1921. Prof. Grierson wrote (p. xiii) of metaphysical poetry of the highest sort that its themes are "the boldest conceptions, the profoundest intuitions, the subtlest and most complex classifications and 'discourse of reason,' if into these too the poet can 'carry sensation,' make of them passionate experiences communicable in vivid and moving imagery."

[5] In the VIIIth of his Clark Lectures (not published) Eliot defined metaphysical poetry as "that in which what is ordinarily apprehensible only by thought is brought within the grasp of feeling, or that in which what is ordinarily only felt is transformed into thought without ceasing to be feeling." In the VIIth Lecture Eliot stressed the difference between Dante and Donne, which I had tried to define myself in *Secentismo e marinismo in Inghilterra,* Firenze, 1925, p. 107.

[6] Cf. "Dante," in *The Sacred Wood:* "About none of Dante's characters is there that ambiguity which affects Milton's Lucifer."

dures sustained comparison with the Florentine. Here are we with the masters; of neither can we say, 'He is the greater'; of each we must say, 'He is unexcelled.' . . . Dante would seem to have the greater imaginative 'vision' . . . Shakespear would seem to have greater power in depicting various humanity, and to be more observant of its foibles." Eliot (pp. 17 and 51) says substantially the same thing: "What I have in mind is that Dante is, in a sense to be defined (for the word means little by itself), the most *universal* of poets in the modern languages. That does not mean that he is 'the greatest', or that he is the most comprehensive—there is greater variety and detail in Shakespeare . . . Dante and Shakespeare divide the modern world between them; there is no third . . . Shakespeare gives the greatest *width* of human passion; Dante, the greatest altitude and greatest depth." The short essay on Dante concludes with these words:

> Dante, more than any other poet, has succeeded in dealing with his philosophy, not as a theory (in the modern and not the Greek sense of that word) or as his own comment or reflection, but in terms of something *perceived*. When most of our modern poets confine themselves to what they had perceived, they produce for us, usually, only odds and ends of still life and stage properties; but that does not imply so much that the method of Dante is obsolete, as that our vision is perhaps comparatively restricted.

We have accounted for the origin of the first portion of this statement. As for the latter part, one must bear in mind what Santayana, to whom Eliot confesses himself indebted, had written (*Three Philosophical Poets*):

> Our poets are things of shreds and patches; they give us episodes and studies, a sketch of this curiosity, a glimpse of that romance; they have no total vision, no grasp of the whole reality, and consequently no capacity for a sane and steady idealization. This age of material elaboration has no sense for perfection. Its fancy is retrospective, whimsical, and flickering; its ideals, when it has any, are negative and partial; its moral strength is a blind and miscellaneous vehemence. Its poetry, in a word, is a poetry of barbarism.

With these poets Santayana contrasts Dante, whom he characterizes with words that Eliot may have remembered:

> Dante gives us a successful example of the *highest species* of poetry. His poetry covers the whole field from which poetry may

be fetched, and to which poetry may be applied, from the inmost recesses of the heart to the uttermost bounds of nature and of destiny. If to give imaginative value to something is the minimum task of a poet, to give value to all things, and to the system which things compose, is evidently his greatest task.

In another passage, this one in the book on Dante, Eliot is taking to task the modern mind (pp. 62–63):

> It appears likely, to anyone who reads the *Vita Nuova* without prejudice, that it is a mixture of biography and allegory; but a mixture according to a recipe not available to the modern mind. When I say the "modern mind," I mean the minds of those who have read or could have read such a document as Rousseau's *Confessions*. The modern mind can understand the "confession," that is, the literal account of oneself, varying only in degree of sincerity and self-understanding, and it can understand "allegory" in the abstract. Nowadays "confessions," of an insignificant sort, pour from the press; everyone *met son cœur à nu,* or pretends to; "personalities" succeed one another in interest. It is difficult to conceive of an age (of many ages) when human beings cared somewhat about the salvation of the "soul," but not about each other as "personalities." Now Dante, I believe, had experiences which seemed to him of some importance; not of importance because they had happened to him and because he, Dante Alighieri, was an important person who kept press-cutting bureaux busy; but important in themselves; and therefore they seemed to him to have some philosophical and impersonal value.

It is interesting, in view of the development which this theory of "impersonality" had received in the essay on "Tradition and the Individual Talent," [7] to trace it back to the reading of Professor Grandgent's *Dante* (New York 1916), a book to which Eliot gives the first place in the list of works that have influenced him. Says Professor Grandgent (pp. 289–90):

---

[7] "The progress of an artist is a continual self-sacrifice, a continual extinction of personality . . . The point of view which I am struggling to attack is perhaps related to the metaphysical theory of the substantial unity of the soul: for my meaning is, that the poet has, not a "personality" to express, but a particular medium, which is only a medium and not a personality, in which impressions and experiences combine in peculiar and unexpected ways. Impressions and experiences which are important for the man may take no place in the poetry, and those which become important in the poetry may play quite a negligible part in the man, the personality."

In no respect, perhaps, do medieval writings differ more patently from modern than in their dignified impersonality. Contrast this attitude for a moment with our present-day effusiveness, our pitiful eagerness to disclose, to anyone who will listen, each petty detail of our bodily and spiritual existence. Think of the flood of trivial self-revelation that pours from the lips of the catchpenny scribbler or the sublimated chorus-girl. And some people must care to read these confidences, else they would not be printed: that is the strangest part of it. Such display would once have seemed almost as indecent as walking naked in the street. If the exhibition of the *ego* was foreign to medieval taste, the observation of self was scarcely less so. Introspection was confined, in the main, to religious experience, where it is legitimate and necessary.

We have thus seen how some of the most characteristic utterances of Eliot as a critic—his theory of the "objective correlative," the other of the "impersonality of the poet"—arose in connection with his study of Dante. The ideas he finds in Santayana and Grandgent witness to that moral idealism and that dread of vulgarity which are typical of the Puritan mind (see Matthiessen, pp. 7–8); the ideas he develops under the stimulus of Pound, *il miglior fabbro*,[8] concern rather the technique of poetry, the finding out of a pattern of clear visual images capable of evoking immediately the underlying emotion. Pound quoted also (p. 150) Arthur Symons on Cary's translation: "To translate Dante is an impossible thing, for to do it would demand, as the first requirement, a *concise* and *luminous* style equal to Wordsworth at his *best*." (The italics are Pound's.)

The blend of these various elements gives to Eliot's interpretation of Dante that peculiar character which is likely to strike an Italian as unfamiliar and curious—as I said at the beginning. Possibly Symons' words have led Eliot to perceive a similarity between the language of Dante and that of Dryden and Pope. The whole first paragraph of his chapter on the *Purgatorio* and the *Paradiso* deserves to be quoted:

> For the science or art of writing verse, one has learned from the *Inferno* that the greatest poetry can be written with the

[8] *The Waste Land* is dedicated to Pound, *il miglior fabbro*, according to the definition of A. Daniel in Dante (*Purg.*, XXVI, 117), which Pound had adopted as the title of the Second Chapter of *The Spirit of Romance*.

greatest economy of words, and with the greatest austerity in the use of metaphor, simile, verbal beauty, and elegance. When I affirm that more can be learned about how to write poetry from Dante than from any English poet, I do not at all mean that Dante is thereby greater than Shakespeare or, indeed, any other English poet. I put my meaning into other words by saying that Dante can do less *harm* to anyone trying to learn to write verse, than can Shakespeare. Most great English poets are *inimitable* in a way in which Dante was not. If you try to imitate Shakespeare you will certainly produce a series of stilted, forced, and violent distortions of language. The language of each great English poet is his own language; the language of Dante is the perfection of a common language. In a sense, it is more pedestrian than that of Dryden or Pope. If you follow Dante without talent, you will at worst be pedestrian and flat; if you follow Shakespeare or Pope without talent, you will make an utter fool of yourself.

It will perhaps surprise Eliot if an Italian qualifies his statement in so far as his own literature is concerned. Whenever Italians have tried to imitate Dante, they have produced sometimes flat and pedestrian verse, but more frequently have written precisely in that stilted and forced style which Eliot thinks proper to the worst imitators of Shakespeare: to witness the two following passages—chosen at random out of many equally to the point—one by Vincenzo Monti, the other by Gabriele D'Annunzio:

> D'italo nome troverai qui tali
>   che dell'uman sapere archimandriti
>   al tuo pronto intelletto impennâr l' ali.
>     (*In Morte di Lorenzo Mascheroni*, I, 82 ff.)

> Ei nella solitudine si gode
>   sentendo sé come inesausto fonte.
>   Dedica l'opre al Tempo; e ciò non ode.
>     (*La Tregua*, in *Laudi*, libro III)

Italians who read Shakespeare, on the other hand, frequently find his language direct and possessing the very accent of life. In either case it could be easily shown that the illusion is caused by the ignorance in which one naturally is of the conventions of a foreign language. What matters for us here is not to ascertain to what extent Dante's style can be considered *simple* (in fact, Dante fits his language to the theme so

that examples of all kinds of style can be found in him), but to know
that to T. S. Eliot that style *seems* simple, that "in twenty years he has
written about a dozen lines in that style successfully; and compared
to the dullest passage of the *Divine Comedy*, they are 'as straw.'"

When Chaucer wanted to imitate Dante, he wrote thus:

> O noble, O worthy Petro, glorie of Spayne,
> Whom Fortune heeld so hye in magestee,
> Wel oghten men thy pitous deth complayne!

and Shelley:

> As in that trance of wondrous thought I lay,
> This was the tenour of my waking dream:—
> Methought I sate beside a public way—

Such passages sound Dantesque enough to an Italian ear, no less
Dantesque than the passages of Monti and D'Annunzio quoted above.
They are conceived in what literary historians call the Dantesque
manner. This Dante, needless to say, has nothing to do with the in-
spirer of the dozen lines or so of which T. S. Eliot is proud.

Eliot's indebtedness to Dante ranges from the quotation and the
adaptation of single lines or passages to the deeper influence in concrete presentation and symbolism.

Actual quotations bear out well Eliot's appreciation of Dante as
the poet who achieves the perfection of a common language, who
teaches "that a straightforward philosophical statement can be great
poetry." All the following passages have in common a quality of plain
statement which is not couched in a form very different from that
it would have in prose:

> Or puoi la quantitate
> comprender de l'amor ch'a te mi scalda,
> quond'io dismento nostra vanitate,
> trattando l'ombre come cosa salda.
> (*Purg.*, XXI, 133–6; motto to *Prufrock*) [9]

> S' i' credesse che mia risposta fosse
> a persona che mai tornasse al mondo,

---

[9] I quote from the "Testo critico della Società Dantesca Italiana." These
lines are given wrongly in the editions of Eliot's *Poems,* thus:
> La quantitate
> Puote veder del amor che a te mi scalda, etc.
Inaccuracies have slipped also into the next quotation; *torno* should be *tornò*.

questa fiamma staria sanza più scosse;
ma però che già mai di questo fondo
non tornò vivo alcun, s'i'odo il vero,
sanza tema d'infamia ti rispondo.
> (*Inf.*, XXVII, 61–6; motto to "The Love Song of
> J. Alfred Prufrock")

E'n la sua volontade è nostra pacè.
> (*Parad.*, III, 85)

La forma universal di questo nodo
credo ch'i' vidi, perché più di largo,
dicendo questo, mi sento ch'i' godo.
> (*Parad.*, XXXIII, 91–3)

These two last quotations are favorites with Eliot; of the whole passage from which the last quotation is taken, he says (p. 54): "Nowhere in poetry has experience so remote from ordinary experience been expressed so concretely, by a masterly use of that imagery of *light* which is the form of certain types of mystical experience." [10]

From such passages one can infer that the influence of Dante could lie for Eliot only in the strengthening of that tendency to use a language not different from the ordinary, and at the same time capable of philosophical turns, that he had found in his early model, Laforgue.

After what Eliot says apropos of the *Commedia,* that "genuine poetry can communicate before it is understood" (p. 16), after what he says elsewhere on the "auditory imagination" (see Matthiessen, Ch. IV), one would expect to find in his poems traces of the rhythm of Dante. However, direct imitation of the *terzina dantesca,* such as poets like Chaucer and Shelley attempted, with little success, is not a thing which would have appealed to a poet as subtle as Eliot. Moreover, the *terzina* is apt to have a somewhat stilted and forced sound; when Eliot says that Dante communicated to him a poetic emotion before he properly understood the text, the appeal to his auditory imagination must have been more an appeal of words than of rhythm in its flow: "The style of Dante has a peculiar lucidity—a *poetic* as distinguished from an *intellectual* lucidity. The thought may be obscure, but the word is lucid, or rather translucent." (p. 18)

---

[10] Cf. Matthiessen, p. 153, for an attempt of Eliot to produce a similar effect in *The Rock.*

Here again, we shall get a clearer idea of the impression Dante's poetry must have made on Eliot's auditory imagination, if we refer to what Ezra Pound felt about *la dolce lingua toscana* (p. 103):

> The best poetry of this time appeals by its truth, by its subtlety, and by its refined exactness. Noffo Bonaguida thus expresses himself and the peculiar introspective tendency of his time:

> Ispirito d'Amor con intelletto
> Dentro dallo meo cor sempre dimora,
> Che mi mantiene in gran gioia e 'n diletto
> E senza lui non viveria un'ora.

In his chapter on *Il Maestro*, Pound remarks (p. 148):

> There are beautiful images in the *Paradiso*, but the chief marvel is not the ornament. Such lines as Canto V, 7–12:

> Io veggio ben sì come già risplende
> nello intelletto tuo l'eterna luce,
> che, vista sola, sempre amore accende;
> e s'altra cosa vostro amor seduce,
> non è se non di quella alcun vestigio
> mal conosciuto, che quivi traluce—[11]

> lose too much in a prose translation, illuminated though they be in essence . . . Though it be true that no man who has not passed through, or nearly approached that spiritual experience known as illumination—I use the word in a technical sense—can appreciate the *Paradiso* to the full, yet there is sheer poetic magic in a line like (Canto VII, 130)—

> Gli angeli, frate, e il paese sincero

> which no lover of the highest art can fail to feel.

Other passages are quoted by Pound in Italian, as their beauty of sound cannot be rendered in any other language; they are passages of philosophical import (e.g. *Parad.,* VII, 136–44), rich in Latin polysyllables, or plain lines, whose charm would strike only a refined ear, like the line quoted above from *Parad.,* VII, or:

> In queste stelle, che intorno a lor vanno

---

[11] This is the text given by Pound; the "Testo critico" is somewhat different.

(from the same Canto, 138) which possibly conveys to Pound more than to an average Italian ear, for he says that "with the suave blending of the elided vowels, [it] has in its sound alone more of the serene peace from that unsullied country than can be conveyed in any words save those flowing from the lips of a supreme genius."

In a similar way, Eliot's feeling for syllable and rhythm in Dante is more for the common qualities of the *dolce lingua toscana* than for the actual metrical skill of the poet.

In Eliot's imitations of Dantesque lines, true, we detect an echo of Dante's unmistakable *endecasillabo*:

> A crowd flowed over London Bridge, so many,
> *I had not thought death had undone so many.*
> (*The Waste Land*, 62–3)

>                    sì lunga tratta
> di gente, ch' io non averei creduto
> *che morte tanta n'avesse disfatta.*
> (*Inf.*, III, 55–7)

> Highbury bore me. Richmond and Kew
> Undid me.
> (*The Waste Land*, 293–4)

> Siena mi fe', disfecemi Maremma.
> (*Purg.*, V, 133)

> Issues from the hand of God, the simple soul
> ("Animula")

> *Esce di mano a lui che la vagheggia*
> . . . . .
> l'anima semplicetta che sa nulla
> (*Purg.*, XVI, 85–8)

But such passages need not detain us for long: one can find similar deft insertions in dozens of other poets. The shock of surprise they give us adds no doubt to the effect of the poem,[12] but it is not from them that we can learn what Dante's influence has meant for Eliot.

That influence is closely connected with Eliot's interpretation of Dante's allegory along the lines suggested by Ezra Pound—as we

---

[12] See Matthiessen, p. 20, for an analysis of these insertions.

have seen above. Clear visual images, a concise and luminous language: these are the two qualities of Dante Eliot has in mind. The former is the "objective correlative" of the emotions they intend to suggest, the latter appeals to the auditory imagination: there is an element of extreme precision and an element of vagueness in both; for the mind of the reader is stirred by the symbolical import of the precise images, whereas—in contrast with the apparent terseness of the vocabulary—"the feeling for syllable and rhythm penetrates far below the conscious levels of thought and feeling, invigorates every word; sinks to the most primitive and forgotten, returns to the origin and brings something back, seeks the beginning and the end" (essay on Arnold).

How much a Dantesque influence of this kind differs from a traditional imitation, can be seen reading side by side Eliot's "La Figlia Che Piange" and Rossetti's "Blessed Damozel":

Stand on the highest pavement of the stair—
Lean on a garden urn—
Weave, weave the sunlight in your hair—
Clasp your flowers to you with a pained surprise. . . .

The blessèd Damozel leaned out
  From the gold bar of Heaven;
. . . . . . .
She had three lilies in her hand,
  And the stars in her hair were seven.

Rossetti's images are directly derived from the *stil nuovo*, but are almost degraded to stage properties; they suggest only an archaic ornamentation, while their original spirit has vanished. The poet speaks in disguise. It is interesting to read what Eliot says of Rossetti's poem (*Dante*, p. 48): "First by my rapture and next by my revolt, [it] held up my appreciation of Beatrice by many years." When Eliot wrote *his* "Blessed Damozel," "La Figlia Che Piange," the pattern of the Pre-Raphaelite poem may have haunted the dim corners of his memory, but the clear visual images which rose in his mind had nothing of the stiff fastidiousness of Rossetti; the picture conjured up is taken from our everyday experience, not from the exquisite conventions of a *fondo oro;* but how much more suggestive of light is Eliot's image than Rossetti's! "Weave, weave the sunlight in your hair"—"And the stars in her hair were seven": we have only to read these two lines one after the other to become fully aware of the difference of the two methods. That "The Blessed Damozel" was actually at the back of Eliot's mind while writing "La Figlia Che Piange" may be seen also from the curious recurring of the Rossettian pattern in the last stanza:

> She turned away, but with the autumn weather
> Compelled my imagination many days,
> Many days and many hours:
> Her hair over her arms and her arms full of flowers . . .

Compare:

> . . . to them she left, her day
> Had counted as ten years.
> (To one, it is ten years of years.
> . . . Yet now, and in this place,
> Surely she leaned o'er me—her hair
> Fell all about my face . . .
> Nothing: the autumn fall of leaves . . .

In *Ash Wednesday,* however, Eliot's method seems to come strangely near to Rossetti's. The beginning of the second section of that poem appears difficult to distinguish from the Pre-Raphaelite manner:

> Lady, three white leopards sat under a juniper-tree
> In the cool of the day, having fed to satiety
> On my legs my heart my liver and that which had been contained
> In the hollow round of my skull. And God said
> Shall these bones live? shall these
> Bones live?

We seem instantly to breathe the atmosphere of the *Vita Nuova,* with its quaint allegorical devices (the famous dream in the third chapter, Love feeding the Lady with the poet's heart), and its mixture of the sensuous and the ethereal. Besides, the poem begins with that significant address, "Donna" (Lady), which had quite a special connotation in Dante's circle..It is only in the following lines that we find Eliot again the admirer of the plain philosophical statements of Dante, with their lucid polysyllables: [13]

---

[13] For other instances of this style see "Burnt Norton," in *Poems,* 1936.

And that which had been contained
In the bones (which were already dry) said chirping:
Because of the goodness of this Lady
And because of her loveliness, and because
She honours the Virgin in meditation,
We shine with brightness.

Evidently the Lady of the poet is a sister of Dante's *donne benedette*. When we read further:

The Lady is withdrawn
In a white gown, to contemplation, in a white gown—

and, in the fifth section:

Will the veiled sister pray
. . . . . . .
Will the veiled sister between the slender
Yew trees pray . . .

our recollection becomes more precise. Have we not met this Lady in those last cantos of the *Purgatorio* of which Ezra Pound exalted the magnificence? The connection of those cantos with the *Vita Nuova* is stressed by Eliot (*Dante*, p. 48): "We cannot understand fully Canto XXX of the *Purgatorio* until we know the *Vita Nuova*"; and he proceeds immediately to quote:

sovra candido vel cinta d'uliva
donna m'apparve
(*Purg., XXX, 31-2*)

All commentators explain that white is the hue of faith. Eliot continues in *Ash Wednesday*:

Let the whiteness of bones atone to forgetfulness.
There is no life in them. As I am forgotten
And would be forgotten, so I would forget
Thus devoted, concentrated in purpose.

Eliot's poem seems to be written in the same key as Canto XXX of the *Purgatorio*: "In the dialogue that follows we see the passionate conflict of the old feelings with the new; the effort and triumph of a new renunciation, greater than renunciation at the grave, because a renunciation of feelings that persist beyond the grave. In a way, these cantos are those of the greatest *personal* intensity in the whole poem

. . . it is in these last cantos of the *Purgatorio,* rather than in the *Paradiso,* that Beatrice appears most clearly." If we assume that Eliot found in those cantos the inspiration of *Ash Wednesday,* the symbolism of this poem seems to become suddenly transparent. The three white leopards belong to the same animal symbolism as the eagle, the fox, and the dragon in *Purgatorio,* XXXII, and, of course, the three beasts in *Inferno,* I. And we seem to discover an uncanny correspondence between the bones "scattered and shining" (II), and the "membra in terra sparte" (*Purg.,* XXXI, 50-1), between the fountain (IV) and the "fontana" (XXVIII, 124),[14] between the "jewelled unicorns" which "draw by the gilded hearse" and the triumphal chariot of Dante's vision (XXIX, 106 ff.), between the wings which "are no longer wings to fly" (I), and "non ti dovea gravar le penne in giuso" (XXXI, 58); and no doubt between the beginning of the fourth section of Eliot's poem and the apparition of Matelda:

> Who *walked* between *the violet and the violet*
> Who walked between
> The *various* ranks of *varied green* . . .

> una donna soletta che *si gia*
> cantando e scegliendo *fior da fiore*
> . . . . . . .
> la gran *variazion* de' freschi *mai*
> (*Purg.,* XXVIII, 40-1, 36)

The "sovegna vos" of the fourth section, from the "Ara vos prec" passage in Canto XXVI, explains the use of the word "dolour" a few lines before ("Sovegna vos a temps de ma *dolor*"), while "Our peace in His will" translates the famous line of the *Paradiso* "E 'n la sua volontade è nostra pace." Definite suggestions from the *Purgatorio* are not only the stairs in the third section, as has already been noticed (Matthiessen, p. 117), but also the landscape dimly seen at the end of the second: "in the cool of the day, with the blessing of sand . . . the quiet of the desert" (*Purg.,* I: "ora mattutina," "lito deserto").

The pattern of the images in *Ash Wednesday* seems thus suggested by Dante, but in a very peculiar way. It is as if Eliot had been reading Dante without giving much heed to the meaning, but letting himself be impressed by a few clear visual images: these he re-

---

[14] "But the fountain sprang up . . ." "L'acqua che vedi . . . esce di fontana salda e certa."

arranges in his own mind just as in a kaleidoscope the same colored glasses can give a no less harmonious (though different) design than the previous one.

Now this kind of influence fits singularly well what Eliot says of the first impression made on him by Dante (pp. 22–23) : "It is really better, at the start, not to know or care what they do mean . . . clear visual images are given much more intensity by having a meaning —we do not need to know what the meaning is, but in our awareness of the image we must be aware that the meaning is there too." Thus the influence of Dante's allegory on Eliot consists in producing what Matthiessen has called a "paradoxical precision in vagueness"; the faces and shapes the poet sees on the stairway (*Ash Wednesday*, III) have a distant resemblance to those which Dante beholds in ecstatic vision while on his way on the stairs of Purgatory (Canto XV); but Eliot's images convey a sense of foreboding which is hardly found in Dante. Indeed Eliot achieves in that section of *Ash Wednesday* an effect at which the French symbolists of the *fin de siècle* are seen striving in their too frequently disappointing poems: to conjure up a haunting presence by partly very vivid, partly elusive traits. A similar effect is attempted in the fifth section of *The Waste Land*.[15]

Apart from the allegory, *Ash Wednesday* reveals a Dantesque in-

---

15 What is the city over the mountains
   Cracks and reforms and bursts in the violet air
   . . . . . .
   A woman drew her long black hair out tight
   And fiddled whisper music on those strings
   And bats with baby faces in the violet light
   Whistled, and beat their wings
   And crawled head downward down a blackened wall
   And upside down in air were towers. . . .
This vision recalls to me the apocalyptical one of the Canzone II of the *Vita Nuova*, which Pound (p. 111) quotes in Rossetti's translation:
   Then saw I many broken hinted sights,
   In the uncertain state I stepped into
   Me seemed to be I know not in what place,
   Where ladies through the streets, like mournful lights,
   Ran with loose hair, and eyes that frighten'd you
   By their own terror, and a pale amaze
   . . . . . .
   And birds dropp'd in mid-flight out of the sky;
   And earth shook suddenly, . . .

fluence also in the labored cadences of many lines.[16] Of course repetitions and assonances like:

> I no longer strive to strive towards such things . . .
> Because I know I shall not know . . .
> Blown hair is sweet, brown hair over the mouth blown . . .
> . . . stops and steps of the mind over the third stair . . .
> Against the Word the unstilled world still whirled . . .
> . . . though I do not wish to wish these things . . .

and still more passages like:

> Both in the day time and in the night time
> The right time and the right place are not here
> No place of grace for those who avoid the face
> No time to rejoice for those who walk among noise and deny
> the voice—[17]

recall first of all the technique of G. M. Hopkins to an English reader.[18] But Hopkins' technique appears the more legitimate in a piece where the influence of Dante is so strong, in that Dante himself had delighted in the *bisticci* which Hopkins only revived, but did not invent (the vogue was mainly started by Guittone d'Arezzo). Readers of Dante are familiar with such lines as:

> ch' i' fui per ritornar più volte volto
> (*Inf.*, I, 36)

> Fuor sei dell'erte vie, fuor sei dell'arte
> (*Purg.*, XXVII, 132)

> Per grazia fa noi grazia che disvele
> (*Purg.*, XXXI, 136)

---

[16] The beginning of the poem is a literal rendering of Guido Cavalcanti's famous *ballata:* "Perch' i' non spero di tornar giammai." An echo of the words of this poem: "la Donna mia Che per sua cortesia Ti farà molto onore" may be found in the passage: "Because of the goodness of this Lady . . ."

[17] See also "Burnt Norton," III: "Distracted from distraction by distraction."

[18] Cf. Hopkins, *Poems,* 1918; p. 12: "I am soft sift In an hourglass"; p. 13: "glow, glory in thunder"; p. 29: "I caught this morning morning's minion"; p. 35: "of the best we boast"; p. 44: "deserve to and do serve God to serve to . . ."; and chiefly *The Leaden Echo and the Golden Echo.*

fur negletti
li nostri vóti, e vòti in alcun canto
(*Parad.*, III, 57)

Cred' io ch' ei credette \ch' io credesse
(*Inf.*, XIII, 25)

infiammò contra me gli animi tutti
e gl'infiammati infiammâr sì Augusto . . .
(*Inf.*, XIII, 67–8)

assai ten prego
e riprego che il prego vaglia mille
(*Inf.*, XXVI, 65–6)

come piante novelle
rinnovellate di novella fronda
(*Purg.*, XXXIII, 143–4)

ella che vedea il tacer mio
nel veder di colui che tutto vede
(*Parad.*, XXI, 49–50)

To come back to the use of images in Eliot: apropos of "Geron-tion" Matthiessen writes (p. 62):

> As he [Eliot] said once in conversation, the images here are "consciously concrete"; they correspond as closely as possible to something he has actually seen and remembered. But he also believes that if· they are clearly rendered, they will stand for something larger than themselves; they will not depend for their apprehension upon any private reference, but will become "unconsciously general."

References in that poem to Mr. Silvero, Hakagawa, Madame de Torn-quist, Fräulein von Kulp, De Bailhache, etc.; prayers "for Guiterriez, avid of speed and power, for Boudin, blown to pieces" in "Animula," and similar allusions throughout Eliot's verse to definite people, and to significant details of scenery (for instance in "The Journey of the Magi": "and three trees on the low sky,/And an old white horse galloped away in the meadow, etc."), may be said also to partake of

Dante's method, which Professor Grandgent describes thus (pp. 272–3), contrasting it with Bunyan's:

> The one starts from an abstract concept and gives it a semblance of material form; the other takes something real and makes it stand for the quality it exemplifies . . . One begets a character called Arrogancy; the other, to embody that vice, introduces an arrogant Florentine, Filippo Argenti, notorious for his unbridled temper . . . In nondramatic literature . . . the difference between the two is noteworthy, the second offering far better opportunities for vividness and illusion. Had Dante been a symbolist of the same kind as Bunyan, he would not have told his story in the first person; the hero would have been a shadowy Christian . . . he would have been obstructed, not by a leopard, a lion and a wolf, but by three monsters called, perhaps, Immoderateness, Violence, and Deceit . . .

After what Pound says (p. 161) of the *Divina Commedia*, that it is "in fact, a great Mystery Play, or better, a cycle of mystery plays," one turns to Eliot's mystery plays, *The Rock* and *Murder in the Cathedral*, expecting to find in them a Dantesque influence. This, however, if it can be said to exist at all, is put into the shade by the strong and evident Greek influence. The Greek chorus and the Bible are the models of Eliot in his dramas, as they were for authors with whom he does not claim kinship: Milton and Swinburne. No wonder then if some passages of those dramas have an odd Swinburnian ring. Is it again the case of an unsought-for return to an early favorite (we know that Swinburne, no less than Rossetti, influenced the formative years of Eliot's adolescence—see Matthiessen, p. 21) through a devious path?

# CLEANTH BROOKS *

THOUGH much has been written on *The Waste Land*, it will not be difficult to show that most of its critics misconceive entirely the theme and the structure of the poem. There has been little or no attempt to deal with it as a unified whole. F. R. Leavis and F. O. Matthiessen have treated large sections of the poem in detail, and I am obviously indebted to both of them. I believe, however, that Leavis makes some positive errors of interpretation. I find myself in almost complete agreement with Matthiessen in his commentary on the sections which he deals with in his *Achievement of T. S. Eliot,* but the plan of his book does not allow for a complete consecutive examination of the poem.

In view of the state of criticism with regard to the poem, it is best for us to approach it frankly on the basis of its theme. I prefer, however, not to raise just here the question of how important it is for the reader to have an explicit intellectual account of the various symbols and a logical account of their relationships. It may well be that such rationalization is no more than a scaffolding to be got out of the way before we contemplate the poem itself as poem. But many readers (including myself) find the erection of such a scaffolding valuable—if not absolutely necessary—and if some readers will be tempted to lay more stress upon the scaffolding than they should, there are perhaps still more readers who, without the help of such a scaffolding, will be prevented from getting at the poem at all.

The basic symbol used, that of the waste land, is taken of course, from Miss Jessie Weston's *From Ritual to Romance.* In the legends which she treats there, the land has been blighted by a curse. The crops do not grow and the animals cannot reproduce. The plight of the land is summed up by, and connected with, the plight of the lord of the land, the Fisher King, who has been rendered impotent by maiming or sickness. The curse can be removed only by the appear-

---

* *The Waste Land: Critique of the Myth,* from MODERN POETRY AND THE TRADITION, pp. 136–172, Copyright, 1939, by the University of North Carolina Press, Chapel Hill, North Carolina.

ance of a knight who will ask the meanings of the various symbols which are displayed to him in the castle. The shift in meaning from physical to spiritual sterility is easily made, and was, as a matter of fact, made in certain of the legends. As Eliot has pointed out, a knowledge of this symbolism is essential for an understanding of the poem.

Of hardly less importance to the reader, however, is a knowledge of Eliot's basic method. *The Waste Land* is built on a major contrast —a device which is a favorite of Eliot's and is to be found in many of his poems, particularly his later poems. The contrast is between two kinds of life and two kinds of death. Life devoid of meaning is death; sacrifice, even the sacrificial death, may be life-giving, an awakening to life. The poem occupies itself to a great extent with this paradox, and with a number of variations upon it.

Eliot has stated the matter quite explicitly himself in one of his essays. In his "Baudelaire" he says: "One aphorism which has been especially noticed is the following: *la volupté unique et suprême de l'amour gît dans la certitude de faire le mal.* This means, I think, that Baudelaire has perceived that what distinguishes the relations of man and woman from the copulation of beasts is the knowledge of Good and Evil (of *moral* Good and Evil which are not natural Good and Bad or puritan Right and Wrong). Having an imperfect, vague romantic conception of Good, he was at least able to understand that the sexual act as evil is more dignified, less boring, than as the natural, 'life-giving,' cheery automatism of the modern world. . . . So far as we are human, what we do must be either evil or good; so far as we do evil or good, we are human; and it is better, in a paradoxical way, to do evil than to do nothing: at least, *we exist* [italics mine]." The last statement is highly important for an understanding of *The Waste Land.* The fact that men have lost the knowledge of good and evil, keeps them from being alive, and is the justification for viewing the modern waste land as a realm in which the inhabitants do not even exist.

This theme is stated in the quotation which prefaces the poem. The Sybil says: "I wish to die." Her statement has several possible interpretations. For one thing, she is saying what the people who inhabit the waste land are saying. But she may also be saying what the speaker of "The Journey of the Magi" says: ". . . this Birth was/ Hard and bitter agony for us, like Death, our death/. . . I should be glad of another death."

I

The first section of "The Burial of the Dead" develops the theme of the attractiveness of death, or of the difficulty in rousing oneself from the death in life in which the people of the waste land live. Men are afraid to live in reality. April, the month of rebirth, is not the most joyful season but the cruelest. Winter at least kept us warm in forgetful snow. The idea is one which Eliot has stressed elsewhere. Earlier in "Gerontion" he had written

> In the juvescence of the year
> Came Christ the tiger
> . . . . . . . . . . . . . . . . . . . . . . . .
> The tiger springs in the new year. Us he devours.

More lately, in *Murder in the Cathedral,* he has the chorus say

> We do not wish anything to happen.
> Seven years we have lived quietly,
> Succeeded in avoiding notice,
> Living and partly living.

And in another passage: "Now I fear disturbance of the quiet seasons." Men dislike to be roused from their death-in-life.

The first part of "The Burial of the Dead" introduces this theme through a sort of reverie on the part of the protagonist—a reverie in which speculation on life glides off into memory of an actual conversation in the Hofgarten and back into speculation again. The function of the conversation is to establish the class and character of the protagonist. The reverie is resumed with line 19.

> What are the roots that clutch, what branches grow
> Out of this stony rubbish?

The protagonist answers for himself:

> Son of man,
> You cannot say, or guess, for you know only
> A heap of broken images, where the sun beats,
> And the dead tree gives no shelter, the cricket no relief,
> And the dry stone no sound of water.

In this passage there are references to Ezekiel and to Ecclesiastes, and these references indicate what it is that men no longer know: The

passage referred to in Ezekiel 2, pictures a world thoroughly secularized:

> 1. And he said unto me, Son of man, stand upon thy feet,
> and I will speak unto thee.
> 2. And the spirit entered into me when he spake unto me,
> and set me upon my feet, that I heard him that spake unto me.
> 3. And he said unto me, Son of man, I send thee to the
> children of Israel, to a rebellious nation that hath rebelled
> against me: they and their fathers have transgressed against me,
> even unto this very day.

Other passages from Ezekiel are relevant to the poem, Chapter
37 in particular, which describes Ezekiel's waste land, where the
prophet, in his vision of the valley of dry bones, contemplates the
"burial of the dead" and is asked: "Son of man, can these bones live?
And I answered, O Lord God, thou knowest. 4. Again he said unto
me, Prophesy over these bones, and say unto them, O ye dry bones,
hear the word of the Lord."

One of Ezekiel's prophecies was that Jerusalem would be conquered and the people led away into the Babylonian captivity. That
captivity is alluded to in Section III of *The Waste Land,* line 182,
where the Thames becomes the "waters of Leman."

The passage from Ecclesiastes 12, alluded to in Eliot's notes, describes the same sort of waste land:

> 1. Remember now thy Creator in the days of thy youth,
> while the evil days come not, nor the years draw nigh, when
> thou shalt say, I have no pleasure in them;
> 2. While the sun, or the light, or the moon, or the stars, be
> not darkened, nor the clouds return after the rain;
> 3. In the day when the keepers of the house shall tremble,
> and the strong men shall bow themselves, and the grinders cease
> because they are few, and those that look out of the windows
> be darkened,
> 4. And the doors shall be shut in the streets, when the
> sound of the grinding is low, and he shall rise up at the voice
> of the bird, and all the daughters of musick shall be brought low;
> 5. Also when they shall be afraid of that which is high, and
> fears shall be in the way, and the almond tree shall flourish, and
> the grasshopper shall be a burden, *and desire shall fail* [italics
> mine]: because man goeth to his long home, and the mourners
> go about the streets;

6. Or ever the silver cord be loosed, or the golden bowl be broken, or the pitcher be broken at the fountain, or the wheel broken at the cistern.

7. Then shall the dust return to the earth as it was: and the spirit shall return unto God who gave it.

8. Vanity of vanities, saith the preacher; all is vanity.

A reference to this passage is also evidently made in the nightmare vision of Section V of the poem.

The next section of "The Burial of the Dead" which begins with the scrap of song quoted from Wagner (perhaps another item in the reverie of the protagonist), states the opposite half of the paradox which underlies the poem: namely, that life at its highest moments of meaning and intensity resembles death. The song from Act I of Wagner's *Tristan und Isolde,* "*Frisch weht der Wind,*" is sung in the opera by a young sailor aboard the ship which is bringing Isolde to Cornwall. The "*Irisch kind*" of the song does not properly apply to Isolde at all. The song is merely one of happy and naïve love. It brings to the mind of the protagonist an experience of love—the vision of the hyacinth girl as she came back from the hyacinth garden. The poet says

> . . . my eyes failed, I was neither
> Living nor dead, and I knew nothing,
> Looking into the heart of light, the silence.

The line which immediately follows this passage, "*Oed' und leer das Meer,*" seems at first to be simply an extension of the last figure: that is, "Empty and wide the sea [of silence]." But the line, as a matter of fact, makes an ironic contrast; for the line, as it occurs in Act III of the opera, is the reply of the watcher who reports to the wounded Tristan that Isolde's ship is nowhere in sight; the sea is empty. And, though the "*Irisch kind*" of the first quotation is not Isolde, the reader familiar with the opera will apply it to Isolde when he comes to the line "*Oed' und leer das Meer.*" For the question in the song is in essence Tristan's question in Act III: "My Irish child, where dwellest thou?" The two quotations from the opera which frame the ecstasy-of-love passage thus take on a new meaning in the altered context. In the first, love is happy; the boat rushes on with a fair wind behind it. In the second, love is absent; the sea is wide and empty. And the last quotation reminds us that even love cannot exist in the waste land.

The next passage, that in which Madame Sosostris figures, calls for further reference to Miss Weston's book. As Miss Weston has shown, the Tarot cards were originally used to determine the event of highest importance to the people, the rising of the waters. Madame Sosostris has fallen a long way from the high function of her predecessors. She is engaged merely in vulgar fortune-telling—is merely one item in a generally vulgar civilization. But the symbols of the Tarot pack are still unchanged. The various characters are still inscribed on the cards, and she is reading in reality (though she does not know it) the fortune of the protagonist. She finds that his card is that of the drowned Phoenician Sailor, and so she warns him against death by water, not realizing any more than do the other inhabitants of the modern waste land that the way into life may be by death itself. The drowned Phoenician Sailor is a type of the fertility god whose image was thrown into the sea annually as a symbol of the death of summer. As for the other figures in the pack: Belladonna, the Lady of the Rocks, is woman in the waste land. The man with three staves, Eliot says he associates rather arbitrarily with the Fisher King. The term "arbitrarily" indicates that we are not to attempt to find a logical connection here. (It may be interesting to point out, however, that Eliot seems to have given, in a later poem, his reason for making the association. In "The Hollow Men" he writes, speaking as one of the Hollow Men:

> Let me also wear
> Such deliberate disguises
> Rat's coat, crowskin, crossed staves
> In a field
> Behaving as the wind behaves.

The figure is that of a scarecrow, fit symbol of the man who possesses no reality, and fit type of the Fisher King, the maimed, impotent king who ruled over the waste land of the legend. The man with three staves in the deck of cards may thus have appealed to the poet as an appropriate figure to which to assign the function of the Fisher King, although the process of identification was too difficult to expect the reader to follow and although knowledge of the process was not necessary to an understanding of the poem.)

The Hanged Man, who represents the hanged god of Frazer (including the Christ), Eliot states in a note, is associated with the hooded figure who appears in "What the Thunder Said." That he is hooded accounts for Madame Sosostris' inability to see him; or rather, here again the palaver of the modern fortune-teller is turned to new and important account by the poet's shifting the reference into a new and serious context. The Wheel and the one-eyed merchant will be discussed later.

After the Madame Sosostris passage, Eliot proceeds to complicate his symbols for the sterility and unreality of the modern waste land by associating it with Baudelaire's *"fourmillante cité"* and with Dante's Limbo. The passages already quoted from Eliot's essay on Baudelaire will indicate one of the reasons why Baudelaire's lines are evoked here. In Baudelaire's city, dream and reality seem to mix, and it is interesting that Eliot in "The Hollow Men" refers to this same realm of death-in-life as "death's dream kingdom" in contradistinction to "death's other kingdom."

The references to Dante are most important. The line, "I had not thought death had undone so many," is taken from the Third Canto of the *Inferno;* the line, "Sighs, short and infrequent, were exhaled," from the Fourth Canto. Mr. Matthiessen has already pointed out that the Third Canto deals with Dante's Limbo which is occupied by those who on earth had "lived without praise or blame." They share this abode with the angels "who were not rebels, nor were faithful to God, but were for themselves." They exemplify almost perfectly the secular attitude which dominates the modern world. Their grief, according to Dante, arises from the fact that they "have no hope of death; and their blind life is so debased, that they are envious of every other lot." But though they may not hope for death, Dante calls them "these wretches who never were alive." The people described in the Fourth Canto are those who lived virtuously but who died before the proclamation of the Gospel—they are the unbaptized. They form the second of the two classes of people who inhabit the modern waste land: those who are secularized and those who have no knowledge of the faith. Without a faith their life is in reality a death. To repeat the sentence from Eliot previously quoted: "So far as we do evil or good, we are human; and it is better, in a paradoxical way, to do evil than to do nothing: at least, we exist."

The Dante and Baudelaire references, then, come to the same thing as the allusion to the waste land of the medieval legends; and these various allusions, drawn from widely differing sources, enrich the comment on the modern city so that it becomes "unreal" on a number of levels: as seen through "the brown fog of a winter dawn"; as the medieval waste land and Dante's Limbo and Baudelaire's Paris are unreal.

The reference to Stetson stresses again the connection between the modern London of the poem and Dante's hell. After the statement, "I could never have believed death had undone so many," follow the words, "After I had distinguished some among them, I saw and knew the shade of him who made, through cowardice, the great refusal." The protagonist, like Dante, sees among the inhabitants of the contemporary waste land one whom he recognizes. (The name "Stetson" I take to have no ulterior significance. It is merely an ordinary name such as might be borne by the friend one might see in a crowd in a great city.) Mylae, as Mr. Matthiessen has pointed out, is the name of a battle between the Romans and the Carthaginians in the Punic War. The Punic War was a trade war—might be considered a rather close parallel to our late war. At any rate, it is plain that Eliot in having the protagonist address the friend in a London street as one who was with him in the Punic War rather than as one who was with him in the World War is making the point that all the wars are one war; all experience, one experience. As Eliot put the idea in *Murder in the Cathedral*:

> We do not know very much of the future
> Except that from generation to generation
> The same things happen again and again

I am not sure that Leavis and Matthiessen are correct in inferring that the line, "That corpse you planted last year in your garden," refers to the attempt to bury a memory. But whether or not this is true, the line certainly refers also to the buried god of the old fertility rites. It also is to be linked with the earlier passage—"What are the roots that clutch, what branches grow," etc. This allusion to the buried god will account for the ironical, almost taunting tone of the passage. The burial of the dead is now a sterile planting—without hope. But the advice to "keep the Dog far hence," in spite of the tone, is, I believe, well taken and serious. The passage in Webster goes as follows

> But keep the wolf far thence, that's foe to men,
> For with his nails he'll dig them up again.

Why does Eliot turn the wolf into a dog? And why does he reverse the point of importance from the animal's normal hostility to men to its friendliness? If, as some critics have suggested, he is merely interested in making a reference to Webster's darkest play, why alter the line? I am inclined to take the Dog (the capital letter is Eliot's) as Humanitarianism [1] and the related philosophies which, in their concern for man, extirpate the supernatural—dig up the corpse of the buried god and thus prevent the rebirth of life. For the general idea, see Eliot's essay, "The Humanism of Irving Babbitt."

The last line of "The Burial of the Dead"—"You! hypocrite lecteur!—mon semblable,—mon frère!" the quotation from Baudelaire, completes the universalization of Stetson begun by the reference to Mylae. Stetson is every man including the reader and Mr. Eliot himself.

II

If "The Burial of the Dead" gives the general abstract statement of the situation, the second part of *The Waste Land,* "A Game of Chess," gives a more concrete illustration. The easiest contrast in this section—and one which may easily blind the casual reader to a continued emphasis on the contrast between the two kinds of life, or the two kinds of death, already commented on—is the contrast between life in a rich and magnificent setting, and life in the low and vulgar setting of a London pub. But both scenes, however antithetical they may appear superficially, are scenes taken from the contemporary waste land. In both of them life has lost its meaning.

I am particularly indebted to Mr. Allen Tate's comment on the first part of this section. To quote from him, "The woman . . . is, I believe, the symbol of man at the present time. He is surrounded by the grandeurs of the past, but he does not participate in them; they don't sustain him." And to quote from another section of his commentary: "The rich experience of the great tradition depicted in the room receives a violent shock in contrast with a game that symbolizes the inhuman abstraction of the modern mind." Life has no meaning; history has no meaning; there is no answer to the question: "What shall we ever do?" The only thing that has meaning is the abstract

---

[1] The reference is perhaps more general still: it may include Naturalism, and Science in the popular conception as the new magic which will enable man to conquer his environment completely.

game which they are to play, a game in which the meaning is assigned and arbitrary, meaning by convention only—in short, a game of chess.

This interpretation will account in part for the pointed reference to Cleopatra in the first lines of the section. But there is, I believe, a further reason for the poet's having compared the lady to Cleopatra. The queen in Shakespeare's drama—"Age cannot wither her, nor custom stale/Her infinite variety"—is perhaps the extreme exponent of love for love's sake, the feminine member of the pair of lovers who threw away an empire for love. But the infinite variety of the life of the woman in "A Game of Chess" *has* been staled. There is indeed no variety at all, and love simply does not exist. The function of the sudden change in the description of the carvings and paintings in the room from the heroic and magnificent to "and other withered stumps of time" is obvious. But the reference to Philomela is particularly important, for Philomela, it seems to me, is one of the major symbols of the poem.

Miss Weston points out (in *The Quest of the Holy Grail*) that a section of one of the Grail manuscripts, which is apparently intended to be a gloss on the Grail story, tells how the court of the rich Fisher King was withdrawn from the knowledge of men when certain of the maidens who frequented the shrine were raped and had their golden cups taken from them. The curse on the land follows from this act. Miss Weston conjectures that this may be a statement, in the form of a parable, of the violation of the older mysteries which were probably once celebrated openly, but were later forced underground. Whether or not Mr. Eliot noticed this passage or intends a reference, the violation of a woman makes a very good symbol of the process of secularization. John Crowe Ransom makes the point very neatly for us in *God Without Thunder*. Love is the aesthetic of sex; lust is the science. Love implies a deferring of the satisfaction of the desire; it implies a certain asceticism and a ritual. Lust drives forward urgently and scientifically to the immediate extirpation of the desire. Our contemporary waste land is in large part the result of our scientific attitude—of our complete secularization. Needless to say, lust defeats its own ends. The portrayal of "the change of Philomel, by the barbarous king" is a fitting commentary on the scene which it ornaments. The waste land of the legend came in this way; the modern waste land has come in this way.

This view is corroborated by the change of tense to which Edmund Wilson has called attention: "And still she *cried*, and still the world *pursues* [italics mine]." Apparently the "world" partakes in the barbarous king's action, and still partakes in that action.

To "dirty ears" the nightingale's song is not that which filled all the desert with inviolable voice—it is "jug, jug." Edmund Wilson has pointed out that the rendition of the bird's song here represents not merely the Elizabethans' neutral notation of the bird's song, but carries associations of the ugly and coarse. The passage is one, therefore, of many instances of Eliot's device of using something which in one context is innocent but in another context becomes loaded with a special meaning.

The Philomela passage has another importance, however. If it is a commentary on how the waste land became waste, it also repeats the theme of the death which is the door to life, the theme of the dying god. The raped woman becomes transformed through suffering into the nightingale; through the violation comes the "inviolable voice." The thesis that suffering is action, and that out of suffering comes poetry is a favorite one of Eliot's. For example, "Shakespeare, too, was occupied with the struggle—which alone constitutes life for a poet—to transmute his personal and private agonies into something rich and strange, something universal and impersonal." Consider also his statement with reference to Baudelaire: "Indeed, in his way of suffering is already a kind of presence of the supernatural and of the superhuman. He rejects always the purely natural and the purely human; in other words, he is neither 'naturalist' nor 'humanist.'" The theme of the life which is death is stated specifically in the conversation between the man and the woman. She asks the question, "Are you alive, or not?" Compare the Dante references in "The Burial of the Dead." (She also asks, "Is there nothing in your head?" He is one of the Hollow Men—"Headpiece filled with straw.") These people, as people living in the waste land, know nothing, see nothing, do not even live.

But the protagonist, after this reflection that in the waste land of modern life even death is sterile—"I think we are in rats' alley/Where the dead men lost their bones"—remembers a death that was transformed into something rich and strange, the death described in the song from *The Tempest*—"Those are pearls that were his eyes."

The reference to this section of *The Tempest* is, like the Philomela reference, one of Eliot's major symbols. A general comment
on it is therefore appropriate here, for we are to meet with it twice
more in later sections of the poem. The song, one remembers, was
sung by Ariel in luring Ferdinand, Prince of Naples, on to meet
Miranda, and thus to find love, and through this love, to effect the re-
generation and deliverance of all the people on the island. Ferdinand,
hearing the song, says:

> The ditty does remember my drowned father.
> This is no mortal business, nor no sound
> That the earth owes . . .

The allusion is an extremely interesting example of the device of
Eliot's already commented upon, that of taking an item from one
context and shifting it into another in which it assumes a new and
powerful meaning. The description of a death which is a portal into
a realm of the rich and strange—a death which becomes a sort of
birth—assumes in the mind of the protagonist an association with
that of the drowned god whose effigy was thrown into the water as
a symbol of the death of the fruitful powers of nature but which was
taken out of the water as a symbol of the revivified god. (See *From
Ritual to Romance*.) The passage therefore represents the perfect
antithesis to the passage in "The Burial of the Dead": "That corpse
you planted last year in your garden," etc. It also, as we have already
pointed out, finds its antithesis in the sterile and unfruitful death "in
rats alley" just commented upon. (We shall find that this contrast
between the death in rats' alley and the death in *The Tempest* is made
again in "The Fire Sermon.")

We have yet to treat the relation of the title of the second section,
"A Game of Chess," to Middleton's play, *Women Beware Women,*
from which the game of chess is taken. In the play, the game is used
as a device to keep the widow occupied while her daughter-in-law
is being seduced. The seduction amounts almost to a rape, and in a
*double entendre,* the rape is actually described in terms of the game.
We have one more connection with the Philomela symbol, therefore.
The abstract game is being used in the contemporary waste land,
as in the play, to cover up a rape and is a description of the rape itself.

In the latter part of "A Game of Chess" we are given a picture of
spiritual emptiness, but this time, at the other end of the social scale,

as reflected in the talk between two cockney women in a London pub. (It is perhaps unnecessary to comment on the relation of their talk about abortion to the theme of sterility and the waste land.)

The account here is straightforward enough, and the only matter which calls for comment is the line spoken by Ophelia in *Hamlet,* which ends the passage. Ophelia, too, was very much concerned about love, the theme of conversation between the women in the pub. As a matter of fact, she was in very much the same position as that of the woman who has been the topic of conversation between the two ladies whom we have just heard. And her poetry, like Philomela's, had come out of suffering. We are probably to look for the relevance of the allusion to her here rather than in an easy satiric contrast between Elizabethan glories and modern sordidness. After all, Eliot's criticism of the present world is not merely the sentimental one that this happens to be the twentieth century after Christ and not the seventeenth.

III

"The Fire Sermon" makes much use of several of the symbols already developed. The fire is the sterile burning of lust, and the section is a sermon, although a sermon by example only. This section of the poem also contains some of the most easily apprehended uses of literary allusion. The poem opens on a vision of the modern river. In Spenser's "Prothalamion" the scene described is also a river scene at London, and it is dominated by nymphs and their paramours, and the nymphs are preparing for a wedding. The contrast between Spenser's scene and its twentieth century equivalent is jarring. The paramours are now "the loitering heirs of city directors," and, as for the nuptials of Spenser's Elizabethan maidens, in the stanzas which follow we learn a great deal about those. At the end of the section the speech of the third of the Thames-nymphs summarizes the whole matter for us.

The waters of the Thames are also associated with those of Leman—the poet in the contemporary waste land is in a sort of Babylonian Captivity.

The castle of the Fisher King was always located on the banks of a river or on the sea shore. The title "Fisher King," Miss Weston shows, originates from the use of the fish as a fertility or life symbol.

This meaning, however, was often forgotten, and so his title in many of the later Grail romances is accounted for by describing the king as fishing. Eliot uses the reference to fishing for reverse effect. The reference to fishing is part of the realistic detail of the scene—"While I was fishing in the dull canal." But to the reader who knows the Weston references, the reference is to that of the Fisher King of the Grail legends. The protagonist is the maimed and impotent king of the legends.

Eliot proceeds now to tie the waste-land symbol to that of *The Tempest,* by quoting one of the lines spoken by Ferdinand, Prince of Naples, which occurs just before Ariel's song, "Full Fathom Five," is heard. But he alters *The Tempest* passage somewhat, writing not, "Weeping again the king my father's wreck," but

> Musing upon the king my brother's wreck
> And on the king my father's death before him.

It is possible that the alteration has been made to bring the account taken from *The Tempest* into accord with the situation in the Percival stories. In Wolfram von Eschenbach's *Parzival,* for instance, Trevrezent, the hermit, is the brother of the Fisher King, Anfortas. He tells Parzival, "His name all men know as Anfortas, and I weep for him evermore." Their father, Frimutel, is dead.

The protagonist in the poem, then, imagines himself not only in the situation of Ferdinand in *The Tempest* but also in that of one of the characters in the Grail legend; and the wreck, to be applied literally in the first instance, applies metaphorically in the second.

After the lines from *The Tempest,* appears again the image of a sterile death from which no life comes, the bones, "rattled by the rat's foot only, year to year." (The collocation of this figure with the vision of the death by water in Ariel's song has already been commented on. The lines quoted from *The Tempest* come just before the song.)

The allusion to Marvell's "To His Coy Mistress" is of course one of the easiest allusions in the poem. Instead of "Time's winged chariot" the poet hears "the sound of horns and motors" of contemporary London. But the passage has been further complicated. The reference has been combined with an allusion to Day's "Parliament of Bees." "Time's winged chariot" of Marvell has not only been changed to the modern automobile; Day's "sound of horns and hunting" has changed to the horns of the motors. And Actaeon will not be brought face to face with Diana, goddess of chastity; Sweeney, type of the vulgar bourgeois, is to be brought to Mrs. Porter, hardly a type of chastity. The reference in the ballad to the feet "washed in soda water" reminds the poet ironically of another sort of foot-washing, the sound of the children singing in the dome heard at the ceremony of the foot-washing which precedes the restoration of the wounded Anfortas (the Fisher King) by Parzival and the taking away of the curse from the waste land. The quotation thus completes the allusion to the Fisher King commenced in line 189—"While I was fishing in the dull canal."

The pure song of the children also reminds the poet of the song of the nightingale which we have heard in "The Game of Chess." The recapitulation of symbols is continued with a repetition of "Unreal city" and with the reference to the one-eyed merchant.

Mr. Eugenides, the Smyrna merchant, is the one-eyed merchant mentioned by Madame Sosostris. The fact that the merchant is one-eyed apparently means, in Madame Sosostris' speech, no more than that the merchant's face on the card is shown in profile. But Eliot applies the term to Mr. Eugenides for a totally different effect. The defect corresponds somewhat to Madame Sosostris' bad cold. He is a rather battered representative of the fertility cults: the prophet, the *seer*, with only one eye.

The Syrian merchants, we learn from Miss Weston's book, were, along with slaves and soldiers, the principal carriers of the mysteries which lie at the core of the Grail legends. But in the modern world we find both the representatives of the Tarot divining and the mystery cults in decay. What he carries on his back and what the fortune-teller is forbidden to see is evidently the knowledge of the mysteries (although Mr. Eugenides himself is hardly likely to be more aware of it than Madame Sosostris is aware of the importance of her function). Mr. Eugenides, in terms of his former function, ought to be inviting the protagonist into the esoteric cult which holds the secret of life, but on the realistic surface of the poem, in his invitation to "a weekend at the Metropole" he is really inviting him to a homosexual debauch. The homosexuality is "secret" and now a "cult" but a very different cult from that which Mr. Eugenides ought to represent. The end of the new cult is not life but, ironically, sterility.

In the modern waste land, however, even the relation between

man and woman is also sterile. The incident between the typist and
the carbuncular young man is a picture of "love" so exclusively and
practically pursued that it is not love at all. The tragic chorus to the
scene is Tiresias, into whom perhaps Mr. Eugenides may be said to
modulate, Tiresias, the historical "expert" on the relation between
the sexes.

The fact that Tiresias is made the commentator serves a further
irony. In *Oedipus Rex*, it is Tiresias who recognizes that the curse
which has come upon the Theban land has been caused by the sinful
sexual relationship of Oedipus and Jocasta. But Oedipus' sin has
been committed in ignorance, and knowledge of it brings horror and
remorse. The essential horror of the act which Tiresias witnesses in
the poem is that it is not regarded as a sin at all—is perfectly casual,
is merely the copulation of beasts.

The reminiscence of the lines from Goldsmith's song in the
description of the young woman's actions after the departure of her
lover, gives concretely and ironically the utter break-down of traditional standards.

It is the music of her gramophone which the protagonist hears
"creep by" him "on the waters." Far from the music which Ferdinand
heard bringing him to Miranda and love, it is, one is tempted to
think, the music of "O O O O that Shakespeherian Rag."

But the protagonist says that he can *sometimes* hear "the pleasant
whining of a mandoline." Significantly enough, it is the music of the
fishmen (the fish again as a life symbol) and it comes from beside
a church (though—if this is not to rely too much on Eliot's note—
the church has been marked for destruction). Life on Lower Thames
Street, if not on the Strand, still has meaning as it cannot have meaning for either the typist or the rich woman of "A Game of Chess."

The song of the Thames-daughters brings us back to the opening
section of "The Fire Sermon" again, and once more we have to do
with the river and the river-nymphs. Indeed, the typist incident is
framed by the two river-nymph scenes.

The connection of the river-nymphs with the Rhine-daughters of
Wagner's *Götterdämerung* is easily made. In the passage in Wagner's
opera (to which Eliot refers in his note), the opening of Act III, the
Rhine-daughters bewail the loss of the beauty of the Rhine occasioned by the theft of the gold, and then beg Siegfried to give them
back the Ring made from this gold, finally threatening him with

death if he does not give it up. Like the Thames-daughters they too have been violated; and like the maidens mentioned in the Grail legend, the violation has brought a curse on gods and men. The first of the songs depicts the modern river, soiled with oil and tar. (Compare also with the description of the river in the first part of "The Fire Sermon.") The second song depicts the Elizabethan river, also evoked in the first part of "The Fire Sermon.' (Leicester and Elizabeth ride upon it in a barge of state. Incidentally, Spenser's "Prothalamion" from which quotation is made in the first part of "The Fire Sermon" mentions Leicester as having formerly lived in the house which forms the setting of the poem.)

In this second song there is also a definite allusion to the passage in *Antony and Cleopatra* already referred to in the opening line of "A Game of Chess."

> Beating oars
> The stern was formed
> A gilded shell

And if we still have any doubt of the allusion, Eliot's note on the passage with its reference to the "barge" and "poop" should settle the matter. We have already commented on the earlier allusion to Cleopatra as the prime example of love for love's sake. The symbol bears something of the same meaning here, and the note which Eliot supplies does something to reinforce the "Cleopatra" aspect of Elizabeth. Elizabeth in the presence of the Spaniard De Quadra, though negotiations were going on for a Spanish marriage, "went so far that Lord Robert at last said, as I [De Quadra was a bishop] was on the spot there was no reason why they should not be married if the queen pleased." The passage has a sort of double function. It reinforces the general contrast between Elizabethan magnificence and modern sordidness: in the Elizabethan age love for love's sake has some meaning and therefore some magnificence. But the passage gives something of an opposed effect too: the same sterile love, emptiness of love, obtained in this period too: Elizabeth and the typist are alike as well as different. (One of the reasons for the frequent allusion to Elizabethan poetry in this and the preceding section of the poem may be the fact that with the English Renaissance the old set of supernatural sanctions had begun to break up. See Eliot's various essays on Shakespeare and the Elizabethan dramatists.)

The third Thames-daughter's song depicts another sordid "love" affair, and unites the themes of the first two songs. It begins "Trams and *dusty* trees." With it we are definitely in the waste land again. Pia, whose words she echoes in saying "Highbury bore me. Richmond and Kew/Undid me" was in Purgatory and had hope. The woman speaking here has no hope—she too is in the Inferno: "I can connect/Nothing with nothing." She has just completed, floating down the river in the canoe, what Eliot has described in *Murder in the Cathedral* as

    . . . the effortless journey, to the empty land
    ·     ·     ·     ·     ·     ·     ·

    Where those who were men can no longer turn the mind
    To distraction, delusion, escape into dream, pretence,
    Where the soul is no longer deceived, for there are no objects, no tones,
    No colours, no forms to distract, to divert the soul
    From seeing itself, foully united forever, nothing with nothing,
    Not what we call death, but what beyond death is not death . . .

Now, "on Margate Sands," like the Hollow Men, she stands "on this beach of the tumid river."

The songs of the three Thames-daughters, as a matter of fact, epitomize this whole section of the poem. With reference to the quotations from St. Augustine and Buddha at the end of "The Fire Sermon" Eliot states that "the collocation of these two representatives of eastern and western asceticism, as the culmination of this part of the poem, is not an accident."

It is certainly not an accident. The moral of all the incidents which we have been witnessing is that there must be an asceticism—something to check the drive of desire. The wisdom of the East and the West comes to the same thing on this point. Moreover, the imagery which both St. Augustine and Buddha use for lust is fire. What we have witnessed in the various scenes of "The Fire Sermon" is the sterile burning of lust. Modern man, freed from all restraints, in his cultivation of experience for experience's sake burns, but not with a "hard and gemlike flame." One ought not to pound the point home in this fashion, but to see that the imagery of this section of the poem furnishes illustrations leading up to the Fire Sermon is the necessary requirement for feeling the force of the brief allusions here at the end to Buddha and St. Augustine.

IV

Whatever the specific meaning of the symbols, the general function of the section, "Death by Water," is readily apparent. The section forms a contrast with "The Fire Sermon" which precedes it—a contrast between the symbolism of fire and that of water. Also readily apparent is its force as a symbol of surrender and relief through surrender.

Some specific connections can be made, however. The drowned Phoenician Sailor recalls the drowned god of the fertility cults. Miss Weston tells that each year at Alexandria an effigy of the head of the god was thrown into the water as a symbol of the death of the powers of nature, and that this head was carried by the current to Byblos where it was taken out of the water and exhibited as a symbol of the reborn god.

Moreover, the Phoenician Sailor is a merchant—"Forgot . . . the profit and loss." The vision of the drowned sailor gives a statement of the message which the Syrian merchants originally brought to Britain and which the Smyrna merchant, unconsciously and by ironical negatives, has brought. One of Eliot's notes states that the "merchant . . . melts into the Phoenician Sailor, and the latter is not wholly distinct from Ferdinand Prince of Naples." The death by water would seem to be equated with the death described in Ariel's song in *The Tempest*. There is a definite difference in the tone of the description of this death—"A current under sea/Picked his bones in whispers," as compared with the "other" death—"bones cast in a little low dry garret,/Rattled by the rat's foot only, year to year."

Further than this it would not be safe to go, but one may point out that whirling (the whirlpool here, the Wheel of Madame Sosostris' palaver) is one of Eliot's symbols frequently used in other poems (*Ash Wednesday,* "Gerontion," *Murder in the Cathedral,* and "Burnt Norton") to denote the temporal world. And I may point out, supplying the italics myself, the following passage from *Ash Wednesday:*

Although I do not hope to *turn* again

.    .    .    .    .    .    .

Wavering between the *profit and the loss*
In this brief transit where the dreams cross
The dreamcrossed twilight *between birth and dying.*

At least, with a kind of hindsight, one may suggest that "Death by Water" gives an instance of the conquest of death and time, the "perpetual recurrence of determined seasons," the "world of spring and autumn, birth and dying" through death itself.

v

The reference to the "torchlight red on sweaty faces" and to the "frosty silence in the gardens" obviously associates Christ in Gethsemane with the other hanged gods. The god has now died, and in referring to this, the basic theme finds another strong restatement:

> He who was living is now dead
> We who were living are now dying
> With a little patience

The poet does not say "We who *are* living." It is "We who *were* living." It is the death-in-life of Dante's Limbo. Life in the full sense has been lost.

The passage on the sterility of the waste land and the lack of water provides for the introduction later of two highly important passages:

> There is not even silence in the mountains
> But dry sterile thunder without rain—

lines which look forward to the introduction later of "what the thunder said" when the thunder, no longer sterile, but bringing rain, speaks.

The second of these passages is, "There is not even solitude in the mountains," which looks forward to the reference to the Journey to Emmaus theme a few lines later: "Who is the third who walks always beside you?" The god has returned, has risen, but the travelers cannot tell whether it is really he, or mere illusion induced by their delirium.

The parallelism between the "hooded figure" who "walks always beside you," and the "hooded hordes" is another instance of the sort of parallelism that is really a contrast. In the first case, the figure is indistinct because spiritual; in the second, the hooded hordes are indistinct because completely *unspiritual*—they are the people of the waste land—

> Shape without form, shade without colour,
> Paralysed force, gesture without motion—

to take two lines from "The Hollow Men," where the people of the waste land once more appear. Or to take another line from the same poem, perhaps their hoods are the "deliberate disguises" which the Hollow Men, the people of the waste land, wear.

Eliot, as his notes tell us, has particularly connected the description here with the "decay of eastern Europe." The hordes represent, then, the general waste land of the modern world with a special application to the breakup of Eastern Europe, the region with which the fertility cults were especially connected and in which today the traditional values are thoroughly discredited. The cities, Jerusalem, Athens, Alexandria, Vienna, like the London of the first section of the poem are "unreal," and for the same reason.

The passage which immediately follows develops the unreality into nightmare, but it is a nightmare vision which is something more than an extension of the passage beginning, "What is the city over the mountains"—in it appear other figures from earlier in the poem: the lady of "A Game of Chess," who, surrounded by the glory of history and art, sees no meaning in either and threatens to rush out into the street "With my hair down, so," has here let down her hair and fiddles "whisper music on those strings." One remembers in "A Game of Chess" that it was the woman's hair that spoke:

> . . . her hair
> Spread out in fiery points
> Glowed into words, then would be savagely still.

The hair has been immemorially a symbol of fertility, and Miss Weston and Frazer mention sacrifices of hair in order to aid the fertility god.

As we have pointed out earlier, this passage is also to be connected with the twelfth chapter of Ecclesiastes. The doors "of mudcracked houses," and the cisterns in this passage are to be found in Ecclesiastes, and the woman fiddling music from her hair is one of "the daughters of musick" brought low. The towers and bells from the Elizabeth and Leicester passage of "The Fire Sermon" also appear here, but the towers are upside down, and the bells, far from pealing for an actual occasion or ringing the hours, are "reminiscent." The civilization is breaking up.

The "violet light" also deserves comment. In "The Fire Sermon" it is twice mentioned as the "violet hour," and there it has little more

than a physical meaning. It is a description of the hour of twilight.
Here it indicates the twilight of the civilization, but it is perhaps
something more. Violet is one of the liturgical colors of the Church.
It symbolizes repentance and it is the color of baptism. The visit to
the Perilous Chapel, according to Miss Weston, was an initiation—
that is, a baptism. In the nightmare vision, the bats wear baby faces.

The horror built up in this passage is a proper preparation for the
passage on the Perilous Chapel which follows it. The journey has not
been merely an agonized walk in the desert, though it is that; nor is
it merely the journey after the god has died and hope has been lost;
it is also the journey to the Perilous Chapel of the Grail story. In Miss
Weston's account, the Chapel was part of the ritual, and was filled
with horrors to test the candidate's courage. In some stories the
perilous cemetery is also mentioned. Eliot has used both: "Over the
tumbled graves, about the chapel." In many of the Grail stories the
Chapel was haunted by demons.

The cock in the folk-lore of many people is regarded as the bird
whose voice chases away the powers of evil. It is significant that it is
after his crow that the flash of lightning comes and the "damp
gust/Bringing rain." It is just possible that the cock has a connection
also with *The Tempest* symbols. The first song which Ariel sings to
Ferdinand as he sits "Weeping again the king my father's wreck"
ends

> The strain of strutting chanticleer,
> Cry, cock-a-doodle-doo.

The next stanza is the "Full Fathom Five" song which Eliot has used
as a vision of life gained through death. If this relation holds, here we
have an extreme instance of an allusion, in itself innocent, forced
into serious meaning through transference to a new context.

As Miss Westen has shown, the fertility cults go back to a very
early period and are recorded in Sanscrit legends. Eliot has been
continually, in the poem, linking up the Christian doctrine with the
beliefs of as many peoples as he can. Here he goes back to the very
beginnings of Aryan culture, and tells the rest of the story of the
rain's coming, not in terms of the setting already developed but in
its earliest form. The passage is thus a perfect parallel in method to
the passage in "The Burial of the Dead":

You who were with me in the ships *at Mylae!*
That corpse you planted *last year* in your garden . . .

The use of Sanscrit in what the thunder says is thus accounted for. In addition, there is of course a more obvious reason for casting what the thunder said into Sanscrit here: onomatopoeia.

The comments on the three statements of the thunder imply an acceptance of them. The protagonist answers the first question, "What have we given?" with the statement:

> The awful daring of a moment's surrender
> Which an age of prudence can never retract
> By this, and this only, we have existed.

Here the larger meaning is stated in terms which imply the sexual meaning. Man cannot be absolutely self-regarding. Even the propagation of the race—even mere "existence"—calls for such a surrender. Living calls for—see the passage already quoted from Eliot's essay on Baudelaire—belief in something more than "life."

The comment on *dayadhvam* (sympathize) is obviously connected with the foregoing passage. The surrender to something outside the self is an attempt (whether on the sexual level or some other) to transcend one's essential isolation. The passage gathers up the symbols previously developed in the poem just as the foregoing passage reflects, though with a different implication, the numerous references to sex made earlier in the poem. For example, the woman in the first part of "A Game of Chess" has also heard the key turn in the door, and confirms her prison by thinking of the key:

> Speak to me. Why do you never speak. Speak.
> What are you thinking of? What thinking? What?
> I never know what you are thinking. Think.

The third statement made by the thunder, *damyata* (control), follows the condition necessary for control, sympathy. The figure of the boat catches up the figure of control already given in "Death by Water"—"O you who turn the wheel and look to windward"— and from "The Burial of the Dead" the figure of happy love in which the ship rushes on with a fair wind behind it: *"Frisch weht der Wind . . ."*

I cannot accept Mr. Leavis' interpretation of the passage, "I sat upon the shore/Fishing, with the arid plain behind me," as meaning that the poem "exhibits no progression." The comment upon what the thunder says would indicate, if other passages did not, that the poem does "not end where it began." It is true that the protagonist does not witness a revival of the waste land; but there are two important relationships involved in his case: a personal one as well as a general one. If secularization has destroyed, or is likely to destroy, modern civilization, the protagonist still has a private obligation to fulfill. Even if the civilization is breaking up—"London Bridge is falling down falling down falling down"—there remains the personal obligation: "Shall I at least set my lands in order?" Consider in this connection the last sentences of Eliot's "Thoughts After Lambeth": "The World is trying the experiment of attempting to form a civilized but non-Christian mentality. The experiment will fail; but we must be very patient in awaiting its collapse; meanwhile redeeming the time: so that the Faith may be preserved alive through the dark ages before us; to renew and rebuild civilization, and save the World from suicide."

The bundle of quotations with which the poem ends has a very definite relation to the general theme of the poem and to several of the major symbols used in the poem. Before Arnaut leaps back into the refining fire of Purgatory with joy he says: "I am Arnaut who weep and go singing; contrite I see my past folly, and joyful I see before me the day I hope for. Now I pray you by that virtue which guides you to the summit of the stair, at times be mindful of my pain." This theme is carried forward by the quotation from *Pervigilium Veneris:* "When shall I be like the swallow." The allusion is also connected with the Philomela symbol. (Eliot's note on the passage indicates this clearly.) The sister of Philomela was changed into a swallow as Philomela was changed into a nightingale. The protagonist is asking therefore when shall the spring, the time of love, return, but also when will he be reborn out of his sufferings, and—with the special meaning which the symbol takes on from the preceding Dante quotation and from the earlier contexts already discussed—he is asking what is asked at the end of one of the minor poems: "When will Time flow away."

The quotation from "El Desdichado," as Edmund Wilson has pointed out, indicates that the protagonist of the poem has been disinherited, robbed of his tradition. The ruined tower is perhaps also the Perilous Chapel, "only the wind's home," and it is also the whole tradition in decay. The protagonist resolves to claim his tradition and rehabilitate it.

The quotation from *The Spanish Tragedy*—"Why then Ile fit you. Hieronymo's mad againe"—is perhaps the most puzzling of all these quotations. It means, I believe, this: The protagonist's acceptance of what is in reality the deepest truth will seem to the present world mere madness. ("And still she cried . . . 'Jug Jug' to dirty ears.") Hieronymo in the play, like Hamlet, was "mad" for a purpose. The protagonist is conscious of the interpretation which will be placed on the words which follow—words which will seem to many apparently meaningless babble, but which contain the oldest and most permanent truth of the race:

> Datta. Dayadhvam. Damyata.

Quotation of the whole context from which the line is taken confirms this interpretation. Hieronymo, asked to write a play for the court's entertainment, replies:

> Why then, I'll fit you; say no more.
> When I was young, I gave my mind
> And plied myself to fruitless poetry;
> Which though it profit the professor naught,
> Yet it is passing pleasing to the world.

He sees that the play will give him the opportunity he has been seeking to avenge his son's murder. Like Hieronymo, the protagonist in the poem has found his theme; what he is about to perform is not "fruitless."

After this repetition of what the thunder said comes the benediction:

> Shantih     Shantih     Shantih

The foregoing account of *The Waste Land* is, of course, not to be substituted for the poem itself. Moreover, it certainly is not to be considered as representing *the method by which the poem was composed*. Much which the prose expositor must represent as though it had been consciously contrived obviously was arrived at unconsciously and concretely.

The account given above is a statement merely of the "prose meaning," and bears the same relation to the poem as does the "prose meaning" of any other poem. But one need not perhaps apologize for setting forth such a statement explicitly, for *The Waste Land* has been almost consistently misinterpreted since its first publication. Even a critic so acute as Edmund Wilson has seen the poem as essentially a statement of despair and disillusionment, and his account sums up the stock interpretation of the poem. Indeed, the phrase, "the poetry of drouth," has become a cliché of left-wing criticism. It is such a misrepresentation of *The Waste Land* as this which allows Eda Lou Walton to entitle an essay on contemporary poetry, "Death in the Desert"; or which causes Waldo Frank to misconceive of Eliot's whole position and personality. But more than the meaning of one poem is at stake. If *The Waste Land* is not a world-weary cry of despair or a sighing after the vanished glories of the past, then not only the popular interpretation of the poem will have to be altered but also the general interpretations of post-War poetry which begin with such a misinterpretation as a premise.

Such misinterpretations involve also misconceptions of Eliot's technique. Eliot's basic method may be said to have passed relatively unnoticed. The popular view of the method used in *The Waste Land* may be described as follows: Eliot makes use of ironic contrasts between the glorious past and the sordid present—the crashing irony of

> But at my back from time to time I hear
> The sound of horns and motors, which shall bring
> Sweeney to Mrs. Porter in the spring.

But this is to take the irony of the poem at the most superficial level, and to neglect the other dimensions in which it operates. And it is to neglect what are essentially more important aspects of his method. Moreover, it is to overemphasize the difference between the method employed by Eliot in this poem and that employed by him in later poems.

The basic method used in *The Waste Land* may be described as the application of the principle of complexity. The poet works in terms of surface parallelisms which in reality make ironical contrasts, and in terms of surface contrasts which in reality constitute parallelisms. (The second group sets up effects which may be described as the obverse of irony.) The two aspects taken together give the effect of chaotic experience ordered into a new whole, though the realistic surface of experience is faithfully retained. The complexity of the experience is not violated by the apparent forcing upon it of a predetermined scheme.

The fortune-telling of "The Burial of the Dead" will illustrate the general method very satisfactorily. On the surface of the poem the poet reproduces the patter of the charlatan, Madame Sosostris, and there is the surface irony: the contrast between the original use of the Tarot cards and the use made by Madame Sosostris. But each of the details (justified realistically in the palaver of the fortune-teller) assumes a new meaning in the general context of the poem. There is then, in addition to the surface irony, something of a Sophoclean irony too, and the "fortune-telling," which is taken ironically by a twentieth-century audience, becomes *true* as the poem develops—true in a sense in which Madame Sosostris herself does not think it true. The surface irony is thus reversed and becomes an irony on a deeper level. The items of her speech have only one reference in terms of the context of her speech: the "man with three staves," the "one-eyed merchant," the "crowds of people, walking round in a ring," etc. But transferred to other contexts they become loaded with special meanings. To sum up, all the central symbols of the poem head up here; but here, in the only section in which they are explicitly bound together, the binding is slight and accidental. The deeper lines of association only emerge in terms of the total context as the poem develops—and this is, of course, exactly the effect which the poet intends.

This transference of items from an "innocent" context into a context in which they become charged and transformed in meaning will account for many of the literary allusions in the poem. For example, the "change of Philomel" is merely one of the items in the decorative detail in the room in the opening of "A Game of Chess." But the violent change of tense—"And still she cried, and still the world pursues"—makes it a comment upon, and a symbol of, the modern world. And further allusions to it through the course of the poem gradually equate it with the general theme of the poem. The allusions to *The Tempest* display the same method. The parallelism between Dante's Hell and the waste land of the Grail legends is fairly close; even the equation of Baudelaire's Paris to the waste land is fairly obvious. But the parallelism between the death by drowning in *The Tempest* and the death of the fertility god is, on the surface, merely accidental, and the first allusion to Ariel's song is merely an irrelevant and random association of the stream-of-consciousness:

> Is your card, the drowned Phoenician Sailor,
> (Those are pearls that were his eyes. Look!)

And on its second appearance in "A Game of Chess" it is still only an item in the protagonist's abstracted reverie. Even the association of *The Tempest* symbol with the Grail legends in the lines

> While I was fishing in the dull canal
>
> .     .     .     .     .     .     .     .
>
> Musing  upon  the  king  my  brother's  wreck

and in the passage which follows, is ironical merely. But the associations have been established, even though they may seem to be made in ironic mockery, and when we come to the passage, "Death by Water," with its change of tone, they assert themselves positively. We have a sense of revelation out of material apparently accidentally thrown together. I have called the effect the obverse of irony, for the method, like that of irony, is indirect, though the effect is positive rather than negative.

The melting of the characters into each other is, of course, an aspect of this general process. Elizabeth and the girl born at Highbury both ride on the Thames, one in the barge of state, the other supine in a narrow canoe, and they are both Thames-nymphs, who are violated and thus are like the Rhine-nymphs who have also been violated, etc. With the characters as with the other symbols, the surface relationships may be accidental and apparently trivial and they may be made either ironically or through random association or in hallucination, but in the total context of the poem the deeper relationships are revealed. The effect is a sense of the oneness of experience, and of the unity of all periods, and with this, a sense that the general theme of the poem is true. But the theme has not been imposed—it has been revealed.

This complication of parallelisms and contrasts makes, of course, for ambiguity, but the ambiguity, in part, resides in the poet's fidelity to the complexity of experience. The symbols resist complete equation with a simple meaning. To take an example, "rock" throughout the poem seems to be one of the "desert" symbols. For example, the "dry stone" gives "no sound of water'; woman in the waste land is "the

Lady of the Rocks," and most pointed of all, there is the long delirium passage in "What the Thunder Said": "Here is no water but only rock," etc. So much for its general meaning, but in "The Burial of the Dead" occur the lines

> Only
> There is shadow under this red rock,
> (Come in under the shadow of this red rock).

Rock here is a place of refuge. (Moreover, there may also be a reference to the Grail symbolism. In *Parzival,* the Grail is a stone: "And this stone all men call the grail . . . As children the Grail doth call them, 'neath its shadow they wax and grow.") The paradox, life through death, penetrates the symbol itself.

To take an even clearer case of this paradoxical use of symbols, consider the lines which occur in the hyacinth girl passage. The vision gives obviously a sense of the richness and beauty of life. It is a moment of ecstasy (the basic imagery is obviously sexual); but the moment in its intensity is like death. The protagonist looks in that moment into the "heart of light, the silence," and so looks into—not richness—but blankness: he is neither "living nor dead." The symbol of life stands also for a kind of death. This duality of function may, of course, extend to a whole passage. For example, consider:

> Where fishmen lounge at noon: where the walls
> Of Magnus Martyr hold
> Inexplicable splendour of Ionian white and gold.

The function of the passage is to indicate the poverty into which religion has fallen: the splendid church now surrounded by the poorer districts. But the passage has an opposed effect also: the fishmen in the "public bar in Lower Thames Street" next to the church have a meaningful life which has been largely lost to the secularized upper and middle classes.

The poem would undoubtedly be "clearer" if every symbol had a single, unequivocal meaning; but the poem would be thinner, and less honest. For the poet has not been content to develop a didactic allegory in which the symbols are two-dimensional items adding up directly to the sum of the general scheme. They represent dramatized instances of the theme, embodying in their own nature the fundamental paradox of the theme.

We shall better understand why the form of the poem is right and inevitable if we compare Eliot's theme to Dante's and to Spenser's. Eliot's theme is not the statement of a faith held and agreed upon (Dante's *Divine Comedy*) nor is it the projection of a "new" system of beliefs (Spencer's *Faerie Queene*). Eliot's theme is the rehabilitation of a system of beliefs, known but now discredited. Dante did not have to "prove" his statement; he could assume it and move within it about a poet's business. Eliot does not care, like Spenser, to force the didacticism. He prefers to stick to the poet's business. But, unlike Dante, he cannot assume acceptance of the statement. A direct approach is calculated to elicit powerful "stock responses" which will prevent the poem's being *read* at all. Consequently, the only method is to work by indirection. The Christian material is at the center, but the poet never deals with it directly. The theme of resurrection is made on the surface in terms of the fertility rites; the words which the thunder speaks are Sanscrit words.

We have been speaking as if the poet were a strategist trying to win acceptance from a hostile audience. But of course this is true only in a sense. The poet himself is audience as well as speaker; we state the problem more exactly if we state it in terms of the poet's integrity rather than in terms of his strategy. He is so much a man of his own age that he can indicate his attitude toward the Christian tradition without falsity only in terms of the difficulties of a rehabilitation; and he is so much a poet and so little a propagandist that he can be sincere only as he presents his theme concretely and dramatically.

To put the matter in still other terms: the Christian terminology is for the poet a mass of clichés. However "true" he may feel the terms to be, he is still sensitive to the fact that they operate superficially as clichés, and his method of necessity must be a process of bringing them to life again. The method adopted in *The Waste Land* is thus violent and radical, but thoroughly necessary. For the renewing and vitalizing of symbols which have been crusted over with a distorting familiarity demands the type of organization which we have already commented on in discussing particular passages: the statement of surface similarities which are ironically revealed to be dissimilarities, and the association of apparently obvious dissimilarities which culminates in a later realization that the dissimilarities are only superficial—that the chains of likeness are in reality fundamental. In this way the statement of beliefs emerges *through* confusion and cynicism—not in spite of them.

# LEONARD UNGER

IN his essay on Babbitt, T. S. Eliot has said, "Given the most highly organized and temporally powerful hierarchy, with all the powers of inquisition and punishment imaginable, still the idea of the religion is the *inner* control—the appeal not to a man's behaviour but to his soul." We may assume that a devotional poem written by Eliot will constitute a record of the poet's religious experience—the personal matter of *"inner* control." The continuity which has been often remarked as existing in Eliot's work becomes definitely apparent after a study of his longer poems. *The Waste Land* looks forward, we can see now, to such a poem as *Ash Wednesday;* especially indicative are these lines from the earlier poem:

> I sat upon the shore
> Fishing, with the arid plain behind me
> Shall I at least set my lands in order?
> London Bridge is falling down falling down falling down
> *Poi s'ascose nel foco che gli affina.* . . .

Setting one's lands in order amounts to approaching the practice of inner control; Cleanth Brooks, Jr., observes: "The protagonist resolves to claim his tradition and rehabilitate it." In the later poem it is evident that he has been pursuing his resolution and that *Ash Wednesday* is uttered, so to speak, from *el foco che gli affina.*

In his essay on Baudelaire Eliot has implied what he considers essential for the possession—more accurately, the pursuit—of Christianity: "the greatest, the most difficult, of the Christian virtues, the virtue of humility." Significantly enough, he uses for the title of his devotional poem the name of that day in the Catholic calendar which begins a season of humility, thus indicating the tone and theme of the poem, so that Ash Wednesday comes to stand for a state of mind, a state of the soul.

---

* From *The Southern Review,* Vol. IV, pp. 745–770, Copyright, 1939, by Leonard Unger.

The relationship which Eliot has indicated as existing between *The Waste Land* and Miss Weston's *From Ritual to Romance* is paralleled, as we shall soon observe, by that existing between *Ash Wednesday* and *The Dark Night of the Soul*, a prose work of the sixteenth-century Spanish mystic, St. John of the Cross. *The Dark Night of the Soul* is a companionpiece to *The Ascent of Mount Carmel*, both of which the saint wrote to expound his mystical *Stanzas of the Soul*. In each of these St. John gives counsel for the religious experience of purgation and explains that those who would attain union with God must enter a condition of the soul called the "dark night." This condition is of two stages: the dark night of sense and the dark night of spirit, in which sense and spirit respectively are purged. The *Ascent*, counsel for the active way of purgation, is intended for proficients; the *Dark Night*, counsel for the passive way, for beginners. "The passive way is that wherein the soul does nothing, and God works in the soul, and it remains, as it were, patient." It is in keeping with the theme of *Ash Wednesday*, humility, that its plan comes from the counsel for the passive way.

The statements of the speaker in Section I of *Ash Wednesday* impart a sense of the debility, humility, and vexation which are to be endured by St. John's beginner, who, to enter the dark night for the purgation of desire, must achieve a "spiritual detachment from all things, whether sensual or spiritual, and a leaning on pure faith alone and an ascent thereby to God."

> . . . those who at this time are going on to perfection . . . progress by means of humility and are greatly edified, not only thinking naught of their own affairs, but having very little satisfaction with themselves; they consider all others as far better, and usually have a holy envy of them, and an eagerness to serve God as these do. . . . And thus He leaves them so completely in the dark that they know not whither to go with their sensible imagination and meditation; for they cannot advance a step in meditation, as they were wont to do aforetime, their inward senses being submerged in this night and left with such dryness that not only do they experience no pleasure and consolation in the spiritual things and good exercises wherein they were wont to find their delights and pleasures, but instead, on the contrary, they find insipidity and bitterness in the said things. . . .

When the soul enters the dark night, it brings these kinds of love under control. It strengthens and purifies the one, namely that which is according to God; and the other it removes and brings to an end; and in the beginning it causes both to be lost sight of. . . .

St. John's description of genuine purgation is recognizably expressed by Eliot in *Burnt Norton:*

> Descend lower, descend only
> Into the world of perpetual solitude,
> World not world, but that which is not world,
> Internal darkness, deprivation
> And destitution of all property,
> Dessication of the world of sense,
> Evacuation of the world of fancy,
> Inoperancy of the world of spirit;
> This is the one way, and the other
> Is the same, not in movement
> But abstention from movement, while the world moves
> In appetency, on its metalled ways
> Of time past and time future.

## I

The first section of *Ash Wednesday*—indeed, the whole poem—not only reflects superficially *The Dark Night of the Soul,* but also contains allusions which, by their contextual significance, are in accord with St. John's purgational system. A structural similarity between *Ash Wednesday* and *The Waste Land* is thus suggested, for the allusions have their place in the devotional poem by sympathetic association with the idea of the *Dark Night.* A preoccupation with the purging of desire, with the condition of "Internal darkness, deprivation, etc.," would bring a sharpened sensitivity to whatever might suggest the condition, would impose something of itself upon all experience and come to include within itself what has been incidentally reminiscent of the personal problem.

The opening line is a literal translation of the first line of a *ballata* by Guido Cavalcanti: *Perch'io non spero di tornar giammai.* Rossetti's translation of it begins: "Because I think not ever to return/ Ballad, to Tuscany,—/Go therefore thou for me/ Straight to my lady's face,/ Who, of her noble grace,/ Shall show thee courtesy." The statements of waning vital powers, the torment to heart and soul,

352

T. S. ELIOT

the condition of the "body being now so nearly dead" and of the "dead mind" make evident a correspondence between the afflictions expressed by this contemporary of Dante and the condition of St. John's beginner, whose sensitivity, both physical and spiritual, has almost ceased to function, while the soul is in a state of despair:

> For indeed, when this purgative contemplation is most severe, the soul feels very keenly the shadow of death and the lamentations of death and the pains of hell, which consists in its feeling itself to be without God, and chastised and cast out, and unworthy of Him; . . . it believes that it is so with it forever.

Cavalcanti's line, as it is used in *Ash Wednesday,* performs much of its original function, for, as we shall note in dealing with later sections, the ideas of devotion to a woman and the religious experience of approaching union with God are held by Eliot in a single conceptual pattern.

In addition to the implications of devotion and distress which arise from the source of the line "Because I do not hope to turn again," there is yet another and perhaps more immediate meaning. To turn would be to depart from the state of purgation and humility and enter the state of existence of the hollow men who "go round the prickly pear." Eliot has used this turning elsewhere (at the beginning of his choruses from *The Rock* and in Section V of *Ash Wednesday*) as a symbol of sterile activity and empty existence, applying it particularly to the modern world. But turning also symbolizes something else, something opposed to the sterile secular motion. The souls in Dante's *Purgatorio* are turning as they move up the winding mount which leads to heaven, the state of blessedness and divine love. In Section III of *Ash Wednesday* the turning stair represents this conception of the motion. Eliot states the difference of these turnings in *Burnt Norton,* and also reminds us of the *Dark Night:*

> Here is a place of disaffection
> Time before and time after
> In a dim light: neither daylight
> Investing form with lucid stillness
> *Turning shadow into transient beauty*
> *With slow rotation suggesting permanence*
> Nor darkness to purify the soul
> Emptying the sensual with deprivation

Cleansing affection from the temporal.
Neither plenitude nor vacancy. Only a flicker
Over the strained time-ridden faces
Distracted from distraction by distraction
Filled with fancies and empty of meaning
Tumid apathy with no concentration
*Men and bits of paper, whirled by the cold wind*
That blows before and after time, . . . [*Italics mine*]

The dual meaning of this turning suggests the condition of the *Dark Night*, for, by having no hope to turn, the protagonist has no hope of responding either to the worldly or the spiritual; the faculties for doing so are become incapacitated. The portions of the line which are repeated state the different shades of meaning contained in the line: the lack of hope; and the condition of being devoid of two kinds of sensibility.

A striking illustration of the sympathetic association by which allusions are present is the line "Desiring this man's gift and that man's scope," quoted with the change of one word from Shakespeare's twenty-ninth sonnet:

When, in disgrace with fortune and men's eyes,
I all alone beweep my outcast state,
And trouble deaf heaven with my bootless cries,
And look upon myself and curse my fate,
Wishing me like to one more rich in hope,
Featured like him, like him with friends possess'd,
Desiring this man's art and that man's scope,
With what I most enjoy contented least;
Yet in these thoughts myself almost despising,
Haply I think on thee, and then my state,
Like to the lark at break of day arising
From sullen earth, sings hymns at heaven's gate;
    For thy sweet love remember'd such wealth brings
    That then I scorn to change my state with kings.

It may be observed that the condition expressed here is in all its details consonant with the accompaniments and signs of purgation set forth by St. John of the Cross.

Although probably not a functional allusion, the "agèd eagle" may have reference to the *Dark Night*. The term *old man* is often used for the unpurged condition of the soul:

. . . God makes it to die to all that is not naturally God, so that, once it is stripped and denuded of its former skin, He may begin to clothe it anew. And thus its youth is renewed like the eagle's and it is clothed with the new man, which, as the Apostle says, is according to God.

"Why should I mourn/ The vanished power of the usual reign?" implies the futility of attempting to do anything about the condition of despair and affliction. To return to the "vanished power of the usual reign" would be a regression, a return to the state that existed before purgation began. By this implication the question becomes a statement of definite religious experience, for to suffer these afflictions is, according to St. John, to be on the way toward union with God. There is no hope of knowing the "infirm glory of the positive hour" or the "one veritable transitory power," which are respectively the modes of worldly and spiritual relief. The place "where trees flower, and springs flow" is a symbol of dual meaning, representing the consolations of sense and of spirit which are attenuated by the dark night. The protagonist, oppressed by the mere self-identity and ephemeral actuality of time and place, further expresses his wretchedness by dwelling upon the static semblance of his condition:

> time is always time
> And place is always and only place
> And what is actual is actual only for one time
> And only for one place. . . .

The rejoicing which proceeds from this realization is a gesture of utter resignation, an acceptance of what seems to be irrevocable misery. So absolute is the hopelessness of his condition that it leads him to renounce the "blessed face" and the "voice" which symbolize hope and guidance. (The *face* and *voice* obviously refer to the "Lady" of Section II, as well as Cavalcanti's lady, who, reflected by the spiritual guide of *Ash Wednesday,* is also an object of spiritual devotion in her original context.) This renunciation has a parallel in the *Dark Night*. St. John says of the soul that "since it believes . . . that its evil will never end . . . it suffers great pain and grief, since there is added to all this (because of the solitude and abandonment caused in it by this dark night), the fact that it finds no consolation or support in any instruction nor in any spiritual master." Of itself, the situation can yield no joy. One positive gesture is, however, possible:

because there is nothing else he can do, the protagonist resigns himself to the situation and accepts it completely. In doing so by his own will, he dismisses the desire to strive and thus gains the satisfaction of consummating a volition. The passage ends with an emphatic restatement of the experience:

> Because I cannot hope to turn again
> Consequently I rejoice, having to construct something
> Upon which to rejoice. . . .

Such rejoicing is constructed upon the resignation to inescapable misery: the positive experience comes into being only by means of the negative experience. This is ironical—and therefore humiliating.

Then come prayer and repentance, and the expressed desire for the passive and unreflective condition counseled by St. John: beginners are "to devote themselves not at all to reasoning and meditation, . . . they will be doing quite sufficient if they persevere in prayer . . . troubling not themselves, in that state, about what they shall think or meditate, . . . being without anxiety, . . ." This aspect of the religious experience appears with more complexity in the paradoxical words

> Teach us to care and not to care
> Teach us to sit still.

Considering the precepts of St. John, it is natural that the protagonist wishes "not to care," to be "without anxiety." On the other hand, the ultimate motive of the desire rests in an actual concern with progressing in the religious experience, for one would want to follow the precept because one really did care. The paradoxical and earnest plea comes as an achievement; it is attained by the resignation contained in the earlier passage. The protagonist would not have it to do over again and hopes that "these words answer/ For what is done, not to be done again." He would now be taught "to care and not to care" because he has made some progress along the way of purgation,

> Because these wings are no longer wings to fly
> But merely vans to beat the air
> The air which is now thoroughly small and dry
> Smaller and dryer than the will. . . .

"Smaller and dryer than the will" is another echo from St. John's *Dark Night:* "To this end God is pleased to strip them of this old man . . . leaving the understanding dark, the will dry, the memory empty. . . ." The prayer and the section end with a quotation from the *Ave Maria* of Catholic ritual, words which are for the penitent who has faith.

II

The purgation continues in Section II, and a state (or station) of the purifying function is expressed by symbolic images, a device which Eliot commends and admires in Dante. In his essay on that poet he says ". . . Hell is not a place but a *state; . . .* Hell, though a state, is a state than can only be thought of, and perhaps only experienced, by the projection of sensory images." He also says:

> What we should consider is not so much the meaning of the images, but the reverse process, that which led a man having an idea to express it in images. We have to consider the type of mind which by nature and *practice* tended to express itself in allegory: and for a competent poet, allegory means *clear visual images*. And clear visual images are given much more intensity by having a meaning—we do not need to know what that meaning is, but in our awareness of the image we must be aware that the meaning is there too.

We may profitably follow Eliot's counsel to consider "not so much the meaning of the images, but the reverse process, that which led a man having an idea to express it in images." The idea is known to be that of purgation. We may know that the images are associated with each other and we may know that they are associated with a particular idea, but we do not know enough until we have learned upon what ground all the associations occur. When this has been learned the images will become meaningful.

We have already noted the connection between the "Lady" of Section II and the lady of Cavalcanti's poem. Mario Praz remarks that the term Lady—"Donna"—"had quite a special connotation in Dante's circle." The *ballata* gives us an instance of the lady's function in the poetry of that circle. Worshipped with religious adoration, she is a type of the Virgin Mary, one who may bring the grace of salvation to her suitor, from whom she receives a personal devotion involving the natural and the supernatural. The sequence of the sections in *Ash Wednesday* is in part founded upon this. The Platonic lover of

Cavalcanti's poem bids his soul to "worship her/ Still in her purity." Such love has a religious quality and is ironically distinct from the sexual formula which describes the performance of the typist and the "young man carbuncular" in *The Waste Land*. The most eminent instance of the love which amounts to religious worship is Dante's devotion to Beatrice. Eliot has stated the idea in his essay on Dante, speaking of the experience [1] in the *Vita Nuova*:

> It is not, I believe, meant as a description of what he *consciously* felt on his meeting with Beatrice, but rather as a description of what that meant on mature reflection upon it . . . the love of man and woman (or for that matter of man and man) is only explained and made reasonable by the higher love, or else is simply the coupling of animals.

It is probably quite valid to associate the Lady with Beatrice, for their function is similar, although it is not necessary for the reader of *Ash Wednesday* to recall any particular appearance of Beatrice from the *Divine Comedy*. Since Eliot's poem deals with purgation, we may take note of his remark: ". . . it is in these last cantos of the *Purgatorio*, rather than in the *Paradiso*, that Beatrice appears most clearly."

Associations of the Lady also involve the "juniper tree." *The Juniper Tree*, one of Jakob Grimm's tales, is an account of a husband and wife who, having no children, but desiring one, finally acquire a boy by supernatural aid. When the wife dies in childbirth the man marries a woman who, having a daughter of her own, Marlinchen, hates the boy. She kills him, makes puddings of his flesh which she gives to her husband for food, and lies about the boy's absence. Mar-

---

[1] "At that moment, I say most truly that the spirit of life, which hath its dwelling in the secretest chamber of the heart, began to tremble so violently that the least pulses of my body shook therewith; and in trembling it said these words: *Ecce deus fortior me, qui veniens dominabitur mihi* ("Here is a deity stronger than I; who, coming, shall rule over me"). At that moment the animate spirit, which dwelleth in the lofty chamber whither all the senses carry their perceptions, was filled with wonder, and speaking more especially unto the spirits of the eyes, said these words: *Apparuit jam beatitudo vestra* ("Your beatitude hath now been made manifest unto you"). At that moment the natural spirit, which dwelleth there where our nourishment is administered, began to weep, and in weeping said these words: *Heu miser! quia frequenter impeditus ero deinceps* ("Alas! how often shall I be disturbed from this time forth!")." *La Vita Nuova* (Rossetti's translation).

linchen carries the boy's bones to a juniper tree. Then there are mist and flames, and a bird appears, singing—

> My mother she killed me,
> My father he ate me,
> My sister little Marlinchen,
> Gathered together all my bones,
> Tied them in a silken handkerchief,
> Laid them beneath the juniper tree,
> Kywitt, kywitt, what a beautiful bird am I!

The bird finally causes the death of the stepmother and becomes a boy again.

The Lady, by her benevolence, corresponds to the sister Marlinchen. The juniper and the bones are additional links. Moreover, the story reminds us of Christian resurrection and the eating of the boy's body parallels the Communion. Eliot's use of this story agrees with his interest in the Christian elements of anthropology manifested by *The Waste Land*. The boy has passed through death and come to life again. Eliot has used devices before to express the idea that life comes through death (*vide The Waste Land, Journey of the Magi,* and *A Song for Simeon*). Another source of "under a juniper tree" strikes the same note. When Elijah was threatened by Jezebel for having slain the prophets of Baal, he went into the wilderness "and came and sat down under a juniper tree: and he requested for himself that he might die." It is possible that the proffering of "my love/ To . . . the fruit of the gourd" derives from another biblical passage of the same nature. When Jonah was afflicted by the sun's heat because the gourd under which he sat had withered, "he fainted, and wished in himself to die."

The bird of Grimm's story has been carried over into the poem. It is not simply for grotesque effect that the bones happen to chirp and sing. In Section IV of *Ash Wednesday* the bird sings "Redeem the time, redeem the dream." Elsewhere in Eliot's poetry the bird and the tree occur together (cf. *The Waste Land*, 1. 356; *Burnt Norton*, I; *Marina*). The bones in the poem reflect the tale, as well as St. John's *Dark Night:* ". . . the yearnings for God become so great in the soul that the very bones seem to be dried up by this thirst, and the natural powers to be fading away."

The book of *Ezekiel* is another source of the bones symbolism.

It may be observed that there are in Section II several allusions to Chapter 37 of *Ezekiel*. After the Lord has passed damning judgment upon many iniquitous peoples, He promises rehabilitation and re-animation to the Israelites. He shows to the prophet a vision symbolic of renewed vitality:

> The hand of the Lord was upon me . . . and set me down in the midst of the valley which was full of bones, . . . they were very dry. And he said unto me, Son of man, can these bones live? . . . So I prophesied . . . and the bones came together . . . and the flesh came up upon them, . . . but there was no breath in them. Then said he unto me, Prophesy unto the wind, prophesy, Son of man. . . . So I prophesied . . . and they lived . . . an exceeding great army.
>
> Then said he unto me, Son of man, these bones are the whole house of Israel: behold, they say, Our bones are dried, and our hope is lost. . . . Therefore prophesy and say unto them, Thus saith the Lord God; . . . ye shall live, and I shall place you in your own land. . . .

The chapter continues with a prophecy of the unity and blessings which God will bestow upon His people. *Ezekiel* ends with instructions for the dividing of the land and the negotiation of inheritance: "(48:29) This is the land which ye shall divide by lot unto the tribes of Israel for inheritance, and these are their portions, saith the Lord God."

It is significant that Eliot's first note to *The Waste Land* (l. 20, "Son of man") refers to *Ezekiel*. (The biblical context of this specific reference has not much importance unless we consider the entire book of *Ezekiel* as relative to *The Waste Land;* space forbids discussion of it.) The second note to *The Waste Land* makes a reference that applies also to Section II of *Ash Wednesday:* "the burden of the grasshopper" holds the same meaning (but for a different purpose) as "the cricket no relief," both deriving from *Ecclesiastes* 12:

> 4 And the doors shall be shut in the streets, when the sound of the grinding is low, and he shall rise up at the voice of the bird, and all the daughters of music shall be brought low; 5 Also when they shall be afraid of that which is high, and fears shall be in the way, and the almond tree shall flourish, and the grass-hopper shall be a burden, and desire shall fail: because man goeth to his long home, and the mourners go about the streets.

It does not seem unlikely that the bird at whose voice "he shall rise up" is connected with the idea of Grimm's tale and Eliot's use of the bird in his poetry. The grasshopper allusion implies the failing of desire. This is an additional association with the purgational dark night, during which the affections are lost sight of.

The loss of legs, heart, and liver reflects Eliot's interest in those aspects of anthropology which seem to bear upon Christian ritual. According to the article on cannibalism in the *Encyclopedia of Religion and Ethics,* a frequent incident in folklore "is that of a child being sent out by the parent to be killed, while the assassin is ordered to bring back the victim's heart, liver, etc. . . . Grimm's story of Snow White is an instance. Here we may see a reminiscence of the practice of eating heart, liver, etc., in order to acquire the strength or soul of their owner." *The Juniper Tree* is cited as another instance. This practice and the Christian Communion are mutually reminiscent; they have become associated with the strength, the salvation, anticipated by the condition of the protagonist. The "three white leopards" which have "fed to satiety" belong to the same association. In the article "Animals" of the encyclopedia the section on the leopard relates that cannibalism and ritualistic flesh-eating are practiced by African tribes in connection with the leopard. There would not necessarily be a relevance between this article and *Ash Wednesday* were it not for an identical phrase appearing in both: "In South Africa a man who has killed a leopard remains in his hut three days; he practices continence and is *fed to satiety* [*Italics mine*]." Although there is no special meaning brought into the poem by the coincidence of phrase with this single passage, its complete context does contain matter which recalls the Communion. The phrase and the leopards are, so to speak, handles of the association; it may very well be an unconscious one for the poet.

A quotation from Chapter 3 of *Genesis* gives the setting of Section II. When the fallen Adam and Eve hid themselves for shame of their nakedness, God walked "in the garden in the cool of the day." Besides the quality the phrase has by its allusiveness, it describes an aspect of the state, the "dream-crossed twilight," which is the subject of the poem. I remarked above that to understand the section it is necessary to learn "upon what ground all the associations occur." This "ground," as we have seen, is the idea of being purified in the purgational dark night. The images in the section, its setting, and the allusions which run through it carry the religious meaning of purgation and the way of purgation.

Eliot has said of Donne that "He knew the anguish of the marrow." As a symptom of intensity words are spoken by "that which had been contained/ In the bones." The words spoken indicate an appreciation of the benevolent guidance of the Lady, as well as the humility of the protagonist. The spiritual guide is responsible for the "brightness," which is faith. Throughout the section faith is signified by the color-symbolism of whiteness. It is by the faith which the Lady inspires that the portions rejected by the leopards are recovered. This faith brings and makes purposeful the "emptiness of the apprehensions" (the forgetfulness) which St. John declares an accompaniment of purgation.

Those familiar with the Catholic litany will appreciate the associations evoked by the solemn liturgical cadences of the words which the bones sing to the Lady of silences. The seeming contradictions which compose the passage are analogous to the paradox ("to care and not to care") upon which the religious experience revolves. The Lady is calm and reposeful by nature. But she is also distressed and worried in her solicitude for the protagonist. By being the Rose of memory and of forgetfulness she is both "Torn and most whole." (As it is convenient, I shall defer a fuller explanation of this to the treatment of Section IV.) She is "Exhausted and life-giving" in the way that Beatrice was, having passed from physical existence to become the inspiration of spiritual life. Her personality is symbolical of all the spiritual aims for which the protagonist strives; sex impulses have been sublimated into religious devotion, so that "The single Rose/ Is now the Garden/ Where all loves end." The torment of "love unsatisfied" is terminated in that it reaches its climax, the satisfaction of its impulse, by a biological performance, such as the typist and the young man enact in *The Waste Land*. This performance, however, is only an incident in the recurring cycle of desire and satisfaction. So long as love is merely a biological urge, forever consuming and forever desiring, there is never ultimate satisfaction. It is in this sense that we have

> The greater torment
> Of love satisfied
> End of the endless
> Journey to no end

> Conclusion of all that
> Is inconclusible
> Speech without word and
> Word of no speech. . . .

The last two lines are a comment upon the emptiness and lack of spiritual meaning which belong to the love that must be forever desiring. A distinction is made between biological desire and spiritual love in *Burnt Norton:* "Desire is itself movement/ Not in itself desirable;/ Love is itself unmoving,/ Only the cause and end of movement,/ Timeless and undesiring. . . ." The chant of the bones ends with a note of thanksgiving. In accordance with the way of purgation the soul being purified is thankful for its present state, "the blessing of sand," from which the garden is to evolve. The scattered bones, shining with faith, say "We are glad to be scattered, we did little good to each other." Much of the irony and all of the bitterness which these words may apparently contain are supplied by the reader. If the protagonist *cares* really, then, according to the direction he has taken, he has good reason *not to care*.

III

When Section III was first published individually it bore the title *Som de l'Escalina* (summit of the stairway), a phrase taken from the familiar *Ara vos prec* passage of the *Purgatorio,* XXVI. The image of the stair is consistent with St. John's *Dark Night,* in which the ladder "of living faith" is used as a symbol and illustration of the purgative contemplation. The soul "is ascending and descending continually," experiencing exaltation and humiliation "until it has acquired perfect habits; and this ascending and descending will cease, since the soul will have attained to God and become united with Him, which comes to pass at the summit of the ladder; for the ladder rests and leans upon Him." St. John describes the ladder as consisting of ten steps. Eliot is most probably referring to these steps with "the figure of the ten stairs" in *Burnt Norton,* and "the saint's stair" in *A Song for Simeon.*

The progress of the protagonist, now signified by turning, is objectified by the "projection of sensory images." The terms "The same shape," "I left them twisting, turning below," and "stops and steps of the mind over the third stair" suggest the changing from one state of mind to another, or rather the function of a single dynamic state of mind. The *shape* and one of *them* are in each case the protagonist. In *Burnt Norton* the poet ponders this movement which is "neither arrest nor movement. And do not call it fixity." The "fetid air" is a sign of purification, representing that which is spiritually foul and unhealthy as the issue of purgation. The cleansing process is illustrated in the *Dark Night* by the example of fire consuming wood: ". . . it brings out and drives away all the dark and unsightly accidents which are contrary to the nature of fire." The devil with "The deceitful face of hope and of despair" embodies the tempting idea of departure from the intense submission to purgation. To persist along the way of purification it is necessary "to care and not to care." This is no ordinary attitude; it is difficult to maintain when confronted by the easy but futile adjustments of mere hope and despair, which are customary and therefore dangerously attractive.

The lurid images which are suggested to the protagonist need not be symbolical, for they occur within a symbol, one that is dramatic: the difficult effort to ascend a stair. However, the picture called to mind for the protagonist by the passage along the stair—"an old man's mouth drivelling, beyond repair"—reminds us of the *old man* that is being cast off by the experience.

"At the first turning of the third stair/ Was a slotted window bellied like the fig's fruit. . . ." There is nothing extraordinary about the presence of the window. One is led to conceive of a tower with a window near the landing below the third flight. Whatever other meaning there may be is to this extent objectified. But a pertinent meaning is suggested. The preceding images readily connote despair; it may therefore be expected that the "deceitful face of hope" follows. The "slotted window" is, besides being superficially consistent, a sexual image. The fig is associated with lust. By taking window in a figurative sense one may arrive at quite a literal interpretation, if not an image: that of the female genital organ. The form of the window is a symbolic frame for the symbolic scene of beautiful sensuous images on which it opens. The "broadbacked figure" suggests a pagan fertility deity who is responsible for an appealing "Distraction, music of the flute." This sensuous beauty is hostile to the purposes of the protagonist; when it fades he gains strength. *Ash Wednesday* is again consistent with the *Dark Night:*

For to some the angel of Satan presents himself—namely, the
spirit of fornication—that he may buffet their senses with
abominable and violent temptations, and may trouble their spirits
with vile considerations and representations which are most visible to the imagination, which things at times are a greater affliction to them than death.

The protagonist has passed through disability of the affections,
achieved some success in attaining the paradoxical position of caring
and not caring, and now gains "strength beyond hope and despair."
The part of man that is vexed by the foibles of hope and despair is
being purged.

Catholic ritual supplies the final words of the section. In the Mass,
just before the priest consumes the Body and drinks the Blood of
Christ, he repeats three times this prayer, while he bows low over
the chalice and patin and strikes his breast thrice: "Lord, I am not
worthy that thou shouldst enter under my roof. But speak the word
only, and my soul shall be healed." Besides the religious connotations
which the words have, they bespeak humility and faith, and an
earnest dependence upon the will of God. The protagonist is still
"Climbing the third stair"—with fervor and humility.

IV

*Ash Wednesday* may be divided into two parts, the first ending
with Section III. In the earlier sections the protagonist has been moving farther along through the dark night, ascending the stair according to the pattern. He reaches the third stair and is still climbing it
at the end of the first part of the poem. In the last three sections he
is trying to realize the causality by which he is conditioned, as well
as the condition itself.

The series of questions which opens Section IV implies wonder as
to the identity of the Lady, the spiritual guide "who moves in the time
between sleep and waking." Although the several questions imply
the same answer, each of them is in terms that have a special significance. Mario Praz remarks that there is a correspondence between
the floral setting and the vision of Matilda in *Purgatorio,* XXVIII:
"a lady solitary, who went along singing, and culling flower after
flower, wherewith all her path was painted." One feels urged to cor-
relate the lines with passages in other portions of Eliot's work. "Be-

tween the violet and the violet" recalls from *The Waste Land* the "violet hour" and the "violet light." Brooks observes that violet, as a quality of the twilight, has symbolic connections with a moment of time and, also, with an experience. It may be that we have here in the violet the last link in a chain of symbols: an experience, a moment of time, a sensory quality of the moment; so that "between the violet and the violet" is ultimately synonymous with "the time between sleep and waking." It is only at such moments, under such conditions, that the protagonist can consciously seize upon the one who "made strong the fountains and made fresh the springs," for it was at such a moment that her influence was first experienced. That these terms are put in the form of questions indicates that the protagonist has not completely established his hold upon her and has not the intimate realization which Dante had of Beatrice. Eliot expresses the belief that the sexual experience of childhood which Dante describes in the *Vita Nuova*

> could only have been written around a personal experience. If so the details do not matter: whether the lady was the Portinari or not, I do not care; it is quite likely that she is a blind for someone else, even for a person whose name Dante has forgotten or never known. But I cannot find it incredible that what has happened to others, should have happened to Dante with much greater intensity.

The protagonist is questioning because he does not specifically remember (or visualize) the one by whom he would be led to a higher love. This is why in Section II the "Lady of silences" is "Torn and most whole/ Rose of memory/ Rose of forgetfulness." These lines from *Marina* involve the same meaning:

> What is this face, less clear and clearer
> The pulse in the arm, less strong and stronger—
> Given or lent? more distant than stars and
> nearer than the eye
>
> . . . . . . . . . . . . . .
>
> I made this, I have forgotten
> And remember.

The original of the Lady, like the earthly Beatrice, was an ordinary and natural person, "Talking of trivial things." She was unaware of the effect her presence and behavior had upon the protagonist, yet the details of the experience remain significant for him, so that he imputes to her a "knowledge of eternal dolour."

The preceding sections of the poem are an account of her having made the fountains and springs of spiritual life appealing and having brought the protagonist closer to them. She has made his situation less dismal, for now the dry rock has been cooled and the sand is firm, whereas in *The Waste Land* there

> is no water but only rock
> Rock and no water and the sandy road . . .
> Sweat is dry and feet are in the sand . . . .

The words of Arnaut Daniel, the poet in purgatory, are used by the protagonist as an entreaty to the spiritual guide: "Sovegna vos"—"be mindful." Thus he expresses his desire, his willingness, to proceed further in the experience of purgation.

"Here are the years that walk between, . . ." *Here* is the present condition. All the years that have passed since the first sexual-religious experience are involved in it; they have brought the condition by removing distractions, "the fiddles and the flutes." And it is only through the passage of time that this momentary experience can be recaptured, that the dreamlike person "who moves in the time between sleep and waking" can be restored. As it is stated in *Burnt Norton*, "Only through time time is conquered." The experiences and conditions recorded in the Bible, in folklore, in the writings of Dante and St. John of the Cross—"the ancient rhyme"—are restored by faith and suffering, "through a bright cloud of tears." The protagonist pleads: "Redeem/ The time. Redeem/ The unread vision in the higher dream." We find the phrase "redeeming the time" at the end of "Thoughts after Lambeth":

> The World is trying the experiment of attempting to form a civilized but non-Christian mentality. The experiment will fail; but we must be very patient in awaiting its collapse; meanwhile redeeming the time: so that the Faith may be preserved alive through the dark ages before us; to renew and rebuild civilization, and save the World from suicide.

(In each case the phrase may be an echo of *Ephesians* 5:15, and *Colossians* 4:6.) "Redeem the time," then, implies a desire that such a time as was conducive to "the higher dream" be restored and the present time atoned for. F. R. Leavis has noted that "the higher dream" is reminiscent of some remarks in Eliot's essay on Dante. Discussing the "pageantry" of the *Paradiso*, Eliot observes: "It belongs to the world of what I call the *high dream*, and the modern world seems capable only of the *low dream*." Though in the modern world the vision—which is paradise and all it stands for—is unread, this does not mean that it has been permanently lost. It belongs to a world different from the modern, one capable of the high dream, and it is this world, this time, which the protagonist wishes to be redeemed. Notice that it is not simply the dream that is requested, but the more concrete vision. The difference becomes appreciable in conjunction with Eliot's statement in *Dante* upon the Italian poet's "visual imagination . . . the trick of which we have forgotten, . . . a more significant, interesting, and disciplined kind of dreaming." The protagonist himself imagines a vision as an accompaniment to the redemption which he pleads: "While jewelled unicorns draw by the gilded hearse." As Leavis observes, the unicorn belongs to the world of vision, of disciplined dreaming. The image is completed with "the gilded hearse." These objects and their embellishment constitute a scene of imaginative pageantry, one that suggests, in addition to the picture, Eliot's conception of a new life attained through death. The protagonist associates the time capable of the vision in the higher dream with the ritual of the funeral. Moreover, the unicorns (creatures of the imagination) have an important function in the ritual of death—death being the eve of the wished-for life.

The supplication is, of course, addressed to the Lady. That she should be pictured "Between the yews, behind the garden god/ Whose flute is breathless" and in Section V as "The veiled sister between the slender/ Yew trees" indicates that there is some ritualistic significance in the precise arrangement of the elements in the figure. The protagonist's reflection upon his condition is equated with the contemplation of a ritualistic symbol. The Lady's position emphasizes the difficulty with which the state is achieved, for she can be revealed thus only when the flute of the garden god has become breathless: in Section III the "music of the flute" is distraction. In other words, she becomes actual in proportion to the success of the protagonist in sublimating into religious devotion the impulses symbolized by the garden god. The yew, an evergreen, is symbolical of immortality. The

Lady being placed between the trees, we may conceive her as gathering up within herself "time past and time future," in short, all reality. We find in *Burnt Norton* that past and future, though equally real with the present, are *actual* only in the present: "At the still point. . . . Where past and future are gathered. . . . Except for the point, the still point,/ There would be no dance, and there is only the dance." That is to say, we may approach reality only through actuality, and the Lady is here the concentrated symbol of the great past and future realities which can in no other way be perceived. The protagonist's perception of her is imperfect, however. A complete intimacy would predicate complete revelation, and she merely "bent her head and signed but spoke no word." Although she adds nothing of revelation, still she gives an encouraging sign. The fountain springs up, making secure his spiritual awareness; the bird reaffirms his petition. So long as there is no complete revelation the protagonist is right in seeking to redeem the dream, for it is a symbol of what is as yet unrevealed, the "token of the word unheard, unspoken." He must continue in purgation until he reaches that state at which the immortal and spiritual essence is entirely realized, "Till the wind shake a thousand whispers from the yew." Such is also the implication in "And after this our exile," a liturgical echo from one of the "Prayers after Low Mass": "Turn then, most gracious advocate, thine eyes of mercy towards us. And after this our exile, show unto us the blessed fruit of thy womb, Jesus."

v

   In Section V the protagonist is pondering upon the *word*, the revelation which the world is resolutely incapable of receiving. Nonetheless, he says, the word exists. It is lost, spent, unheard, and unspoken only because unattained. And it is *the Word*, the very Word that the apostle John speaks of. "The centre of the silent Word" about which "the unstilled world still whirled" is equivalent to "the still point of the turning world. . . . Where past and future are gathered" of *Burnt Norton*. A source of the idea is probably the point "where every *where* and every *when* is focused" of *Paradiso*, XXIX. We have previously noted the whirling movement as symbolical of the world's non-Christian attitude and activity. The modern world has violated its actual relationship to the unchanging and divine essence. But the Word is not destroyed. It is still "within/ The world and for the world."

Notice that the line "O my people, what have I done unto thee" is punctuated by a period rather than a question mark. The line is from *Micah* 6:3: "O my people, what have I done unto thee? and wherein have I wearied thee? testify against me." These words occur also in "The Adoration of the Cross" for Good Friday, a penitential ritual. We may infer, then, that the protagonist recalls the words and exclaims them because of his religious humility and his wonder at the condition of the world. Having faith in God and the divine love, it is puzzling to him that the world should have moved "Against the Word."

He asks where the *word* shall be found, and answers himself exhaustively and emphatically, recognizing that the condition of the modern world is prohibitive of the experience which he desires. St. John's dark night is naturally suggested by the words "those who walk in darkness." The modern world does not afford the realities ("The right time and the right place") which are necessary for those who have only begun to be purged and would continue in purgation. Here in the world that is real at present there is neither "a place of grace" nor a "time to rejoice" for the partially purged, and it is inevitable that they "avoid the face" and "deny the voice." Ability to do otherwise depends not upon desire but upon condition. And the condition of the protagonist, and others like him, is that of participating in the temporal and sensual. They are of the modern world and must inescapably "walk among noise." This opinion, because one of disillusionment, is both realistic and religious. In his essay on Bradley, Eliot declares that "wisdom consists largely of scepticism and uncynical disillusion. . . . And scepticism and disillusion are a useful equipment for religious understanding." An inference of the protagonist's understanding and achievement naturally follows.

Having contemplated the circumstances, he asks whether the spiritual guide, the "veiled sister," will pray for those in the state of purgation, "those who wait/ In darkness." In enduring the contradictions which make up their paradoxical condition they are "torn on the horn," for, although they desire the divinely spiritual life, they remain unpurged of worldly inclinations. They are attracted by two opposing directions, and so are torn between the seasons, times, hours, words, and powers of the worldly and the divine: at the gate of a more spiritual life, they "will not go away and cannot pray." The protagonist pleads that the "veiled sister" intercede for them.

As in the preceding section, the Lady is pictured between yew trees. From the protagonist's humble point of view, she is offended, for the insufficiently purged would enlist her solicitude. These are terrified by the world which is hostile to their interests, and by their own apparently inalterable condition. The divinely spiritual is, of course, their highest desire, and this they "affirm before the world." But when they return to their own reality, "between the rocks," and face the chosen direction, they do not *will* to advance: their denial is implicit in their condition.

The quality of the rocks (which are red and dry in *The Waste Land*) signifies that those who have chosen the spiritual way and made some progress have gained an existence more tolerable than that from which they set out, the latter being the merely secular and sensually appetitive world. Their progress may be arrested, but they have reached the last stage at which the world is an impediment to their further advancement, "the last desert between the last blue rocks/ The desert in the garden the garden in the desert/ Of drouth." The difference between the desert and the garden is of qualitative degree. Each is contained in the other: as the purgation of the individual continues, the desert condition is evolving toward the garden condition, which is the state of spiritual salvation. Drouth, representing spiritual want, also represents the function by which all that is foreign to the spiritual is purged away. This purgation is symbolized in "spitting from the mouth the withered apple-seed," evidently an allusion to the forbidden fruit eaten by Adam and Eve. The apple-seed, withered and being spit out, symbolizes the attenuated mundane desires which are being cast off by purgation.

VI

The first lines of the poem are repeated, except for the change of one word, as the opening lines of the final section, thus imparting formality and the quality of an expressive pattern which are characteristic of ceremonial incantation. Furthermore, this difference of one word emphasizes, by comparison with the protagonist's initial condition, the condition ultimately achieved in *Ash Wednesday*. At the first he despaired of the possibility of ever being sensible to physical and spiritual attractions. But the condition has altered. He has passed through temptations and has arrived at the token, at least, of divine actuality. Now, according to his spiritual limitations and the choice he has made, his inclinations should be at a standstill. But they are not so. The purgation which has diminished the faculty for finding pleasure in the world has brought, since it was not complete, a nostalgic attraction to the pleasures that have to a great extent receded. The choice has been made and there is no question of considering the consequences in terms of reward, of "Wavering between the profit and the loss." However, though he has no desire to wish for the pleasures of the world, he inclines toward them. A confession of this follows the phrase "(Bless me father)." Among Catholics the usual form for beginning a confession is: "Bless me father; I confess to almighty God and to you, father, that I have sinned."

Attraction is exerted by the natural earth itself and its broad range of delightful manifestations. Hence the "wide window." The nostalgic quality of the appeal is reflected by the terms of the experience:

> And the *lost* heart stiffens and rejoices
> In the *lost* lilac and the *lost* sea voices
> And the *weak* spirit quickens to *rebel*
> For the *bent* golden rod and the *lost* sea smell
> Quickens to *recover*
> The cry of quail and the whirling plover
> And the blind eye creates
> The empty forms between the ivory gates
> And smell *renews* the salt savor of the sandy earth . . . .

The protagonist is aware that his actual need can in no way be satisfied by the phenomena of the earth, although he is, against his wish, attracted by them. This is again implied by the *"blind* eye" which creates the *"empty* forms between the ivory gates." That is, the weakened faculties of mundane conception are indulged to experience the false promises of worldly pleasures. "Ivory gates" is an allusion to the passage in the *Aeneid* where Aeneas and the Sibyl, journeying through Hades, are informed by Anchises, Aeneas' father, of the two gates of Sleep: "Two gates of Sleep there are, whereof the one is said to be of horn, and thereby an easy outlet is given to true shades; the other gleaming with the sheen of polished ivory, but false are the dreams sent by the spirits to the world above."

The condition of the protagonist is a "brief transit" and a "time of tension" because it is not one of repose, but a straining in two opposing directions, the worldly and the spiritual. The end of the one and the beginning of the other are a twilight, a transition from one state to another. It is in this sense a condition between the death of the worldly and the birth of the spiritual, "between dying and birth." The same purgation that would utterly remove the mundane attachment would concurrently introduce one entirely spiritual. "The place of solitude where three dreams cross" is, of course, "the time of tension." Past, present, and future are the three dreams. We have previously noted that the coexistence of these is stressed in *Burnt Norton*. These times (dreams, perhaps) meet each other at one point, the transitional condition. Other terms may be substituted for these with an addition of meaning. The three times may be respectively called the conditions unpurged, partially purged, and completely purged.

The "place of solitude" is, as in the preceding section, "Between blue rocks." In the discussion of Section IV it was observed that the protagonist will maintain his position until a divine revelation comes, "Till the wind shake a thousand whispers from the yew." It was also noted that the two yews between which the Lady is placed are representative of past and future times. The protagonist now pleads

> But when the voices shaken from the yew-tree drift away
> Let the other yew be shaken and reply.

That is, "when worldly experiences and the memory of them have passed, I hope for a revelation from the divine."

*Ash Wednesday* ends with a plea to the feminine principle of spiritual guidance. The first request is clear enough; the falsehoods with which spiritual pilgrims might mock themselves are, among others, complacency, the deceits of hope and despair, the "empty forms." Recurrence of the lines

> Teach us to care and not to care
> Teach us to sit still

has the same ritualistic effect as the opening lines. In connection with the earlier instance of the plea it was observed that caring and not caring constitute the patience and humility counseled by St. John of the Cross, as well as the motivating devotion. This paradox which introduces and punctuates the poem is a motif of the purgation. We have seen how it operates in Section II: the images and statements which reflect a condition of defeat are symptomatic of hope and progress. The consonance which the condition has with *The Dark Night of the Soul* saves it from ironic emphasis. "Strength beyond hope and despair" of Section III is at once an attainment and a resolution of the paradox. The necessity for caring and not caring persists from one stage of purgation to another. In the final stage of *Ash Wednesday* the protagonist wishes to learn "to sit still/ Even among these rocks." Out of humility and devotion he seeks to maintain patience and gratefulness for the degree of progress he has been granted. Peace may be found even in an incomplete detachment from the world, in partial purgation, by realizing that the condition is in accord with the will of God. It is with hesitation that I remark at all upon the line "Our peace in His will," which is a translation of Dante's well-known line *"la sua voluntade e nostra pace."* T. S. Eliot's own comment upon it inspires my hesitation:

> And the statement of Dante seems to me *literally true*. And I confess that it has more beauty for me now, when my experience has deepened its meaning, than it did when I first read it. So I can only conclude that I cannot, in practice, wholly separate my poetic appreciation from my personal beliefs.

"Spirit of the river, spirit of the sea" suggests Aphrodite, goddess of fertility. In this symbolism the idea of fertility has been spiritualized; the protagonist seeks a spiritual birth, the divine revelation, through the solicitous intercession of the Lady. The concluding words, which are a plea for continuation of the spiritual contact, are quotations from Catholic ritual. "Suffer me not to be separated from Thee" occurs in "Devotions of the Forty Hours," Visit IV. "And let my cry come unto Thee" is the response to the versicle "O Lord, hear my prayer." The last two lines are, as they occur in the poem, dramatically emphatic of the situation. Because of all that has gone before, they issue effectually as the protagonist's utterance, their full significance including, besides their intrinsic suitability to their place in the poem, the ritualistic force and religious meaning for which they serve in a specific ceremonial performance. The individual experience of the protagonist brings him to traditional worship.

## 2. T. S. ELIOT'S ROSE GARDEN *

The purpose of this essay is to focus attention upon a specific aspect of continuity in the poetry of T. S. Eliot. I shall attempt to follow what I believe to be an important strand, a basic and persistent theme in Eliot's poetry throughout the course of his career. Consideration of this theme may begin by first taking notice of its appearance in Eliot's prose. In his essay on Dante (1929) he discusses the experience of ecstasy in childhood described in the *Vita Nuova:*

> Now Dante, I believe, had experiences which seemed to him of some importance . . . important in themselves; and therefore they seemed to him to have some philosophical and impersonal value. I find in it an account of a particular kind of experience: that is, of something which had actual experience (the experience of the "confession" in the modern sense) *and* intellectual and imaginative experience (the experience of thought and the experience of dream) as its materials; and which became a third kind. It seems to me of importance to grasp the simple fact that the *Vita Nuova* is neither a "confession" nor an "indiscretion" in the modern sense, nor is it a piece of Pre-Raphaelite tapestry. If you have that sense of intellectual and spiritual realities that Dante had, then a form of expression like the *Vita Nuova* cannot be classed either as "truth" or "fiction."
>
> In the first place, the type of sexual experience which Dante describes as occurring to him at the age of nine years is by no means impossible or unique. My only doubt (in which I found myself confirmed by a distinguished psychologist) is whether it could have taken place so *late* in life as the age of nine years. The psychologist agreed with me that it is more likely to occur at about five or six years of age. It is possible that Dante developed rather late, and it is also possible that he altered the dates to employ some other significance of the number nine. But to me it appears obvious that the *Vita Nuova* could only have been written around a personal experience. If so, the details do not matter: whether the lady was the Portinari or not, I do not care; it is quite likely that she is a blind for some one else, even for a person whose name Dante may have forgotten or never known.

* From *The Southern Review,* Vol. VII, pp. 667–689, Copyright, 1942, by Leonard Unger.

But I cannot find it incredible that what has happened to others should have happened to Dante with much greater intensity.

The attitude of Dante to the fundamental experience of the *Vita Nuova* can only be understood by accustoming ourselves to find meaning in the *final causes* rather than in origins. It is not, I believe, meant as a description of what he *consciously* felt on his meeting with Beatrice, but rather as a description of what that meant on mature reflection upon it. The final cause is the attraction towards God.

Several details of Eliot's comment are of particular interest to us. He ascribes an obscurity and yet peculiar reality to the experience. He regards the experience as one not uncommon among men nor restricted to any single period or kind of period in history. He acknowledges that the experience may be variously interpreted, and he himself finds it significant beyond its phenomenal and experiential details: the experience is for him derivative of a supernatural cause; it represents implicitly and symbolically meanings that are of some intellectual complexity, meanings that are philosophical and religious.

This experience and the interpretation put upon it constitute the theme which we shall observe operating by various uses throughout Eliot's writings, from his earliest poetry to his most recent. I shall try to treat the poetry, as nearly as possible, in chronological order of its appearance. According to this plan, it seems natural and profitable to begin with a consideration of the French poem, *Dans le Restaurant,* which appears in *Poems* (1920). This poem is made up, until the final section, of talk made by a shabby old waiter, uncouth and repellent in manners, to a "respectable" diner, who occasionally interrupts with indignance. For my own convenience I shall translate from the French, omitting here the diner's interruptions. The words of the "garcon délabré qui n'a rien à faire":

> In my country there is rainy weather,
> Wind, much sunshine, and rain;
> There is what one calls a beggar's wash-day.
>
> . . .
>
> The willows drenched, and blossoms on the hedges—
> It is there, in a shower, that one takes shelter.
> I was seven, she was even younger.
> She was completely soaked, I gave her some primroses.
>
> . . .

I tickled her, in order to make her laugh.
I experienced a moment of power and ecstasy.

At this point the diner's interruption is—

Come now, old lecher, at that age . . .

But the waiter continues reminiscing:

Sir, the fact is a hard one.
A large dog came and bothered us;
I was frightened, I left her half-way up the path.
What a pity.

And now the diner finally has his say:

Come now, you have your nerve!
Go and wipe the streaks from your face.
Here's my fork, scratch your head with it.
By what right do you have experiences like mine?
Now, here are ten sous, for the bath-house.

Conspicuous in the words of the waiter, obviously central to the poem, is the childhood experience. Its potential significance is suggested by the intensity with which the old waiter is haunted by this experience, so haunted that he must tell of it to an unsympathetic and complete stranger. That Eliot intended the experience portrayed here as of the kind discussed in his essay on Dante is, I believe, beyond any doubt. Its being ascribed to the undignified old man illustrates that its source is basic in human nature and (to follow Eliot) in a nature beyond that. This is further emphasized by the statement of the snobbish patron: "De quel droit payes-tu des expériences comme moi?"

In his fine analysis of *The Waste Land* Mr. Cleanth Brooks has explicated the English version of the passage on the drowned Phoenician, pointing out its symbols and allusions, its several levels of meaning. But we should determine its coherent status in the French poem. To observe that the passage on drowning follows a reference to the waiter's need of a bath seems to me to be more than simply amusing. Here, as elsewhere in Eliot's poetry, water is symbolic of spiritual rebirth—a pre-requisite of return to the obsessive experience. The manner by which the waiter is shown to be in need of water and the shift to the drowned man thus constitute a characteristic irony. And the shift illustrates again the "commonness" of the experience, bringing the lives of the two modern men and the ancient Phoenician within a single category. The Phoenician's death is cryptically, ironically, meant as a rebirth. The under-sea current (symbol of a spiritual force) carries him "aux étapes de sa vie antérieure," presumably to an ecstatic moment in childhood and its *final cause*. The return by stages suggests a progress according to purification or purgation.

In *Dans le Restaurant* there are certain elements which, we shall notice, repeatedly characterize the theme. These are the images of water, foliage, the little girl and the proffered flowers. Another recurrent element is the waiter's remorse—remembering that he left the girl half-way up the path—for having withdrawn from the situation: "C'est dommage." The more-than-scenic significance of the images is well established in poems earlier even than *Dans le Restaurant*. For example, this obtains in *La Figlia Che Piange* where, in addition to the images, there is the peculiar quality of the departure, the "pained surprise" and "resentment" of the girl—conversely related to the man's remorse. The speaker of the poem is, moreover, obviously involved in the scene; his final comment on it is explicit enough:

> I should have lost a gesture and a pose.
> Sometimes these cogitations still amaze
> The troubled midnight and the noon's repose.

Other thematic elements, incidental in the earlier poems but later to be elaborated and defined, occur in *The Love Song of J. Alfred Prufrock* and *Portrait of a Lady*.

> We have lingered in the chambers of the sea
> By sea-girls wreathed with seaweed red and brown
> Till human voices wake us, and we drown.

Prufrock's last words are a generalization. We bungle our adventures in the actual world because we are out of our true element, having strayed from the sea-girls and sea-chambers, the dreamworld that is an approach to spiritual reality. A similar hint of the "experience" is found in the *Portrait*.

> I keep my countenance,
> I remain self-possessed
> Except when a street piano, mechanical and tired
> Reiterates some worn-out common song
> With the smell of hyacinths across the garden

> Recalling things that other people have desired.
> Are these ideas right or wrong?

Here the speaker is distracted from his composure on the "actual" level by a reminder of the experience that is lost and neglected. These observations on *Prufrock* and *Portrait* are perhaps an over-reading of the poems taken singly. But I believe that they are justified in the light of later poems, and that the early passages become increasingly significant of the theme as one finds it more centrally and extensively treated in later compositions. Indeed, even the later poems will, in a sense, be over-read. Our emphasis is upon the theme, and it is often dominant in the work, but never the exclusive import—neither in *Dans le Restaurant* nor in *The Waste Land*. But on the other hand, with regard to Eliot's work as a whole, the theme is always basic as a point of view, even when there is no direct suggestion of the child-hood experience.

In *Gerontion* the dramatic and imagistic details of the experience or any explicit reference to it are not to be found. To the extent that this poem is allied with the theme, it is so allied generally and conceptually. If one recognizes the theme in the poems where its elements are more openly displayed, one will also see it as underlying *Gerontion,* and consequently find that poem additionally meaningful. The title and the senility portrayed throughout—the old man—represent a sense of remoteness from the experience of sexual-religious ecstasy and its significance. A similar representation (the agèd eagle) is later to be observed in the first section of *Ash Wednesday*. *Gerontion* opens with the scene of old age. Next is the statement of the coming in spring of *Christ the Tiger*. This, I believe, is equivalent to the *experience*. There is then the picture of Mr. Silvero, Hakagawa, etc., and their adjustment (or maladjustment) to it; and the old man again. The passage that follows is of special significance, "key" for our purposes:

> After such knowledge, what forgiveness? Think now
> History has many cunning passages, contrived corridors
> And issues, deceives with whispering ambitions,
> Guides us by vanities. Think now
> She gives when our attention is distracted
> And what she gives, gives with such supple confusions
> That the giving famishes the craving. Gives too late

> What's not believed in, or if still believed,
> In memory only, reconsidered passion. Gives too soon
> Into weak hands, what's thought can be dispensed with
> Till the refusal propagates a fear.

As I read the passage, it is a statement of the difficulty of recapturing the experience, and yet of the need to return to it; of the distractions which lead away from it. There is from this point of view a criticism of man's world, a picture of the individual's predicament. What History gives is the experience. And we find here, as elsewhere, the expression of inadequate response to it, of inability for a serious and effective attempt to reconstruct it. Further along in the poem I find the idea of removal, of the *lost experience,* even more particularized. It seems to me that this passage is an apostrophe to the girl, the Lady, the partner in the experience:

> I that was near your heart was removed therefrom
> To lose beauty in terror, terror in inquisition.
> I have lost my passion: why should I need to keep it
> Since what is kept must be adulterated?
> I have lost my sight, smell, hearing, taste and touch:
> How should I use them for your closer contact?

We shall meet again in later poems the "terror" here mentioned, and the loss of passion and the sensual faculties.

In discussing the theme as it is present in *The Waste Land* I shall not review that poem in its entirety, but refer the reader to Mr. Brooks' analysis. He will find, I believe, that the observations made here are consistent with Mr. Brooks' conclusions. The theme is evident in the first section, *The Burial of the Dead.* Following the song quoted from *Tristan and Isolde* is a passage comparable in its descriptive details to the scene in *Dans le Restaurant:*

> "You gave me hyacinths first a year ago;
> "They called me the hyacinth girl."
> —Yet when we came back, late, from the Hyacinth garden,
> Your arms full, and your hair wet, I could not
> Speak, and my eyes failed, I was neither
> Living nor dead, and I knew nothing,
> Looking into the heart of light, the silence.
> *Oed' und leer das Meer.*

The correspondence between the two garden scenes is surely obvious. And here, too, there is the tone of remorse. It may be noticed that the protagonist recalls not the experience in the garden, but his removal from it, his failure to see its meaning. The experience was both *life* and *death,* but its absence is neither.

The theme appears again at the end of the section, in the protagonist's speech to *Stetson.* In this passage the experience is attributed to all men of all times, to the man who was on King William Street and in the ships at Mylae, and attributed—with the quotation from Baudelaire—even to the reader. In addition to whatever other meanings it may have, I take the "corpse" to be a reference to the sexual-religious experience which has been neglected and repressed—or buried. (I am struck by the presence of the "Dog" here and the "gros chien" in *Dans le Restaurant,* but am not prepared to make anything of it.)

The section *Death by Water,* as it appears in Eliot's French poem, and its relationship to the theme have been discussed above. The theme appears conspicuously again at the end of *The Waste Land,* in the passages respectively introduced by *Datta, Dayadhvam, Damyatta.* There is first the statement of the intensity and persistent importance of the experience: "The awful daring of a moment's surrender." And then it is characterized as an unforgettable and desirable moment of freedom and communion: "I have heard the key / Turn in the door once and turn once only." And finally the experience is again referred to in terms nostalgic and remorseful: especially significant are the words *would have responded:*

> The boat responded
> Gaily, to the hand expert with sail and oar
> The sea was calm, your heart would have responded
> Gaily, when invited, beating obedient
> To controlling hands.

I have already discussed *Ash Wednesday* at some length, indicating that the two ideas basic to the conceptual structure of the poem are the course of purgation prescribed by St. John of the Cross in his *Dark Night of the Soul,* and the principle of spiritual guidance symbolized by the "Lady" who appears prominently throughout the poem. In *Ash Wednesday* the theme which we discuss is more centrally and elaborately employed than in earlier poems, especially with regard to its religious aspect. I shall attend here only to salient points, those most obviously involved in the continuity of the theme.

The first section of *Ash Wednesday* expresses the senility and weakened sensual faculties which represent remoteness from the experience and despair of renewing it:

> Because I know I shall not know
> The one veritable transitory power . . .

The second section is addressed by the bones to the Lady. Among the abundant and complex elements of this section are those which refer to the nature of the experience, especially in the song of the bones to the "Lady of silences":

> Rose of memory
> Rose of forgetfulness . . .
> The single Rose
> Is now the Garden
> Where all loves end
> Terminate torment
> Of love unsatisfied
> The greater torment
> Of love satisfied . . .
> Grace to the Mother
> For the Garden
> Where all love ends.

The *memory* and *forgetfulness* recall Eliot's remark that "Dante may have forgotten or never known" the name of the person represented by Beatrice. This stated obscurity and elusiveness recurs in his subsequent writings. It appears again in the form of questions at the opening of the fourth section of *Ash Wednesday*: "Who walked between the violet and the violet. . . ." A passage from this same section will illustrate the manner in which the theme is dramatically and symbolically developed throughout *Ash Wednesday*, as well as the significance put upon it:

> Here are the years that walk between, bearing
> Away the fiddles and the flutes, restoring
> One who moves in the time between sleep and waking . . .

The protagonist speaks from his condition of religious purgation. The present moment is seen as one resulting from and therefore containing the spiritual activity since the initial experience. This idea, it may be observed, is in accord with the co-existence of all times, as expressed elsewhere in *Ash Wednesday,* in *The Waste Land* and *Four Quartets.* The experience is regarded as not being subject to temporal flux but as the timeless unchanging reality. It is, nevertheless, sought and approached by temporal means. For until the experience has been recreated one must act in the world of past, present, and future. Thus, intimations of the experience, the appearance of the Lady, come under special conditions, "in the time between sleep and waking." It may be noticed that in this poem and in others such moments are always characterized by a dream-like, twilight atmosphere, as in the final section:

> In this brief transit where the dreams cross
> The dreamcrossed twilight between birth and dying . . .

In *Ash Wednesday,* more clearly and fully than in earlier poems, restoration of the childhood experience is identified with the goal of religious life, its meaning "on mature reflection upon it . . . the attraction towards God."

Similar to *Ash Wednesday* in its basic meaning, as well as in its lyrical quality, is the poem "Marina," for which Eliot derived his "objective correlative" from Shakespeare's *Pericles.* The speaker of Eliot's poem is Pericles, Prince of Tyre, who, after years of believing that his daughter Marina is dead, finds to his amazement that she is still alive. The following passage is from the recognition scene (V, i) between father and daughter:

> *Per.* But are you flesh and blood?
> Have you a working pulse? and are no fairy?
> Motion! Well; speak on. Where were you born?
> And wherefore call'd Marina?

The usefulness of this scene for Eliot's purposes is apparent: the unusual meeting between father and daughter is made dramatically to symbolize a restoration of the experience:

> What is this face, less clear and clearer
> The pulse in the arm, less strong and stronger—
> Given or lent? more distant than the stars and nearer than the eye
>
> Whispers and small laughter between leaves and hurrying feet
> Under sleep, where all the waters meet . . .

Obviously significant here are the dreamlike quality and the telling reference to the children among the foliage. And Eliot repeats in this poem the half-remembered character of the experience, the self-conscious effort for its recreation:

> I made this, I have forgotten
> And remember . . .
> Made this unknowing, half conscious, unknown, my own.

*Burnt Norton,* even more than *Ash Wednesday*—more than any other of Eliot's poems—displays clearly on its surface the spiritual quest, the constant endeavor to interpret the experience and thus to re-live it. The poem is a kind of essay, including within its range scenic description of the *garden* and philosophic discourse on the ultimate significance of the experience. In this poem Eliot repeats in effect and amplifies the passages in his essay on Dante. *Burnt Norton* opens with a statement of the co-existence of all times, the ever-presence of past and future. An implication of this is that the lost experience of the past and the desired experience of the future are in no way repetitions, but exist identically in the timeless reality that is possibly available at any actual moment. As the first section of the poem progresses, it is granted, perhaps ironically, that the experience may not have actually occurred, may be only imagined; yet it is significantly implied that the experience is a goal to which one might *return,* as if it should have happened but did not, through a fault of human nature.

> What might have been is an abstraction
> Remaining a perpetual possibility
> Only in a world of speculation.
> What might have been and what has been
> Point to one end, which is always present.
> Footfalls echo in the memory
> Down the passage which we did not take
> Towards the door we never opened
> Into the rose-garden. My words echo
> Thus, in your mind.
> But to what purpose
> Disturbing the dust on a bowl of rose-leaves
> I do not know.

Not having had the experience is comparable to a refusal of it; it is real for each of us, though we may not be awakened to that fact

—just as God may exist despite the opinion of a world of infidels. In the next passage a bird speaks, beckoning "Into our first world," leading excitedly to the experience. But this is the "deception of the thrush," the deception of phenomenal details which seem by association to recall the experience: the scene that follows is not genuine, but mechanical and devitalized; the music is "unheard" and "hidden"; privacy is spoiled by an "unseen eyebeam" and the roses have the "look of flowers that are looked at." The details of the situation have been forcibly willed—"as our guests, accepted and accepting." For an instant the dry concrete pool is filled, the lotus rises (with sexual significance). But the pool is "water out of sunlight," a mirage, and disappears when a cloud passes over. The effort is thus one of torment, disappointing in its partial and insufficient revelation. And yet, even in such attenuated form, an intimation of the hidden experience is an unbearable strain on the limited human capacity:

> Go, said the bird, for the leaves were full of children,
> Hidden excitedly, containing laughter.
> Go, go, go, said the bird: human kind
> Cannot bear very much reality.

The second section begins with a discourse upon the reconciliation of extremes; all oppositions ("forgotten wars"), all that seems disparate in life and in the universe, are finally discernible in a harmonious pattern which has issued from a single source. And this source is the "still point," describable only in paradoxical terms: "Neither from nor towards . . . neither arrest nor movement." It is comparable to, perhaps derives from, the point in *Paradiso*, XXIX, "where every *where* and every *when* is focused." In Dante's poem the point is at the center of the nine circles representing the blessed orders, and the point itself represents the creative love of God, as it does in Eliot's poem:

> I can only say, *there* we have been: but I cannot say where.

The "experience" is, thus, allied with the point and partakes of its quality:

> a grace of sense, a white light still and moving,
> *Erhebung* without motion, concentration
> Without elimination, both a new world
> And the old made explicit, understood

In the completion of its partial ecstasy,
The resolution of its partial horror.

This recalls the "terror" that follows the experience in *Gerontion*. And here again are the hardly bearable reality and the circumstantial details of the temporal world by which it can be approached:

Time past and time future
Allow but a little consciousness
To be conscious is not to be in time
But only in time can the moment in the rose-garden,
The moment in the arbour where the rain beat,
The moment in the draughty church at smokefall
Be remembered; involved with past and future.
Only through time time is conquered.

The third section presents a picture of the barrier to the conquest of time and a means by which this barrier may be overcome. The barrier is the spiritual desolation of the world; it is to be overcome by the purgational system of St. John of the Cross—the descent into darkness and "perpetual solitude"—stated in compressed form at the end of the section.

A symbolic expression of St. John's *Dark Night* opens the fourth section: the day has been buried and the sun obscured. There follows then an eager questioning, "Will the sunflower turn to us," asking in effect whether life, rebirth, will come to one who waits in the prescribed passivity of purgation. And the section ends with an answer:

After the kingfisher's wing
Has answered light to light, and is silent, the light is still
At the still point of the turning world.

The "kingfisher" I associate with the Fisher King of the *waste land,* which will be redeemed by a divine act. The passage thus means that there will be a rebirth when, through grace, the world is restored to contact with the "still point."

Many of the elements we have often observed so far are recapitulated in the final section of *Burnt Norton*. Spiritual aims, the timeless reality which is the beginning and end of all experience, are attainable only through discipline—"by the form, the pattern"—like the discipline of art. But the world presents a hindrance to discipline: "Shrieking voices . . . voices of temptation . . . The loud lament

of the disconsolate chimera." And the poem concludes reaffirming
the principle with which it began, the "one end, which is always
present":

> Desire itself is movement
> Not in itself desirable;
> Love is itself unmoving,
> Only the cause and end of movement,
> Timeless, and undesiring
> Except in the aspect of time
> Caught in the form of limitation
> Between un-being and being.
> Sudden in a shaft of sunlight
> Even while the dust moves
> There rises the hidden laughter
> Of children in the foliage
> Quick now, here, now, always—
> Ridiculous the waste sad time
> Stretching before and after.

A distinction is made here between appetitive pursuit and the spiritual
love which is the final "satisfaction" beyond temporal activity. The
"waste sad time" is all mortal time. This passage embraces the systematic range of Eliot's conceptual materials, from the childhood experience of the rose-garden to a religious and philosophic ideology.

One who is already familiar with the several aspects of this theme
would surely recognize them in Eliot's play, *The Family Reunion,*
even upon a first reading. Apart from the superficial structure of the
play—the action-plot and the family relationships—are distinguish-
able Harry's many remarks upon time, experience, and a special kind
of consciousness, remarks which all the family but Agatha consider
nonsense and insanity. As the play develops it becomes more and
more apparent that Harry's problem is not whether or not he murdered his wife, a moral problem, but a spiritual problem of longer
standing to which the murder is only incidental. And this is what
Harry finally discovers for himself. He is beset by a peculiar need,
one which his family and the world do not understand. This need is
the "experience," the advance toward spiritual rebirth and the peace
of religious love—variously represented throughout Eliot's poetry and
described in *Burnt Norton* as the "inner freedom from the practical
desire."

I shall take notice of several instances in the play which clearly echo the theme in terms which we have seen to be its most specific representation. The first of these is in the long conversation between Harry and Mary. They discuss their childhood, their most intimate attitudes; and to Harry's question—"Is the spring not an evil time, that excites us with lying voices?"—Mary responds with surprising sympathy and understanding:

> Pain is the opposite of joy
> But joy is a kind of pain
> I believe the moment of birth
> Is when we have knowledge of death
> I believe the season of birth
> Is the season of sacrifice . . .

And thus for a moment the "experience" is suggested to Harry:

> You bring me news
> Of a door that opens at the end of a corridor,
> Sunlight and singing; when I had felt sure
> That every corridor only led to another,
> Or to a blank wall . . .

But Mary's brief communion with Harry soon fails, and it remains for his aunt Agatha to lead him to the door of the rose-garden.

The climactic scene of the play is the long dialogue of Harry and Agatha, in which she tells him of the loveless and bitter relationship of his father and mother, of her own love for his father whom she prevented from killing his mother, and of her emotional attachment to Harry himself. Just before giving this information Agatha introduces the motif of the "experience":

> There are hours when there seems to be no past or future,
> Only a present moment of pointed light
> When you want to burn. When you stretch out your hand
> To the flames. They only come once,
> Thank God, that kind. Perhaps there is another kind,
> I believe, across a whole Thibet of broken stones
> That lie, fang up, a lifetime's march. I have believed this.

And after Agatha's account, Harry exclaims—

> Look, I do not know why,
> I feel happy for a moment, as if I had come home.

> It is quite irrational, but now
> I feel quite happy, as if happiness
> Did not consist in getting what one wanted
> Or in getting rid of what can't be rid of
> But in a different vision. This is like an end.

At this point I wish to refer to the penetrating study of *The Family Reunion* made by Mr. C. L. Barber, whose critical judgments I accept in large part. Mr. Barber presents an extremely interesting and persuasive criticism of the play from the psychoanalytic point of view. Yet I differ with his attitude that the play cannot be meaningfully interpreted except by this approach, which is illustrated by his comment on the verses just quoted:

> Just because statements like this cannot be otherwise understood, one must employ psychoanalytic interpretation to get at their content—interpretation, that is, appropriate to non-communicative, asocial psychic products. In pursuing the meaning of the play, gaps appear which cannot be bridged except by following out unconscious symbolic associations.

Mr. Barber's application of the psychoanalytic terms may be wholly accurate. But I think it is evident that passages such as the one on which he comments here *are* otherwise meaningful, and meaningful as the author consciously intended. It is true that one could hardly expect an audience or reader to grasp this meaning without a special preparation, a familiarity with its repeated occurrence throughout Eliot's work. If, however, one considers the play in the light of the already established continuity, the theme is no less understandable here than elsewhere. One so prepared would surely recognize the significance of the passage that comes toward the end of the dialogue between Harry and Agatha:

> *Agatha:* I only looked through the little door
> When the sun was shining on the rose-garden:
> And heard in the distance tiny voices
> And then a black raven flew over.
> And then I was only my own feet walking
> Away, down a concrete corridor
> In a dead air . . .
>
> *Harry:* In and out, in an endless drift
> Of shrieking forms in a circular desert . . .

*Agatha:* Up and down, through the stone passages
Of an immense and empty hospital . . .

*Harry:* To and fro, dragging my feet
Among inner shadows in the smoky wilderness . . .
I was not there, you were not there, only our phantasms
And what did not happen is as true as what did happen,
O my dear, and you walked through the little door
And I ran to meet you in the rose-garden.

*Agatha:* This is the next moment. This is the beginning.
We do not pass twice through the same door
Or return to the door through which we did not pass.
I have seen the first stage: relief from what happened
Is also relief from that unfulfilled craving
Flattered in sleep and deceived in waking.
You have a long journey.

The picture of agonized effort which is portrayed in the trance-like speeches of Harry and Agatha is that put upon one by the experience, the spiritual quest in an unsympathetic world. After the revelation by Agatha Harry is suddenly changed. Now he welcomes the presence of the Eumenides. Now it is clear to him that he "must go," that he must follow the "bright angels," which formerly he fled in horror. And thus once again Eliot invokes the paradoxical discipline of St. John's *Dark Night of the Soul.* We recall that the way to salvation begins in *Ash Wednesday* with spiritual and sensual debility, in *Burnt Norton* with the descent into darkness; and toward the end of the play it is stated in Harry's decisive words:

Where does one go from a world of insanity?
Somewhere on the other side of despair.
To the worship in the desert, the thirst and deprivation,
A stony sanctuary and a primitive altar,
The heat of the sun and the icy vigil
A care over lives of humble people,
The lesson of ignorance, of incurable diseases.
Such things are possible. It is love and terror
Of what waits and wants me, and will not let me fall.

As I have said, I agree with Mr. Barber's critical judgments. The play has serious failings. Most important among these, it seems to me, is the degree of obscurity in which Eliot keeps his most important symbols; and also, his failure to integrate fully action and motivation with the dominant theme. Except for Harry and Agatha, none of the characters realizes what is happening. The central character's existence in a world of his own, though he admits it, prevents a true dramatic situation. The other characters do not know this world and refuse to know it. The nearest they come to it is their impersonal statement in the final Chorus: "We do not like the maze in the garden, because it too closely resembles the maze in the brain." But Eliot's experiment was a bold one.

The theme, as we have followed it so far, appears in a peculiarly personal application, not related to subjects that are public and historical in the most common sense. In the earlier work the experience is simply portrayed, referred to, or reflected fragmentarily. And then in *Ash Wednesday, Burnt Norton,* and *The Family Reunion* it is developed conceptually and dramatically. In Eliot's most recent work, the poems which with *Burnt Norton* have been brought together under the title *Four Quartets,* we find the theme no less personal in its significance, but also recognizably and directly related to the social scene, the World Wars and present chaos; that is, the meaning of the theme is extended from the individual to society.

*East Coker* has been discussed with illuminating information and sound comment in an article by Mr. James Johnson Sweeney. As a brief supplement to Mr. Sweeney's interpretation I shall indicate the presence of the "experience" in *East Coker*. The first two sections of the poem are a commentary on the cycle of history, the Renaissance and the world today, with the conclusion that there is "only a limited value / In the knowledge derived from experience," that the only wisdom is humility. In Section III the darkness of the modern scene is equated with the spiritual darkness defined by St. John of the Cross: "let the darkness come upon you / Which shall be the darkness of God." Thus the darkness is a prefiguring of redemption: "the darkness shall be the light, and the stillness the dancing." And the redemption, the restoration to which purgation by humility and abjectness leads, is again represented by the "experience":

> Whisper of running streams, and winter lightning.
> The wild thyme unseen and the wild strawberry,
> The laughter in the garden, echoed ecstasy
> Not lost, but requiring, pointing to the agony
> Of death and birth.

>            You say I am repeating
> Something I have said before. I shall say it again.
> Shall I say it again? In order to arrive there,
> To arrive where you are, to get from where you are not,
>      You must go by a way wherein there is no ecstasy.

The fourth section represents the spiritual suffering by which Christian salvation is to be attained. The last section of *East Coker* is a personal statement of the effort for discipline that has been made, of the meager and humble result, and yet of determination to continue, despite the increasing difficulty of the times. And now, not the "experience" alone is seen as significant of the essential reality in which *beginning* and *end* are identical, but all life, all history:

> Home is where one starts from. As we grow older
> The world becomes stranger, the pattern more complicated
> Of dead and living. Not the intense moment
> Isolated, with no before and after,
> But a lifetime burning in every moment
> And not the lifetime of one man only
> But of old stones that cannot be deciphered.

The discourse on history and its relation to the "experience" and spiritual reality which was begun in *East Coker* is continued in *The Dry Salvages*. As in *East Coker*, the meaning of reality is extended beyond the experience:

> The moments of happiness—not the sense of well-being,
> Fruition, fulfillment, security or affection,
> Or even a very good dinner, but the sudden illumination—
> We had the experience but missed the meaning,
> And approach to the meaning restores the experience
> In a different form, beyond any meaning
> We can assign to happiness. I have said before
> That the past experience revived in the meaning
> Is not the experience of one life only
> But of many generations—not forgetting
> Something that is probably quite ineffable:
> The backward look behind the assurance
> Of recorded history, the backward half-look
> Over the shoulder, towards the primitive terror.

The "primitive terror" is represented in the poem by three principle symbols: the river, the ocean, and the rocks, all of which seem to be

controlled by secular civilization but which continue actually as
menacing and destructive. I have not space here to dwell upon the
full meaning of the ocean, except to indicate that, in its immense
shapelessness, it represents history as other than "sequence" and "development." It is thus already symbolical at the end of *East Coker:*

> We must be still and still moving . . .
> Through the dark cold and the empty desolation,
> The wave cry, the wind cry, the vast waters . . .

In *The Dry Salvages* the symbolism is continued with the representation as "seamen" of those who are to live into the future, and with
the exclamation to them, "Not fare well, / But fare forward, voyagers."
The final section of the poem repeats that the spiritual reality is ap-
proachable not alone in the ecstatic moment, but by a way of life:

> Men's curiosity searches past and future
> And clings to that dimension. But to apprehend
> The point of intersection of the timeless
> With time, is an occupation for the saint—
> No occupation either, but something given
> And taken, in a lifetime's death in love,
> Ardour and selflessness and self-surrender.
> For most of us, there is only the unattended
> Moment, the moment in and out of time,
> The distraction fit, lost in a shaft of sunlight,
> The wild thyme unseen, or the winter lightning
> Or the waterfall, or music heard so deeply
> That it is not heard at all, but you are the music
> While the music lasts.

And the poem ends affirming that life, even though it is short of
saintliness and lacks the given ecstatic moment, may be meaningful
and purposeful:

> And right action is freedom
> From past and future also.
> For most of us this is the aim
> Never here to be realized;
> Who are only undefeated
> Because we have gone on trying;
> We, content at the last
> If our temporal reversion nourish

(Not too far from the yew tree)
The life of significant soil.

The three poems which follow *Burnt Norton* all make reference to World War II. Whereas the theme in *Burnt Norton* is developed on an abstract level and with no indication of an application other than personal, in the other poems the meaning of the theme is enlarged, applied to particular events in history, and thus extended beyond the personal. This tendency is more pronounced in each succeeding poem, and is most fully developed in *Little Gidding*, which is also the poem which reflects the war most fully and most immediately. In *Burnt Norton* the "waste sad time" which stretches before and after the personal experience is called ridiculous. In *The Dry Salvages* not only the personal experience but "right action is freedom/ From past and future also." Thus all moments and all actions can be regarded as spiritually significant, as related to the timeless reality. In this sense, as it is stated in the final section of *Little Gidding*, "history is a pattern/ Of timeless moments. . . . History is now and England." And in the statement "The moment of the rose and the moment of the yew-tree/Are of equal duration," we see the rose garden theme related to time and history—for the yew-tree, symbolic of death, is also symbolic of eternity, in which the pattern of history exists.

With the closing lines of *Little Gidding* the experience in the rose garden is again clearly evoked:

Through the unknown, remembered gate
When the last of earth left to discover
Is that which was the beginning;
At the source of the longest river
The voice of the hidden waterfall
And the children in the apple-tree
Not known, because not looked for
But heard, half-heard, in the stillness
Between two waves of the sea.
Quick now, here, now, always—
A condition of complete simplicity
(Costing not less than everything) . . .

This passage is rich in symbols, themes and ideas which are the immediate materials of *Four Quartets,* and which can be followed back through all of Eliot's poetry. In this passage, as in the whole body of the poetry, the theme of the experience in the rose garden is of central significance. We begin to see a pattern that is both intricate and intelligible when we focus our attention on this point.

# JAMES JOHNSON SWEENEY *

$S$INCE its first appearance in the spring of 1940,[1] T. S. Eliot's *East
Coker* has been widely applauded as his most considerable poetic
achievement of the last eighteen years. Since the publication of *The
Waste Land* Eliot's use of literary allusion and adapted quotation has
become familiar and expected. In spite of this, with the publication of ·
*East Coker* in book form [2] we again began to hear criticisms and com-
plaints reminiscent of those which greeted *The Waste Land* two
decades ago.

In his essay "Tradition and the Individual Talent" republished
in *The Sacred Wood* (1920) we read: "the historical sense involves
a perception, not only of the pastness of the past, but of its presence."
Again in his introduction to Mark Wardle's translation of Valéry's
*Le Serpent* (1924) he wrote: "One of the qualities of a genuine poet
. . . is that in reading him we are reminded of remote predecessors,
and in reading his remote predecessors we are reminded of him."

Between the publication of these two statements *The Waste Land*
appeared, when the presence and necessity of notes provoked impa-
tience and censure on the part of many critics. But as I. A. Richards
put it in his *Principles of Literary Criticism:* "A more reasonable complaint would have been that Mr. Eliot did not provide a larger apparatus of elucidation."

But it appears that the reviewers are still reluctant to make the
effort to read him carefully before passing judgment on him. For
example, in *The New Statesman and Nation* of September 14, 1940,
we have such a perceptive critic as G. W. Stonier writing in the body
of a generally sympathetic review as follows:

> Again his [Eliot's] use of quotation, by which he so often im-
> parts a nostalgic flavour to his verse, has curious lapses. In *East*

* *East Coker: A Reading,* from *The Southern Review,* Vol. VI, No. 4,
pp. 771–791, Copyright, 1941, by Louisiana State University.
[1] London: *The New English Weekly,* March 20, 1940; New York: *Partisan Review,* May–June, 1940.
[2] London: Faber & Faber. One shilling.

*Coker* there are examples of both success and failure. The section beginning

> O dark dark dark. They all go into the dark,
> The vacant interstellar spaces, the vacant into the vacant,
> The captains, merchant bankers, eminent men of letters . . .

makes excellent use of a well-known passage in Samson ("Dark, dark, dark! The moon . . . hid in her vacant interlunar cave"). But how do the last lines of the following passage, delightful in its scene, strike the reader?

> In that open field,
> If you do not come too close, if you do not come too close,
> On a summer midnight, you can hear the music
> Of the weak pipe and the little drum,
> And see them dancing around the bonfire,
> The association of man and woman
> In daunsinge, signifying matrimonie—
> A dignified and commodious sacrament,
> Two and two, necessary conjunction,
> Holding eche other by the hand or the arm
> Whiche betokeneth concorde.

There the Elizabethan spelling imparts no flavour save perhaps one of pedantry; its only effect is to make us think, "Well, I suppose Eliot, when he wrote that, was thinking of passages in Spenser's Epithalamion." Yet obviously to Eliot the whiff of the antique has an immediate, an emotional effect, like the reminiscences of Haydn in Prokofieff's Classical Symphony. This is a purely literary failure . . .

Such a conclusion is an injustice. And it is particularly difficult to understand since Stonier concludes this sentence with the words: ". . . the more odd because of all poets Eliot is in certain directions the most precise in his effects."

A reader who has confidence in Eliot's precision that Stonier claims to have and is as familiar with Eliot's allusive technique, should not be satisfied to identify such a pointed emphasis on the archaic as a mere willful infusion of pedantry. He should endeavor to find what specific allusion is embodied in the passage and why the poet sought to underscore these lines in the text by setting them apart from the rest in archaic spelling. In Eliot's manner of doing it there is certainly no attempt at disguise or mystification. We are clearly invited to associate the lines with some specific feature of the literary past. And had Stonier seriously considered this point he would have had to look no further for a cue than the poem's title and the author's name.

Coker is a small village near Yeovil on the borders of Dorsetshire and Somersetshire in England, reputedly the birthplace of Sir Thomas Elyot (?–1546), the author of *The Boke named The Gouvernour* (1531). Chapter XXI of The Firste Boke is entitled "Wherefore in the good ordre of daunsinge a man and a woman daunseth to gether." And the opening paragraph of this chapter reads:

> It is diligently to be noted that the associatinge of man and woman in daunsing, they bothe obseruinge one nombre and tyme in their meuynges, was not begonne without a speciall consideration, as well for the *necessarye coniunction* of those *two persones,* as for the intimation of sondry vertues, whiche be by them represented. And for as moche as *by the association of a man and a woman in daunsinge may be signified matrimonie,* I coulde in declarynge *the dignitie and commoditie of that sacrament* make intiere volumes . . .

Then further along we come across a passage:

> In euery daunse, of a moste auncient custome, there daunseth to gether a man and a woman, *holding eche other by the hande or the arme, whiche betokeneth concorde.*

Here we have clearly the source of those lines. Their roots turn out to be Tudor not Elizabethan. And thanks to that "flavour of pedantry," or more exactly archaism, to which Stonier objects, one aspect of Eliot's approach to his theme in *East Coker* begins to take shape for us.

*The Boke named The Gouvernour* was one of the first of those works partly on politics, partly on education, which the study of the classics and more particularly that of Plato, multiplied at the end of the Renaissance throughout Europe. *The Gouvernour* has been described as the earliest treatise on moral philosophy in the English language.

Sir Thomas Elyot was an ardent monarchist, a scholar deeply influenced by the writings of such continental humanists as Pico della Mirandola and Erasmus, and a thorough churchman—at one time the intimate of Sir Thomas More, but always a loyal adherent to the Church of his sovereign. We are at once struck by the link between

Sir Thomas Elyot's interests and T. S. Eliot's famous declaration of faith as a "Classicist in literature, royalist in politics, and anglo-catholic in religion" which appeared in his 1928 preface to *For Lancelot Andrewes*. A common emphasis is apparent in the title of T. S. Eliot's essay *The Idea of a Christian Society* and Elyot's translation of Pico della Mirandola's *Rules of a Christian Life;* just as we find a community of viewpoint between T. S. Eliot's later poems and Sir Thomas Elyot's work entitled *Cyprianus, a Swete and Devoute Sermon of the Holy Saynt Cyprian on the Mortality of Man*.

Finally, a fundamental feature of Sir Thomas Elyot's interests was language—words in particular. He was very conscious of the poverty of the Anglo-Saxon of his time as compared with other languages and desired above all things to augment its vocabulary. In 1536 he undertook the compilation of a dictionary, the *Bibliotheca Eliotae* subsequently known as *Eliotes Dictionaire*. And from a purely linguistic viewpoint *The Gouvernour* may be regarded as a connecting link between the English of the time of Chaucer and the English of the time of Bacon. Its style for the period is peculiar; for many of the words or phrases it employed were even then going out of use, while, on the other hand, many new words are recognizable, apparently original importations.

We now see the picture beginning to arrange itself: a twentieth century Eliot, who feels he has certain spiritual links with a Tudor Elyot, communing with himself in the dark spring following the outbreak of the second world war within little more than two decades. Although Sir Thomas Elyot of Coker may have died without issue, there is a sufficient kinship in their interests to draw the contemporary Eliot to him in thought. Something is amiss with contemporary civilization, its mode of conduct or philosophy of life. The elder Elyot had tried through *The Boke named The Gouvernour* to suggest for his period a pattern of harmonious living and concord based on the Platonic ideals of the Renaissance. The younger man, faced by the darkness of the present moment, feels a certain irony in the parallels which he recognizes between his own interests and those of his precursor. In spite of all the confidence in intellectual progress of Sir Thomas Elyot's time, it is evident, today, that the neo-classical, individualist approach of the Renaissance led to a mechanical view and a spiritual poverty and produced the cataclysm which has overwhelmed the present age.

In my beginning is my end.

This is the theme which dominates the whole work. Like a musical phrase it is woven back and forth through the entire texture of the composition, now stated in one key of meaning, now in another.

The actual wording of the theme is possibly an echo of the inscription

En ma fin est mon commencement

embroidered upon the chair of state of Mary, Queen of Scots. In 1931 Maurice Baring published an historical study of the Scottish queen under this title. In his preface we read:

The title of this book needs some explanation. The inscription:

In my End is my Beginning

was the motto embroidered upon the Chair of State of Mary, Queen of Scots. This inscription perplexed Mr. Nicholas White, a friend of Cecil's, who, on his road to Ireland in the spring of the year 1569, paid a visit of curiosity to the Queen of Scots during her captivity at Tutbury, the house of the Earl of Shrewsbury.

He wrote as follows: "In looking upon her cloth of estate, I noticed this sentence embroidered: 'en ma fin est mon commencement,' which is a riddle I understand not" . . .

Baring continues:

Her motto was symbolic in more ways than one. Putting aside the question of whether the death of the Queen of Scots was, as some think, the triumph of a martyred saint awaiting canonization in the future, or a consummate piece of playacting, there is no doubt that practically and politically the end of the Queen of Scots was her beginning; for at her death her son, James Stuart, became heir to the crowns of England and Scotland and he lived to wear both crowns.

A more remote source of the theme, yet a source which has been rich in suggestion for so much of Eliot's mature poetry, is the philosophical remains of Heraclitus of Ephesus. For example here we read:

The beginning and the end are common. [LXX]
Fire lives in the death of earth, air lives in the death of fire,

water lives in the death of air, and earth lives in the death of water. [XXV]

Throughout the poem we find this theme given two contrasting interpretations: a spiritual one, and a material or temporal one. In the spiritual interpretation the "beginning" is seen as that "highest type of knowledge—the intuition of pure being" which Christopher Dawson regards as "the starting point of human progress" in his study *Progress and Religion;* and man's end—goal or purpose—is the knowledge of the Divine Order, or God, which can only come by intuition, through love. The material or temporal interpretation stresses the cyclic nature of history, the temporality of material achievement, and the mortality of man in the spirit of the admonition: "Remember, man, that thou art dust and unto dust thou shalt return."

These two interpretations of the dominant theme are played back and forth until their final combination in that victorious reversal of the introductory statement that closes the poem:

In my end is my beginning.

I

Man as a physical being has his cycle of life; its opening predicates its close.

Like every other form of animal life man is the creature of environment, heredity and function. "Consequently his culture is not an abstract intellectual construction, but a material organization of life, which is submitted to the same laws of growth and decay, of 'generation and corruption,' as the rest of the material world." [Christopher Dawson, *op. cit.,* p. 74] As in Heraclitus' view, all is one eternal flux, all is involved in ceaseless round of life, death, growth, and decay. The Logos, the element of law or order, is the only stable factor in the ever shifting world:

> . . . In succession
> Houses rise and fall, crumble, are extended
> Are removed, destroyed, restored . . .

Houses—whether the term be taken literally to signify buildings, the material components of a village such as Coker, or figuratively, as dynasties—houses rise and fall, houses live and die.

> . . . there is a time for building
> And a time for living and for generation
> And a time for the wind to break the loosened pane
> And to shake the wainscot where the field-mouse trots
> And to shake the tattered arras woven with a silent motto.

In the passing of Mary Queen of Scots, we see the fugitive character of temporal glory and we have its symbolization in the fluttering of the tattered arras embroidered with her motto.

To Eliot, as he looks back from the dark moment after the outbreak of a new, disillusioning war, the village of Coker in its association with Sir Thomas Elyot represents a beginning—the beginning of a period which had looked forward idealistically and hopefully to a future of intellectual achievement and conquest. You can still imagine Sir Thomas Elyot's ideal dancers in their dance "around the bonfire" symbolizing human harmony and concord, yet at the same time reminding us, through "the rhythm of their dancing," of the laws of growth and decay, of generation and corruption—

> Eating and drinking. Dung and death.

And the poet is brought back to the reality of the present. For that period is completely behind us,

> Dawn points, and another day
> Prepares for heat and silence.

All that survives, from the period just closed, on which we can hope to build for the future, is what that period already had at its outset— "the intuition of pure being."

> Out at sea the dawn wind
> Wrinkles and slides. I am here
> Or there, or elsewhere. In my beginning.

II

So what has the present day to do with these hopes of a younger time? Eliot asks himself in the opening lines of the second section

> What is the late November doing
> With the disturbance of the spring
> And creatures of the summer heat . . . ?

In these "sproutings" of

> That corpse you planted last year in your garden,

we feel an echo of *The Waste Land* and a renunciation of the earlier attitude of that poem and of *Gerontion*.

> Do not let me hear . . .

The pattern and content of these poems he sums up in the first seventeen lines of Section II of *East Coker,* with subtle echoes of their rhythms and imagery. Late November, like *The Waste Land*'s "winter dawn," now hears "thunder rolled by the rolling stars . . . whirled in a vortex that shall bring" the world, eventually, through fire, as preached in the "Fire Sermon," and through devastation to "the peace that passeth understanding," even as *The Waste Land* saw this prefigured in

> The sound of horns and motors, which shall bring
> Sweeney to Mrs. Porter in the spring

But "the poetry does not matter." To start again is the important thing. As Christopher Dawson says in *Progress and Religion*: ". . . intellectually, at least, man's development is not so much from the lower to the higher as from the confused to the distinct." The materialist approach did not help us to this. In spite of Sir Thomas Elyot's enthusiasm, zeal and optimism, things did not work out as they were expected to. The autumn of civilization did not bring the serenity and calm that was expected. Did those quiet-voiced elders, such as Sir Thomas Elyot and the Renaissance leaders, deceive us more with their confidence in man and his powers of intellectual achievement, or the despairful author of *Gerontion?*

> There is, it seems to us,
> At best, only a limited value
> In the knowledge derived from experience.
> The knowledge imposes a pattern, and falsifies,
> For the pattern is new every moment.

For in the Heraclitean saying, no man ever bathes twice in the same stream, just as we may speak of the ever-changing bather the stream receives. Or according to the late F. H. Bradley, for whom Eliot has long had a great admiration: If views are dependent on needs and needs are culturally and individually determined, the whole Universe seems too subject to the individual knower. What is given counts for so little and the arrangement counts for so much, while in fact the arranger, if we are to have real knowledge, seems so dependent on the world. But the individual who knows is here wrongly isolated, and then, because of that, is confronted with a mere alien Universe. And the individual, as so isolated, I agree, could do nothing, for indeed he is nothing. My real personal self which orders my world is in truth inseparably one with the Universe. Behind me the absolute reality works through and in union with myself, and the world which confronts me is at bottom one thing in substance and in power with this reality. There *is* a world of appearance and there *is* a sensuous curtain, and to seek to deny the presence of this or to identify it with reality is mistaken. But for truth I come back always to that doctrine of Hegel, that "there is nothing behind the curtain other than that which is in front of it."

Again we read in Eliot's 1939 essay *The Idea of a Christian Society:*

. . . so long as we consider "education" as a good in itself . . . , without any ideal of the good life for society or for the individual, we shall move from one uneasy compromise to another. To the quick and simple organization of society for ends which, being only material and worldly, must be as ephemeral as worldly success, there is only one alternative. As political philosophy derives its sanction from ethics, and ethics from the truth of religion, it is only by returning to the eternal source of truth that we can hope for any social organization which will not, to its ultimate destruction. ignore some essential aspect of reality.

In other words, the solution is clearly not through the accumulation of encyclopaedic knowledge in accord with the ideal of the Renaissance, or a scientific exploration of our physical world in keeping with that of the last two centuries, but through a return to the beginning—through the intuition of pure being—to the eternal source of truth. The increase of human knowledge only brings us the satisfaction of feeling ourselves undeceived

Of that which, deceiving, could no longer harm.

At the same time the passionate pursuit of material knowledge which has characterized the last five centuries of European history has steadily more and more discouraged any interest in spiritual values.

As a result we find ourselves today like Dante in the opening lines
of the *Inferno:*

> In the middle of the journey of our life
> I found myself in a dark wood,
> having lost the straight path.

"Life has become" for us, as it had for Dr. Watson in A. Conan
Doyle's *The Hound of the Baskervilles,* "like that great Grimpen
Mire, with little green patches everywhere into which one may sink
and with no guide to point the track." And Eliot has both these pictures in mind when he sees himself in *East Coker*

> In the middle, not only in the middle of the way
> But all the way, in a dark wood, in a bramble,
> On the edge of a grimpen, where there is no secure foothold,
> And menaced by monsters, fancy lights,
> Risking enchantment.

And in this predicament after depending so long on the misleading
advice and the empty promises of our elders, Eliot resolves that we
should put aside all notions of "the wisdom of old men." "Do not
let me hear" he writes, "Of the wisdom of old men, but rather of
their folly . . . ," which is their vanity. In reality they are nothing
more than infinitesimal details of the Divine pattern. And their notion of their importance as individuals, their dread of losing their
imagined spiritual autonomy—their fear "of belonging to another, or
to others or to God" is only another heritage of the Renaissance individualist approach. At best it is merely the wisdom of the children of
this world in their generation—a short-term wisdom. For if we face
facts frankly we will realize that

> The only wisdom we can hope to acquire
> Is the wisdom of humility: humility is endless.

This is especially clear today when we consider the emptiness of
the material civilization we have so long adulated. It was a dream, a
delusion even as Eliot's present-day vision of Sir Thomas Elyot's
dancers. And in the concluding lines of Section II of *East Coker* Eliot
caustically underscores its fragile passing with a parody of the line
of Stevenson's "Requiem": "Home is the sailor, home from the sea,/
And the hunter home from the hill"—

The houses are all gone under the sea.
The dancers are all gone under the hill.

### III

The third section of the poem opens on this note—the darkness in which the disappearance of these illusions has left the world:

Oh dark dark dark. They all go into the dark,
The vacant interstellar spaces, the vacant into the vacant,
The captains, merchant bankers, eminent men of letters,
The generous patrons of art, the statesmen and the rulers,
Distinguished civil servants, chairmen of many committees,
Industrial lords and petty contractors, all go into the dark,
And dark the Sun and Moon, and the Almanach de Gotha
And the Stock Exchange Gazette, the Directory of Directors,
And cold the sense and lost the motive of action.
And we all go with them . . .

In the present world-crisis Eliot sees illustrated the broader spiritual problem which faces us. In his editorial valedictory "Last Words" in the final issue of *The Criterion*, January, 1939, he wrote: "The period immediately following the war of 1914 is often spoken of as a time of disillusionment: in some ways and for some people it was rather a period of illusions." And in the concluding paragraph of *The Idea of a Christian Society* published in the autumn of 1939, we read:

I believe that there must be many persons who, like myself, were
deeply shaken by the events of September 1938; persons to whom
that month brought a profounder realization of a general plight
. . . a feeling of humiliation which seemed to demand an act
of personal contrition, of humility, repentance and amendment;
a doubt of the validity of a civilization . . . Was our society,
which had always been so assured of its superiority and rectitude,
so confident of its unexamined premises, assembled round anything more permanent than a congeries of banks, insurance com-
panies, and industries, and had it any beliefs more essential
than a belief in compound interest and the maintenance of
dividends?

And in this context—its association with the present eclipse of such formerly powerful sources of information as the Almanach de Gotha, the Stock Exchange Gazette and the Directory of Directors—the line

And cold the sense and lost the motive of action

affords a subtle, ironic commentary through an echo it brings us of the line from Swinburne's "The Last Oracle" (*Poems and Ballads—Second Series*): "Dark the shrine and dumb the fount of song thence welling."

To Milton's Samson the darkness in his eyes was a source of lamentation:

> O dark, dark, dark, amid the blaze of noon,
> Irrecoverably dark, total Eclipse
> Without all hope of day!

To Eliot, on the contrary, the first closing-in of darkness brings promise of a sounder road to truth and enlightenment. We already had a suggestion of this in the echo of Vaughan's "Ascension Hymn"—

> They are all gone into the world of light!

—in the first line of Section III:

> O dark dark dark. They all go into the dark.

The clearing away of material, distracting ambitions, the blacking-out of the "fancy lights," open a way to the poet to return to his beginning—to "the starting point of human progress, the intuition of pure being."

> I said to my soul, be still, and let the dark come upon you
> Which shall be the darkness of God.

For the poet, this darkness is the darkness of the Isa Upanishad:

> Into blind darkness enter they
> That worship ignorance;
> Into darkness, as it were, greater
> They that delight in knowledge.
> Other, indeed, they say, than knowledge!
> Other, they say, than non-knowledge!

It is the transitional stage between periods—Jung's *Night Journey* of the Rebirth Pattern—with a suggestion of the present war in the possible ambiguity of interpretation afforded by the "hollow rumble of wings":

As, in a theatre,
The lights are extinguished, for the scene to be changed
With a hollow rumble of wings, with a movement of
                        darkness on darkness . . .

But from a spiritual viewpoint such a darkness and such a realization
of the emptiness of material achievement awaken in Eliot above all
thoughts of *The Dark Night of the Soul,* that passive night, that intense purification with which God, according to St. John of the Cross,
visits the soul. To such as desire purification St. John of the Cross
says:

> Advice must be given to learn to abide attentively and to pay
> no heed either to imagination or its workings; for here, as we
> may say, the faculties are at rest, and are working not actively
> but passively by receiving that which God works in them.

And in this spirit Eliot tells us

> I said to my Soul, be still, and wait without hope
> For hope would be hope for the wrong thing; wait without love
> For love would be love of the wrong thing; there is yet faith
> But the faith and the love and the hope are all in the waiting.
> Wait without thought, for you are not ready for thought:
> So the darkness shall be the light, and the stillness the dancing.

In the first half of this line we hear once again an echo of Milton's
*Samson:*

> O first created Beam, and thou great Word,
> Let there be light, and light was over all;
> Why am I thus bereav'd thy prime decree?

And in the concluding clause—"And the stillness the dancing," another echo of Sir Thomas Elyot of Coker: "There daunseth to gether
a man and a woman, holding eche other by the hande or the arme,
which betokeneth concorde."

To recover purity of vision, which must not be regarded as hope-
lessly lost, we must learn from nature the need of undergoing

the agony
Of death and birth

—that is to say "rebirth"—a return through the agony of death (near
at hand for "old men") to "the beginning," "the intuition of pure

being." The way to this, according to Eliot, is St. John of the Cross'
*Dark Night of the Soul* as we have it explained in the concluding
lines of Section III:

> In order to arrive there,
> To arrive where you are, to get from where you are not,
> You must go by a way wherein there is no ecstasy.
> In order to arrive at what you do not know
> You must go by a way which is the way of ignorance.

And it is clear that Eliot wants the source of these lines to be
readily recognizable in order that his reference may enjoy the advantage of all the accumulated commentary and explanation linked
to St. John of the Cross' mystical philosophy. We can see this from
the closeness with which he makes them echo a translation of the
saint's own words:

> ——In order to arrive at having pleasure in everything,
> Desire to have pleasure is nothing . . .
> ——In order to arrive at a knowledge of everything,
> Desire to know nothing.
> ——In order to arrive at that wherein thou hast no pleasure,
> Thou must go by a way wherein thou hast no pleasure.
> ——In order to arrive at that which thou knowest not,
> Thou must go by a way that thou knowest not.
> ——In order to arrive at that which thou possessest not,
> Thou must go by a way that thou possessest not.
> ——In order to arrive at that which thou art not,
> Thou must go through that which thou art not.

This is clearly not defeatism or apathy. Nor is it a philosophy of
escape such as so many critics are constantly seeing in Eliot's writings.
To these, Agatha, in Eliot's *Family Reunion* (Part II, Scene II), has
already replied in her answer to Amy's taunt—"So you *will* run
away,":

> In a world of fugitives
> The person taking the opposite direction
> Will appear to run away.

Stonier, in his review of *East Coker,* writes that Eliot "having abjured
ecstasy, allows himself to fall into a mental trance." What Eliot actually advocates is far from an apathetic passivity. In *Ash Wednesday*
he prayed

Teach us to care and not to care
Teach us to sit still.

But "to sit still" in the sense advocated by St. John as a necessary step to spiritual purgation. For Eliot feels with St. John of the Cross, that we must undergo not only the mortification of the flesh by *The Ascent of Mount Carmel* but also the trial of *The Dark Night of the Soul,* before we can hope for that perfect union of the soul with God in love, and for the divinization of all our faculties described by St. John of the Cross in *The Spiritual Canticle* and *The Living Flame of Love.*

Then in summing up his conclusions from the advocated approach of St. John of the Cross, Eliot returns in the last three lines of Section III to Heraclitus, "The Dark"—the unity of opposition, the harmony of strife:

And what you do not know is the only thing you know
And what you own is what you do not own
And where you are is where you are not.

For among the Heraclitean fragments we read

The unlike is joined together, and from differences results most beautiful harmony, and all things take place by strife. [XLVI]

It is this Heraclitean note combined with echoes of the seventeenth century English metaphysical poets which will characterize the entire following section of the poem.

### IV

There, in the opening lines, the poet sees Christ, with His hands bleeding from the nail wounds, as the wounded surgeon in a similar light to that in which Pascal sees Him: "Jesus suffers in His passions the torments which men inflict on Him; but in His agony He suffers the torments He inflicts on Himself." [*Pensées,* No. 552] And at the same time in these lines we have another echo of Heraclitus:

The physicians, therefore, . . . cutting and cauterizing, and in every way torturing the sick, complain that the patients do not pay them fitting reward for thus effecting these benefits—and sufferings. [LVIII]

The soul, according to St. John of the Cross, during *The Dark Night* is "under medical treatment for the recovery of its health, which is God Himself." The steel that questions the distempered part is God's love; for, as St. John of the Cross describes it in the *Living Flame of Love:* ". . . the soul will be conscious of an assault upon it made by a seraph armed with a dart of most enkindled love, which will pierce the soul . . ." Still the compassion of the Surgeon is always evident. For the soul "amidst these gloomy and loving pains, is conscious of a certain companionship and inward strength which attends upon it." [*The Dark Night of the Soul*]

"Our only health is our disease" since the soul must suffer "that it may become meet for the divine love." The constant care of God "is not to please," "for as God sets the soul in this dark night to the end that He may quench and purge its sensual desire, He allows it not to find attraction or sweetness in anything whatsoever."

Furthermore, "To be restored, our sickness must grow worse" for only through the most complete suffering can we hope for complete purgation.

Throughout all these stanzas we see the Heraclitean play of opposites persevering. But an echo which this line brings up gives us another key to the undercurrent thought of this section: the vital need to put aside the blinding, confining interests of the body and of the world. For here, rhythm and figures both are clearly intended to recall those of Marvell's "A Dialogue between the Soul and the Body" in which the soul complains of its imprisonment in the confining flesh:

> Soul:    O Who shall, from this Dungeon, raise
> A Soul inslav'd so many wayes? . . .
> Here blinded with an Eye; and there
> Deaf with the drumming of an Ear . . .
> Constrain'd not only to indure
> Diseases, but what's worse, the Cure:
> And ready oft the Port to gain
> Am Shipwrackt into Health again.

"The whole earth is our hospital, endowed by ruined millionaire," Adam, with original sin. As T. E. Hulme put it in a passage quoted by T. S. Eliot in his introduction to Baudelaire's *Journaux Intimes,* "in the light of these absolute values, man himself is judged to be essentially limited and imperfect. He is endowed with Original Sin."

The cure is a fever cure—through the fever of love which is kindled in burning away impurities until the ascending chill will bring a calm similar to that which will be brought into the world by

> that destructive fire
> Which burns before the ice-cap reigns.

The purgation must grow from a purgation of the flesh to a purgation of the mind.

> The chill ascends from feet to knees,
> The fever sings in mental wires.

We are reminded of the "trilling wires of the blood" in *Burnt Norton*. But here the experience has to do with the spirit rather than with the flesh. And we remember that Eliot feels that "the great mistake made about Christianity is to suppose it primarily a religion and emotion when it is primarily dogma and intellectual." [*The Idea of a Christian Society*]

Suffering is the basis of our cure—a penetential suffering and a thorough period of trial. We try constantly to blind ourselves to the need for humility and penance with notions of the importance of man and with materialistic emphases—

> . . . we like to think
> That we are sound, substantial flesh and blood

—but at bottom we recognize the necessity of penance, and the fact that even our own penance would be feeble without the divine atonement made by Christ on our behalf. This is the reason that we ". . . call this Friday good"—the day on which the anniversary of Christ's sufferings is observed. And just as we saw Eliot in *Ash Wednesday* commemorating a victory over the temptation in the wilderness and announcing his spiritual entrance upon a penitential period, this Good Friday note in *East Coker* celebrates the culmination of suffering and purgation, and an anticipation of the Resurrection to the light.

### v

So now the poet feels, "here I am, in the middle way," returning to his earlier echo of "nel mezzo del cammin." He feels lost in the dark wood

> . . . having had twenty years—
> Twenty years largely wasted, the years of *l'entre deux guerres*—
> Trying to learn to use words.

He has come to feel with Pico della Mirandola, one of the exemplars of his precursor, Sir Thomas Elyot, that:

> We shall live for ever, not in the school of word-catchers, but in the circle of the wise, where they talk not of the mother of Andromache or of the sons of Niobe, but of the deeper causes of things human and divine; he who looks closely will see that even the barbarians had intelligence not on the tongue, but in the breast.

In *Burnt Norton,* Eliot had already expressed a similar sentiment:

> Words move, music moves
> Only in time; but that which is only living
> Can only die. Words, after speech, reach
> Into the silence.

But, in the opening chorus of *The Rock,*

> The endless cycle of idea and action,
> Endless invention, endless experiment,
> Brings knowledge of motion, but not of stillness;
> Knowledge of speech, but not of silence;
> Knowledge of words, and ignorance of the Word.

Again in *Burnt Norton:*

> . . . Only by the form, the pattern,
> Can words or music reach
> The stillness, as a Chinese jar still
> Moves perpetually in its stillness . . .

Today the poet has come to realize that each venture in "trying to learn to use words" is merely

> . . . a new beginning, a raid on the inarticulate
> With shabby equipment always deteriorating
> In the general mess of imprecision of feeling,
> Undisciplined squads of emotion.

He feels with Heraclitus that

> It is a weariness to labour at the same things and to be always beginning afresh. [LXXXII]

Emotion in Eliot's opinion is primarily a contributor of confusion. In *The Idea of a Christian Society* we read, "It is not enthusiasm, but dogma, that differentiates a Christian from a pagan society." And Eliot feels with T. E. Hulme, whom he quotes substantially in the closing paragraph of his preface to Baudelaire's *Journaux Intimes,* that a man "can only accomplish anything of value by discipline— ethical and poetical. Order is thus not merely negative, but creative and liberating. Institutions are necessary." Emotion upsets order. The lack of order, or discipline overwhelmed by emotion, only throws us back "into the general mess of imprecision of feeling." Whenever and wherever this occurs, according to Eliot, ground is lost. What there is to conquer

> By strength and submission, has already been discovered
> Once or twice, or several times, by men whom one cannot hope
> To emulate . . .

Or in Heraclitus' words: "Much learning does not teach one to have understanding, else it would have taught Hesiod and Pythagoras, and again Xenophanes and Hecataeus." [LVI]

> There is only the fight to recover what has been lost
> And found and lost ᵔgain and again: and now, under conditions
> That seem unpropitious. But perhaps neither gain nor loss.
> For us, there is only the trying. The rest is not our business.

Humility outweighs individualism and material achievement. In the end it is only "the still point" of which *Burnt Norton* spoke which matters.

> . . . there the dance is,
> But neither arrest nor movement. And do not call it fixity.
> . . . Except for the point, the still point
> There would be no dance, and there is only the dance.
> I can only say, *there* we have been: but I cannot say where.
> And I cannot say, how long, for that is to place it in time.

With the opening line of the second half of Section V we have a restatement of the main theme in a new wording

> Home is where one starts from

But

> As we grow older
> The world becomes stranger, the pattern more complicated
> Of dead and living. Not the intense moment
> Isolated, with no before and after,
> But a lifetime burning in every moment
> And not the lifetime of one man only
> But of old stones that cannot be deciphered.

We are assailed increasingly by distractions and interests of the world about us, whereas

> Love is most nearly itself
> When here and now cease to matter.

"Old men ought to be explorers": they should not be satisfied with the world at hand, but be ready to "put off the old man and put on the new." Whether we are

> Here and there does not matter

—for love, according to St. John of the Cross, "is like a fire, which ever ascends, hastening to be absorbed in the centre of its sphere." [*The Dark Night of the Soul*]

> We must be still and still moving
> Into another intensity
> For a further union, a deeper communion.

As Pascal urged [*Pensées,* No. 524] "there must be feelings of humility, not from nature, but from penitence, not to rest in them, but to go on to greatness,"—

> Through the dark cold and the empty desolation,
> The wave cry, the wind cry, the vast waters
> Of the petrel and the porpoise.

For, even now,

> Dawn points, and another day
> Prepares for heat and silence. Out at sea the dawn wind
> Wrinkles and slides.

"In my end is my beginning."

# C. L. BARBER *

IN *The Family Reunion* Mr. Eliot has attempted for the first time to dramatize the issues which concern him without the support of the visible forms of his faith. His task in the theater has been the extraordinarily difficult one of presenting the action of redemption to audiences for the most part unconvinced that such an action exists. In *The Rock* and *Murder in the Cathedral,* he sought to mitigate the gap between himself and his audiences by staying within the church, writing about church issues for church audiences. This procedure permitted him to "assume some moral attitude in common with his audience" and so avoid in a measure the didacticism of imposing his assumptions. But the effect of staying within the church was also to make his productions special, as the precincts of the church are special for the general modern public. The public at large beat a path, it is true, to *Murder in the Cathedral.* But most of them went as sightseers, ready to forget their own standards when these were burlesqued in the murderers' Erastian apologies, but in a spirit which regarded as historical not only the events, but also the Christian values and standards of the play. In *The Family Reunion* Eliot has deliberately made impossible any such facile acceptance of the reality of the supernatural. He has sought to confront the modern world with the necessity of redemption at its starkest, without benefit of clergy. Christian terms are virtually excluded from both action and verse; the intention is to have the Christian view of man's condition emerge from a commonplace setting of secular modern life. The difference between a natural and supernatural view of man's destiny is put squarely in the middle of the action—not, as before, on the periphery, where it could be left by the audience in abeyance, outside their experience of the play.

Eliot's purpose in cutting away all traditional props is illuminated

* *Strange Gods at T. S. Eliot's "The Family Reunion"* from *The Southern Review,* Vol. VI, No. 2, pp. 387–416, Copyright, 1940, by Louisiana State University.

by his remarks about the relation of Baudelaire's Satanism to traditional Christianity:

> He is beginning, in a way, at the beginning; and being a discoverer, it is not altogether certain what he is exploring and to what it leads; he might almost be said to be making again, as one man, the effort of scores of generations. . . . His business was not to practice Christianity, but—what was much more important for his time—to assert its *necessity*.

The exclusion of Christian terms in *The Family Reunion* is part of an effort to begin again at the beginning, at the point where the decay of faith has left modern men. Eliot's hero, Harry Lord Monchensy, is represented as the uncertain and tormented discoverer, "making, as one man, the effort of scores of generations." The Eumenides who pursue and finally confront him are intellectually appropriate to embody what he discovers, since they are symbols conceived before the birth of Christ as the supernatural agents of retribution. To assert "the necessity" of Christianity, the dramatist presents his hero in the grip of the irrational dread and horror of life which naturalistic thought regards as characteristic of neurotic maladjustment. Like a neurotic, Harry is chained to a past which, as he says, "is always present," and which destroys his life; and like a neurotic, he is subject to the "instinct to return to the point of departure." These motives bring him back home to "Wishwood," in search of illusory childhood satisfactions, after he has broken free from the exile of a disastrous marriage by murdering his wife. Once back home, his intensely hostile relations with his mother conform to what might be called the Orestes variant of the Oedipus pattern—where the son's attachment leads not to incest, but to matricide. Eliot is very much aware of the part which the Oedipus pattern has played in modern naturalistic thought about the issue of freedom and determinism. In adapting the Greek original to his own view of life, he puts all his emphasis on the supernatural element which naturalism ignores or reinterprets. When the Furies appear to Harry, their objective presence is intended to reveal that the ground of his anguish is not a complex, "not something inside me," but a curse. Although at first they seem to be pursuing him for the murder of his wife, this concrete and personal source of guilt proves illusory. The Furies follow Harry not for what he himself has done, but for a sin of his father, the origin of the curse under whose compulsion the hero has acted. In this supernatural predicament, Harry discovers the necessity of Christianity, for resolution can come only by accepting an original sin which was not his own, but his father's, only by following the Furies instead of seeking to escape in flight. The intention is thus to show that what in natural terms appears complete neurotic failure, involving the destruction of wife and mother, is really "a kind of preparation" for crossing the boundary to "the other side of despair."

If to employ a fully elaborated Christian framework for a drama today is to assume too much with audiences for whom the Christian tradition is something external, the highly intelligent scheme of *The Family Reunion* suffers disastrously from the complementary difficulty that the author can rely on no living tradition whatever. To represent religion "at the beginning," the dramatist undertakes the job of virtually creating a religious symbolism. Ancient Greece is too far away to contribute more than a mere blank pattern for the Eumenides. And to succeed, Eliot's scheme requires him to make his apparitions seem more real than the contemporary setting from which they incongruously emerge. His failure is extremely interesting as an example of what can happen when, in the absence of support from society, an artist tries to do everything himself. The play's defects are all the more interesting and revealing because Eliot is so very competent and honest a craftsman. One can see the consequences of his social isolation working themselves out in spite of his art. The technical defects seem to me to go back to such causes, and I shall try to show them in that light. Fundamental among them is the split between the modern setting and the supernatural action, between Harry and "the family," which Mr. Francis Fergusson pointed out in his brilliant comments on the play as theater in a recent *Southern Review*. This cleavage is the difference between Eliot and his times, become part of the play instead of remaining outside, as it did when he stayed within the church. Its artistic consequences extend right through the work, and include the defects of the verse.

The lack of any basis in social behavior for the religious symbols accounts further for a fundamental failure to control them: their significance as religious symbols is not made to grow satisfactorily out of their immediate emotional content. Their religious meaning remains either impractically abstract, or vague and obscure, a matter of dark hints and fugitive suggestions; Eliot strikingly fails to make it dramatically and emotionally intelligible. On the other hand, the feeling about the Eumenides which he does make artistically objective fails to coalesce with their supernatural significance. Whenever Harry's anguished horror at them actually comes through the verse, it is, concretely, a horror of *being looked at*. This irrational and apparently arbitrary feeling can be understood if the Furies are recognized as symbols in an exhibitionistic fantasy latent in the play. They turn out to correspond exactly to the *voyeurs* in the typical nightmare of nakedness which Freud has described in *The Interpretation of Dreams*.

This element in the play raises interesting and fundamental questions about the use of such symbols in poetry and drama. In the view of the matter I shall try to work out, it is not an objection to artistic or religious symbols that they draw support from unconscious impulses which many psychologists classify as sexual. To point out this support does not of itself compromise their objective validity. On the contrary, living religious traditions and living poetry get much of their strength by being able to include such impulses in a common way of feeling and acting and so use them to reinforce human values. What *is* fatal for an artist is to use irrational symbolic significance without making it a part of a socially meaningful action, without drawing it up into the regions of life men have in common. In so far as a writer does this, his production is really asocial, like a dream—a work of fantasy rather than a work of art. The decay of religious tradition—the lack of forms at once symbolic and social—has of late led inward writers in this asocial direction, under such banners as that of Surrealism. I think that in *The Family Reunion* Eliot has gone the same way in spite of his concern for orthodoxy, and that this has happened because, to use his own terms, there was no living tradition or social "way of feeling and acting" about the Eumenides to help control their irrational significance. The latent exhibitionistic fantasy which attaches to them is asocial and unacceptable, and so must withdraw from direct expression even while seeking to assert itself. Its presence largely explains the artistic failure. It also explains the astonishingly ruthless and unchristian way that its hero pursues his destiny. From the standpoint of orthodoxy, the Eumenides prove to be Strange Gods: their revelation is antinomian heresy which places their follower above social morality. That their author created them is explicable only because society makes the motive they serve unconscious, so that he could not know them for what they are.


2


First to define the play's artistic deficiencies, before offering a psychological explanation for them. Eliot's failure adequately to objectify the religious significance of the Eumenides can best be approached by examining the structure of contrasts running through the play. To dramatize the difficulty of beginning at the beginning, he constantly emphasizes the incongruity of Harry's encounter with the supernatural, the difference between the reality which confronts him and his ordinary material surroundings. The fatuous aunts and uncles who are at the family reunion serve to dramatize this difference by their timid and helpless incomprehension of what is really happening; and Harry's constant unsuccessful attempts to explain to them the grounds of his obsession emphasize his helplessness. The use of this kind of contrast constitutes a return to the structure which Eliot adopted to handle the same motif of obsession in the unfinished *Sweeney Agonistes* of fifteen years ago. The line from the *Choephoroi* which served as an epigraph for *Sweeney:* "You don't see them, you don't —but *I* see them . . ." is spoken almost verbatim by Harry just after his first entrance. Doris, Dusty, Krumpacker, and the rest, who "don't see them" in *Sweeney,* have been replaced in the new play by the much more genteel family, but the family serves the same purpose in the author's effort to get a kind of ghost story effect from the apparition of spiritual reality.

Eliot himself explained, in *The Use of Poetry,* how in *Sweeney* this structure was an attempt to solve the problem of writing for a heterogeneous audience, most of whom would not be aware of the higher levels of spiritual significance the dramatist wanted to put across. In this connection he advanced his now familiar theory of levels of significance to account for Shakespeare's broad appeal:

> For the simplest auditors there is the plot, for the more thoughtful the character and conflict of character, . . . and for the auditors of greater sensitiveness and understanding a meaning which reveals itself gradually.

In his experiment with *Sweeney,* his intention

> was to have one character whose sensibility and intelligence
> should be on the plane of the most sensitive and intelligent mem-
> bers of the audience; his speeches should be addressed to them
> as much as to the other personages in the play—or rather, should
> be addressed to the latter who were to be material, literal-minded
> and visionless, with the consciousness of being overheard by the
> former. There was to be an understanding between this pro-
> tagonist and a small number of the audience, while the rest of
> the audience would share the responses of the other characters in
> the play. Perhaps this was all too deliberate, but one must experi-
> ment as one can.

On reflection, this plan appears to be an extraordinary way to attempt
to solve the problem Eliot has so well stated. Such a discontinuity of
levels really works counter to the aim of including the whole audience: most of the audience by the author's deliberate plan are not expected to understand the protagonist! Much in Shakespeare's plays,
it is true, must escape the less sensitive auditor, or any auditor at first
hearing. But in Shakespeare this higher meaning is latent in the concrete plot, clustered about a hard core of action from which it emerges
but from which it can never be detached. In Eliot's scheme, on the
contrary, the higher meaning is set over against the obvious and
tangible surroundings. The irrelevance for Eliot of what in the
modern world is tangible and obvious is in the last analysis what
makes such an opposition necessary. The visible life and the traditions
of Shakespeare's time provided him with materials for plots at once
obvious to the simplest auditor and capable of containing the play-
wright's higher meanings. Eliot's meaning cannot in this direct
fashion find a body in contemporary life and symbols, with the result that when he uses a modern setting he must set spiritual in
opposition to material. As it works out in *The Family Reunion,* what
is material remains insignificant, while what is spiritual is not adequately objectified. And the dramatizing of the opposition amounts
at times to dramatizing the writer's difficulty of expression, his difficulty in making "spiritual" meaning concrete. His isolation from
the greater part of his audience becomes part of the play as the isolation of his protagonist from its "visionless" characters.

Lacking a core of meaning, the husk which constitutes the setting is inert and purposeless.

A curse is written
On the under side of things
Behind the smiling mirror
And behind the smiling moon. . . .

In his scenes of manners, the author holds the mirror up to nature merely to provide something which the Reality of the curse can break through. The trick, however, is obvious, because he does not succeed in making plausible characters whose *raison d'etre* is to be unreal. Each is endowed with an Individual Characteristic which each exhibits in a self-trivializing fashion. There are the back-biter, the silly-sweet flower lover, the London Clubman with a girl buried somewhere in his past—and Uncle Gerald, the retired Anglo-Indian, who performs as follows when Harry confronts the family:

HARRY:  But how can I explain, how can I explain to *you*?
You will understand less after I have explained it.
All that I could hope to make you understand
Is only events: not what has happened.
And people to whom nothing has ever happened
Cannot understand the unimportance of events.

GERALD:  Well, you can't say that nothing has
happened to *me*.
I started as a youngster on the North
West Frontier—
Been in tight corners most of my life
And some pretty nasty messes.

Clubman Uncle Charles then remarks that there isn't much that would surprise or shock *him*. If these background figures had been kept consistently on a highly conventional level, they might perhaps have been put across as a species of Eliot's "here-we-go-round-the-prickly-pear" macabre. Unfortunately, however, the shift up the social scale from Doris, Klipstein, and the rest, who don't understand Sweeney, to "the family," who don't understand Harry, goes with a shift from the traditions of music hall entertainment to those of English parlor drama. The stock cast of Piccadilly is too debilitated even to support burlesque. Moreover, Eliot is at cross-purposes about burlesque: he wants his setting to *seem* real, blandly and prosaically normal, so he cannot afford to let his audience laugh it out of existence. To make it plausible, he keeps a realistic base to his action, and includes a great deal of circumstantial elaboration of the parlor drama variety: country-constable, family doctor, parlor-maid, etc. Perhaps sections of a London audience, accustomed to mistake parlor drama for reality, could be expected to make the same mistake about the family's reunion. It would then come as a dramatic shock to hear Harry repeatedly tell aunts and uncles that they do not really exist. For others there can be no shock to the explosion of an Appearance so obviously made of theatrical straw.

One even feels a certain indignation at the high-handed treatment of these fussy maiden aunts and bumbling uncles, because Eliot is continually taking advantage of them. He dismisses them as unreal without ever having created them. They are even made to dismiss themselves, in choruses like the following, spoken while waiting for Harry to arrive home:

### Chorus
Why do we feel embarrassed, impatient, fretful, ill at ease,
Assembled like amateur actors who have not been assigned their parts?
Like amateur actors in a dream when the curtain rises, to find themselves dressed for a different play, or having rehearsed the wrong parts,
Waiting for the rustling in the stalls, the titter in the dress circle, the laughter and catcalls in the gallery?

### Charles
I might have been in St. James's Street, in a comfortable chair rather nearer the fire.

### Ivy
I might have been visiting Cousin Lily at Sidmouth, if I had not come to this party.

### Gerald
I might have been staying with Compton-Smith, down at his place in Dorset.

### Violet
I should have been helping Lady Bumpus, at the Vicar's American Tea.

### Chorus
Yet we are here at Amy's command, to play an unread part in some monstrous farce, ridiculous in some nightmare pantomime.

A tedious quotation is necessary to show how the verse gets nowhere. It is obviously written to fill a void: the details evoke no total reality, but merely the abstract classifications from which they have been selected; elaboration proceeds through intellectual rather than imaginative connections, notably in the baldly systematic analysis of the audience's amusement. The monstrous farce might have saved the play, but of course it is never staged; there is not enough energy for such goings-on. Instead, what we get is the random bit about Lady Bumpus, which is characteristic of most of the comedy in the play. There is no social satire, because there is no social standard of value, but only the standard furnished by the Eumenides. The tendency of the humor is simply to dismiss its object.

Some of the choruses by the aunts and uncles are better than this. But throughout, the basic trouble with both their futility and their fatuity is that neither is felt with pathos. In Eliot's poems, Uncle Gerald and the others would be part of the crowd which flowed over London Bridge, "so many, I had not thought death had undone so many." He has often expressed the state of spiritual death they represent in images charged with pity and disgust:

> . . . the strained time-ridden faces
> Distracted from distraction by distraction. . . .
>
> Men and bits of paper, whirled by the cold wind. . . .
>
> Eructation of unhealthy souls
> Into the faded air. . . .

In the attempt to elaborate stage personalities to fill the "twittering world" thus described in *Burnt Norton,* the informing emotion has disappeared: no cold wind whirls Uncle Gerald. The elaboration has only got in the poet's way, because the social details it involves are not relevant to what he wants to express, and so his imagination cannot dominate them. The verse in the scenes of manners suffers accordingly—not from lack of control, but from lack of anything to control. He frequently uses, in a rather restrained way, the technique of organizing his verse rhythms by units corresponding to breath impulses, which worked so well in some of the choruses of *Murder in the Cathedral:* "Clean the air! clean the sky! wash the wind! take stone from stone and wash them. . . ." The feeling necessary to support such rhythms is lacking in much of the new play, however, with the result that the poetry often has a sighing, tired quality, the lines ending in a gratuitous dying fall. And the iteration of key words which characterizes much of this type of verse occurs frequently when what is re-echoed is of no significance. Although the diction is never pretentious, the presence of such excess of form over content, unobtrusive but pervasive, leaves one with a feeling of being clogged with unevacuated language—a feeling which accumulates almost unnoticed from passages like this:

> GERALD: Even so, we don't want Downing to know
> Any more than he knows already.
> And even if he knew, it's very much better
> That he shouldn't know that we knew it also.

While the insignificance of the material setting enervates its expression, when the verse strives to express the significant issues at the heart of the play, it suffers from the failure to embody the spiritual action in immediate dramatic terms. Isolated as he is, the hero has to express the crucial reality of the play almost single-handed, aided only by the cryptic remarks of his Cassandra-like Aunt Agatha. They stand in the middle of the parlor, while what matters remains behind the mirror. Hence to reach the real issues, the discourse must move away from the immediate circumstances in which it is spoken instead of rising out of them. The contribution of the dramatic situation is merely negative, to emphasize by its irrelevance or unimportance the difficulty of communicating what really matters. The result is that much of the best poetry is not dramatic poetry, and suffers from the lack of a dramatic context to give it precision and receive its impact. For example, in the episode between Harry and his cousin Mary, Harry jumps off into space in passages like this:

> What I see
> May be one dream or another; if there is nothing else
> The most real is what I fear. The bright colour fades
> Together with the unrecapturable emotion,
> The glow upon the world, that never found its object. . . .

The fact that Harry is speaking to Mary does not greatly matter. The necessary context must be gathered from afar through the characteristically veiled allusion to the Eumenides. Like many similar allusions, this dark hint is probably impractical on the stage, for the Furies have not yet appeared to the audience. But more important

still is the indeterminateness which afflicts even such good poetry as
this because of the lack of specific dramatic reference. Harry gives
his spiritual autobiography in a number of similar passages. They
express spiritual or emotional *states,* not actions, and the framework of
the play merely occasions them and obscures their real relation one
to another, which is like that of analogous passages in the poems.

The material setting does serve one purpose: by insisting on its
unreality Harry can express indirectly the intensity of what is real
for him. We have already heard him telling the family that they can
understand "only events, not what has happened." When a motor
accident prevents his younger brother John from arriving at the reunion, the family's concern gives Harry occasion to remark that

> A minor trouble like a concussion
> Cannot make very much difference to John.
> A brief vacation from the kind of consciousness
> That John enjoys, can't make very much difference
> To him or to anyone else. If he was ever really
>     conscious,
> I should be glad for him to have a breathing spell:
> But John's ordinary day isn't much more than
>     breathing.

Out of its context, this may sound like kidding the kid brother, but
Harry is fully in earnest. When his relatives rebuke him for his lack
of feeling, he continues with

> It's only when they see nothing
> That people can always show the suitable emotions—
> And so far as they feel at all, their emotions are
>     suitable.
> They don't understand what it is to be awake,
> To be living on several planes at once
> Though one cannot speak with several voices at once.
> I have all of the rightminded feeling about John
> That you consider appropriate. Only, that's not
>     the language
> That I choose to be talking. I will not talk yours.

This is a taste of Harry's social feeling—a ruthless impulse to eliminate
other people because he finds their irrelevant presence exasperating. It
is obviously intended to be in excess of any provocation furnished

by John, the excess serving to convey the pressure of the supernatural facts Harry faces. This indirect method of expression is easily worn out, however, and Eliot uses it with a wanton persistence which suggests that some of Harry's exasperation is his own. The fact that the same dismissing tendency appears in the handling of the aunts and uncles strengthens this impression that the writer has failed to keep an objective attitude towards his hero. Instead he slips over into identifying himself with Harry's point of view, affirming Harry's values instead of dramatizing Harry's state of mind. So too with the hero's constant insistence that what he knows and feels is inexpressible: one cannot avoid feeling that the protagonist is voicing the frustration of his creator. Harry makes literally dozens of remarks like:

> I talk in general terms
> Because the particular has no language. . . .
>
> O, there *must* be another way of talking
> That would get us somewhere. . . .
>
> Do you think that I believe what I said just now? . . . .
> I was talking in abstractions: and you answered
> in abstractions.

This device of turning the artistic process back upon itself soon reaches a point of diminishing return. Of course, one of the things Eliot wants to convey is just the difficulty of communicating the terrible fact of supernatural retribution his hero is discovering. But he does not give his audience an adequate point of vantage outside Harry, with the result that they are as uncertain as the hero about "what he is discovering and to what it leads."

One is reminded of Eliot's remarks in *Hamlet and his Problems* about the lack of an objective correlative in *Hamlet:*

> Hamlet (the man) is dominated by an emotion which is inexpressible, because it is in *excess* of the facts as they appear. And the supposed identity of Hamlet with his author is genuine to this point: that Hamlet's bafflement at the absence of an objective equivalent to his feelings is a prolongation of the bafflement of his creator in the face of his artistic problem. Hamlet is up against the difficulty that his disgust is occasioned by his mother, but that his mother is not an adequate equivalent for it; his disgust envelops and exceeds her. . . . And it must be noticed that the

very nature of the *données* of the problem precludes objective
equivalence. To have heightened the criminality of Gertrude
would have been to provide the formula for a totally different
emotion in Hamlet; it is just *because* her character is so negative
and insignificant that she arouses in Hamlet the feeling which
she is incapable of representing.

All this acute criticism applies directly to *The Family Reunion*. Eliot
has deliberately set out "to express the inexpressibly horrible," the
"intense feeling, ecstatic or terrible, without an object or exceeding its
object," which he felt to be the underlying emotion in Hamlet. He remarked in passing that this feeling "is doubtless a subject of study for
pathologists"—with an ironic suggestion that pathologists in general
and Ernest Jones in particular are off the point. In attempting in his
latest play what "proved too much" for Shakespeare, he evidently
thought that he had discovered in the Eumenides the objective equivalent Shakespeare lacked, just as he has himself found in the Christian supernatural the object of this intense feeling without a human
object. He relies on the Eumenides to escape the dilemma he so accurately formulates. It is "they" who are to embody Harry's torment
adequately:

> If I tried to explain, you could never understand . . .
> There is only one way for you to understand
> And that is by seeing.

But, as Mr. Fergusson remarks, these Furies are "figments" "whom
no carpenter, no electrician could show us as anything but fake."
Their significance must be conveyed by Harry, but it is just their
significance which he is never able to state. One can note in passing
that whereas Shakespeare's play is saved because Hamlet is a man
in society, a prince who acts a great part in high events, Eliot's Harry
exists only in those inward regions where Eliot found Hamlet's problems.

The Eumenides fail as an objective correlative because Harry's
relation to them exists exclusively on a symbolic level which cannot
be adequately dramatized in social terms. The relation of a man with
the Christian God can be made dramatic because, whatever its symbolic content, the church and tradition give it a form analogous to a
social relation, and it has consequences in physical behavior among
men. Becket's decision among the tempters issues in action: "UNBAR

THE DOORS!" and the blood which follows. Harry's decision to follow the Furies can be conceived only as a new disposition of the soul. His mother's downright "where are you going?" is an awkward question; he can answer nothing but

> I shall have to learn. That is still unsettled.
> I have not yet had the precise directions.
> Where does one go from a world of insanity?
> Somewhere on the other side of despair.
> To the worship in the desert, the thirst and deprivation,
> A stony sanctuary and a primitive altar,
> The heat of the sun and the icy vigil,
> A care over lives of humble people,
> The lesson of ignorance, of incurable diseases.
> Such things are possible. It is love and terror
> Of what waits and wants me, and will not let me fall.
> Let the cricket chirp. John shall be the master.
> All I have is his. No harm can come to him.
> What would destroy me will be life for John. . . .
> I must follow the bright angels.

The family conclude from this that Harry is going to be a missionary: "A missionary! That's never happened in our family!" Harry tells them, once more, that they are off the point; but this does not cover up the circumstance that, after all, no physical destination has been provided for him. The poetry suffers, characteristically, from having to avoid the concrete. The weak assertion: "Such things are possible," is quite unconvincing, for the suggestions about "thirst and deprivation," the "lesson of incurable diseases" and the rest are no more than suggestions. They seem to be thrown out almost grudgingly, because people will ask questions. As always when Harry is talking to the family, he protects himself by a kind of spiritual *snobisme* which scorns to explain, since

> All that I could hope to make you understand
> Is only events: not what has happened.

"What has happened" never does become fully clear, because Eliot has not found "a chain of events which shall be the formula of that particular emotion" he wants to express.

3

If the resolution of the play is a wish-fulfillment of impulses which cannot be openly expressed, since they have no accepted place in social life, this would explain the failure to represent them in concrete social events. It would also explain the hero's resistance to making a final explanation, in spite of the fact that he himself cannot leave his obsession alone. To get at "the underside of things" in the play, it will be necessary to make an analysis, somewhat bald and laborious, first of the irrational content of Harry's encounter with the Furies, and then of his relations with his family. On the manifest or explicit level of the play, much that I shall investigate is shrouded in doubt and beset with ambiguities. Harry himself repeatedly insists on the irrational character of what he is experiencing: "Look," he says to his Aunt Agatha,

> . . . I do not know why,
> I feel happy for a moment, as if I had come home.
> It is quite irrational, but now
> I feel quite happy. . . .

Just because statements like this cannot be otherwise understood, one must employ psychoanalytic interpretation to get at their content—interpretation, that is, appropriate to noncommunicative, asocial psychic products. In pursuing the meaning of the play, gaps appear which cannot be bridged except by following out unconscious symbolic associations. If objectivity had been achieved, such analysis would be superfluous or merely supplementary. Unfortunately, psychoanalytic methods and thought, developed from the treatment of illness, carry the presumption about art that it is *all* simply a neurotic by-product, that the final reality behind it is an individual deficiency. Actually, however, a fully successful literary work is not subject to analytic reduction from a manifest meaning to latent personal "intentions," because these are fully expressed at a social level: to explore them can enrich but cannot undercut the work as it stands. The analytical approach is perverse when employed to explain away artistic success; but resentment at the abuse of it should not blind us to its usefulness in explaining certain kinds of artistic failure. This is the case when failure results not from a deficiency of properly expressive powers in the artist, but from the unacceptable character of what he wants to express. Thus with Eliot's play, if we can get at the underlying content, we can explain why the work is uncommunicative in the light of a conflict of latent and manifest meanings. This does not involve pursuing the origin of these meanings in the biography of the author, for what concerns us is in the play. It does not matter for criticism what particular life experiences, perhaps not overt at all, lie behind a typical symbolic structure which recurs again and again; and in any case only the individual's free associations could bring these to light. Nor need we explore the difficult question just how far Eliot was conscious of what he was doing: one can be conscious of the same thing in so many different ways, differently at different times, and under so many different names.

I cannot pretend to apply psychological concepts to the play with full accuracy, or to reconcile contradictions between current schematizations of the neurosis with which psychologists themselves are struggling. But the neurotic characteristics are there, and despite the blurred edges of theoretical systems they are worth describing because their artistic consequences are so interesting. One can see merely "by inspection" that *The Family Reunion* attempts to express two socially incompatible motives without sacrificing either, according to the pattern Dr. Karen Horney has made familiar in *The Neurotic Personality of Our Time*. On the one hand, the action is the vehicle for hostile impulses towards wife and mother, and towards the world in general as represented by the family. Yet on the other, the representation is also arranged to satisfy the need to feel secure while being hostile. In Harry, the neurotic necessity of finding reassurance and safety is finally achieved by being perfect and by being loved. Harry is provided with a higher destiny to justify his superior hostility; and at the reunion he rediscovers in his Aunt Agatha a "real" mother who gives him her affection and approval. Remorse and repentance might resolve the conflict of these motives towards hostility and perfection, but remorse is appallingly lacking in Eliot's predestined hero. Although Harry suffers in general, he does not suffer for *his* sins: to do so would involve renouncing the underlying hostility. The absence of remorse is thus a measure of the neurotic contradiction in the play, and also of the involuntary immorality which is implicit in the neurotic demand to have one's cake and eat it too. If one agrees with

Dr. Horney, as I do, that such neurotic character is socially determined and maintained, then one can add that the real criticism of the society which produced Harry is not what he says about it, but what he is within it.

However, this judgment is contingent upon what one makes of the Eumenides, for their function is precisely to justify Harry's ruthlessness, and to shift the hero's guilt from himself to the compulsion of "the curse upon the house." If Eliot had made this curse fully intelligible, my argument would have to be metaphysical: does or does not such supernatural compulsion exist? As the play stands, however, the unintelligibility of the curse and the Furies who convey it forces us to look for unconscious symbolic meanings, and these reveal the Eumenides to be elements in a fantasy which supports the contradictory social impulses we have noticed.

A crucial statement which leaves us up in the air when taken at face value is Harry's remark when he decides to follow the Furies:

> I know that you are ready,
> Ready to leave Wishwood, and I am going with you.
> You followed me here, where I thought I should
> escape you—
> No! you were already here before I arrived.
> Now I see at last that I am following you. . . .

What do we know on a manifest level to make this "discovery" intelligible? The Eumenides are already at Wishwood, and Harry has been following them, because they embody the curse upon the house. Harry has just learned of the curse from his Aunt Agatha. Its origin is in the sin of his dead father, who violated a loveless marriage with Harry's mother, Amy, under the compulsion of a deep passion for Agatha. This sin of Agatha and his father, together with his father's sin of intention to kill Amy, is what Harry must expiate. In some fashion which is never made explicit, the sin has haunted his life: indeed, the failure of his life by ordinary standards has been "a kind of preparation for something else," an unconscious pursuit of his purgatorial destiny. When I describe thus directly how the Furies are represented as visiting the sin of the father on the son, I can give no conception of the fragmentary, abstract and riddling way this is conveyed in the play. The pattern is something that must be reconstructed from dark hints. The nearest thing to a direct expression of it, and one of the very few passages where the curse comes to the surface, occurs in a speech of Agatha's more than a hundred lines before Harry's cryptic remarks to the Furies, when she says,

> What we have written is not a story of detection,
> Of crime and punishment, but of sin and expiation.
> It is possible that you have not known what sin
> You shall expiate, or whose, or why. It is certain
> That the knowledge of it must precede the expiation.
> It is possible that sin may strain and struggle
> In its dark instinctive birth, to come to consciousness
> And so find expurgation. It is possible
> You are the consciousness of your unhappy family,
> Its bird sent flying through the purgatorial flame.

Here again, as with Harry's account of his destination, the poetry withdraws from committing itself fully: the repetition of "it is possible" acts to protect what Agatha says from being taken at full value. Yet this is all we get to make intelligible Harry's crucial remarks about the Eumenides. Most of the scene preceding their apparition is about something apparently quite unrelated—his reunion with his aunt. Moreover, although the whole necessity of purgation springs from the evil of his father's sin, this is never presented so that we feel it as evil; on the contrary, its "dark instinctive birth" has an ambiguous fascination. This fact is crucial, because we could feel the action of the curse to be valid *only* if this sin which is its source were felt to be immediately present, here and now, unredeemed and requiring redemption.

Confronted with the failure to make explicitly or emotionally intelligible Harry's remark that he now sees he has really been following the Furies while he thought he fled from them, we can look for an explanation in a symbolic emotional significance which has not been made explicit. If the Eumenides have the symbolic character of *voyeurs* in an exhibitionistic dream or fantasy, and if Harry's experience corresponds to that of the dreamer, then his at once fleeing and pursuing them can be understood as ambivalence. At one level, to be looked at by them is horrible; at another deeper level, it is something which he seeks. Before the decision to follow them, the anguish alone is expressed in consciousness, while the positive element is repressed, appearing only in his obsession with the pursuers—the "grip" they have on him. Because their attraction is repressed, they seem to come from outside, independent of the will; in fact Harry's repeated insistence that they *are* outside is a way of confirming the repression. Freud describes this ambivalence in connection with his discussion of exhibition dreams: "According to our unconscious purpose, the exhibition is to proceed; according to the demands of the censorship, it is to come to an end." The anguish or embarrassment felt by the dreamer is "the feeling of inhibition." It represents "the reaction . . . to the fact that the exhibitionistic scene which has been condemned by the censorship has nevertheless succeeded in presenting itself." With Harry's decision to pursue the Eumenides, the positive element of his ambivalent attitude emerges into consciousness in the recognition that he has been following them all along. His decision itself consists in accepting the subconscious wish; the impulse to exhibitionism is fulfilled symbolically by following the Furies. With the decision goes a reintegration of Harry's personality which can now be understood. The conflict between the perverse or infantile impulse and the social morality requiring its repression has been resolved *by embracing the perversion*. Of course this can be done only because the Furies are elevated and spiritualized, and their subconscious content is heavily disguised. The opposition of society reappears, however, in Harry's otherwise superfluous self-justification and his conviction that he cannot be understood. His exalted though vague imperative justifies him in dismissing his family and the claims of his antipathetic, "material" mother, who dies when her hopes of a "normal" life for him collapse.

The specific symbolic content of the Eumenides must be submerged when they have become bright angels whom Harry is following; it can come closer to the surface when he is pursued, because then the conscious emotion of horror serves as a disguise. It is in these encounters that the experience of being looked at is made concrete, as nothing else in the relation is, in sensuous imagery. Eliot has dramatized Harry's entrance very effectively by arranging that the family should be sitting in the drawing-room after dusk with the curtains still open. When Harry enters he *"stops suddenly at the door and stares at the window,"* catching a glimpse of his pursuers. His first words are:

> How can you sit in this blaze of light for all
>       the world to look at? . . .
> Do you like to be stared at by eyes through a
>       window?

From Aeschylus's line, "—but I see them: they are hunting me
down . . ." Eliot omits the notion of physical violence and substitutes
"but I see them, And they see me." The poetry which expresses this
feeling about being seen is distinguished by a special quality of its
own from the staple verse of the play:

> In Italy, from behind the nightingales' thicket,
> The eyes stared at me, and corrupted that song.

The constrained but intense quality of this, its combination of an un-
emotional form of statement with a substratum of strong feeling, recurs later, more desperately, when the Eumenides first directly confront Harry:

> I tell you, it is not me you are looking at,
> Not me you are grinning at, not me your
>       confidential looks
> Incriminate, but that other person, if person,
> You thought I was: let your necrophily
> Feed upon that carcass.

It is notable that when the avengers actually appear their character is
not that of avengers. Their grinning and their confidential, incrimi-
nating looks suggest rather partners in an illicit relationship from
whom the hero struggles to disassociate his conscious personality.

Freud observes that the spectators in a dream of exhibition are
never very clearly defined: instead of presenting the actual spectator
who was the "object" of the infantile sexual experience revived in the
dream, the censorship substitutes "a number of strangers" who, like
Harry's Furies, remain individually vague. Behind these substitutes,
however, free association reveals a particular person to whom the still
active but repressed impulse became attached in childhood. In the
dream the association of the experience with childhood can take the
form of the dreamer's returning home, or being at home, when the
exhibition situation intervenes. When Harry returns home, he actually finds this particular person in Agatha: the real reunion, the
reunion which is not "a cheat," is with her, and with the Eumenides

who are her symbolic substitutes. With Agatha Harry resumes the
child's status, and in this relation rediscovers the tenderness of mother
and son. Agatha and Amy, the two most fully realized characters in
the play, constitute figures of the mother at different times or on different levels of consciousness. Strong-willed and uncomprehending,
Amy is Harry's mother *now*, in the "hither world" of waking life.
Harry is given occasion to describe in retrospect how she sought to
impose a "normal" life on her son without giving him up; she has at
once preserved and frustrated his unresolved attachment and so con-
verted it from love to exasperated antagonism. But Agatha is his
mother *then*, as she was in childhood, and as she still exists in the
region of consciousness where the "curse" has its operation:

> . . . in the night time
> And in the nether world
> Where the meshes we have woven
> Bind us to each other.

The scene immediately preceding the final decision to follow the
Furies is a discovery scene, in which Harry finds *now* his mother of
*then*. Reunion brings

> . . . relief from that unfulfilled craving
> Flattered in sleep, and deceived in waking.

Harry gains strength from Agatha to follow the Furies. It is
notable that this dream mother understands his decision and says repeatedly, "You must go." Amy, by contrast, cannot comprehend the
necessity of his mission and regards it as running away. Agatha steps
into the empty window embrasure after the Eumenides have left it,
to recite, in a trance-like state, a lyric which concludes

> O my child, my curse,
> You shall be fulfilled:
> The knot shall be unknotted
> And the crooked made straight.

Although she herself cannot be represented as the partner in this fulfillment, she for a moment literally takes the place of her symbolic
substitutes, and she is made to approve the pursuit of them. Shortly
afterwards, she and Amy square off in a fight over the question of

Harry's leaving. Agatha's aloof references to a spiritual necessity which "in this world . . . is inexplicable" baffle Amy and justify Harry: his mother *then* is set in victorious opposition to his mother *now*. Before he goes it is made clear that his departure will result in Amy's death, but he "must go," so that in the end the mother who opposes following the Furies is destroyed by a sort of spiritual stab in the back.

The scene with Agatha would be sentimental if Eliot had simply presented the fulfillment of a longing to return to home and mother; but the necessary incompleteness of this longing, the pathos of the relation of son and mother, is also objectified in the action as the sin of Agatha and Harry's father. This sin, by exiling Agatha from Harry's childhood home, has been what has kept her from him during the long years when both have suffered from their separation. An equivalent is thus provided for the limitation which in fact prevents the consummation of a son's attachment to his mother, the sense of guilt involved in his desire to take his father's place in her affections. No overt physical desire need, of course, be involved. We can understand the ambiguous fascination of the curse, which acts as a bond between Harry and Agatha at the same time that it keeps them apart, if we recognize that the guilt involved in it has been thus *displaced* in the dramatic representation. It is in fact the guilt attaching to the son's relation with the mother—or to the Eumenides, her substitute, who as we noticed are horrible to Harry as the partners rather than the avengers of a crime. By being displaced upon the father, the sin is made sufficiently external to Harry's feelings for Agatha so that these feelings need not be inhibited. It is more respectable to inherit guilt than to make it. Of course an objective supernatural causation is assumed in the curse. But precisely this causation is never made intellectually or emotionally comprehensible. Instead, what the scene makes us feel is the flow of tenderness which goes with Agatha's revelation of the sin and her recognition of Harry as his father's successor. The sin is what they have in common.

The compulsive influence ascribed to the curse also serves to lighten Harry's burden of guilt for the murder of his wife. At his first entrance, he describes to the horrified family how his marriage has been a destructive experience from which he had sought to escape—

For a momentary rest on the burning wheel
That cloudless night in the mid-Atlantic
When I pushed her over.

His account of his experience in marriage:

The partial anaesthesia of suffering without feeling
And partial observation of one's own automatism
While the slow stain sinks deeper through the skin . . .

is a description of a man whose feelings of tenderness have been
fixated by an earlier attachment. The marriage relation consequently
becomes an "automatism" which only aggravates his sense of guilt.
Although it seems at first that the Eumenides are pursuing Harry for
this crime of murder, what we have said already about their symbolic
relation to his fixation suggests that they are really the cause rather
than the result of his getting rid of his wife.[1] And this fact, that they
are the cause, is precisely what Harry learns when he discovers that
he has really been following them. This discovery can act as a release
from guilt only, of course, because "they" and the curse are represented as a higher order of reality outside Harry. By this higher interpretation, the murder has only been a recapitulation, under the
stress of supernatural compulsion, of the action of his father in de-

---

[1] The Furies stand in the way of love in another connection also, for they
intervene just as Harry is establishing a relation with his childhood playmate
Mary, whom he finds at home. Mary is the "hyacinth girl," or *la figlia che
piange,* in the play: the continuity of Eliot's key scenes and personages was
underlined by Eliot himself when he had her enter on the London stage actually
carrying hyacinths. The scene between Mary and the hero, when the trembling
possibility of love is cut off by the Eumenides, appeared in *The Waste Land* as:
"You gave me hyacinths first a year ago;
"They called me the hyacinth girl."
—Yet when we came back, late, from the Hyacinth garden,
Your arms full, and your hair wet, I could not
Speak, and my eyes failed, I was neither
Living nor dead, and I knew nothing,
Looking into the heart of light, the silence.
*Oed' und leer das Meer.*
"The heart of light" reappears in the crucial childhood "moment in the rose
garden" of *Burnt Norton,* which is quoted below. It is another symbol of the
infantile motive which reasserts itself just when adult fulfillment appears pos-
sible.

siring to kill Amy. Indeed, to get rid of her has been a necessary step in pursuing his destiny, however construed: at the same time that it releases the Furies to follow him, it releases him to follow the Furies.

The scene with Agatha is the most moving and the most dramatic in the play, because in getting back to childhood Harry gets back into a positive relation with other people. There are moments when he can express himself by responding with feeling instead of describing his feelings; and the significance of his general reflections can at last be felt in relation to a specific dramatic context. At the climax of reunion, Agatha tells him how she intervened to prevent his father from killing Amy, because "You were due in three months time," and

> I did not want to kill *you!* . . .
> If that had happened, I knew I should have carried
> Death in life, death through lifetime, death in my womb.
> I felt that you were in some way mine!
> And that in any case I should have no other child.

HARRY:   And have me. That is the way things happen.
> Everything is true in a different sense,
> A sense that would have seemed meaningless before.
> Everything tends towards reconciliation
> As the stone falls, as the tree falls. And in the end
> That is the completion which at the beginning
> Would have seemed the ruin.
> Perhaps my life has only been a dream
> Dreamt through me by the minds of others. Perhaps
> I only dreamt I pushed her.

AGATHA:      So I had supposed. What of it?
> What we have written is not a story of detection,
> Of crime and punishment, but of sin and expiation.
> It is possible that you have not known what sin, . . .

Reconciliation "as the tree falls" takes significance from what is happening, from the circumstance that Harry is returning to a child's status. Yet even here there is an evasive quality about the poetry which comes, in the last analysis, from the latent content it conveys. After Harry's gesture of feeling in "And have me," a resistance intervenes to force the poetry up to the level of general reflection. The climax of wish-fulfillment is to turn the tables by imposing the character of a dream on all the failures of waking life. Harry's "Perhaps I only dreamt I pushed her" has led some reviewers to conclude that his crime, like his father's, was only in intention. But the play will not bear this construction: Eliot goes to some trouble to furnish independent testimony from Harry's valet that the murder really happened. Agatha's "What of it?" is therefore intended to dismiss the actual murder as inconsequential. Her remark condenses into three appalling words the quality of the perverse spirituality of the play, a spirituality which does not grow out of real events but serves the purpose of denying and escaping them. The wish to impose fantasy on actuality accounts, in the last analysis, for the artistic defects of the poetry, the evasiveness apparent in the repetition of "perhaps" and "it is possible." It cannot be firm and strong, because what it affirms must be over and above the facts, not in them.

In making a judgment about the consequences for art of a wish-fulfillment motive, we must keep clear the distinction that it is not the use of irrational symbolism which is fatal, but the use of such symbolism to resolve a conflict in a fashion which is in fact impossible. This difference can be examined if we consider how Eliot has used the same material employed in *The Family Reunion* successfully in his poised and moving poem *Burnt Norton*. The central "moment in the rose-garden" in that poem reappears in the play. In *Burnt Norton* it embodies the spiritual reality, "out of time," about which the unreality of "time past" and "time future" are delicately balanced. In the play it is the crucial moment of fulfillment, or near fulfillment, which Harry and Agatha had together during his childhood. She exclaims,

> I only looked through the little door
> When the sun was shining on the rose-garden:
> And heard in the distance tiny voices
> And then a black raven flew over.
> And then I was only my own feet walking
> Away, down a concrete corridor
> In a dead air.

Harry responds with

> O my dear, and you walked through the little door
> And I ran to meet you in the rose-garden.

And Agatha adds,

> This is the next moment.

This expression of the pathos of lost tenderness is very moving. The episode as it is described in *Burnt Norton* is more beautiful still, one of the most beautiful things in Eliot's poetry. Yet if we examine its symbolic content, we discover the same exhibitionistic motive which underlies the play.

> And the pool was filled with water out of sunlight,
> And the lotos rose, quietly, quietly,
> The surface glittering out of heart of light,
> And they were behind us, reflected in the pool.
> Then a cloud passed, and the pool was empty.

"They" are, indifferently, the adults, Agatha, or the Eumenides when these last are "accepted and accepting": "they" see the lotus, which carries an obvious phallic significance. It is superfluous here to explore the complex symbolism further, except to remark that the episode is described from within "our first world" and that the manifold associations with childhood include the children in the leaves, "hidden excitedly, containing laughter." They are excited because they are about to *discover* themselves in a child's game of peek-a-boo. Now to point out this latent content does not damage the spiritual significance of the episode in *Burnt Norton*. Its innocence is secure, because it evokes the tenderness of childhood, and there is nothing inconsistent or immoral about such tenderness' being based on exhibitionistic satisfactions. One can note too that the episode is presented in a fashion which preserves an ambiguity as to whether it ever happened: the poem objectifies not only the episode, but its relation to present consciousness:

> Footfalls echo in the memory
> Down the passage which we did not take
> Towards the door we never opened
> Into the rose-garden. My words echo
> Thus, in your mind.

Compared to the poise of this, even Agatha's "I only looked through the little door . . ." one of the best things in the play, is crude because it affirms too much.

The rest of *Burnt Norton* presents the effort to recapture in later life, through spiritual discipline and through art, the emotional state evoked by the moment in the garden. The poem thus explores and utilizes the profound connections between such experience in childhood and the well-springs of spiritual experience in later life. The play also seeks to objectify this deep connection by representing Harry's return home as an effort, finally successful, to get back to the sources of spiritual fertility. But the crucial difference is that the poem uses the childhood episode only to define a state of feeling, which in later life is sought not in the objects of childhood, but in other, socially acceptable objects. This quest can be expressed successfully, because such resolution is in fact possible. The play, by contrast, seeks to recapture the same feeling in the action and in the objects of childhood, by representing the childhood moment *happening over again* in the adult present. But this is not possible—this wish is self-contradictory—because for an adult to reënact the same moment is no longer innocent but perverse. Hence the necessity of censorship, of a "spirituality" which denies the facts, of hiding and riddling—hence, in short, the play's artistic failure.

Exhibitionistic motifs appear frequently throughout Eliot's poems, from Prufrock, with his shy efforts to show off. This does not mean that the subject of the poems is the quest for exhibitionistic satisfactions—the trouble with *The Family Reunion* is that its subject comes down to that. In the successful poems, what the exhibitionistic pattern contributes is a fundamental structure within which Eliot's adult experience is given form. To take one example almost at random, *The Hollow Men* is haunted by eyes, at once attractive and terrible: "Eyes I dare not meet in dreams" are associated with "that final meeting" which might bring back reality, but which the empty men avoid, "behaving as the wind behaves." The sexually charged imagery of seeing provides the form to express something quite objective: the sterility of a society without faith.

Another problem about the use of wish-fulfillment motives in art, and particularly in tragedy, is presented by the attempt in *The Family Reunion* to use the compulsion of the curse to justify the hero's destruction of his wife and mother. This element in the action clearly serves as the vehicle for perverse hostility. But Aeschylus's trilogy of the house of Atreus undoubtedly appeals to perverse and destructive impulses latent in our nature, the same impulses, in fact, that underlie Eliot's play. Wishful fulfillment of destructive or self-destructive impulses is an essential element in tragedy: the wish provides the motive force of the representation, the fascination of the terrible story. At one level, we *want* Orestes to kill Clytemnestra, or Othello to kill Desdemona; we desire the Erinyes to pursue Orestes. The compulsive character of the events in tragedy, as of those in nightmare, expresses the power of the sympathy for such terrible actions which is the submerged component of our ambivalent feeling about them. A tragedian can heighten the grip of his story by finding an objective equivalent for this compulsion: filial piety obliges Orestes to kill his mother; Shakespeare has Othello talk sublimely and irrationally, a few moments before he acts, about his duty of killing Desdemona. But always in successful tragedy the other side of such ambivalent feeling is kept uppermost, the terror or anguish which overlies the forbidden wish. This distress is essential because it expresses the violence done to the social prohibition of fulfillment: full representation of the enactment of the destructive wish is conditional upon experiencing it with suffering: otherwise the representation would be immoral. In Eliot's play the attempt to justify following the Furies, to licence a normally submerged wish, goes with a failure to express adequately the horror of his hero's destructive acts. No remorse is ever expressed by Harry for the murder of his wife; the emphasis is all on the action of pushing her over, not at all on the consequences for her; Agatha's devastating "What of it?" finally makes her death morally immaterial. The indirect murder of his mother when Harry pursues his bright angels is carried out in a mood of similarly "spiritual" exaltation. It is true, of course, that Harry expresses a great deal of suffering; but his suffering and his actions are expressed separately: he suffers in general but is exonerated in particular. In this respect what Eliot has made of Greek myth may be likened to what Seneca made of it. In Seneca, too, action and suffering are disassociated; the suffering gets expressed in stoical sentences, while the dread crimes of the Greek heroes are portrayed with such uninhibited participation that the representation sometimes amounts to a pornography of the violent passions. Nothing so violent occurs in *The Family Reunion,* where a far finer-grained moral sensibility restrains expression; but the irrational wish motive latent in the Greek drama has in a similar fashion swept all before it at the moments of dramatic crisis. A further similarity appears in the shift in emphasis which tends to make the suffering of the tragic hero the justification instead of the consequence of his crimes. His greater intensity of feeling sets him apart, not merely in stature, but morally.

Eliot had Becket say that "action is suffering and suffering is action": his failure to express the two together in *The Family Reunion* is obviously not the result of any lack of conscious understanding of the tragedian's problem. But conscious understanding is not enough, precisely because the great and terrible motives which he has employed spring from regions outside its range. Their control must consequently be largely indirect, through attitudes and feelings about irrational impulses established in community life. It was the lack of such traditions in modern society that led Eliot to set his hero's desperation above social restraints; but once Harry was isolated in this way, there was nothing to prevent his plunging off after strange gods. The unconscious character of their appeal accounts at once for their appearing god-like and for the failure to be conscious that they are not true gods. A social nemesis, nevertheless, pursues and reveals the aberration: although the hero seems to escape, the play is overtaken.

# LOUIS L. MARTZ *

$\mathbf{M}$ ARIANNE MOORE once acutely remarked that Eliot's poems "are so consistently intricated that one rests on another and is involved with what was earlier." Thus *Four Quartets* rests firmly on a basis of imagery and theme built up by Eliot's other works; and this may be said of all his poems: any given one is best apprehended in the context provided by the body of Eliot's achievement. This is true of all poets in some degree; indeed, assessing the degree of "intrication" among a poet's various works may be one element in deciding the problem of greatness. With these concerns in mind, I should like to explore Eliot's symbol of "the still point," the dominant symbol of his poetry since *The Waste Land;* and at the same time to stress, in relation to the body of his poetry, the significance of one work which has been neglected in recent essays on Eliot—*Murder in the Cathedral.*

The relation of this play to the core of Eliot's poetry is shown in Becket's first words, addressed to the priest who has been rebuking the Chorus for its lamentations:

> Peace. And let them be, in their exaltation.
> They speak better than they know, and beyond your under-
> standing.
> They know and do not know, what it is to act or suffer.
> They know and do not know, that acting is suffering
> And suffering is action. Neither does the actor suffer
> Nor the patient act. But both are fixed
> In an eternal action, an eternal patience
> To which all must consent that it may be willed
> And which all must suffer that they may will it,
> That the pattern may subsist, for the pattern is the action
> And the suffering, that the wheel may turn and still
> Be forever still.

* *The Wheel and the Point: Aspects of Imagery and Theme in Eliot's Later Poetry,* from *The Sewanee Review,* Winter, 1947, pp. 126-147, Copyright, 1947, by The University of the South.

One must first recognize the double meanings in the words, *suffering, patient,* and *patience. Suffering* is not simply undergoing *misery* or *pain;* it is also *permitting, consenting;* he who consents to an action must suffer for it, must accept responsibility for it. The Chorus of Women of Canterbury, the "type of the common man," understands no such responsibility as the play begins: "For us, the poor, there is no action,/But only to wait and to witness." It is this responsibility that the women strive to evade as they realize they are being "drawn into the pattern of fate"; this is what they finally admit at their great moment of exaltation and vision: "I have consented, Lord Archbishop, have consented." It is the admission of sin which Eliot describes and demands in his prose writings—in the essay on Baudelaire's *Journaux Intimes,* for example, where he insists that "the recognition of the reality of Sin is a New Life," and finds the greatness of Baudelaire (like the greatness of the Chorus here) to reside in his capacity for suffering pain in the knowledge of good which comes from the knowledge of evil. It is the view expressed in one of Eliot's notes to *The Idea of a Christian Society:* "The notion of communal responsibility, of the responsibility of every individual for the sins of the society to which he belongs, is one that needs to be more firmly apprehended."

Thus, too, the *patient* is everyone, martyr, murderer, and spectator: he is at once suffering pain and permitting action; in Becket and the Chorus, he is also self-controlled. The same ideas are seen in the lyric of "East Coker," where the "hospital" patient is saved by Christ from "Adam's curse": "Beneath the bleeding hands we feel/The sharp compassion of the healer's art." Becket is the Christ of his age, who by suffering heals those who also suffer, as he explains just before his martyrdom:

> We are not here to triumph by fighting, by stratagem, or by
>     resistance,
> Not to fight with beasts as men. We have fought the beast
> And have conquered. We have only to conquer
> Now, by suffering. This is the easier victory.
> Now is the triumph of the Cross, now
> Open the door!

This eternally decreed pattern of suffering, which is also action, and of action, which is also suffering, Eliot symbolizes by the image of the wheel which always turns, yet, at the axis, always remains still. This image lies at the heart of Eliot's poetry. In *Ash Wednesday:*

> Against the Word the unstilled world still whirled
> About the centre of the silent Word.

In the two *Coriolan* poems:

> O hidden under the dove's wing, hidden in the turtle's breast,
> Under the palmtree at noon, under the running water
> At the still point of the turning world. O hidden.

Above all, in the two fragments from Heracleitus which are prefaced to "Burnt Norton" and announce the theme of all the *Four Quartets.* The first fragment is closely related to the above passage from *Ash Wednesday:* "But though the Word is common [*central,* in Eliot's image], the many live as though they had a wisdom of their own." The wheel image is more clearly suggested in the second fragment, which is best read with the fragment (LXX) and editorial note immediately following in the Loeb Library edition, for the words of Fragment LXX echo throughout the *Four Quartets:*

> LXIX. The road up and the road down is one and the same.
> LXX.  The beginning and end are common.

"Heracleitus is referring to a point on the circumference of a circle." These fragments appear in "The Dry Salvages": "And the way up is the way down, the way forward is the way back"; but the image of the wheel is presented most extensively in Section II of "Burnt Norton," opening with the image of "the bedded axle-tree," and continuing with the familiar words:

> At the still point of the turning world. Neither flesh nor fleshless;
> Neither from nor towards; at the still point, there the dance is,
> But neither arrest nor movement.

Here is *Peace*—Becket's first word in the play—the end which all patients and actors in the play, guided or misguided, seek after in their various ways: the Knights by violent worldly action; the Priests by flight and barricade; the Chorus by an attempt to remain unconscious, inactive, seeking a "peace" which is only the refuge of animals: "And the labourer bends to his piece of earth, earth-colour, his own colour,/Preferring to pass unobserved"; Becket alone by the true path of conscious submission to the central Word, as explained by his definition of *Peace* in the Christmas sermon. Becket's death is thus the still point of the world that turns within the play.

This is the theme which unifies Eliot's poetry from the words of Buddha and St. Augustine in *The Waste Land* to "the unimaginable zero summer," the still point symbolized by the ascetic ritual of Little Gidding. Becket and the religious community of Nicholas Ferrar have for Eliot much the same symbolic meaning—a meaning also found by Eliot in Pascal and the religious community of Port-Royal. Indeed, the implication of the whole body of Eliot's writing is nowhere better illustrated than in the interrelation between *Murder in the Cathedral*, "Little Gidding," and Eliot's essay on the *Pensées* of Pascal. Becket, Ferrar, and Pascal are, as this essay suggests, symbols of "one kind of religious believer, which is highly passionate and ardent, but passionate only through a powerful and regulated intellect . . . facing unflinchingly the demon of doubt which is inseparable from the spirit of belief." Of all three it might be said that "he had the knowledge of worldliness and the passion of asceticism, and in him the two are fused into an individual whole." All are symbols to be recommended "to those who doubt, but who have the mind to conceive, and the sensibility to feel, the disorder, the futility, the meaninglessness, the mystery of life and suffering, and who can only find peace through a satisfaction of the whole being."

This still point of peace is variously symbolized throughout Eliot's poetry, and the variety of the symbols has led readers to miss the connection between Eliot's image of the "rose-garden" and Becket. The "rose-garden," as Mr. Unger explains in his study of this image (THE SOUTHERN REVIEW, Spring, 1942), represents in Eliot a moment of contact with reality, a moment of rare consciousness and "sudden illumination," which flashes across the drab flux of ordinary life as the only meaningful moment (or moments) of that life— an experience which the individual may try constantly and unsuccessfully to recapture. It is, in short, the "still point" in the life of the individual.

The image of the rose-garden is used most clearly in *Ash Wednesday*, "Burnt Norton," and *The Family Reunion*, but with important differences of reference. In *Ash Wednesday* the rose is explicitly religious in significance, suggesting Dante's "rosa sempiterna" of Paradise. In "Burnt Norton" and *The Family Reunion* the image appears to draw part of its power and meaning from two other sources in literature which have not been generally noted. Mr. Eliot has remarked in conversation upon the importance of *Alice in Wonderland* here. As most readers will recall, Alice, near the beginning of her adventures, is wandering about "in a long, low hall" where she finds a "golden key" that fits the lock of "a little door."

> Alice opened the door and found that it led into a small passage . . . she knelt down and looked along the passage into the loveliest garden you ever saw. How she longed to get out of that dark hall, and wander about among those beds of bright flowers and those cool fountains, but she could not even get her head through the doorway.

From then on, despite her adventures, Alice never forgets "the little door into that lovely garden"; "I've got back to my right size: the next thing is, to get into that beautiful garden—how *is* that to be done, I wonder?" It is not until well past the middle of her story that she finally walks "down the little passage: and *then*—she found herself at last in the beautiful garden, among the bright flower-beds and the cool fountains." True, it is not a rose-garden, but it does contain the famous white rose-tree, where the gardeners are busily painting the roses red.

In "Burnt Norton," ·

> Footfalls echo in the memory
> Down the passage which we did not take
> Towards the door we never opened
> Into the rose-garden.

The experience of Alice becomes in Eliot a symbol of the longing to be born again, a symbol of the search for spiritual refreshment, for a change of heart, a change of vision, as in this dream-scene of "Burnt Norton," where "the leaves were full of children,/ Hidden excitedly, containing laughter." The Alice-imagery carries the same suggestions in *The Family Reunion*:

> You bring me news
> Of a door that opens at the end of a corridor,
> Sunlight and singing. . . .
>
> I only looked through the little door
> When the sun was shining on the rose-garden:
> And heard in the distance tiny voices. . . .

And what did not happen is as true as what did happen,
O my dear, and you walked through the little door
And I ran to meet you in the rose-garden.

But other echoes inhabit this garden. The imagery of Alice seems
to be merged with memories of another garden-experience, related
in D. H. Lawrence's story, "The Shadow in the Rose Garden" (in
*The Prussian Officer,* 1914), which Eliot praises and discusses at
some length in *After Strange Gods.* If one adds the traditional associations between human love and love of the divine, the experience
of the woman in Lawrence's story is very close in symbolic meaning
to Eliot's conception of the still point in "Burnt Norton":

> To be conscious is not to be in time
> But only in time can the moment in the rose-garden,
> The moment in the arbour where the rain beat,
> The moment in the draughty church at smokefall
> Be remembered; involved with past and future.
> Only through time time is conquered.

Lawrence's woman seeks to recapture the experience of an early love
by revisiting the rose-garden where the experience had occurred, a
garden in bright sunlight, with "blue sea" visible beyond:

> . . . she came to a high wall by the wayside. Under this she went
> slowly, stopping at length by an open doorway, which shone like
> a picture of light in the dark wall. There in the magic beyond
> the doorway, patterns of shadow lay on the sunny court. . . .
> She tiptoed nervously into the courtyard. . . . Irresolutely she
> took a step forward, and again forward, leaning, yearning, to-
> wards the garden beyond. . . .

> Slowly she went down one path, lingering, like one who has
> gone back into the past. Suddenly she was touching some heavy
> crimson roses that were soft as velvet, touching them thought-
> fully, without knowing, as a mother sometimes fondles the hand
> of her child. . . . Then she wandered on in abstraction. Some-
> times a flame-coloured, scentless rose would hold her arrested. She
> stood gazing at it as if she could not understand it. . . . So,
> slowly, like a white, pathetic butterfly, she drifted down the
> path, coming at last to a tiny terrace all full of roses. They seemed
> to fill the place, a sunny, gay throng. She was shy of them, they
> were so many and so bright. They seemed to be conversing and

laughing. She felt herself in a strange crowd. It exhilarated her,
carried her out of herself. . . .

Then she started cruelly as a shadow crossed her and a figure
moved into her sight. It was a man who had come in slippers,
unheard. He wore a linen coat. The morning was shattered, the
spell vanished away.

It is her lover, whom she had thought dead, but who is now amazingly
before her in the flesh—beyond redemption, as she realizes "with horror," for he is insane:

The woman turned and walked swiftly, blindly, between the
sunny roses, out from the garden, past the house with the blank,
dark windows, through the sea-pebbled courtyard to the street.
Hastening and blind, she went forward without hesitating, not
knowing whither.

The doorway, the sunlight, the water, the roses, the illusion of a
crowd, the laughter, the shattered moment of illumination—all point
inevitably toward "Burnt Norton" and *The Family Reunion*:

I only looked through the little door
When the sun was shining on the rose-garden:
And heard in the distance tiny voices
And then a black raven flew over.
And then I was only my own feet walking
Away, down a concrete corridor
In a dead air. Only feet walking
And sharp heels scraping.

I believe, too, that in Eliot's line, "The moment in the arbour
where the rain beat," one finds added significance by recalling Joyce's
story, "The Dead," which Eliot praises and discusses at length, along
with Lawrence's story, in *After Strange Gods*. In "The Dead" the
significant moment is the wife's sudden vision of her long-dead
lover, standing in the garden in heavy rain, "at the end of the wall
where there was a tree."

As these stories show, the "moment" may be an experience
actually consummated, as in Lawrence, or an experience only desired, never achieved, as in "The Dead," "Burnt Norton," and *The
Family Reunion*. But the desire for this still point where all desires
end is the saving grace; the unredeemable or unconsummated mo-

ment in the worldly garden is related to and indeed leads on to the Rose of Paradise, for the object of desire is a moment of timeless reality, apprehended in the world of time. Indeed, the rose-garden scene of "Burnt Norton" suggests the words of St. Bernard in Dante's Paradise: "That thou mayest consummate thy journey perfectly . . . fly with thine eyes throughout this garden; for gazing on it will equip thy glance better to mount through the divine ray." (Canto xxxi) The religious implications of this imagery are enhanced by the echoes of St. Augustine's *Confessions* which, I think, introduce and conclude the description of the rose-garden in "Burnt Norton." Recall Eliot's meditation here on the theme that "Time past and time future . . ./Point to one end, which is always present"; recall that "Footfalls echo in the memory," that "My words echo/Thus, in your mind," leading to the evocation of the imagery of the rose-garden as a memory of a possible childhood experience. Then read Augustine's section on the problem of time (*Confessions,* Book XI), especially this passage:

> For if there be times past, and times to come; fain would I know where they be: which yet if I be not able to conceive, yet thus much I know, that wheresoever they now be, they are not there future or past, but present. For if there also, future they be, then are they not there yet: if there also they be past, then are they not there still. Wheresoever therefore and whatsoever they be, they are not but as present. Although as for things past, whenever true stories are related, out of the memory are drawn not the things themselves which are past, but such words as being conceived by the images of those things, they, in their passing through our senses, have, as their footsteps, left imprinted in our minds. For example, mine own childhood, which at this instant is not . . . but as for the image of it, when I call that to mind, and tell of it, I do even in the present behold it, because it is still in my memory. (Ch. XVIII, Loeb Library trans.)

Indeed, in this book of the *Confessions* (Ch. XI) Augustine expresses the central question of Eliot's later poetry:

> Who will hold [the heart of man], and so fix it, that it may stand a while, and a little catch at a beam of light from that ever-fixed eternity, to compare it with the times which are never fixed, that he may thereby perceive how there is no comparison between them . . . and that all both past and to come, is made

up, and flows out of that which is always present? Who now
shall so hold fast this heart of man, that it may stand, and see,
how that eternity ever still standing, gives the word of command
to the times past or to come, itself being neither past nor to come?
Can my hand do this, or can the hand of my mouth by speech,
bring about so important a business?

The difficulty is that the search for the still point involves the
grasping of so many false points—a confusion represented in the
*Coriolan* poems, which are closely related to *Murder in the Cathedral.*
In "Triumphal March" the crowd is seeking desperately for "light,"
for a still point in the meaningless flux of life without faith, where
the Sanctus bell announces only "crumpets." As they watch the
parade of death and daily banality, they find the supreme moment,
mistakenly, in their glimpse of the worldly Leader. The terror of
clinging to such a "point" is displayed in "Difficulties of a Statesman," where the Leader, lost in the flux of worldly affairs, is himself
desperately searching for "a still moment, repose of noon." Becket's
career, as presented in the play, provides the best commentary on
*Coriolan.* The still point of peace for which all cry is not of this world,
though it may be glimpsed in this world, as Becket's Christmas sermon shows: "He gave to His disciples peace, but not peace as the
world gives."

To this theme of the timeless reality glimpsed in the world of
time Eliot returns again and again in *Four Quartets,* with constant
parallels to *Murder in the Cathedral.* Thus, in "The Dry Salvages":

> Men's curiosity searches past and future
> And clings to that dimension. But to apprehend
> The point of intersection of the timeless
> With time, is an occupation for the saint—
> No occupation either, but something given
> And taken, in a lifetime's death in love,
> Ardour and selflessness and self-surrender.
> For most of us, there is only the unattended
> Moment, the moment in and out of time,
> The distraction fit, lost in a shaft of sunlight. . . .

Among the saints who are thus prepared to recognize the moment
when it comes are Augustine, Becket, Pascal, and the devotees of
Little Gidding; the Chorus of the play represents "most of us," unable
to anticipate, to understand, or to arrest the timeless moment.

The death of Becket, then, is one of these moments of illumination, equivalent to a moment in the rose-garden: a parallel enforced by Eliot's use of an identical sentence after the illumination in both "Burnt Norton" and *Murder in the Cathedral:* "Human kind cannot bear very much reality." Consideration of Eliot's use of these words in both works would have solved Mr. Wheelwright's difficulty in interpreting the first section of "Burnt Norton" (*Chimera,* Autumn, 1942). He asks: "What is the reality of which humankind cannot bear too much? I cannot agree with Mr. Unger that the garden itself is meant; that, while it lasts, is not reality but nostalgic illusion, and is very easily borne." But Mr. Unger is essentially correct, though I should explain the "moment" somewhat differently:

> Other echoes
> Inhabit the garden. Shall we follow?
> Quick, said the bird, find them, find them,
> Round the corner. Through the first gate,
> Into our first world, shall we follow
> The deception of the thrush? Into our first world.

The deception, I think, is chiefly the illusion that peace and vitality and fruition can be fully realized and sustained on this earth:

> Dry the pool, dry concrete, brown edged,
> And the pool was filled with water out of sunlight,
> And the lotos rose, quietly, quietly,
> The surface glittered out of heart of light,
> And they were behind us, reflected in the pool.
> Then a cloud passed, and the pool was empty.
> Go, said the bird, for the leaves were full of children,
> Hidden excitedly, containing laughter.
> Go, go, go, said the bird: human kind
> Cannot bear very much reality.

The experience is at once real and illusory. It is real because it represents one of those rare moments when humanity recognizes its deep need for contact with the "heart of light"—the still point, the Word, Dante's "deep light." As in any mirage, the sight of water signifies an intense feeling of need. The vision, however, is illusory, because it can only be experienced through the insubstantial forms of "time." For average humanity this effect of illusion is necessary, since such a moment of perception is too intense to be borne for long:

            the enchainment of past and future
          Woven in the weakness of the changing body,
          Protects mankind from heaven and damnation
          Which flesh cannot endure.

For the saint, however, such a perception is neither unbearable
nor illusory, since he understands the true significance of the earthly
moment and sees the higher realm in which the need will be satisfied.
Hence Becket is able to explain the torment of the Chorus in its great
cry, "I have smelt them, the death-bringers," which ends with the
recognition of deep guilt and of deep need for a Mediator:

          I have consented, Lord Archbishop, have consented.
          Am torn away, subdued, violated,
          United to the spiritual flesh of nature,
          Mastered by the animal powers of spirit,
          Dominated by the lust of self-demolition,
          By the final utter uttermost death of spirit,
          By the final ecstasy of waste and shame,
          O Lord Archbishop, O Thomas Archbishop, forgive us,
                forgive us, pray for us that we may pray for you, out
                of our shame.

The agony of the Women here, as the sexual imagery shows, comes
from recognizing the degradation of humanity into the animal; and
the echo of Shakespeare's "The expense of spirit in a waste of shame"
extends the horror. In suffering their Lord to die, they feel "torn
away" from the Source of Light. Becket's answer is very close to
"Burnt Norton":

          Peace, and be at peace with your thoughts and visions.
          These things had to come to you and you to accept them.
          This is your share of the eternal burden,
          The perpetual glory. This is one moment,
          But know that another
          Shall pierce you with a sudden painful joy
          When the figure of God's purpose is made complete.
          You shall forget these things, toiling in the household,
          You shall remember them, droning by the fire,
          When age and forgetfulness sweeten memory
          Only like a dream that has often been told
          And often been changed in the telling. They will seem unreal.
          Human kind cannot bear very much reality.

These passages in "Burnt Norton" and the play may seem far apart, since one relates to a vision of beauty and the other to a vision of ugliness. But the two visions lead to one end. Either is an escape from the world of Hollow Men, which, says Eliot in "Burnt Norton,"

> . . . is a place of disaffection
> Time before and time after
> In a dim light: neither daylight
> Investing form with lucid stillness
> Turning shadow into transient beauty
> With slow rotation suggesting permanence
> Nor darkness to purify the soul
> Emptying the sensual with deprivation
> Cleansing affection from the temporal.

The "daylight" is equivalent to the moment in the rose-garden; the darkness is equivalent to that "Dark Night of the Soul" of St. John of the Cross, the religious purgation which has been well explained by Mr. Unger in relation to *Ash Wednesday* and "Burnt Norton," and by Mr. Sweeney in relation to "East Coker" (THE SOUTHERN REVIEW, Spring, 1939, 1941, 1942). Both ways lead to reality and to salvation, though they appear to be moving in opposite directions ("the way up is the way down"). The way of the Dark Night leads down through a stage of utter disgust with the physical (as in the above chorus) and reaches at the bottom a state of vacancy, where sense and spirit alike are momentarily nullified—a low point from which one can only return upward to grace. It is this state which the Chorus describes in its final chant as "the loneliness of the night of God, the surrender required, the deprivation inflicted."

One may clarify the interrelation of these symbols by dividing them into three channels to reality. The average man has two approaches. The first is through the physical and sensuous: through the rose-garden and its related symbols of natural beauty, freshness, and fertility: the hyacinth girl, childish laughter, the bird's song. The second is the opposite, religious way of the Dark Night. The third way, reserved for superior individuals, is also religious, but it leads directly upward, "Light upon light, mounting the saint's stair," as Eliot says in "A Song for Simeon."

Hence Becket and the Chorus simultaneously achieve stillness at opposite poles: Becket in a vision of ultimate being, the Chorus in a vision of ultimate nullity:

Becket:  I have had a tremor of bliss, a wink of heaven, a whisper,
         And I would no longer be denied; all things
         Proceed to a joyful consummation.

Chorus:  Emptiness, absence, separation from God;
         The horror of the effortless journey, to the empty land
         Which is no land, only emptiness, absence, the Void,
         Where those who were men can no longer turn the
            mind
         To distraction, delusion, escape into dream, pretence,
         Where the soul is no longer deceived, for there are no
            objects, no tones,
         No colours, no forms to distract, to divert the soul
         From seeing itself, foully united forever, nothing with
            nothing. . . .

This experience of purgation is similar to that of *Ash Wednesday*. The Chorus is detached from the world to face a moment of reality, and the vision of utter destruction which it sees is really the road to exaltation. The passage just cited is the lowest point of the Chorus, although horror reaches greater intensity in the next chant, during the murder of Becket. In the latter the Women are really on the upward way, but, as usual, they misunderstand, "They know and do not know":

Clear the air! clean the sky! wash the wind! take stone from stone
   and wash them.
The land is foul, the water is foul, our beasts and ourselves defiled
   with blood.
A rain of blood has blinded my eyes. Where is England? where is
   Kent? where is Canterbury?
O far far far far in the past: and I wander in a land of barren
   boughs: if I break them, they bleed; I wander in a land of
   dry stones: if I touch them they bleed.

The blood of Becket is purification, not defilement, for those who are contrite and ask for cleansing. The rain of blood is akin to Eliot's usual symbol of redemption, the water for which the Waste Land cries. And in this passage, together with suggestions of an Egyptian plague, of the land of Polydorus, of the stones leading to Dante's river of Blood, and of the bleeding boughs of the Suicides in the *Inferno* (Cantos xii and xiii), we have a specific echo of Eliot's own Waste

Land: "And the dead tree gives no shelter, the cricket no relief,/And the dry stone no sound of water."

The Chorus, in fact, has begun the play in exactly the state described in the opening lines of *The Waste Land:* the state of those who fear a conscious life:

> Now I fear disturbance of the quiet seasons:
> Winter shall come bringing death from the sea,
> Ruinous spring shall beat at our doors,
> Root and shoot shall eat our eyes and our ears,
> Disastrous summer burn up the beds of our streams
> And the poor shall wait for another decaying October.

As in "Burnt Norton," these things are seen "in a shaft of sunlight," though the Chorus would avoid the illumination, "living and partly living"—living, that is, an animal existence, not the full life of conscious humanity. Salvation comes through the gradual growth of consciousness and the acknowledgment of Sin.

The choruses of the play thus echo and prophesy the whole development of Eliot's poetry. The chorus opening Part II, which was substituted in the second edition of the play for the ecclesiastical procession of the original version, is closely related to the garden scene of "Burnt Norton," to "A Song for Simeon," to "Marina," to the *Landscapes,* "New Hampshire," "Rannoch," and "Cape Ann," and, in its imagery of the bird's song amid barrenness, to the many other places where Eliot uses this imagery of desired fertility and rebirth. This revision seems to me an improvement over the original Biblical chants, partly because it strengthens the play's unity by showing the effect of Becket's sermon on the Chorus, which here no longer fears the coming of Spring; and also because the revision is closer to the heart of Eliot's poetry and thus draws strength, as do the other choruses, from connection with the body of the poet's work.

To illustrate these relations fully, I should like to concentrate upon the difficult chorus already cited, that of "the death-bringers." Readers have disagreed widely in the evaluation of this, some placing it among "the greatest poetry of our day," others declaring that its "force is just violence, not really poetic force." Misunderstanding and dissatisfaction arise from viewing this chorus as simply "a prescience of evil"; it is certainly this, but not simply this. Eliot is creating here the vision of a universe without order, a vision given in the only way in which the "type of the common man" can realize it, by all the "quickened senses." The order of time is abolished: the merry fluting of a summer afternoon is heard at night mingled with the owl's "hollow note of death." Bats, with the huge scaly wings of Lucifer, slant over the noon sky. The creative mind of God and Man is gone; the scavengers and the least sensitive, least conscious forms of life take over. The threat of Death exists even in the most delicate flowers. And with this disorder humanity feels its involvement: "I have lain on the floor of the sea and breathed with the breathing of the sea-anemone, swallowed with ingurgitation of the sponge." But, paradoxically, the Women are saved, not lost, by such a vision, for here gradually emerges the human consciousness at highest intensity, recognizing all creation as part of a pattern which points to this moment, seeing themselves as "death-bringers," admitting Sin, crying for absolution. The disorder in the first two-thirds of this chorus, with its long, irresolute lines, changes to a balanced order of versification, phrasing, and thought as the Chorus recognizes its responsibility:

> Have I not known, not known
> What was coming to be? It was here, in the kitchen, in the
>     passage,
> In the mews in the barn in the byre in the market place
> In our veins our bowels our skulls as well
> As well as in the plottings of potentates
> As well as in the consultations of powers.

Comparison with *The Waste Land* and "The Dry Salvages" shows this chorus as central to the body of Eliot's poetry. Here is "What the Thunder Said": the "Murmur of maternal lamentation," the vision of the dissolution of human order and history, which lead to the Chapel Perilous and the "damp gust/Bringing rain." The opening of "The Dry Salvages" creates much the same feeling of the dissolution of human order and human time. Here the river is a "death-bringer," always involved with man, however remote it may appear. The rhythm, the time kept by the river is equated with the natural flow of man's life from birth to death, as Miss Gardner has said (*New Writing and Daylight,* Summer, 1942). Miss Gardner has also shown that the movement of the river differs from that of the sea, which is without direction; and this is a crucial distinction in understanding the poem. If man looks beyond the rhythm of his own machines, he can understand the river's movement from source to mouth, which is like the movement from past to future; but when the river, the "brown god," merges with the sea, which contains "Many gods and many voices," man's sense of direction and of time is lost:

> The tolling bell
> Measures time not our time, rung by the unhurried
> Ground swell, a time
> Older than the time of chronometers, older
> Than time counted by anxious worried women
> Lying awake, calculating the future,
> Trying to unweave, unwind, unravel
> And piece together the past and the future. . . .

We watch with wonder the sea and

> Its hints of earlier and other creation:
> The starfish, the hermit crab, the whale's backbone;
> The pools where it offers to our curiosity
> The more delicate algae and the sea anemone.

Here the relation of this *Quartet* to the play becomes clear. The "anxious worried women" are like the Chorus of Women of Canterbury who are attempting to measure events on a human scale, but are dragged, as by the bell tolling with the ground swell, to a bewildering vision of a universe which will not fit into the human order, to a terrifying sense of some relation with the "living things under sea," and finally to a sense of design, not that of past and future, but a design centered upon a timeless moment of illumination, a still point round which the world is ordered: the death of God's martyr, an "instant eternity." The bell of "The Dry Salvages" indicates such a moment, giving significance to a life of which we can otherwise only say, "There is no end, but addition: the trailing/Consequence of further days and hours." The bell, like the death of Becket, is "perpetual angelus," a remembrance of the Incarnation, where, says Eliot in "The Dry Salvages,"

> the impossible union
> Of spheres of existence is actual,
> Here the past and future
> Are conquered, and reconciled. . . .

This, in *Murder in the Cathedral* and *Four Quartets,* is Eliot's tentative answer to his continual exploration of the problem of time and the meaning of history.[1]

Though granting the play's relation to the central themes of Eliot's poetry, some critics have seen little relation between the poetic method of *Murder in the Cathedral* and the method of his non-dramatic poems. Mr. Matthiessen, for example, noting "a relative lack of density" in the play compared with *The Waste Land,* says that this is partly due to the fact that Eliot has not followed his earlier method of employing "symbols which maintained the action continually in the present at the same time that he was exploring analogies with the past." (*Sat. Rev. of Lit.* Oct. 12, 1935) Now it should be admitted that parts of the play lack the necessary substance of poetry: some of the verse spoken by the Priests, the Knights, and Becket is embarrassingly weak. But the play has a density of the whole design which helps to compensate for a lack in density of line. Consider the fields of reference which the whole play holds: The liturgy of the Church, which the choruses resemble. The mystery and miracle plays of the medieval Church. The Morality play, with its Temptations. The Greek drama. *Samson Agonistes,* whom Becket recalls during his own temptation. The book of Job and Biblical style in general. Finally, the symbolism of the history and tradition of Becket, which enables one to defend the work along the lines of Eliot's own statement about *The Divine Comedy:* "The whole poem . . . is, if you like, one vast metaphor."

Even cursory reading in contemporary documents dealing with Becket's murder [2] will show that Eliot has followed the history and tradition of Becket very closely; but the result is not at all the usual method of the historical dramatist. The effect which one feels, particularly in the latter part of the play, is that of the "intersection of the timeless with time." The reported actions and conversations of

---

[1] In addition to valuable help received from the articles cited in the body of this essay, I should like to acknowledge indebtedness to F. R. Leavis's essay on Eliot's later poetry, SCRUTINY, Summer, 1942, and to F. O. Matthiessen's study of the *Quartets,* KENYON REVIEW, Spring, 1943. Quotations from Eliot's works are given by permission of Harcourt, Brace and Co.

[2] See William Holden Hutton, *S. Thomas of Canterbury. An account of his life and fame from the contemporary biographers and other chroniclers,* London, 1889, esp. pp. 234–45.

the year 1170, verified as few medieval events have been, are crossed and exalted by the intermittent cries of the Chorus, which intersect the literal and lift it into the realm of symbol. Thus the arguments between Becket and the Knights hold to reported events in the world of time, while, breaking in, the Chorus cries, "This is out of life, this is out of time." Here, on a large scale, is a development from the poetical method of the earlier Eliot, used still to explore the problems which dominate *The Waste Land*.

Can we admit a certain density of the whole and still agree with those critics who regard the play as a jumble of maladjusted parts? I think not. Aside from the unifying effect of Becket as a symbol, the Chorus shows a unified development toward consciousness; and all parts of the play are organically related to the theme, even the startling prose defences which the Knights present to the audience. It has been charged that these are Shavian imitations which violate the unity of the play, desecrate the tone set by the Chorus and the death, and, in all, form an inexcusable example of Eliot's bad taste in witticism. But the shock of the contrast between the Chorus's final cries and the Knights' feeble apologia is the measure of the difference between the Church and the State, between the religious judgment and the worldly judgment, between the timeless moment and the world of time. The Chorus represents the religious conscience of humanity, the Knights represent the weakness of Parliamentary Debate, Law Court, and Historical Analysis, when unaccompanied by religious faith and religious humility. Viewed thus in relation to the whole play, these speeches of defence balance the speeches of the cynical Herald and the worldly Tempters in Part I. Finally, Becket's sermon, recreated from hints in contemporary accounts of its original, forms a nodus of theme, symbol, and tradition, of past and present, binding the play's two parts, and binding Becket's search for Peace with our own.

The play is not, then, a mere church pageant written to order; it is vitally related to the content and the method of Eliot's other poetry. It does not represent merely the feelings and views of an "isolated" religious group; it represents the public state of mind at the time of its original performance in 1935—a state of mind now reappearing in the aftermath of war. The play begins with fear, foreboding, and shrinking, and closes with the feeling well described by Eliot in his *Idea of a Christian Society,* with reference to the Munich conference:

"a feeling of humiliation, which seemed to demand an act of personal contrition, of humility, repentance and amendment; what had happened was something in which one was deeply implicated and responsible." The play is thus rooted both in our time and in Becket's time. As in the short *Landscapes* and in the longer landscapes which begin each of the *Four Quartets,* Eliot has placed his moment in the world, only to dissolve and to transcend the worldly. Through its "symbol perfected in death," the play presents the "end" of man envisaged in "Burnt Norton":

> The inner freedom from the practical desire,
> The release from action and suffering, release from the inner
> And the outer compulsion, yet surrounded
> By a grace of sense, a white light still and moving. . . .

# BIBLIOGRAPHY

*When an item is a review or study of a work by Eliot and the work is not specified by the title of the item, then the work is named in parenthesis after the item.*

*Items marked with an asterisk are included, whole or in part, in this volume.*

\* Aiken, Conrad, *Scepticisms*, N.Y., Knopf, 1919, 203–205.

—— "The Scientific Critic," *The Freeman*, vol. 2 (1921), 593–594. (*The Sacred Wood*)

—— "An Anatomy of Melancholy," *The New Republic*, vol. 33 (1923), 294–295. (*The Waste Land*)

—— "After *Ash Wednesday*," *Poetry: A Magazine of Verse*, vol. 45 (1934), 161–165. (*After Strange Gods* and *The Rock*)

—— "Homage to T. S. Eliot," *The Harvard Advocate*, vol. 125, no. 3 (1938), 17.

\* Aldington, Richard, "The Poetry of T. S. Eliot," *Literary Studies and Reviews*, N.Y., The Dial Press, 1924, 181–191.

Bailey, Ruth, *A Dialogue on Modern Poetry*, London, Oxford University Press, 1939, *passim*. (*Gerontion*)

Baker, Howard, "Homage to T. S. Eliot," *The Harvard Advocate*, vol. 125, no. 3 (1938), 46–47.

\* Barber, C. L., "T. S. Eliot After Strange Gods," *The Southern Review*, vol. 6, no. 2 (1940), 387–416.

Barnes, T. R., "Poets and the Drama," *Scrutiny*, vol. 4, no. 2 (1935), 189–195. (*The Family Reunion*)

Basler, Roy P., "Psychological Patterns in 'The Love Song of J. Alfred Prufrock,'" *Twentieth Century English* (ed. W. S. Knickerbocker), N.Y., The Philosophical Library, 1946, 384–400.

Bates, Ernest S., "T. S. Eliot: Leisure Class Laureate," *The Modern Monthly*, vol. 7 (Feb. 1933), 17–24.

Battenhouse, Roy W., "Eliot's 'The Family Reunion' As Christian Prophecy," *Christendom*, vol. 10 (1945), 307–21.

Beach, Joseph Warren, *The Concept of Nature in Nineteenth-Century English Poetry,* N.Y., Macmillan, 1936, 554–555.

Bell, Clive, "T. S. Eliot," *The Nation* (London), vol. 33 (1923), 772–773.

Blackmur, R. P., "T. S. Eliot," *Hound & Horn,* vol. 1, nos. 3 & 4 (1928), 187–213, 291–319.

—— "T. S. Eliot in Prose," *Poetry: A Magazine of Verse,* vol. 42 (1933), 44–49.

—— "The Dangers of Authorship," *The Double Agent.* N.Y., Arrow Editions, 1935, 172–183. (*After Strange Gods*)

* —— "T. S. Eliot—From *Ash-Wednesday* to *Murder in the Cathedral,*" *The Double Agent,* N.Y., Arrow Editions, 1935, 184–218.

—— "The Whole Poet," *Poetry: A Magazine of Verse,* vol. 50 (1937), 48–51. (*Collected Poems, 1909–1935*)

—— "Homage to T. S. Eliot," *The Harvard Advocate,* vol. 125, no. 3 (1938), 20.

—— "It is Later Than He Thinks," *The Expense of Greatness,* N.Y., Arrow Editions, 1940, 239–244. (*The Idea of a Christian Society*)

—— "Mr. Eliot and Notions of Culture: A Discussion," *Partisan Review,* vol. 11, no. 3 (1944), 302–304.

Blisset, William, "The Argument of T. S. Eliot's *Four Quartets,*" *University of Toronto Quarterly,* vol. 15, no. 2 (1946), 115–126.

Bodgener, J. H., "Spiritual Life and Literary Trends," *The London Quarterly and Holborn Review,* vol. 170 (1945), 321–327. (*Four Quartets*)

Bodkin, Maud, *The Quest for Salvation in an Ancient and a Modern Play,* London, Oxford University Press, 1941. (*The Family Reunion*)

Borey, J. A., "The Literary Criticism of T. S. Eliot," *American Prefaces,* vol. 1, no. 5 (1936), 67–71.

Boyd, Ernest, *Studies from Ten Literatures,* N.Y., Scribner's, 1925, 315–317. (Eliot's poems in French)

Boynton, Grace M., "Without a Parable: an Encounter with the Poetry of T. S. Eliot," *The Windsor Quarterly,* vol. 1, no. 2 (1933), 102–310.

Bradbrook, M. C., "Eliot's Critical Method," *Focus Three: T. S. Eliot, A Study of His Writings by Several Hands* (ed. B. Rajan), London, Dennis Dobson, 1947, 119–128.

Bradford, C., "Footnotes to *East Coker:* a Reading," *The Sewanee Review,* vol. 52 (1944), 169–175.

Brenner, Rica, "Thomas Stearns Eliot," *Poets of Our Time,* N.Y., Harcourt, Brace, 1941, 159–206.

* Brooks, Cleanth, *"The Waste Land:* Critique of the Myth," *Modern Poetry and the Tradition,* Chapel Hill, The University of North Carolina Press, 1939, 136–173.

* Brooks, Van Wyck, "What is Primary Literature?" *Opinions of Oliver Allston,* N.Y., Dutton, 1941, 218–227.

Brown, Alec, "The Lyric Impulse in the Poetry of T. S. Eliot," *Scrutinies II* (ed. E. Rickword), London, Wishart, 1931.

Brown, E. K., "T. S. Eliot: Poet and Critic," *The Canadian Forum,* vol. 10 (1930), 448.

——— "Mr. Eliot and Some Enemies," *University of Toronto Quarterly,* vol. 8, no. 1 (1938), 69–84.

Brown, W. C. "Mr. Eliot without the Nightingales," *The University of Kansas City Review,* vol. 14, no. 1 (1947), 31–38.

Buck, Philo M., Jr., "Faith of Our Fathers—T. S. Eliot," *Directions in Contemporary Literature,* N.Y., Oxford University Press, 1942, 261–290.

Bullough, Geoffrey, *The Trend of Modern Poetry,* Edinburgh, Oliver and Boyd, 1934, 133–152.

Burke, Kenneth, "The Allies of Humanism Abroad," *The Critique of Humanism* (ed. C. Hartley Grattan), N.Y., Brewer and Warren, 1930, 169–194.

Bush, Douglas, *Mythology and the Romantic Tradition in English Poetry,* Cambridge, Harvard University Press, 1937, 506–518.

Butler, John F., "Tragedy, Salvation and the Ordinary Man," *The London Quarterly and Holborn Review,* vol. 162 (1937), 489–497. (*Murder in the Cathedral*)

Campbell, Harry M., "An Examination of Modern Critics: T. S. Eliot," *Rocky Mountain Review,* vol. 8 (1944), 128–137.

Campbell, Roy, "Contemporary Poetry," *Scrutinies,* (ed. Edgell Rickword), London, Wishart, 1928, 162–179.

Cantwell, Robert, "Mr. Eliot's Sunday Afternoon," *The New Republic,* vol. 72 (1932), 132–133.

Cargill, Oscar, *Intellectual America,* N.Y., Macmillan, 1941, 258–274.

Chaning-Pearce, M., "Little Gidding," *The Nineteenth Century*, vol. 133 (1943), 74–78.

Chase, Richard, "The Sense of the Present," *Kenyon Review*, vol. 7, no. 2 (1945), 218–231.

——— "T. S. Eliot in Concord," *The American Scholar*, vol. 16, no. 4 (1947), 438–443.

Church, Richard, "T. S. Eliot: A Search for Foundations," *Eight for Immortality*, London, Dent, 1941, 83–97.

Church, R. W., "Eliot on Bradley's Metaphysic," *The Harvard Advocate*, vol. 125, no. 3 (1938), 24–26.

Coats, R. H., "An Anchor for the Soul (A Study of Mr. T. S. Eliot's Later Verse)," *The Hibbert Journal*, vol. 44 (1946), 112–118. (*Four Quartets*)

Collin, W. E., "T. S. Eliot," *The Sewanee Review*, vol. 39 (1931), 13–24.

——— "T. S. Eliot the Critic," *The Sewanee Review*, vol. 39 (1931), 419–424.

Collingwood, R. G., *The Principles of Art*, Oxford, Clarendon Press, 1938, 310, 333–335. (*The Waste Land*)

Coomaraswamy, A. K., "Primordial Images," *PMLA*, vol. 61 (1946), 601–603.

* Cowley, Malcolm, "Readings from the Lives of the Saints," *Exiles Return*, N.Y., Norton, 1934, 123–128.

——— "Afterthoughts on T. S. Eliot," *New Republic*, vol. 87 (1936), 49.

Cunliffe, John W., *English Literature in the Twentieth Century*, N.Y., Macmillan, 1933, 323–329.


Daiches, David, "T. E. Hulme and T. S. Eliot" and "T. S. Eliot," *Poetry and the Modern World*, Chicago, University of Chicago Press, 1940, 90–105, 106–127.

Daniells, J. R., "T. S. Eliot and His Relation to T. E. Hulme," *The University of Toronto Quarterly*, vol. 2 (1933), 380–396.

Daniels, Roy, "The Christian Drama of T. S. Eliot," *The Canadian Forum*, vol. 16, no. 187 (1936), 20–21.

Dawson, N. P., "Enjoying Poor Literature," *The Forum*, vol. 69 (1923), 1371–1379.

Deutsch, Babette, *This Modern Poetry*, N.Y., Norton, 1935, 117–132.

—— "T. S. Eliot and the Laodiceans," *The American Scholar,* vol. 9, no. 1 (1939), 19-30.

DeVoto, Bernard, "Waste Land," *The Literary Fallacy,* Boston, Little, Brown, 1944, 108-111.

Dobrée, Bonamy, "T. S. Eliot," *The Lamp and the Lute,* Oxford, Clarendon, 1929, 107-133.

Dobson, Charles A., "Three of Mr. Eliot's Poems," *The New Review* (Calcutta), vol. 12 (1940), 361-372.

Drew, Elizabeth, *Directions in Modern Poetry,* N.Y., Norton, 1940, 37-55, 133-147.

Duncan Jones, E. E., *"Ash Wednesday," Focus Three: T. S. Eliot, A Study of His Writings by Several Hands* (ed. B. Rajan), London, Dennis Dobson, 1947, 37-56.

Dupee, F. W., "Difficulty as Style," *The American Scholar,* vol. 14, no. 3 (1945), 355-357.

Eastman, Max, *The Literary Mind,* N.Y., Scribner's, 1931, 20-23, 110-112.

Eberhart, Richard, "Homage to T. S. Eliot," *The Harvard Advocate,* vol. 125, no. 3 (1938), 18-19.

Elliott, G. R., "T. S. Eliot and Irving Babbitt," *The American Review,* vol. 7 (1936), 442-454.

Evans, B. I., *Tradition and Romanticism,* London, Methuen, 1940, 192-200.

Fergusson, Francis, "T. S. Eliot and His Impersonal Theory of Art," *The American Caravan* (ed. Van Wyck Brooks, et al.), N.Y., Macaulay, 1927, 446-453.

—— "Eliot's Norton Lectures," *Hound & Horn,* vol. 7, no. 2 (1934), 356-358. (*The Use of Poetry and the Use of Criticism.*)

—— "Notes on the Theater," *The Southern Review,* vol. 5, no. 3 (1940), 562-564. (*The Family Reunion*)

—— "Action as Passion: *Tristan* and *Murder in the Cathedral,*" *The Kenyon Review,* vol. 9, no. 2 (1947), 201-221.

Fernandez, Ramon, "The Classicism of T. S. Eliot," *Messages,* N.Y., Harcourt, Brace, 1927, 295-304.

Fletcher, J. G., "Poems in Counterpoint," *Poetry: A Magazine of Verse,* vol. 63 (1943), 44-48. (*Four Quartets*)

Flint, R. W., "The *Four Quartets* Reconsidered." *The Sewanee Review,* vol. 56, no. 1 (1948), 69–81.

* Forster, E. M., "T. S. Eliot," *Abinger Harvest,* N.Y., Harcourt, Brace, 1936, 89–96.

Foster, G. W., "The Archetypal Imagery of T. S. Eliot," *PMLA,* vol. 60 (1945), 567–585.

Fowlie, Wallace, "Eliot and Tchelitchew," *Accent,* vol. 5, no. 3 (1945), 166–170.

Friend, A. C., "T. S. Eliot—An Appreciation," *The St. Louis Review,* vol. 2 (1932), 6–8.

Gardner, Helen L., *"Four Quartets:* A Commentary," *Focus Three: T. S. Eliot, A Study of His Writings by Several Hands* (ed. B. Rajan), London, Dennis Dobson, 1947, 57–77.

George, R. E. G., "The Return of the Native," *The Bookman,* vol. 75 (1934), 423–431.

Gordon, George S., *Poetry and the Moderns,* Clarendon Press, Oxford, 1935.

Greenberg, Clement, "Mr. Eliot and Notions of Culture: A Discussion," *Partisan Review,* vol. 11, no. 3 (1944), 305–307.

Gregory, Horace, "The Unities and Eliot," *Life and Letters Today,* vol. 23 (1939), 53–60. (*The Family Reunion*)

―――― and Zaturenska, Marya, "T. S. Eliot, the Twentieth-Century 'Man of Feeling' in American Poetry," *A History of American Poetry,* Harcourt, Brace, N.Y., 1946, 413–428.

Grierson, H. J. C., and Smith, J. C., "Twentieth Century Poetry: between the Wars, 1919–1939," *A Critical History of English Poetry,* London, Chatto and Windus, 1944, 548–569.

Grudin, Louis, *Mr. Eliot among the Nightingales,* Paris, Lawrence Drake, 1932.

Harding, D. W., "Mr. Eliot at Harvard," *Scrutiny,* vol. 2, no. 3 (1933), 289–292. (*The Use of Poetry and the Use of Criticism*)

―――― *"The Rock,"* *Scrutiny,* vol. 3, no. 2 (1934), 180–183.

―――― "T. S. Eliot, 1925–1935," *Scrutiny,* vol. 5, no. 2 (1936), 171–176.

―――― "Christian or Liberal?" *Scrutiny,* vol. 8, no. 3 (1939), 309–313.

—— "We Have Not Reached Conclusion," *Scrutiny*, vol. 11, no. 3 (1943), 216–219. (*Little Gidding*)

Hausermann, H. W., "*East Coker* and *The Family Reunion*," *Life and Letters Today*, vol. 47 (1945), 32–38.

Hazlitt, Henry, "The Mind of T. S. Eliot," *The Nation*, vol. 135 (1932), 312–313. (*Selected Essays*)

Henderson, Philip, "The Agony of Mr. Eliot," *The Poet and Society*, London, Secker & Warburg, 1939, 154–171.

* Hicks, Granville, *The Great Tradition*, N.Y., Macmillan, 1935, 268–271.

Higinbotham, R. N., "Objections to a Review of *Little Gidding*," *Scrutiny*, vol. 11, no. 4 (1943), 259–261.

Hodin, J. P., "T. S. Eliot on the Condition of Man Today," *Horizon*, vol. 12 (1945), 83–89.

Hook, Sidney, "The Dilemma of T. S. Eliot," *The Nation*, vol. 160 (1945), 69–71.

House, Humphrey, "Mr. Eliot as a Critic," *The New Oxford Outlook*, vol. 1 (1933), 95–105.

Howard, Brian, "Mr. Eliot's Poetry," *The New Statesman*, vol. 36, (1930), 146. (*Ash Wednesday*)

Humphries, Rolfe, "Salvation from Sand in Salt," *Poetry: A Magazine of Verse*, vol. 59 (1942), 338–339. (*The Dry Salvages*)

Jack, Peter Monro, "A Review of Reviews of T. S. Eliot's *Four Quartets*," *American Bookman*, vol. 1, no. 1 (1944), 91–99.

Jameson, R. DeL., "Poetry and Plain Sense," National Tsing Hua University, Peiping, 1931.

Jay, Douglas, "Mr. T. S. Eliot: After Lambeth," *The Oxford Outlook*, vol. 11 (June 1931), 78–85.

Jones, Howard Mumford, "The Legend of T. S. Eliot," *Saturday Review of Literature*, vol. 14 (Sept. 19, 1936), 13–14.

Knickerbocker, W. S., "Bellwether: an Exercise in Dissimulatio," *The Sewanee Review*, vol. 41 (1933), 64–79.

Kronenberger, Louis, "T. S. Eliot as Critic," *The Nation*, vol. 140 (1935), 452–453.

Krutch, Joseph Wood, "A Poem is a Poem," *The Nation*, vol. 137 (1933), 679–680. (*The Use of Poetry and the Use of Criticism*)

* Laski, Harold J., *Faith, Reason and Civilization*, N. Y., Viking, 1944, 96–100, 180–182.

* Leavis, F. R., "T. S. Eliot," *New Bearings in English Poetry*, London, Chatto & Windus, 1932, 75–132.

—— "Mr. Eliot, Mr. Wyndham Lewis, and Lawrence," *Scrutiny*, vol. 3, no. 2 (1934), 184–191.

—— "Mr. Eliot and Education," *Scrutiny*, vol. 5, no. 1 (1936), 84–89. (*Essays Ancient and Modern*)

—— "T. S. Eliot's Later Poetry," *Education and the University*, London, Chatto and Windus, 1943, 87–104. Also, *Scrutiny*, vol. 11, no. 1 (1942), 60–71.

—— "Reflections on the Above," *Scrutiny*, vol. 11, no. 4 (1943), 261–267.

Leighton, Lawrence, "A Note on the Poems," *The Harvard Advocate*, vol. 125, no. 3 (1938), 10, 48. (Eliot's early *Advocate* poems)

Lewis, Wyndham, *Men Without Art*, London, Cassell, 1934, 65–100.

Liebowitz, Martin, "Sense and Sensibility," *Kenyon Review*, vol. 5, no. 2 (1943), 219–227.

Lowell, R. T. S., "Homage to T. S. Eliot," *The Harvard Advocate*, vol. 125, no. 3 (1938), 20, 41.

Lynd, Robert, "Mr. T. S. Eliot as Critic," *Books and Authors*, N.Y., Putnam's, 1923, 277–284.


MacCarthy, Desmond, "New Poets," *The New Statesman*, vol. 16 (1921), 418–420.

MacLeish, Archibald, "Homage to T. S. Eliot," *The Harvard Advocate*, vol. 125, no. 3 (1938), 18.

MacNeice, Louis, *Modern Poetry*, London, Oxford University Press, 1938, 11–15, 56–59, 84–85, 103–105, 144–145, 162–168, 183–184.

Madge, Charles, "In Memoriam T. S. E.," *New Verse*, vol. 31 (1938), 18–21.

Mangan, Sherry, "A Note: On the Somewhat Premature Apotheosis of Thomas Stearns Eliot," *Pagany*, vol. 1, no. 2 (1930), 23–36.

Mankowitz, Wolf, "Notes on 'Gerontion,'" *Focus Three: T. S. Eliot, A Study of His Writings by Several Hands* (ed. B. Rajan), London, Dennis Dobson, 1947, 129–138.

* Martz, Louis L., "The Wheel and the Point: Aspects of Imagery

and Theme in Eliot's Later Poetry," *The Sewanee Review,* vol. 55, no. 1 (1947), 126–147.

Mason, H. A., "Elucidating Eliot," *Scrutiny,* vol. 14, no. 1 (1946), 67–71. (*Four Quartets*)

Masters, Charlie, "Analysis of 'Burnt Norton,'" *American Prefaces,* vol. 6, nos. 2 and 3 (1941), 99–112, 212–231.

\* Matthiessen, F. O., *The Achievement of T. S. Eliot,* London, Oxford University Press, 1935. Revised edition, 1947.

——— "For an Unwritten Chapter," *The Harvard Advocate,* vol. 125, no. 3 (1938), 22–24. (Eliot's plays)

——— *American Renaissance,* N.Y., Oxford University Press, 1941, *passim.*

——— "Eliot's Quartets," *Kenyon Review,* vol. 5, no. 2 (1943), 161–178.

——— "American Poetry, 1920–40," *The Sewanee Review,* vol. 55, no. 1 (1947), 24–55.

McGreevy, Thomas, *Thomas Stearns Eliot,* London, Chatto and Windus, 1931.

Mesterton, Erik, *The Waste Land, Some Commentaries,* Argus Bookshop, 1943.

Meyerhoff, Hans, "Mr. Eliot's Evening Service," *Partisan Review,* vol. 15, no. 1 (1948), 131–138.

Molony, M. F., "Mr. Eliot and Critical Tradition," *Thought,* vol. 21 (1946), 455–474.

Monroe, Harriet, "A Contrast," *Poetry: A Magazine of Verse,* vol. 21 (1923), 325–330. (*The Waste Land*)

——— *Poets and Their Art,* N.Y., Macmillan, 1932, 100–105.

Montgomerie, W., "Harry, Meet Mr. Prufrock (T. S. Eliot's Dilemma)," *Life and Letters Today,* vol. 31 (1941), 115–128.

Moore, Marianne, "It Is Not Forbidden to Think," *The Nation,* vol. 142 (1936), 680–681.

Moore, Merrill, "Homage to T. S. Eliot," *The Harvard Advocate,* vol. 125, no. 3 (1938), 42, 45.

Moore, Dom Sebastian, "East Coker: The Place and the Poem," *Focus Two* (ed. B. Rajan and A. Pearse), London, Dennis Dobson, 1946, 91–103.

\* More, Paul Elmer, "Cleft Eliot," *Saturday Review of Literature,* vol. 9 (1932), 233. Also, *Designed for Reading* (An Anthology Drawn from *The Saturday Review of Literature,* 1924–1934), 333–338.

Morgan, Roberta, and Wohlstetter, Albert, "Observations on 'Prufrock,'" *The Harvard Advocate,* vol. 125, no. 3 (1938), 27-30, 33-38.

Morrison, Theodore, *"Ash Wednesday:* A Religious History," *The New England Quarterly,* vol. 11 (1938), 266-286.

Muir, Edwin, "Contemporary Writers (Mr. T. S. Eliot)," *The Nation,* (London), vol. 37 (1925), 644-646. Also, *Transition,* N.Y., Viking, 1926, 131-146.

Munson, Gorham B., "The Esotericism of T. S. Eliot," *1924,* no. 1 (July 1924), 3-10.

Nicoll, Allardyce, "T. S. Eliot and the Revival of Classicism," *The English Journal* (College Edition), vol. 23 (1934), 269-278.

* Nuhn, Ferner, "Orpheus in Hell: T. S. Eliot," *The Wind Blew from the East,* N.Y., Harper, 1942, 195-255.

O'Connor, William Van, *"Gerontion* and *The Dream of Gerontius," Furioso,* vol. 3, no. 2 (1947), 53-56.

O'Donnell, G. M., "Homage to T. S. Eliot," *The Harvard Advocate,* vol. 125, no. 3 (1938), 17-18.

Oras, Ants, "The Critical Ideas of T. S. Eliot," *Tartu,* vol. BXXVIII, no. 3 (1932).

Palmer, H. E., "The Hoax and Earnest of *The Waste Land," Dublin Magazine,* vol. 8 (1933), 11-19.

Parkes, H. B., *The Pragmatic Test,* San Francisco, The Colt Press, 1941, 178-186.

Parsons, I. M., "Mr. Eliot's Authority," *The Spectator,* vol. 149 (1932), 450-452, 480, 534. (Plus Correspondence with Rebecca West)

Partridge, A., "T. S. Eliot," Publications of the University of Pretoria, Series 3, no. 4 (1937).

Passmore, J. A., "T. S. Eliot," Sydney University Literary Society, 1934.

Peacock, Ronald, "T. S. Eliot," *The Poet in the Theatre,* N.Y., Harcourt, Brace, 1946, 3-25.

Phillips, W., "Mr. Eliot and Notions of Culture: A Discussion," *Partisan Review,* vol. 11, no. 3 (1944), 307-309.

Pope, J. C., "Prufrock and Raskolnikov," *American Literature*, vol. 17, no. 3 (1945), 213–230.

—— "Prufrock and Raskolnikov Again: A Letter from Eliot," *American Literature*, vol. 18, no. 4 (1947), 319–321.

Pound, Ezra, "T. S. Eliot," *Poetry: A Magazine of Verse*, vol. 10 (1917), 264–271. (*Prufrock and Other Observations*)

—— *T. S. Eliot and Others, Answers to a Questionnaire on Modern Poetry*, London Chapbook No. 27, July 1922.

* —— *Polite Essays*, Norfolk, New Directions, no date, 135–138, 141–143.

Powell, Dilys, "T. S. Eliot," *Descent from Parnassus*, N.Y., Macmillan, 1934, 55–100.

*Praz, Mario, "T. S. Eliot and Dante," *The Southern Review*, vol. 2, no. 3 (1937), 525–548.

Preston, Raymond, *Four Quartets Rehearsed*, N.Y., Sheed and Ward, 1946.

Prokosch, Frederick, "Homage to T. S. Eliot," *The Harvard Advocate*, vol. 125, no. 3 (1938), 41.


Quiller-Couch, Arthur, "Tradition and Orthodoxy," *The Poet as Citizen and Other Papers*, N.Y., Macmillan, 1935, 44–65.


Rahv, Philip, "T. S. Eliot," *Fantasy*, vol. 2 (1932), 17–20.

Rajan, B., "The Unity of the Quartets," *Focus Three: T. S. Eliot, A Study of His Writings by Several Hands* (ed. B. Rajan), London, Dennis Dobson, 1947, 78–95.

Ransom, John Crowe, "Waste Lands," *Modern Essays*, (ed. Christopher Morley), N.Y., Harcourt, Brace, 1924, 345–359.

—— "A Cathedralist Looks at Murder," *The World's Body*, N.Y., Scribner's, 1938, 166–172.

—— "T. S. Eliot as a Dramatist," *Poetry: A Magazine of Verse*, vol. 54 (1939), 264–271. (*The Family Reunion*)

* —— "T. S. Eliot: the Historical Critic," *The New Criticism*, Norfolk, New Directions, 1941, 135–208.

—— "The Inorganic Muses," *The Kenyon Review*, vol. 5, no. 2 (1943), 294–300.

Rascoe, Burton, "Pupils of Polonius," *The Critique of Humanism*, (ed. C. Hartley Grattan), N.Y., Brewer and Warren, 1930, 109–130.

Rice, Philip Blair, "Out of The Waste Land," *Symposium,* vol. 3, no. 4 (1932), 422–442.

—— "The Critic as Prophet," *Poetry: A Magazine of Verse,* vol. 50 (1937), 51–54. (*Essays Ancient and Modern*)

*Richards, I. A., "The Poetry of T. S. Eliot," *Principles of Literary Criticism,* N.Y., Harcourt, Brace, 1934, 289–295.

—— "Mr. Eliot and Notions of Culture: A Discussion," *Partisan Review,* vol. 11, no. 3 (1944), 310–312.

Rickword, Edgell, *"Selected Essays,* by T. S. Eliot," *Scrutiny,* vol. 1, no. 4 (1933), 390–393.

—— "The Modern Poet," *Toward Standards of Literature* (ed. F. R. Leavis), London, Wishart, 1933, 100–106.

Ridler, Anne, "A Question of Speech," *Focus Three: T. S. Eliot, A Study of His Writings by Several Hands* (ed. B. Rajan), London, Dennis Dobson, 1947, 107–118.

Roberts, Michael, "The Poetry of T. S. Eliot," *The London Mercury,* vol. 34 (1936), 38–44.

Ross Williamson, H., *The Poetry of T. S. Eliot,* N.Y., Putnam's, 1933.


*Savage, D. S., "The Orthodoxy of T. S. Eliot," *The Personal Principle,* London, Routledge, 1944, 91–112.

Schwartz, Delmore, *"The Criterion, 1922–1939," The Kenyon Review,* vol. 1 no. 4 (1939), 437–449.

*—— "T S. Eliot as the International Hero," *Partisan Review,* vol. 12, no. 2 (1945), 199–206.

Seldes, Gilbert, "T. S. Eliot," *The Nation,* vol. 115 (1922), 614–616.

Shand, John, "Around *Little Gidding," The Nineteenth Century,* vol. 136 (1944), 120–132.

*Shapiro, Karl, *Essay on Rime,* Reynal & Hitchcock, N.Y., 1945, 16–17, 22, 29, 40, 60–61.

Shapiro, Leo, "The Medievalism of T. S. Eliot," *Poetry: A Magazine of Verse,* vol. 56 (1940), 202–213.

Shillito, Edward, "The Faith of T. S. Eliot," *Christian Century,* vol. 51 (1934), 994–995.

Shuster, G. W., "Mr. Eliot Returns," *The Commonweal,* vol. 16 (1932), 581–583.

Sinclair, May, " 'Prufrock: and Other Observations': A Criticism," *The Little Review*, vol. 4 (1917), 8–14.

Sitwell, Edith, *Aspects of Modern Poetry*, London, Duckworth, 1934, 99–140.

────── "Lecture on Poetry since 1920," *Life and Letters Today*, vol. 39 (1943), 86–93.

Slochower, Harry, *No Voice Is Wholly Lost*, N.Y., Creative Age Press, 1945, 181–183.

Smith, Bernard, *Forces in American Criticism*, N.Y., Harcourt, Brace, 1939, 358–359, 382–387.

Smith, F. J., "A Reading of *East Coker*," *Thought*, vol. 21 (1946), 272–286.

Smith, Grover, "Observations on Eliot's 'Death by Water,' " *Accent*, vol. 6, no. 4 (1946), 257–263.

Smith, J. C., see H. J. C. Grierson.

Southworth, J. G., "The Poetry of T. S. Eliot," *Sowing the Spring* (ed. Basil Blackwell), Oxford, 1940, 76–91.

Spencer, Theodore, "The Poetry of T. S. Eliot," *The Atlantic Monthly*, vol. 51 (Jan. 1933), 60–68.

────── "On Murder in the Cathedral," *The Harvard Advocate*, vol. 125, no. 3 (1938), 21–22.

*Spender, Stephen, "T. S. Eliot in His Poetry," and "T. S. Eliot in His Criticism," *The Destructive Element*, Houghton, Mifflin, N.Y., 1936, 132–175.

Stephenson, E. M., *T. S. Eliot and the Lay Reader*, London, The Fortune Press, 1944.

Stevens, Wallace, "Homage to T. S. Eliot," *The Harvard Advocate*, vol. 125, no. 3 (1938), 41.

Stonier, G. W., "Eliot and the Plain Reader," *The Fortnightly Review*, vol. 138 (1932), 620–629. Also, *Gog Magog*, London, Dent, 1933, 140–155.

Strachey, John, *The Coming Struggle for Power*, N.Y., Modern Library, 1935, 224–228.

Strong, Robert, "The Critical Attitude of T. S. Eliot," *The London Quarterly and Holborn Review*, vol. 158 (1933), 513–519.

*Sweeney, J. J., "*East Coker*: A Reading," *The Southern Review*, vol. 6, no. 4 (1941), 771–791.

────── "*Little Gidding*: Introductory to a Reading," *Poetry: A Magazine of Verse*, vol. 62 (1943), 214–223.

Swinnerton, Frank, *The Georgian Literary Scene*, London, Heinemann, 1935, 509–514.


\* Tate, Allen, "T. S. Eliot," *Reactionary Essays*, N.Y., Scribner's, 1936, 210–220. (*Ash Wednesday*)
———— "Homage to T. S. Eliot," *The Harvard Advocate*, vol. 125, no. 3 (1938), 41.
Taupin, René, "The Classicism of T. S. Eliot," *Symposium*, vol. 3 (1932), 64–84.
\*Thompson, T. H., "The Bloody Wood," *The London Mercury*, vol. 29 (1934), 233–239.
Tinckom-Fernandez, W. G., "T. S. Eliot, '10," *The Harvard Advocate*, vol. 125, no. 3 (1938), 5–10, 47–48.
Tindall, William York, *Forces in Modern British Literature, 1885–1946*, N.Y., Knopf, 1947, *passim*.
———— "The Recantation of T. S. Eliot," *The American Scholar*, vol. 16, no. 4 (1947), 431–437.
Turnell, G. M., "Tradition and Mr. T. S. Eliot," *Collosseum*, (June 1934), 44–54.
———— "Mr. Eliot's New Play," *Scrutiny*, vol. 8, no. 1 (1939), 108–114.


\*Unger, Leonard, "Notes on *Ash Wednesday*," *The Southern Review*, vol. 4, no. 4 (1939), 745–770.
\*———— "T. S. Eliot's Rose Garden: A Persistent Theme," *The Southern Review*, vol. 7, no. 4 (1942), 667–689.
Untermeyer, Louis, "T. S. Eliot," *American Poetry Since 1900*, N.Y., Holt, 1923, 352–375.


\*Van Doren, Mark, "Mr. Eliot Glances Up," *The Private Reader*, N.Y., Holt, 1942, 212–216. (*Essays Ancient and Modern*)
Vivas, Eliseo, "The Objective Correlative of T. S. Eliot," *The American Bookman*, vol. 1, no. 1 (1944), 7–18.
Voigt, F. A., "Milton, Thou Shouldst Be Living . . . ," *The Nineteenth Century*, vol. 130 (1943), 211–221.
Voigt, G. P., "Has the Pendulum Started Back?" *The Lutheran Church Quarterly*, vol. 9 (1936), 149–155.

Waggoner, H. H., "T. S. Eliot and the Hollow Men," *American Literature*, vol. 15, no. 1 (1943), 101-126.

Warren, Robert Penn, "Homage to T. S. Eliot," *The Harvard Advocate*, vol. 125, no. 3 (1938), 46.

Wecter, Dixon, "The Harvard Exiles," *Virginia Quarterly Review*, vol. 10 (1934), 244-257.

Weiss, T., "T. S. Eliot and the Courtyard Revolution," *The Sewanee Review*, vol. 54, no. 2 (1946), 289-307.

Wheelwright, Philip, "The Burnt Norton Trilogy," *Chimera*, vol. 1, no. 2 (1942), 7-18.

Wilder, Amos N., "Mr. T. S. Eliot and the Anglo-Catholic Option," *Spiritual Aspects of the New Poetry*, N.Y., Harper, 1940, 205-216.

Williams, Charles, *Poetry at Present*, London, Oxford University Press, 1930, 163-173.

——— "A Dialogue on Mr. Eliot's Poem," *The Dublin Review*, vol. 212 (1943), 114-122. (*Four Quartets*)

Williams, William Carlos, "Homage to T. S. Eliot," *The Harvard Advocate*, vol. 125, no. 3 (1938), 42.

——— "The Fatal Blunder," *The Quarterly Review of Literature*, vol. 2, no. 2 (1945), 125-126.

Williamson, George, "The Talent of T. S. Eliot," *The Sewanee Review*, vol. 35 (1927), 284-295. Also, University of Washington Chapbooks, no. 32 (1929).

Wilson, Edmund, "The Poetry of Drouth," *The Dial*, vol. 73 (1922), 611-616.

——— "T. S. Eliot and the Church of England," *The New Republic*, vol. 58 (1929), 283-284.

*——— "T. S. Eliot," *Axel's Castle*, N.Y., Scribner's, 1931, 93-131.

*Winters, Yvor, "T. S. Eliot, or the Illusion of Reaction," *The Anatomy of Nonsense*, Norfolk, New Directions, 1943, 120-167.

Wohlstetter, A., see Morgan, R.


*Yeats, W. B., *The Oxford Book of Modern Verse*, Oxford, Oxford University Press, 1936, xxi-xxiii.


Zabel, M. D., "T. S. Eliot in Mid-Career," *Poetry: A Magazine of Verse*, vol. 36 (1930), 330-337. (*Ash Wednesday*, "Ariel Poems," and *Dante*)

———— "The Still Point," *Poetry: A Magazine of Verse,* vol. 41 (1932), 152–158. (*Triumphal March* and *Difficulties of a Statesman*)

———— "The Use of the Poet," *Poetry: A Magazine of Verse,* vol. 44 (1934), 32–37. (*The Use of Poetry and The Use of Criticism*)

———— "Poetry for the Theatre," *Poetry: A Magazine of Verse,* vol. 45 (1934), 152–158. (*The Rock*)

———— "Poets of Five Decades," *The Southern Review,* vol. 2, no. 1 (1936), 168–171.

Zaturenska, Marya, see Gregory, H.

# Date Due

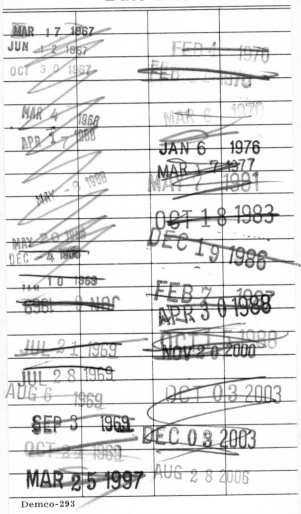

MAR 17 1967
JUN 12 1967
OCT 30 1967

MAR 4 1968
APR 17 1988

MAY 3 1968

MAY 2 1968
DEC 4 1968

JAN 10 1969
JUN 9 1969

JUL 21 1969

JUL 28 1969
AUG 6 1969

SEP 3 1969

OCT 24 1969

MAR 25 1997

FEB 4 1970
FEB 24 1970

MAR 6 1970

JAN 6 1976
MAR 17 1977
MAY 7 1981

OCT 18 1983
DEC 19 1986

FEB 7 1987
APR 30 1988

OCT 1988
NOV 20 2000

OCT 03 2003

DEC 03 2003
AUG 28 2006

Demco-293